THE CALIFORNIA DESERTS

The publisher gratefully acknowledges
the generous contribution to this book
provided by

the General Endowment Fund
of the University of California Press Foundation.

The California Deserts

AN ECOLOGICAL REDISCOVERY

BRUCE M. PAVLIK

UNIVERSITY OF CALIFORNIA PRESS
Berkeley   Los Angeles   London

University of California Press, one of the most distinguished university presses in the United States, enriches lives around the world by advancing scholarship in the humanities, social sciences, and natural sciences. Its activities are supported by the UC Press Foundation and by philanthropic contributions from individuals and institutions. For more information, visit www.ucpress.edu.

University of California Press
Berkeley and Los Angeles, California

University of California Press, Ltd.
London, England

Library of Congress Cataloging-in-Publication Data

Pavlik, Bruce M.
   The California deserts : an ecological rediscovery / Bruce M. Pavlik.
      p. cm.
   Includes bibliographical references and index.
      ISBN 978-0-520-25140-3 (cloth : alk. paper) — ISBN 978-0-520-25145-8 (pbk. : alk. paper)
      1. Desert ecology—California. 2. Deserts—California. I. Title.
QH541.5.D4P38 2008
577.5409794—dc22   2007024427

Manufactured in China
10   09   08
10 9 8 7 6 5 4 3 2 1

The paper used in this publication meets the minimum requirements of ANSI/NISO Z39.48–1992 (R 1997) (Permanence of Paper).

Excerpt pp. 12–13 from Wallace, W. J. 1957. A clay figurine from Death Valley National Monument, California. *The Masterkey*. Courtesy of the Autry National Center/Southwest Museum, Los Angeles, CA.

Excerpt p. 31 and pp. 35–36 from Latta, F. 1979. *Death Valley '49ers*. Reprinted with permission of Chris Brewer, Bear State Books, Exeter, CA.

Excerpt on page 45 from Campbell, E. W. C. and W. H. Campbell. 1937. The archeology of Pleistocene Lake Mojave. The Lake Mojave site. *Southwest Museum Papers*. Courtesy of the Autry National Center/Southwest Museum, Los Angeles, CA.

Excerpt p. 58 from Perkins, Edna Brush. Edited by Peter Wild. *The White Heart of the Mojave: An Adventure with the Outdoors of the Desert*, pp. 93–95. © 2001 (copyright holder). Reprinted with permission of The John Hopkins University Press.

Excerpt pp. 59–61 from Jaeger, Edmund. *Desert Wildlife*. Copyright © 1950, 1961 by the Board of Trustees of the Leland Stanford Jr. University; renewed 1989.

Excerpt pp. 61–63 from *Travels with Charley, in Search of America* by John Steinbeck, © 1961, 1962 by The Curtis Publishing Co., © 1962 by John Steinbeck, renewed © 1990 by Elaine Steinbeck, Thom Steinbeck, and John Steinbeck IV. Used by permission of Viking Penguin, a division of Penguin Group (USA) Inc.

P. 64, "Requiem for Sonora" from *Selected Poems, 1969–1981*, by Richard Shelton, © 1982. Reprinted by permission of the University of Pittsburgh Press.

Artwork p. 134 from *Quaternary Extinctions: A Prehistoric Revolution*, edited by Paul S. Martin and Richard G. Klein © 1984 The Arizona Board of Regents. Reprinted by permission of the University of Arizona Press.

Cover photos: top, bajada in spring (Bruce Pavlik); left, Devil's Hole Pupfish (USFWS); middle left, *Lianthus parryi* (Bruce Pavlik); middle right, Minnie Williams (John Walter and Nancy Peterson Walter); right, Desert Bighorn (Christopher L. Christie).

To my family—
past, present, and future

AURORA VALLEY

Mono Lake

White Mt.
(14,246')

Sierra Nevada

White Mountains

OWENS VALLEY

EUREKA VALLEY

Last Chance Range

Grapevine Mountains

NEVADA

Kings River

Inyo Mountains

SALINE VALLEY

Owens River

Mt. Whitney
(14,495')

Owens Lake

Coso Range

DEATH VALLEY

PANAMINT VALLEY

Argus Range

Telescope Peak
(11,049')

Panamint Mountains

Badwater
(–282')

Ash Meadows

Spring Mountains

Charleston Peak
(11,919')

Las Vegas

Muddy Mountains

Amargosa River

Kingston Range

Nopah Range

Kern River

Avawatz Mountains

Clark Mt.
(7,929')

New York Mountains

Paiute Range

Dead Mountains

Colorado River

Tehachapi Mountains

GARLOCK FAULT

CALIFORNIA

Silver Lake

Soda Lake

Devil's Playground

Providence Mountains

Tejon Canyon Pass

Afton Canyon

Old Woman Mountains

CHEMEHUEVI VALLEY

SAN ANDREAS FAULT

ANTELOPE VALLEY

Mojave River

Newberry Mountains

CADIZ VALLEY

Cajon Pass

LUCERNE VALLEY

Sheephole Mountains

Whipple Mountains

Los Angeles

San Bernardino Mountains

Pinto Mountains

SAN ANDREAS FAULT

Mt. San Jacinto
(10,786')

COACHELLA VALLEY

San Jacinto Mountains

Santa Rosa Mountains

Chuckwalla Mountains

Chocolate Mountains

Algodones Dunes

ARIZONA

Colorado River

PACIFIC OCEAN

Salton Sea

IMPERIAL VALLEY

Vallecitos Mountains

New River

Alamo River

N

San Diego

Gila River

0   50   100 miles

M E X I C O

CONTENTS

Preface · ix

Acknowledgments · xi

INTRODUCTION: THE LOST BASKET · 1

REDISCOVERY · 15

Coming to Explore · 19
Coming to Conquer · 29
Coming to Understand · 40
Coming to Cherish · 54

A CONSPIRACY OF EXTREMES · 65

Geography of a Bioregion · 68
Climate · 71
Geology · 79
Soils · 88
Waters · 92

OPERATIONS AND ORIGINS · 97

Ecosystem Operations in the Desert Bioregion · 99
Origins of the Desert Bioregion · 129

REMARKABLE BIOTA · 147

Biological Diversity: The Richness of Species · 151
Evolving with Drought · 152

GREATER THAN THE SUM OF THE PARTS · 193

    Great Basin Communities · 198
    Mojave Communities · 212
    Sonoran Communities · 232

THE FUTURE OF THIS ARID BIOREGION · 251

    Current Threats · 254
    Ecological Remedies · 290
    Weaving a New Basket · 303

    References · 305
    Art Credits · 329
    Index · 333

PREFACE

This is a book about ecological relationships within the California deserts—how organisms interact with each other and the arid environment. Given the large variety of organisms and the number of possible interactions, there is no way for such a book to be comprehensive, nor to focus on detailed descriptions of the organisms themselves. A desert biophile should refer to field guides (such as those by MacMahon [1985] and Phillips and Comus [2000], or those in the California Natural History Guide series from the University of California Press), floras (for example, *The Jepson Desert Manual* [Baldwin et al. 2002] and *California Desert Flowers* [Morhardt and Morhardt 2004]), faunas (for example, *The Lives of Desert Animals in Joshua Tree National Monument* [Miller and Stebbins 1973]), and Web sites (for example, http://calphotos.berkeley.edu, www.californiaherps.com, and www.mbr-pwrc.usgs.gov/Infocenter/infocenter.html) to obtain information on identification and distribution. Instead, this book is a synthesis that expands on Edmund Jaeger's classic *The California Deserts* (1933) using 75 years of recent ecological research.

I also wanted to include *Homo sapiens* as one of the many organisms that have interacted with the desert. Ancient arrivals, recent immigrants, modern residents, and timeless wanderers all reflect and affect these landscapes. Consequently, we can detect human tolerance of, and adaptation to, desert conditions using archeological and historical evidence. But there are also spiritual components to our desert existence that value beauty and inspire stewardship. In a world where the fate of entire ecosystems depends on human values and attitudes, strict science falls short.

Finally, the California deserts — the Great Basin, Mojave, and Sonoran — are not confined to California. Although the Mojave is centered here, it is probably more correct to say that the Great Basin and Sonoran deserts extend west into this state from Nevada and Arizona, respectively. Utah is the eastern limit of the Great Basin, while Mexico is the southern limit of the Sonoran. Consequently, I have crossed all borders to include some nearby organisms and places not strictly Californian. This allows me to invite all residents of the arid west to discover and rediscover these deserts, these organisms, and these special places.

ACKNOWLEDGMENTS

The mentors in my life made this book possible. Manuel Miranda inspired an early love of biology, allowing me to see that the world was "full of life." Jackie Preciado taught me how to write about it. William Emboden and George Fisler insisted that I really know those organisms, while John Kontogiannis showed me how to integrate field and lab. Mary DeDecker demonstrated the delicate balance between scientist and activist, always insisting that resource management decisions be based on the best available, most objective information. Her skills and enthusiasm were remarkable, her kindness legendary. Michael Barbour taught me that science was as creative as it was rigorous, and that an academic could also be warm and gregarious. Finally, my brother Robert Pavlik has shown me the relevance of human history to understanding and preserving a landscape.

I would particularly like to acknowledge the helpful suggestions and assistance I received from Donna Baker (Camden-Carroll Library at Morehouse State University), Dr. Michael Barbour (University of California at Davis), Chris Brewer (Bear State Books), Diane Boyer (U.S. Geological Survey), Dr. Brian Brown (Natural History Museum of Los Angeles County), Joanne (DeDecker) Busby, Erin Chase (The Huntington Library), John Evarts (Cachuma Press), Dr. Nancy Ferguson (U.S. Fish and Wildlife Service), Jodie Frasier (U.S. Fish and Wildlife Service), Leslie Freund (Phoebe Apperson Hearst Museum of Anthropology), Dr. Mark Giambastiani (ASM Affiliates), Christine Giles (Palm Springs Art Museum), Erika Gorder (Rutgers University Libraries), Kevin Hallaran (Riverside Metropolitan Museum), Meg Hannah (University of California Press), Dr. John Harris (Mills College), Joyce Hilton (Mills College), Kate Hoffman (University of California Press),

Dr. Debra Hughson (Mojave National Preserve), Paul Johnson, Marilyn Kim (Autry National Center, Southwest Museum), Doris Kretschmer (University of California Press), Vincent Lee (California Academy of Sciences), Lisbeth Louderback (University of Nevada at Reno), Dr. Dennis Murphy (University of Nevada at Reno), Scott Norton (University of California Press), Anna O'Leary, Robert Pavlik (California Department of Transportation), Dr. Norman Penny (California Academy of Sciences), Dr. Fred Phillips, Cassie Pinnell (Mills College), Dr. Donald Sada (Desert Research Institute, University of Nevada at Reno), Linda Slater (Mojave National Preserve), Rachelle Smith (Specialized Libraries and Archival Collections, University of Southern California), Susan Snyder (The Bancroft Library), Michael Steward, Dr. Anna Lynn Suer, Jeri Taylor, Kim Walters (Autry National Center, Southwest Museum), Jenny Wapner (University of California Press), Carol (DeDecker) Weins, Dr. Weiping Xie (Natural History Museum of Los Angeles County), John Willoughby (United States Bureau of Land Management), and the photographers, artists, and cartographers whose knowledge and skill captured the remarkable images that illustrate this book. Funds to support publication were provided by BMP Ecosciences and a Faculty Development Grant from Mills College.

South Park
San Francisco, California

The Lost Basket

Human understanding of the California deserts has developed over a very long period of time. Some of that period is historical and relatively well documented by texts, specimens, photographs, and recordings. But the long remaining period predates written history and is recorded by artifacts and oral traditions that are incomplete at best and whose meanings require careful interpretation. How can we fully appreciate all dimensions of that development when confined to the usual, unambiguous forms of evidence?

I have chosen to introduce the science of ecological relationships in a story, part fact and part fiction. The factual part is about self-taught botanist Mary DeDecker, who found, on one of many desert excursions, a basket hidden in a limestone grotto. The fictional part is my account of how the basket was lost. In this way, I attempt to sketch a broader, more humane understanding of discovery and rediscovery in the California deserts.

CIRCA 1850

This basket was old when Tau-ruv was born. A gift from her grandmother, it was woven from grass and willow stems collected near the village. Shaped by ancient *ko onzi* hands for holding the seeds of subsistence, the basket served well for generations. As a young mother, Tau-ruv could not gather without it and several others she cherished. Despite fading colors and recent patches, this old basket was part of an inheritance that ensured a life-giving harvest.

Tau-ruv was gathering seeds in the southern end of the dry valley, where *aiwa*, the sand grass, was lush and bursting with a summer crop. Ayis, her son, followed along, sometimes helping and often distracted by stripe-tailed lizards that bolted from beneath the shrubs. Other women in the party had already left for the village, but mother and son stayed on. They spent most of this day just beyond a canyon mouth that spilled its gravel and sand at the foot of a massive dune. The canyon provided passage home to their deep valley of permanent springs. Her family lived most of the year near one large spring, collecting seeds from these valleys and hunting bighorn sheep on steep mountain slopes.

This had been a particularly good year for seeds. Winter rains were heavy, and the deep sand beneath their feet was still wet. Tufts of *aiwa* had grown thicker and taller than Tau-ruv could recall in all of her 23 years. She walked between the tufts, grabbing stalks and stripping them of the ripe crop. One hand dropped the stems, chaff, and seeds into a large conical basket slung behind her back, while the other hand pulled on another clump of stalks. If the pull was too hard and roots began to lift from the sand, her foot tamped the plant back in place. Once in a while a few seeds were sown back into the ground. "You feed me and I tend you," was murmured like a prayer and offered like an apology. She traded cut hands and aching back for the comfort of a large harvest.

Ayis, however, was tending to himself, still sulking about having to do women's work. Stomping around and waving a threshing stick, he released his frustrations against defiant shrubs. Whack! After all, he caught and skinned rabbits as well as the older boys. Whack! Surely this year would be his last—no mother could make an eight-year-old man

Upper The dunes of the dry valley where Tau-ruv and Ayis collected seeds of *aiwa*. (D. W. Sada)

Lower A way of knowing. Western Shoshone woman gathering *aiwa* in the Great Basin, c. 1935. (Julian H. Steward)

gather seeds. Whack! A lizard scurried away. When everyone finally saw his arsenal of new arrow points, there would be no question about it: he would be allowed to join the hunt.

The still air of the afternoon was hot, and Tau-ruv had not taken a sip of water since early morning. Ayis carried the woven *olla*, its last slosh of water smelling like pine resin. Instead of the bottle, he dropped a thrashing lizard into her hand. Tau-ruv's dry screech turned to laughter and she swatted him gently. They spent a few minutes resting, watching cloud shadows creep across the valley. She decided they had gathered enough and that it was time to break camp and return home. He decided he would never come back here again.

Camp was where seeds were winnowed from the chaff and poured back into storage baskets for the long walk back. It was also where the boy-man practiced chipping, turning glassy black stones into sleek, sharp weapons. Tau-ruv tied everything from camp together into a single, cumbersome bundle to carry on her back. Everything but the old basket, which Ayis grasped by its worn, fibrous handle. "I'll make sure she won't take me again," he thought. Marching off, he began mocking his mother's work by collecting whatever was encountered along the way. Flowers, twigs, pebbles, beetle carcasses, and sand were thrown into the old basket. Crossing over the monstrous dune, Ayis grabbed seeds from "old man grass," a grizzled tangle of stems and dagger-like leaves that often drew blood. More abundant were the insect-shaped seeds of "bug" plants that dangled like beads when ripe and were much less painful to collect. The last dune slope was covered with bug plants, which yielded several handfuls of the dry, black delicacies. "These will be the last seeds I ever gather," he thought, chasing his mother toward the canyon mouth.

Several hours of walking made the daylong thirst unbearable. Tau-ruv and Ayis scrambled up a small, rocky cleft in the canyon that became a waterfall during storms. But on this summer evening no puddles hid among the dry boulders. Walking slowly, Tau-ruv scanned the surrounding gray and orange walls for places that might store a bit of liquid. The cliffs were nearly vertical in this section but riddled with small caves and bowl-like depressions. A golden dragonfly zagged by, as if to encourage their search.

Upper *Aiwa* (Indian ricegrass), its fibrous roots in deep sand. (James M. Andre)

Lower The nutritious grain of *aiwa* (Indian ricegrass), still attached to the floral chaff. (Steve Matson)

Halfway through the canyon Tau-ruv noticed an unusually leafy, bright green shrub perched on the gray rock above. Unlike all others, it glowed with small yellow flowers. "Maybe there's a crack with water," she said to her son. "Stay here. I'll climb up and see."

Tau-ruv carefully took off her burden and scrambled up to the shrub. A woody, twisted stem was growing from a fissure, watered by droplets that meandered from above. "Come," she called, "there's enough." Ayis hurried up, taking a sash of empty *ollas* and the old bas-

Threshing begins by beating *aiwa* stems until chaffy grains fall to the bottom of the pile. Tossing in a winnowing basket separates the grain from the chaff. (Julian H. Steward)

ket of silly treasures. Reaching the ledge, he stashed the basket into the very back of a small cave. "It fits nicely—if I left it behind, she wouldn't want to take me again," he thought spitefully. Turning back around, he pressed fingers into the crack and lifted a few drops into his dry mouth. Relief came slowly. They managed to half-fill one *olla* by pressing it against a mossy spout. "This will make the rest of our trip a little easier," she said, thinking his brooding came from thirst. Ayis shook his head, tied the *olla* back onto the sash, and climbed down.

It was not until they emerged into the deep valley that Ayis told his mother about leaving the old basket behind. The long, tiring walk had brought his petulance to the surface. She was a little hurt by his defiance but aware that he was right; this would be their last gathering trip. The old basket could be retrieved another time. But now she was focused on reaching the flickering lights that pierced the dark, hollow distance before them. Cooking fires signified home and food and water. Tau-ruv led her son back across the long escarpment, finding their willow-branch house just before sunrise. They collapsed into rabbitskin blankets and a deep, well-deserved sleep.

But she never returned to the cave and old basket high on the wall of the canyon. Tau-ruv became ill the next year and, despite the age-old remedies of her grandmother, died on a grief-filled winter day. Her face was ceremoniously washed, her body carefully buried in the hills above the village. Ayis grew into a strong man and skilled hunter. He eventually took a wife from the Owens Valley, as it came to be called, and raised children among its lush, river-fed meadows. He told them stories of his mother, about gathering seeds in the dry valley, and how to track bighorn sheep in the high desert mountains. Soon their lives would tragically change, as "cow men" and soldiers appeared from out of nowhere. But the old basket was secure, sheltered from rain and wind and never bothered by nesting packrats or mischievous coyotes. Its fibers and pigments were just beyond reach of the sun, whose light crept across the mouth of the cave for 50,000 days.

SUMMER 1975

The drive from Independence to the southern end of Eureka Valley had taken about three and a half hours, longer than usual because Mary wanted to look for populations of a rare cactus near Joshua Flat. But the main purpose of the trip was to collect additional specimens of a strange, summer-flowering shrub that she had discovered growing in the steep-walled canyon linking Eureka and Saline valleys.

The Bronco pitched left to right as the front wheel surmounted a chunk of bedrock on the canyon floor. In the early spring, flash flooding had swept away the veneer of gravel, exposing a large rib of limestone Mary had not seen before. "Better stop here," she said to husband Paul, who always drove cautiously in such remote places, "and we can walk the rest of the way." Ahead they saw a low wall of gray stone spanning the narrow canyon, worn smooth by infrequent cascades of raging water. Paul pulled the growling vehicle into a crescent of shade cast by a north-facing cliff. It was hot, but they carried plenty of water and a few tuna sandwiches.

Mary scrambled over the dry waterfall, recalling that she had not really expected to find anything flowering so late in the year. After all, summer in the northern Mojave was dry and hot, and most of the carbonate-loving plants would be dormant. The limestone monkey-flower *(Mimulus rupicola)*, which pokes its harlequin pink flowers out of vertical fissures, is hard to find by mid-June, even in a good rainfall year. But she loved coming back again and again to look for surprises. And last summer she found quite a surprise: a tall, conspicuous, yellow-flowered shrub unlike anything she had seen in her 20 years of desert botanizing. It was similar to wild buckwheats in the genus *Eriogonum* but did not possess all of the necessary diagnostic characteristics. Perhaps it was

Mary and Paul DeDecker in Eureka Valley, March 1978. (Author)

Limestone monkeyflower, its tap root in a fissure of carbonate rock. (Author)

a new species of buckwheat and could be named *eurekensis*, after the great sandy valley to the north of the canyon. As soon as she had returned home, she sent a few flowering branches to James Reveal at the University of Maryland, who, after much study and deliberation, wrote back with exciting news. This was not just a new species, but also a whole new genus of plants that he would name after her — *Dedeckera eurekensis*. "Quite a surprise and an honor," she thought, as the gravel crunched beneath her boot.

A half-mile or so up the canyon Mary and Paul DeDecker stopped to rest. Even shady rocks were hot to the touch, so they took long sips from plastic bottles and daubed wet handkerchiefs over sweaty faces. "It's just a few hundred yards ahead, so let's have lunch when we get there," she whispered to Paul, who nodded. "You know, Mary, we ought to be thinking about getting a new Jeep soon. I'm not sure how much longer we can trust the old Bronco on trips like this." Although seasoned and spry, both were in their seventies and neither relished the idea of getting stuck out in the desert. "The Johnsons are expecting us to arrive at the dune camp before dark, so we should keep moving."

The canyon twisted and turned, getting wide, then narrow, and changing color again and again. Light gray bands of Bonanza King Dolomite glowed in the afternoon sun, alternating with orange bands of sandstone and white bands of limestone. Each band was an ancient seafloor, hundreds of millions of years old, now uplifted, exposed and eroded: a desiccated layer cake left out in the elements. Walking up-canyon brought contact with higher and higher layers, each favored by different assemblages of carbonate-loving plants. Mary had found only a few shrubs of *Dedeckera* growing on Bonanza King and only in the vicinity of this one canyon. "What strange preferences to have," she thought. How did such a plant evolve? Could it be a relict as old as these mountains, persisting after ancestors had long disappeared?

Mary spotted the luminous shrub from a hundred feet away. The bright yellow flowers justified the informal name Mary had given it: July gold. This stout individual had a woody trunk nearly five inches across where it disappeared into the rock face. Desert shrubs as large as this are often several centuries old, and a few have been known to live for more than a thousand years. She gathered some branches while Paul broke out the sandwiches and set up the lunch spot. Each branch was carefully placed into a paper bag, to be carefully pressed back at the car. After a few weeks of drying, she would send them out to university herbaria (libraries of preserved plants), along with detailed information on where and when the collection was made. Specimens of an unusual, newly described plant from a remote corner of California are highly valued by research scientists.

But a new thought began to bother Mary as she ate lunch. The few *Dedeckera* shrubs

Above DeDecker's Blue Butterfly (*Icaricia acmon dedeckera*) feeds only on July gold. (Author)

Left July gold, a rare shrub that grows on the Bonanza King limestone of Inyo County. (M. Austin-McDermon)

she knew about at this spot were all fairly large and probably old. Where were the smaller, younger plants? To be sure, reproduction of desert shrubs is always sporadic, but a healthy population typically consists of seedlings, small individuals, and large individuals in various proportions. Not apparently true here. Was this evidence of a relict species slowly going extinct? Was it a conservation issue, with *Dedeckera eurekensis* a flowering version of the California Condor? "You know, Mary," Paul pointed with his carrot stick, "it looks like a few off-roaders have come up the canyon from Saline Valley pretty recently. Their tires came close to your plant there." Mary agreed, and became even more concerned about the fate of *Dedeckera* and its once remote home. She knew that more and more people would visit this place in the future, and that some might not take care to avoid these old shrubs with their powerful vehicles.

"Paul, I'm going to climb up here a little ways to look for more plants. Maybe I can find some younger ones and get a better idea of whether this population is going to hold its own." Paul knew better than to ask her not to go climbing around in search of plants; that was why they came. "Well, just be careful and don't go too high," he admonished. She stood up tall and placed her weathered hand on the rock. "It's not steep, and these pockmarks give you plenty to hang on to," she said, moving up slowly.

As she left the canyon floor behind, Mary followed the narrow, sloping ledges formed by the erosion of layered dolomite. In some places there were round grottoes, not quite caves, adjacent to the ledges. These were probably made by water dripping through cracks and slowly dissolving the otherwise hard rock. Most were a foot or two in diameter; a few were large enough to sit in. As she made her way, she counted the number of *Dedeckera* shrubs in two simple categories: those taller than her knee and those shorter. So far, none were in the second category.

Paul kept his eye on her the whole time, worrying to himself. At one point she stooped and disappeared. "Paul," she called out. He looked harder, a bit concerned. "Paul, I found a basket," she yelled louder. "A what?" He saw her come back to the edge, beaming a great

Another way of knowing. Specimen of Indian ricegrass deposited in the Jepson Herbarium, University of California at Berkeley. (Steve Matson)

wide smile and holding between her hands a conical object. "It's a woven basket, in good shape. It was just sitting in the back of a small hole. And guess what? There are still seeds in it."

Coming down was, of course, harder than going up, especially given the excitement and the use of only one arm, the other cradling the very old basket. She got back to Paul and held it out to him. "Look, it's so tightly woven. Some of the strands are colored. And the seeds. Look down at the bottom," she laughed with glee. "You can tell, those are *Dicoria* seeds from the dune. They still look like little bugs."

FALL 1999

I visited Mary and Paul at their Independence home before going on a camping trip to the Inyo Mountains. Their smiles were as wide as ever, their invitation to sit and talk as enthusiastic as the last, but they had slowed considerably. Mary took frequent naps on the couch; Paul had become quite hard of hearing. The living room was warm with afternoon sun, and the hollow ticking of a clock was the only sound when voices became quiet. On the wall were watercolors of mountain and desert places, painted with gray green, autumn rust, and pale blue—colors typical of the eastern Sierra. There were many photos of daughters, sons-in-laws, and grandchildren, of weddings, graduations, births, and reunions, of full lives lived on the edge of the Great Basin.

Mary's personal herbarium, which had more than 6,000 specimens, had been recently donated to the Rancho Santa Ana Botanical Garden in Claremont. Field trips out to the far desert were now rare as certain cacti. But they still maintained the important things in their lives: being together, keeping in touch with loved ones, watching the neighborhood change, and keeping track of the wildflower blooms and winter snows.

We talked about family members, camps we had shared at the dunes, conservation issues in the Owens Valley, and odd plants that still presented surprises. "*Dedeckera* was found in Coldwater Canyon, just east of Laws," she told me with a smile. "Way beyond the Eureka-Saline Canyon," now officially named DeDeckera Canyon on the maps, "but still on Bonanza King Dolomite. Such a strange distribution." More was known about its problems with reproduction after several years of study by her son-in-law, Del Weins, at the University of Utah. He came to the conclusion that this was an ancient species, a relict of evolution in the buckwheats that persisted at the edge of extinction in a hot, dry, modern world. This strange plant had made quite a scientific splash.

I wanted to ask her about the basket. "Mary, do you remember the basket you found in the canyon? You told me the story before, but I wanted to check with you."

"Oh yes," she said, "that was really something."

We talked for a while, reconstructing her discovery as best we could. Some details were lost in time. I wondered how it got there: Did the Indians have a nearby camp? Was there a trade route? Could it have been ceremonial? Mary thought that those mountains and Eureka Valley would have been too dry to support any long-term habitation. "There could have been higher rainfall long ago, allowing people to move more freely," I said.

"Yes, that could be. The basket may have been left as a food cache. Or maybe it was just an accident. We don't know," she said with a long breath. "So much time has passed, we'll never know."

Soon after its discovery Mary had taken the basket to the Phoebe Apperson Hearst Museum of Anthropology at the University of California at Berkeley, where it had been added to the collection. "They thought it was two or three hundred years old, at most. They weren't too excited; maybe it was too ordinary for them." Her disappointment passed. "But those seeds made it special." She caught her breath and looked out the window toward the Sierra crest. Mary was getting tired and I knew that the visit should soon end.

After returning home, I arranged to examine the basket and its contents. Leslie Freund, the collections manager at the Hearst Museum, retrieved it from the warehouse of materials that the university had carefully preserved from California and all over the world. This was but one small piece of the collection and had probably not been visited since Mary brought it in. Leslie impressed on me the importance of careful, gloved handling. She even provided an air

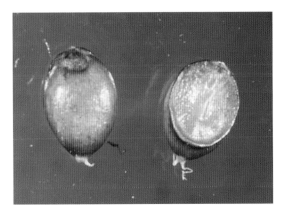

Upper The lost basket and its contents, deposited at the Hearst Museum of Anthropology, University of California at Berkeley. (Author)

Center Bugseeds. (Author)

Lower Grains of Eureka dunegrass. (Author)

pillow surface on which to place the ancient piece. Now that it had survived relatively intact in an open desert cave, she wanted to ensure its future. The dark, humidity-controlled, insect-free cabinet would do that, but I wondered if the basket somehow missed the sanctuary of limestone mountains.

Holding the basket was exciting. In addition to finally seeing its physical form, I could sense integrity, endurance, and mystery. The conical shape was in no way distorted, and it was larger than expected—more than a foot tall and almost a foot in diameter near its broken top. Faint red coloring, perhaps in a banded pattern, was still visible, and there were frayed attachments for a handle or sling. Long ago it had been patched near its pointed

EYE OF THE BEHOLDER

The desert's past is complex. Biologists, archeologists, and historians reevaluate each other's evidence now more than ever, looking for connections and inconsistencies and constructing a more robust understanding of that complex past. Rediscovery is thus aided by reinterpretation, along with lively debate among academic disciplines.

Perhaps this can be illustrated by an example from Death Valley. In 1956 a clay figurine was found in a shallow cave during an archeological survey. Buried beneath a thick layer of dust and debris on a rock ledge, the delicate artifact belonged to one of the many transient inhabitants of the shelter. It was described in a journal article as a "human effigy" similar to those of the Anasazi tradition from further south.

But it may have been a stretch to portray the figurine as human. The renowned archeologist William Wallace wrote:

> An incurving neck separates head from torso. Viewed from above the top of the
> head is flattish. . . . No facial features are portrayed, the blank facial region
> flaring upward to the top. A line of curving incisions around its upper border,
> seemingly made with a small fingernail, may represent hair or even a headdress.

bottom, but the weaving was still tight and strong. The inside had a thin, crusty lining of dried mud, probably the accumulated dust from slow erosion of the cave's ceiling.

Two other items accompanied the basket: one was a ziplock bag full of materials that had once been held by the ancient vessel, the other a note from Mary, dated July 29, 1975, stating where the discovery was made and the scientific name of the plant with the bug-like seeds *(Dicoria canescens* subsp. *clarkiae)*. I asked Leslie if I could carefully sift through the contents of the bag. She provided some pans and tools, as well as a dust mask in case there were disease-causing organisms in the mix. I poured a small pile of seeds, sand, and mud dust into one end of the sloping pan and began coaxing the stuff "downhill"

> The slightly rounded torso is wedge-shaped, tapering from sloping shoulders to a narrow, almost pointed base. Breasts were separately formed from tiny blobs of clay and then applied. The right one has broken away leaving only a roughened spot. . . . A small perforation, slightly below the middle of the body and a little right of center may indicate the navel. Arms and legs were not added.
>
> A double row of small punctuations runs from the tops of the shoulders to somewhat below the breasts. This V-shaped decoration, on the front only, is 2 cm long and 2 mm wide with the rows 1 mm apart. Apparently it depicts a bead necklace.

A biologist examining the same artifact may be struck by its resemblance to pup-fishes *(Cyprinodon)* of the Death Valley region. Although the body shape is not an exact match, the tailfin rays ("hair") and chevrons of scales ("necklace") are consistent with that reinterpretation. Instead of a human fertility symbol, medicinal totem, or doll, could this be a spiritual icon dedicated to a living mystery? Native people certainly knew of the fish and regarded their spring-fed habitats as sacred. T. S. Palmer of the Death Valley Expedition recorded that Indians brought them pupfishes for examination. Besides, other figurines found throughout the American southwest have been less problematic. Clay effigies that portray a grasshopper, horned toad, or bighorn sheep tend to look very realistic. And effigies intended to be human have "well-formed bodies, with modeled faces and anatomical features," according to one recent review. Perhaps examination of other artifacts from the region will provide a new interpretation.

Far left, Death Valley figurine (Edith S. Taylor); **left,** Anasazi effigies (National Park Service); **far right,** pupfish (D. W. Sada).

with a brush. The bugseeds looked typical for the species, with dark color and a fringed edge of short protrusions that resembled stubby legs. There were thousands of these, but occasionally I came across the smaller, flask-shaped grains of Indian ricegrass *(Achnatherum hymenoides)*, a plant known to be of great importance to desert people. It mostly grows in sand, its dense clumps of soft, long leaves found in lush stands on the west side of Eureka Dunes.

After 20 minutes of careful sorting, I found something unexpected and thrilling. It was the large, round grain of a very rare grass, Eureka dunegrass *(Swallenia alexandrae)*, whose entire existence is confined to the dunes of Eureka Valley and nowhere else on the planet. I recognized the grain because of my work on the ecology and conservation of this unusual species. This grass is like no other; its long, solid stems grow quickly to avoid burial by moving sand, forming scraggly hummocks that resemble grizzled beards. Its leaves are stiff and pungent but kept active during the hot summer by water stored deep in the dune. I kept searching the contents of the bag, finding five more Eureka dunegrass grains. The low number indicated that they were probably not a significant foodstuff, but their presence meant that someone had definitely been collecting on the Eureka Dunes and not in some other valley where the bugseeds or ricegrass grains could also be found. Mary would have been delighted by this finding, because we had both speculated many times about Indians and their use of Eureka Dunes. This evidence was irrefutable: native people obviously had a knowledge and appreciation of these desert places and desert resources that was transmitted across generations or, as in this case, passed on to us in the form of a lonely, lovely basket.

WINTER 2008

I have often thought about that basket and its seeds, and traditions developed over centuries, lost for such a long time and then rediscovered. Perhaps that is also true about desert knowledge, carefully woven from accumulated experiences and handed down between generations. As Paiute and Shoshone people were driven from Great Basin homelands, their knowledge of plants, animals, water, and landscapes, and the whole of their desert existence, became a lost inheritance. A few children learned what they could from elders, but most were overwhelmed by a new world of immigrants, prejudice, and modern values. Some of this knowledge persisted into the late twentieth century, when it began to be rediscovered, not just by scientists in the field and curators in museums, but also by the Indian people themselves. The memories and practices of tribal elders have resurfaced in living rooms and on back porches, even taught in classrooms beyond the reservation border. It is my hope that this book reflects the many ways desert knowledge is being rediscovered, amplified by new discoveries and given to future generations. Those generations will come to this place of wonder and beauty to make their own observations and to have their own revelations. This is a book about rediscovery as well as discovery—weaving a new basket, holding it sacred, and passing it on.

Rediscovery

Indians first observed the organisms, processes, and history of California deserts. Over millennia, native people obtained knowledge both practical and esoteric, necessitated by survival in a land of extremes and accumulated by active minds recording how nature worked. Such knowledge became tradition when passed across generations, allowing cultural adjustments to the changing environment. The depth and breadth of their understanding can only be glimpsed or imagined, but should never be minimized. Indians lived within deserts, were born, fed, and raised on them, suffered the extremes and uncertainties, and passed into the ancient, stony soils. Theirs was a discovery so intimate and spiritual, so singular, that we can only commemorate it with our own 10,000-year-long rediscovery of this place and all of its remarkable inhabitants. Our rediscovery has only begun.

Our rediscovery is not based upon living in the deserts, despite a current human population of over one million dwelling east of the Sierra. We do not exist within the ecological context of the land. We are not dependent upon food webs of native plants and

Aha Macav, the Mojave people, depicted in 1853. (H. B. Molhausen)

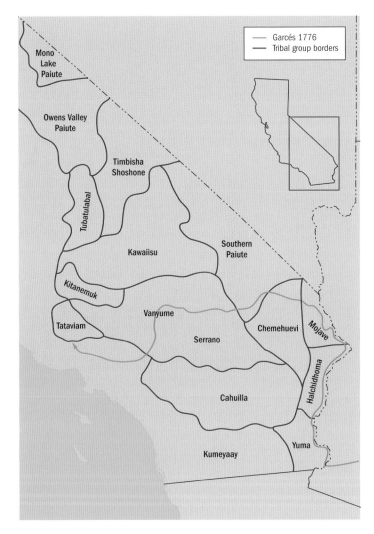

The aboriginal desert, showing linguistic territories and tribal regions.
(Based on Anderson 2005)

animals, nor do we contribute to the development of soils with our own ashes. We import building materials and energy sources and refuse to be fully subjected to the harsh climate or limited by the sparse waters. Instead, our rediscovery rises from a cultural juggernaut of explorers, immigrants, entrepreneurs, scientists, and artists with conflicting motives: some came to explore the deserts, some to conquer, some to understand, and others to cherish. Each motive left its imprint, and each determines the breadth of our rediscovery and the future of this arid region.

The first discovery of California deserts took place during the peopling of North America at the end of the Pleistocene, approximately 12,000 years ago. Glaciers, forests, rivers, and lakes retreated from lowland landscapes, gradually replaced by landforms and species favored by aridity. Such sweeping ecological changes necessitated human exploration because old ways of obtaining food and water became unreliable. The record of chipped stone tools, fish traps, cave dwellings, and other persistent material provides evidence of technological innovation and population migration as diverse peoples expanded or contracted their territories. But even as extreme conditions of drought and heat developed, there were no undiscovered springs, no lost herds of bighorn sheep, no "terra incognita" or "empty" lands. By the time Europeans arrived near the end of the eighteenth century, at least 12 major linguistic tribes, hundreds of cultural groups, and thousands of individuals had completely explored and occupied California's desert lands.

Friar Francisco Garcés, the first European to cross the Mojave Desert. (Unknown artist, USC Libraries)

The rediscovery of the California deserts was begun by Friar Francisco Garcés. Garcés was an intrepid, soft-spoken Franciscan missionary who often traveled alone or with a handful of Indian guides and interpreters. He was described at the time by Friar Pedro Font:

Father Garcés is so well fitted to get along with the Indians and to go among them that he appears to be but an Indian himself. Like the Indians he is phlegmatic in everything. He sits with them in the circle, or at night around the fire, with his legs crossed, and there he will sit musing two or three hours or more, oblivious to everything else, talking with them with much serenity and deliberation. And although the foods of the Indians are as nasty and dirty as those outlandish people themselves, the father eats them with great gusto and says that they are good for the stomach and very fine. In short, God has created him, as I see it, solely for the purpose of seeking out these unhappy, ignorant, and rustic people. (Cous 1900)

Macedonia Canyon, possibly used by Garcés to cross the
Providence Mountains and reach the Mojave River. (Author)

Unlike his contemporaries, Garcés was able to communicate across boundaries of ignorance with respect and kindness. He also was ambitious, introducing native souls to sacraments and attempting to establish a land route from New Mexico to the fledgling missions of California. Required by the crown of Spain to keep a *diario,* Garcés recorded in detail the native people he encountered and the landscapes he traversed. He left the mission of San Xavier del Bac (near Tucson) in 1771, crossed the Colorado River at Yuma, headed south to avoid the Algodones Dunes, entered the Imperial Valley, and traveled far enough north to see the San Bernardino Mountains. Garcés had also accompanied Lieutenant-Colonel Juan Bautista Anza on expeditions in 1774 and 1775, which included caravans of men, women, children, and animals across vast, uncharted terrain. Over his life, Garcés had made five such journeys, or *entradas,* logging more than 5,000 desert miles.

But the most remarkable *entrada* would make him the first European to enter the heart of the California deserts. In February 1776 he followed the Colorado River north from Yuma along with two Indians, a few horses, and some pack mules. After 15 days of rugged travel they reached a village of Mojave people (whom he called Jamajabs — "hama-ha-bees") in the vicinity of present-day Needles. He wrote:

I can say with entire truth that these Indians have great advantages over the Yumas and the rest of the Nations of the Rio Colorado; they are less molestful, and none are thieves; they seem valiant, and nowhere have I been better served. I showed them a picture of the Virgin; it pleased them very much. . . . As I am the first Español who has been in their land they celebrated it beyond bounds. . . .

The female sex is the most comely on the river; the male very healthy and robust. The women wear petticoats of the style and cut that the Yumas [wear]. The men go entirely naked, and in a country so cold this is well worthy of compassion. These say that they are very strong; and so I found them to be, especially in enduring hunger and thirst. It is evident that this nation goes on increasing, for I saw many lusty young fellows, and many more boys; the contrary is experienced in the other nations of the river. They came together to visit me about 20 hundred souls. Abound here certain blankets that they possess and weave of furs of rabbits and otters brought from the west and northwest, with the people of which parts they keep firm friendship.   (Cous 1900)

But the ambitious Garcés was not to remain with these vigorous people in their riverine paradise. Along with three Jamajabs he headed due west on March 4, covering six to 20 miles in a day, being led from one watering hole to another amidst the arid valleys and hills of eastern California. This was a major route for the Mojave people, who routinely traded with coastal tribes hundreds of miles away. Garcés and his party arrived at Cedar Spring in the Providence Mountains, where they met four naked Jamajabs returning from the west with highly prized seashells.

> I was lost in wonder to see that they brought no provisions whatever on a route where there is naught to eat, nor did they carry bows for hunting. They replied to my amazement "the Jamajabs endure hunger and thirst for four days," to give me to understand that indeed are they valiant men.
>
> (Cous 1900)

From these mountains Garcés was the first European to view the interior of this vast desert and its great sea of sand (near present-day Kelso). Descending into the dry lowlands, perhaps through Macedonia Canyon, was a pure act of faith. After two more days the party reached the flowing waters of a "saltish" river, which Garcés named the Arroyo de los Martires. They were somewhere between the south shore of Soda Lake (the terminus of the modern Mojave River) and the gaping mouth of Afton Canyon. The miracle of desert water brought forth cottonwood trees, wild grapes, and lush grass. Over the next 12 days Garcés described small villages of Vanyume people, who harvested the marshes and were skillful basket weavers.

Upper Garcés came to the terminus of the Mojave River at Soda Lake. The white flowers belong to yerba manza (*Anemopsis californica*), a common plant of saline marshes and alkali meadows. (Mona Bourell)

Lower Afton Canyon and the dry bed of the Mojave River. (Robert C. Pavlik)

Although provisions had been sparse (at one point the party killed and entirely consumed one of their horses, and "not even the blood was wasted"), the Vanyume "regaled me with hares, rabbits, and great abundance of acorn porridge, wherewith we relieved the great neediness that we had." This generosity astounded the gray-robed Franciscan:

> The [chief] of these rancherias [villages] presented me with a string of white seashells; and his wife sprinkled me with acorns and tossed the basket, which is a sign among these people of great [veneration]. In a little while after that she brought seashells in a small gourd, and sprinkled me with them in the way which is done when flowers are thrown. . . . I reciprocated these attentions as well as I could, and marveled to see that among these people so rustic are found demonstrations proper to the most cultivated, and a particular prodigality in scattering their greatest treasures, which are the shells.
>
> (Cous 1900)

Turning south with the river near present-day Barstow, they began to ascend the San Bernardino Mountains. Villages became numerous (mostly Serrano people) and more prosperous, as oaks, junipers, and pines formed the vegetation of the headwaters. Reaching the summit on March 21, 1776, Garcés could see the winding course of the Santa Ana River and the shimmering blue Pacific beyond. This epic desert *entrada* had come to an end, but the friar went on to Mission San Gabriel, Tejon Pass, Tulare Lake, and back to the Mojave River, probably by way of Tehachapi Pass and the Antelope Valley. His route established the California section of the Old Spanish Trail that thousands of immigrants would subsequently follow, and his *diario* recorded that singular, fleeting moment of first contact between two previously isolated worlds. One of those worlds would not survive, the world of vibrant indigenous culture and joyous hospitality. In 1781 Garcés himself was killed by Yuma Indians who could no longer tolerate exploitation and brutalization by the Spaniards.

Other explorers came for material, rather than spiritual, purposes, seeking a west-flowing river that would connect the deserts to the Pacific (the mythical Buenaventura River). Jedediah Smith came via Utah in 1826, a trapper searching the fur-producing waters of the continental interior. He had returned from California with several bales of beaver pelts and was seeking another route along the Virgin River in the fall of 1826. Smith was met at the Colorado by the Mojaves, who gave him a supply of "corn, beans, locust bread [made from beans of honey mesquite], and a little Indian flour." After building a raft to cross the river at what would become Fort Mojave, the party traversed the southern end of Lanfair Valley and intercepted the Garcés route at Vontrigger Spring. They crossed the Providence Mountains and Kelso Wash, and reached the Mojave River just as Garcés had done some 50 years before.

Our course was up the River which sometimes runs in sight and then for miles disappeared in the sands [hence he called it the Inconstant River]. In places I found grass and the Sugar Cane [the tall grass *Phragmites communis,* or carrizo] and in some places small Cottonwood. I also saw tracks of horses that had been here during the summer. My guides belonged to a tribe of Indians residing in the vicinity called the wanyumas [Vanyume], not numerous for this barren country could not support them. At this place was some sign of Antelope and Mt sheep. Mr. Rogers killed an antelope which tasted quite strong of wormwood [*Artemisia,* or sagebrush].

(Brooks 1977)

And like Garcés, Smith was greeted with great hospitality by these Vanyume people. They shared loaves of hard, crystalline sugar threshed from vast quantities of cut cane. Trade with upslope tribes provided the same acorn mush that Garcés appreciated, and a sweet bread made from pinyon pine nuts. Smith also witnessed a rabbit hunt:

As there were in the neighborhood a plenty of hares the Indians said they must give us a feast. Several went out for this purpose with a net 80 or 100 yards long. Arriving at a place where they knew them to be plenty the net was extended among the wormwood. Then divided on each wing they moved in such direction as to force the frightened game to the net where they were taken while tangled in its meshes. Being out but a short time they brought in two or three dozen a part of which they gave me. (Brooks 1977)

Other sections of his trip were more arduous, but not without small wonders worthy of a note in the trapper's journal:

I traveled a west course fifteen days over a country of complete barrens, generally traveling from morning until night without water. I crossed a salt plain about 20 miles long and 8 wide [probably Soda Lake]; on the surface was a crust of beautiful white salt, quite thin. Under the surface there was a layer of salt from a half to one and a half inches in depth; between this and the upper layer there is about four inches of yellowish sand. (Brooks 1977)

Smith's party arrived in San Gabriel, headed north to the San Joaquin Valley and east to cross the Sierra for the first time at Ebbetts Pass in May 1827. Passing Walker Lake, he may have been one of the first Europeans to cross the Great Basin of eastern California and central Nevada on his way back to Great Salt Lake. But he never struck the Buenaventura, leaving others to that legendary quest.

Peter Skein Ogden, another fur trapper, followed the Humboldt River across central Nevada in 1829 but headed south from Walker Lake to cross the White-Inyo Range for the first time. His party came to the Owens River, followed it through Owens Valley, past Owens Lake, and all the way to the Gulf of California. But beaver had already become scarce, so they turned north and east back to Utah without finding a better route to the Pacific.

John C. Frémont ("The Pathfinder") led his expeditions in the 1840s with the expressed purpose of finding the Buenaventura (and an unexpressed purpose of conducting military reconnaissance), but he was also the first scientific explorer to enter the California deserts. Trained as a topographic engineer, Frémont also had an appreciation of geology and botany. On his second expedition during the spring of 1844, he and a party (which included the guide Kit Carson) followed the crest of the Transverse Ranges from Tejon Canyon to Cajon Pass, along the southwest edge of the Antelope Valley. They were searching for the western end of the Garcés route, using the Mojave River to go north and east through Tecopa and Las Vegas. He wrote about descending into the desert:

[We] emerged from the *yucca* forest at the foot of an outlier of the Sierra before us, and came among the fields of flowers we had seen in the morning, which consisted principally of the rich orange-colored Californian poppy, mingled with other flowers of brighter tints. Reaching the top of the spur, which was covered with fine bunch grass, and where the hills were very green . . . we

John C. Frémont, explorer, botanist, territorial governor, and presidential candidate. (Unknown artist, Bancroft Library)

continued our beautiful road, and reached a spring in the slope, at the foot of the ridge, running in a green ravine, among granite boulders; here nightshade, and borders of buckwheat, with their white blossoms around the granite rocks, attracted our notice as familiar plants. Several antelopes were seen among the hills, and some large hares. . . .

We continued on through a succession of valleys, and came into a most beautiful spot of flower fields: instead of green, the hills were purple and orange, with unbroken beds, into which each color was separately gathered. A pale straw color, with a bright yellow, the rich red orange of

the poppy mingled with fields of purple, cover the spot with a floral beauty; and, on the border of the sandy deserts, seemed to invite the traveler to go no farther. (Jackson and Spence 1970)

The flower fields are still visible today in the Gorman Hills, Tejon Ranch, and the Antelope Valley California Poppy State Reserve, as are the granitic rocks that lie along this portion of the San Andreas Fault. They camped among the "nut pines," from which Frémont collected the first specimens of pinyon pine *(Pinus monophylla)*, and struck the Old Spanish Trail on April 20 just north of Cajon Pass. Within a day they were following the Mojave River north (past the "narrows" of Victorville), noticing that they were on a rather well-worn road through a rapidly changing wilderness:

We traveled down the right bank of the stream, over sands which are somewhat loose, and have no verdure, but are occupied by various shrubs. A clear bold stream,

Upper   Tejon Canyon Pass, possibly Frémont's route across the Tehachapi Range and into the Mojave Desert. (Author)

Lower   California poppies and Joshua trees in the western Antelope Valley. (Q. T. Luong)

Upper   Upper Narrows of the Mojave River near Victorville, where Garcés and other explorers of this desert must have passed. (Author)

Lower   Riparian forest along the Mojave River near Camp Cady, dominated by Fremont cottonwood (*Populus fremontii*). (Author)

60 feet wide, and several feet deep, had a strange appearance, running between perfectly naked banks of sand. The eye, however, is somewhat relieved by willows, and the beautiful green of the sweet cottonwoods [later to be named *Populus fremontii*] with which it is well wooded. As we followed along its course, the river, instead of growing constantly larger, gradually dwindled away, as it was absorbed by the sand. We were now careful to take the old camping places of the annual Santa Fe caravans, which, luckily for us, had not yet made their yearly passage. A drove of several thousand horses and mules would entirely have swept away the scanty grass at the watering places.

(Jackson and Spence 1970)

Cautiously venturing beyond the dry riverbed, they made their way past present-day Barstow, obtaining water from shallow wells that coyotes had dug into the wet sands. The sun burned, the air was hot, and a strong wind drew moisture from every breath. The progression toward aridity changed the country into a series of desolate basins separated by rocky slopes and serrated ridges. Nevertheless, Frémont continued his botanical observations:

> But, throughout this nakedness of sand and gravel, were many beautiful plants and flowering shrubs, which occurred in many new species, and with greater variety than we had been accustomed to see in the most luxuriant prairie countries; this was a peculiarity of this desert. Even where no grass would take root, the naked sand would bloom with some rich and rare flower, which found its appropriate home in the arid and barren spot.
>
> Scattered over the plain, and tolerably abundant, was a handsome leguminous shrub, three or four feet high, with fine bright-purple flowers. It is a new *psoralea*, and occurred frequently henceforward along our road. [The shrub would later be named *Psorothamnus fremontii*.]
>
> (Jackson and Spence 1970)

This was at least 60 years before the biological study of home would be called *ecology* and more than 100 years before the Mojave's richness of unique plant species would be fully documented. And his observations of floral diversity (and beauty) were not just made from the perch of a saddle, 10 feet above the soil surface. The flowers of many species barely overtop the surrounding pebbles. It is amusing to imagine John C. Frémont, who eventually led the Bear Flag Rebellion and became territorial governor, stooped before a patch of "belly plants" enthusiastically cataloging the desert flora.

Upper   Fremont's indigobush (*Psorothamnus fremontii*), one of many plants named for "The Pathfinder." (Gary A. Monroe)

Lower   The flowers told Frémont that the "handsome leguminous shrub" he discovered belonged to the pea family. (James M. Andre)

The expedition turned north to intersect the Amargosa River where it flows into Death Valley (near the Salt Creek Hills). More plants were collected as they passed through the narrow river canyon (including both species of mesquite and the caperlike *Oxystylis* known

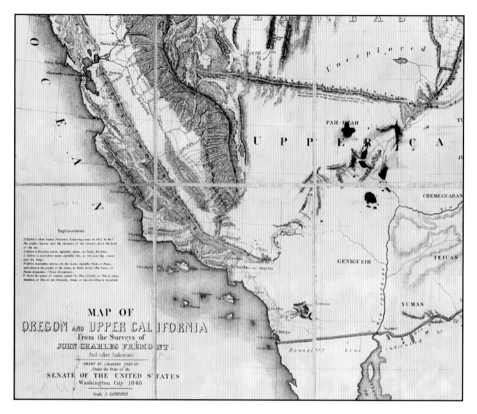

Imagine crossing the vast intermountain west using John Frémont's map of 1848. (From Lines 1999)

only from this drainage). Crossing the Ibex Hills and the ancient, eroded bed of Lake Tecopa, he wrote:

[W]e traversed a part of the desert, the most sterile and repulsive that we had yet seen. Its prominent features were dark *sierras*, naked and dry; on the plains a few straggling shrubs — among them cactus of several varieties. Fuentes pointed out one called the Spaniards *bisnada* [probably *Ferocactus cylindraceus*], which has a juicy pulp, slightly acid, and is eaten by the traveler to allay thirst. Our course was generally north; and, after crossing an intervening ridge, we descended into a sandy plain or basin, in the middle of which was the grassy spot, with its springs and willow bushes, which constitutes a camping place in the desert, and is called the *Archilette*.

(Jackson and Spence 1970)

The grassy spot was probably the lush marshes fed by Tecopa Springs, surrounded by ice age lake sediments and layers of volcanic ash. They stopped at Resting Springs to bury the bodies of a Mexican man and boy who had been killed and mutilated by vengeful Indians, and went on to make Las Vegas ("the meadows") by May 3.

When he finally returned to the eastern states, half of Frémont's 1,400 plant specimens had not survived the journey. Some were lost by accident, others destroyed or damaged during river crossings or by "the dreadful flood of the Kansas." The remainder was given to Frémont's academic counterpart, Dr. John Torrey, who began the process of describing and naming many species previously unknown to science. Convention and modesty prevented Torrey from naming these plants after himself or Frémont, but authorship of each species description was shared and remains valid today (for example, desert trumpet is still officially known as *Eriogonum inflatum* Torrey and Fremont). Frémont published his epic, often flamboyant report in 1845, which became a best seller among those following his adventures and those who would soon aspire to westward migration.

COMING TO CONQUER

To overland immigrants, California was separated from the rest of the continent by two great obstacles: the Sierra Nevada and the "Great American Desert." Frémont's expeditions convinced them the obstacles could be surmounted, while Marshall's discovery of gold convinced them the effort would pay off. Although passage from Salt Lake City into southern Nevada was filled with challenge, the Old Spanish Trail through arid California was considered especially dangerous. Jim Bridger and Kit Carson had followed it on horseback and warned against taking wagons, women, and children by that route. The essential elements of water, wood, grass, and game were in short supply, and much of the region remained unmapped until 1861. Frémont simply labeled much of this desert country as "unexplored" on his map of 1848, but the lure of California was overpowering.

The first wagon train to attempt the desert crossing was led by Jefferson Hunt in 1849. Having spent 30 days in a long caravan from Salt Lake City, Hunt's party of 107 wagons and 500 cattle, horses, and oxen had become fragmented and spread across an increasingly difficult landscape. A small splinter group, guided by William Manley, found their way to Ash Meadows in western Nevada by early December. The springs and grass of "Relief Valley" (now called Amargosa Valley) provided a boost before pushing toward the snowy mountain (Telescope Peak) they mistook for the final Sierran barrier. Manley wrote his famous, detailed memoir in 1894:

Some who had read Frémont's travels said that the range immediately west of us must be the one he described, on the west of which was beautiful country, of rich soil and having plenty of cattle, and horses and containing some settlers, but on the east all was barren, dry rocky, sandy desert as far as could be seen. We know this eastern side answered well the description and believed that this was really the range described, or at least was close by.

The view of snowy Telescope Peak, which haunted William Manley's party during the winter of 1849/1850. (Charles Webber)

Ahead of the Manley party were the "Jayhawkers," a group of exuberant, impetuous, and youthful gold seekers that believed they could cross this false Sierra to the north, over what is now called Towne Pass. But first they had to traverse the deep, salty valley that lay ahead, a valley deceptive in size and difficult of passage. Manley scouted it with determination, hoping that the route was not as bad as it looked:

I was pretty near the summit, where a pass through the rocky range [between the Funeral and Black mountains] had been found and on this mountain not a tree or shrub or spear of grass could be found—desolation beyond conception. I carried my gun along every day, but for the want of a chance to kill any game a single load would remain in my gun for a month. Very seldom a rabbit could be seen, but not a bird of any kind, not even a hawk, buzzard or crow made their appearance here.

In one of the perpendicular portions [of Furnace Creek Canyon] it seemed to be a variegated clay formation, and a little water seeped down its face. Here the Indians had made a clay bowl and fastened it to the wall so that it could collect and retain about a quart of water, and I had a drink of water, the first one since leaving the running stream.

Manley unknowingly led his wagon train into the driest, hottest, lowest, and least vegetated valley in North America. Determination and optimism rapidly gave way to the reality of this extreme desert. Juliette Brier recalled in 1897:

The '49ers cross Death Valley. (Unknown artist, Bancroft Library)

We reached the top of the divide between Ash Meadows and Death Valley, and oh! what a desolate country we looked down upon. The men said they could see what looked like springs down in the valley. . . .

I was sick and weary, and the hope of a good camping place was all that kept me up. Poor little Kirk [her two-year-old son] gave out and I carried him on my back, barely seeing where I was going, until he would say, "Mother, I can walk now." Poor little fellow! He would stumble on a little ways over the salty marsh and sink down crying, "I can't go any farther." Then I would carry him again and soothe him the best I could. . . .

I was ready to drop, and Kirk was almost unconscious, moaning for a drink. Mr. Brier took him on his back and we hastened to camp to save his life. It was 3 o'clock Christmas morning when we reached the springs [Travertine Springs near the mouth of Furnace Creek Wash]. I only wanted to sleep; but my husband said I must eat and drink or I would never wake up.   (Latta 1979)

Mrs. Brier was one of the first three white women to enter Death Valley, along with Abigail Arcan and Sarah Bennett. Their fortitude had already been tested, but the party was still more than 200 miles north of Los Angeles and almost 300 miles from the Pacific Ocean, with several intervening mountain ranges and the western Mojave to cross. The journey was now desperate, but many of the hardships had been self-imposed. The historian Frank Latta pointed out:

(text continues on page 35)

ALONG THE MOJAVE RIVER IN 1863

Originating on Butler Peak in the San Bernardino Mountains (8,535 feet), the east fork of the Mojave River brings snowmelt into the hot, dry desert. During wet years the surge of water extends to Helendale, the former site of an extensive freshwater marsh. Deep sands absorb most of the runoff beyond this point, but local drainages and bedrock basins can bring flows back to the surface. Re-emerging in Afton Canyon, the Mojave picks up groundwater tinged with alkali, which it delivers to the sink of Soda Lake (937 feet elevation).

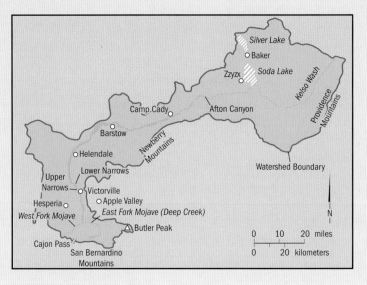

The Mojave River system: ancient remnant, historical landmark, modern treasure. (Based on Lines 1999)

Along its 120-mile-long course, the "Inconstant River" not only provided the water and feed that made desert exploration possible, it also offered psychological comfort in a frightful and foreboding landscape. Traveling from east to west in 1853, Gwynne Heap captured the fear of crossing the dry expanse from the Colorado River to Soda Lake:

> The solitude was unrelieved by the song of bird or the chirp of insect; the mournful murmur of the breeze, as it swept over the desert, was the only sound that broke the silence. In many places a deceptive mirage spread fictitious lakes and spectral groves to our view, which a puff of wind or a change in our position, suddenly dissolved. . . .

The pale moon occasionally overshadowed by clouds threw a ghostly light over the desert, and skeletons of animals glistening in her beams, strewed the way, adding horror to the scene.

And he also conveyed the sense of relief after this section of the journey had been passed and the Mojave River was reached:

Beginning a desert journey at Cajon Pass Tollhouse along the Government Road, 1863. (Rudolph D'Heureuse, Bancroft Library)

The sandy soil through which the Mohaveh flows absorbs nearly all its water, and where we struck it [east of Daggett] was no longer a running stream. Grass, however, was everywhere abundant together with a thick growth of willows, reed, mesquite bushes, interlaced with grapevines; and in some places there were beautiful groves of cottonwoods.

Where we crossed the Mohaveh [two days later] it was a rapid stream, twenty-five yards in breadth and one foot in depth, but its water was too warm to be drinkable. Passed several fine meadows near the river and saw bands of antelopes, also hares and partridges. . . . The road leading up to an extensive plain thickly covered with cedars and pines [California junipers and pinyon], intermingled with palmyra cactus and aloes [Joshua trees and Mojave yucca].

The western section of the river route, from Cajon Pass to Camp Cady, remained an important corridor for travel into the twentieth century (much of it was later paralleled by U.S. Highway 66). But the drier, eastern section of the Garcés route, from Soda Lake to the Colorado River, was replaced in 1858 with a new road that could support wagons and large numbers of immigrants. This "Government Road" took advantage of several strong, well-positioned springs (Government, Rock, Marl) that had been surveyed along the 35th parallel. It was built by Edward F. Beale, who received funding from the U.S. Army and who used camels to support the construction effort. Small earthen forts (redoubts) were established at key locations to protect the flow of mail, soldiers, and travelers from hostile Chemehuevis and Southern Paiutes. Lieutenant Milton Carr described Hancock's Redoubt at Soda Springs (near present-day Zzyzx) after completion in June 1860:

Lay over to-day to rest the horses and finish the Redoubt. Had it finished so that a small party of men can hold it securely against any number of Indians

➤

Upper left   Bed of the Mojave River above Afton Canyon. Dr. Stark examines the sandy, open banks. (Rudolph D'Heureuse, Bancroft Library)

Lower left   The redoubt at Camp Cady. (Rudolph D'Heureuse, Bancroft Library)

Right   First botanical photo from the California deserts. The lineup includes (left to right) beavertail cactus, silver cholla, California barrel cactus, creosote bush, Mojave yucca, and barrel cactus. (Rudolph D'Heureuse, Bancroft Library)

that will ever be likely to be in that part of the country. Loop-holes are so arranged around the top, that men inside of the redoubt can command all the ground around, without exposing themselves to the fire of the Indians. Had the front traverse so arranged, also, that it will afford secure shelter to three or four horses.   (Duffield-Stoll 1994)

The first photographer of the California deserts, Rudolph D'Heureuse, traveled along the Mojave River and the Government Road with Philadelphia Company in 1863. His photos show the journey from Cajon Pass to the Colorado River, including "Narrows," "Lanes Crossing," and the "Caves," places that Garcés would have recognized from the century before. Wagons and lone travelers are shown against the pristine landscape—no salt cedar or other weeds are visible. The first deliberate botanical photo from the bioregion was taken near Rock Springs, as men posed with arranged specimens of beavertail cactus *(Opuntia basilaris)*, silver cholla *(O. echinocarpa)*, and California barrel cactus *(Ferocactus cylindraceus)*, along with Mojave yucca *(Yucca schidigera)* and creosote bush *(Larrea)*. In another haunting image, a Dr. Stark

Upper left Philadelphia Company poses at Rock Springs, 1863, an important water supply along the Government Road. (Rudolph D'Heureuse, Bancroft Library)

Lower left Dr. Stark with Mojave women in "modern" dresses made from traditional materials. (Rudolph D'Heureuse, Bancroft Library)

Right Author poses at Rock Springs, 2005, now in the Mojave National Preserve. (Richard Hiett)

stands awkwardly beside two young Mojave women wearing rabbit-fur clothes and shell necklaces from a culture that would soon disappear. And when Philadelphia Company finally reached the great Colorado, its riverbed was open, rocky, and un-vegetated, revealing a long history of terrible floods. These precious photos are the last glimpses of an ancient, intact desert bioregion in California.

In addition, their improvidence regarding the use and conservation of drinking water soon becomes apparent to one who reads about Death Valley '49ers. They made no intelligent use of the Indians who occupied almost every portion of the great desert across which they were traveling. A few presents of coffee, sugar or beads would have caused the Indians to lead them to water or to the trail of the Hunt party, which was, during most of the time, only a few days' travel south of them. News of such treatment would have traveled days ahead of them and would have paved the way for their safe and speedy passage to California.

Instead of cultivating the acquaintance and friendship of the Indians, they stole corn, squashes and other foodstuffs from them and gave them every reason to keep out of sight.

Indians were following the party at all times. . . . The Indians were actually trying to help them. At the head of Searles Lake Valley a small group of Indians presented themselves to Jay Hawk Deacon Richards, led him to the water which the '49ers called Providence Spring and unquestionably saved the lives of some forty struggling, famished persons.

It became necessary for the Bennett-Arcan party to set up camp near Tule Springs, almost 280 feet below sea level, and wait for Manley and John Rogers to go on ahead to Los Angeles and return with food and knowledge of the route. The 26-day rescue, like the journey as a whole, was both heroic and foolhardy. They returned to find most of the party still alive, maniacal with gratitude and anxious to surmount the looming Panamint Range. After several days of a long, rocky climb, Manley recalled:

Just as we were ready to leave and return to camp we took off our hats, and then overlooking the scene of so much trial, suffering and death spoke the thought uppermost saying: — "Good bye Death Valley!" then faced away and made our steps. . . . Ours was the first visible footsteps, and we the party named it the saddest and most dreadful name that came to us first from its memories.

Eventually they would make their way through Panamint, Searles, and Indian Wells valleys, joining the Joe Walker Trail and turning south toward Soledad Canyon near Palmdale. They would not arrive in the oak-filled canyons and luxurious meadows of Ranch San Francisquito (Newhall) until March 7, 1850.

Other parties of immigrants wisely avoided the Death Valley region entirely. Some kept farther south to connect with the drainage of the Mojave River and Cajon Pass; others followed the eastern Sierra from Reno through Owens Valley before linking up with the Walker Trail. A third option was westward from Tucson to Yuma and north into the Coachella Valley and San Gorgonio Pass. A steadily increasing stream of people led to commercial transportation and government engineering projects. Stagecoaches were already operating in northern California before the '49ers had left Death Valley. Regular service across arid lands was established by 1860. Roads soon proliferated, some constructed of wood planks on shifting sands, others hand-cut into solid rock. Now the desert and its inhabitants could be conquered by a flood of people in search of land, as well as gold.

European settlement of Owens Valley began in 1861 with the establishment of ranches in lush, creek-fed meadows. Until this time more than 2,000 Owens Valley Paiutes had harvested bulbs and roots from these meadows *(pitana patu)*, even developing an irrigation system and cultivation practices that greatly increased natural productivity. Violence soon erupted south of present-day Bishop, beginning a conflict that required military intervention. Lt. Colonel George Evans of the Second Cavalry, California Volunteers, was dispatched with a garrison to engage the Indians, tempting them to fight by destroying their food caches. On July 1 he wrote to commanders in San Francisco:

The Indians claim the valley as belonging to them, and still insist upon it that no white man shall settle, or, as they term it, sit down in the valley. They say that whites may locate in the hills and work the mines, but must not sit down on the grass patches.

These Indians subsist at this season of the year entirely upon the grass seeds and nuts gathered in the valley from the lake up, and the worms gathered at the [Owens] lake. They gather this food in large quantities during the summer and prepare it for winter use, which together with the pinon nuts gathered in the mountains in the fall of the year, is their only subsistence. Without this food gathered and laid up they cannot possibly subsist through the winter. From the facts set forth above, the nature of these Indians and the surrounding country, it does seem to me that the only way in which they can be chastised and brought to terms is to establish a temporary post, say for one winter, at some point near the center of the valley, from which point send and keep scouts continually ranging through the valley, keep the Indians out of the valley and in the hills, so that they can have no opportunity of gathering and preserving their necessary winter supplies, and they will be compelled to sue for peace before spring and grass come again.

(McGrath 1988)

By 1862 Camp Independence had been established and a truce signed with the starved and subjugated Paiutes. The ranchers and miners returned, and the Visalia Delta reported on September 25:

The Indian troubles have finally ceased to scare the timid or retard our progress, from the fact that a military post has been established on Owens' River. So those wishing to pay us a visit need have no fears of leaving their scalps.

(McGrath 1988)

But hostilities were soon renewed in the spring of 1863 with the death of Joaquin Jim, who had led the Paiutes. The lives of 200 Indians and 30 whites were soon lost by mutual atrocity, but the ultimate blow to indigenous Owens Valley culture was to separate the Paiute from their "grass patches," seeds, nuts, and worms. Separation led to desperate dependency, as a militiaman from Lone Pine related to the Visalia Delta (January 11, 1865):

We have fed them all summer, and it is a pretty hard thing now, because we are unable to do it any longer on account of County Taxes, high price of living, and altogether are unable to do it any longer to have our throats cut and butchered. Only last week an Indian drew his knife on my wife because she would not let him take possession of the kitchen and give him sugar in his coffee.

(McGrath 1988)

Immigration and settlement would continue to drive a wedge between native peoples and their lands, withering a long tradition of desert knowledge. The Vanyume tribe, first

A Cahuilla man tends beans and transforms the Imperial Valley from desert into farm. (George W. James)

encountered by Garcés near Afton Canyon, had already been collected into missions between 1820 and 1834 and driven to extinction before the end of the century. Government subdivision of the "vacated" territory had begun in 1855, with the first European crops planted along the Mojave River in 1872.

The rush of progress accelerated after a series of railroad surveys were launched in the 1850s, with construction begun in the 1870s and 1880s. The purpose of the surveys was to find routes to serve industrial mining and agricultural development, as well as westward expansion. Eventually the desert would be crossed by five major lines, with a dozen or more smaller branch operations that facilitated the transport of ore, produce, and cattle. The stage had been set for burgeoning commerce and land speculation, to be finally and completely unleashed when desert waters were driven into canals and pipelines. As he chronicled the hopeful agrarian spirit of this era, George Wharton James wrote (1914):

In the Antelope Valley, on the Mohave desert, . . . astonishing transformations have taken place. . . . Forty, fifty years ago, herds of antelope roamed over this valley in vast numbers, hence the name. Standing at what is now Palmdale one can look over about 640,000 acres, of what in those early days were regarded as absolutely irreclaimable desert. Thirty years ago, before the day of the gasoline engine and cheap pumping-plant, settlers came to this gaunt land of yuccas, brush, grass and sage. They dug wells, and found enough water for their own use near enough to the surface. . . .

In 1909 it was discovered that one of these men who, seventeen years before, had planted pear trees, was receiving $2,000 per acre *gross*, from his crop. . . . The result can be well imagined. . . . Here, as in so many other regions of California, the constant cry is for more capital for development, and as fast as it comes it is being put into good use—use that will soon convert land that has been "desert" for centuries into orchards of beauty and great monetary value.

To some mentalities, however, there may not seem to be much beauty in the romantic transformation of the desert, yet there are few who can look upon these vast fields of green alfalfa, the immense areas of olive, orange, lemon, peach, apricot, pomegranate and fig orchards, with the stately groves of tropical date-palms, the miles and miles of luscious melons and cantaloupes, and the thousands of acres of growing cotton with its fluffy balls of purest white making the green all the more delicious, without feeling a quick wave of admiration sweep over him.

All that has been said of the remarkable development of the Imperial Valley applies with equal force to the Coachella Valley, except that the source of the water, which has worked the transformation is different. . . . [A] few years ago the government, in seeking to aid the Indian, sunk a trial artesian well. At great depth a marvelous flow of pure water was struck, which came forth with such force as to demonstrate the existence of a great underground flow. Since then scores of wells have been put in from above Indio to below Mecca, with gratifying results. . . . In 1913 I put in a well on land I had purchased from the Southern Pacific Company. We went down in the neighborhood of nine hundred feet, and there came rushing out [the water], with great force over the casing.

James describes the rapid progress of the late nineteenth century that would finally conquer these desert lands. Mass migration, settlement, military enforcement, establishment of reservations, access, and modern agriculture would displace the original inhabitants, humans and otherwise. Once its wildness was subdued, the "Great American Desert" would no longer be feared, but instead regarded as a vast interior in need of reclamation. Even tourism would come with the easy access afforded by the first railroads and highways, supported by mission-style rest stops in the wilderness (for example, Kelso Depot), and even grand hotels in Barstow (Casa del Desierto) and Needles (El Garcés). Outsiders with romantic and often bizarre notions of this changing landscape and its people could now follow the ancient footpaths in luxury. The text of a Santa Fe Railroad postcard from the early 1900s proclaimed the sad juxtaposition of old and new:

Close to Needles live the remnants of the once powerful and warlike tribe of Indians, the Mojaves, now beggarly hangers-on to civilization, who love to congregate around the trains and offer their wares to passengers.

Postcard from the El Garcés Hotel along the Santa Fe Railroad at Needles. (Unknown photographer, California Historical Society)

The Chemehuevi people expressed their understanding of the California deserts in myth and ritual song. As transcribed from tribal elders by the anthropologist Alfred Kroeber in the early twentieth century:

The heros are Coyote and his elder brother Puma . . . who build a house on Nuvant [Charleston Peak] while the world is still covered with water. When the earth has become dry through the instrumentality of an old woman in the west, [they] could not find men. Coyote marries a louse, from whose eggs spring many tribes. The Chemehuevi themselves, however, the Mohave, and other southerners come from Coyote's own voidings [scat]. As shamans dream of Nuvant, they see there Coyote and Puma and Yunakat, the personification of food. The shamans acquire their songs and powers from these or other mythological beings at Nuvant. A man "dreams" of the time when the earth was still wet from the primeval flood and without mountains, when the cane sprang up and Older Brother Puma instructed him in detail how to make each part of bow and arrow . . . [and] to flake arrowheads.

Such tales of origins, animal deities, sacred mountains, and knowledge were probably told during rituals. A cyclic ritual, consisting of 100 or 200 songs about a single myth, often began an elaborate ceremony that could last for days. The Chemehuevi had four song cycles, entitled "Salt," "Deer," "Mountain Sheep," and "Shaman's," while the Mojave people had 30. "Salt" told the story of four mountain-sheep brothers traveling from the Aha'av'ulype [Providence Mountains] toward Yava'avi-ath'i [near Daggett] along portions of the lower Mojave River:

On the way they saw and talked or disputed about their tears, their powers and future, several insects, rats, birds, and tobacco plants, meteors and constellations, and a lake which they took to be the sea. Then they turned southeastward across the desert, and finally at Himekuvauva [west of Parker], their tears turned into salt and they into stone. The Chemehuevi now gather salt there, the Mohave say, and sing what they have dreamed about Salt.

The myths and songs, rendered in dream states and visions, were nevertheless inspired by the reality of the desert. Memories of vast lakes, the arrival of aridity, and the deposition of salt were part of the collective understanding of the landscape in which the Chemehuevi lived. These facts were rediscovered by expeditions that included observant military officers and scientists. This is illustrated in the report of William P. Blake, who served as geologist on the 1853 railroad survey of Lt. R. S. Williamson of the Army Corps of Topographical Engineers. While crossing the Salton Basin, he noted:

On turning around the point, I saw a discoloration of the rocks extending for a long distance in a horizontal line on the side of the mountains. On approaching this, it was found that the white color was produced by a calcareous incrustation, extending over the whole surface, and into every cavity and crevice. This crust had evidently been deposited under water, and, when seen at a distance of a few yards, its upper margin appeared to form a distinct line, which indicated the former level of the water under which it was deposited. This water-line, at the point where it was first observed, was only about fifteen feet above the general level of the clay, but it could be traced along the mountain sides, following all the angles and sinuosities of the ridges for many miles—always preserving its horizontality—sometime being high up above the plain, and again intersecting long and high slopes of gravel and sand; on such places a beach-line could be traced. These evidences of a former submergence were so vivid and conclusive that it became evident to every one in the train [of wagons] that we were traveling in the dry bed of a former deep and extended sheet of water, probably an *Ancient Lake* or an extensive bay. . . .

In the interstices of the incrustation, and in its mass, many small spiral shells were found; they were also very abundant upon the surface of the clay. . . . They were so numerous in some places. Five or six species of the genera, *Planorbis, Anodonta, Physa,* and *Amnicola,* were soon collected, and showed that the former lake was of fresh water. . . .

The adjoining valleys in the mountains, and the upper portions of the slope of the Desert are inhabited by a tribe of Indians called Cohillas. Up to the time of our arrival their country had never been visited by the whites with a train of wagons. . . .

The chief, or "capitan," and the principal men having collected for a talk with Lieutenant Parke, they learned

Upper   The waterline of ancient Lake Cahuilla, on the west side of the Salton Trough. (Author)

Lower   Shells of freshwater mollusks embedded in desert soils of the Salton Trough, evidence of Lake Cahuilla. (Author)

the object of our visit, and appeared much pleased. When questioned about the shore-line and water marks of the ancient lake, the chief gave an account of a tradition they have of a great water *(agua grande)* which covered the whole valley and was filled with fine fish. There was also plenty of geese and ducks. Their fathers lived in the mountains and used to come down to the lake to fish and hunt. The water gradually subsided *"poco a poco"* (little by little) and their villages were moved down from the mountains, into the valley it had left. They also said that the waters once returned very suddenly and overwhelmed many of the people and drove the rest back to the mountains.

The Indians had a grand feast and dance during the night, keeping us awake by their strange songs and indescribable noises. At 4 A.M. the temperature of the spring was 56 degrees and the air 52 degrees.

Fish traps precisely mark the shoreline of ancient Lake Cahuilla where it is now desert scrub. (Author)

Clearly, Blake had rediscovered ancient Lake Cahuilla, which had been filled most recently by the Colorado River in prehistoric times and was over 100 miles long and 300 feet deep. Along its shallows the Indians built fish traps that still mark the shoreline high on valley slopes. Although the lake had been dry for almost 400 years before he arrived, its beauty, bounty and decline (over a period of 55 to 60 years) were perfectly preserved in Cahuilla song. His journals record for the first time the idea that the desert had undergone great transitions in its past, from wet and lush to dry and sparse.

The effects of the distant past were also emerging in studies of Mono Lake by geologist Israel Russell, published in 1889:

Reaching the plain, which we shall call Aurora Valley, after the mining town on the hills above, we find its surface a level-floored desert, scantily clothed with sage-brush and bunch-grass. From obscure terraces about the base of the hills we are enabled to determine that this was once the bed of a lake. In the lowest part of the basin the water was formerly 250 feet deep. We can trace the ancient water lines with tolerable certainty about the northern border of the basin, and are thus assured that the ancient lake did not overflow in that direction. . . .

When the cold wave of the Quaternary had passed its climax and begun to decline, the snow and ice were melted from the mountains and increased the flood of the lowlands. This change

The now exposed tufa towers of Mono Lake were formed underwater long ago. Israel Russell linked the lake's history, and the history of the Great Basin, to Sierran glaciers of the Pleistocene. (George Hawxhurst)

was similar to that which now takes place each year in the same region with the advance of summer. The maximum expansion of the lakes in the inclosed basins at the eastern base of the mountains followed the maximum extension of the glaciers.

We pass on down the sloping plain leading to Lake Mono and after a monotonous ride of ten or twelve miles through sage-brush, over sand dunes, and across ancient lake beaches, reach Warm Springs, on the eastern shore of the lake. When I gained this camping place in the spring of 1881, the only evidence that it had been frequented by man was a trail leading to a spring. A year later I found a railroad crossing the valley, and a station near where I had previous camped. . . .

While riding along the shore of Lake Mono, one's attention is continually attracted to the islands that break the monotony of its surface. . . . In seeking names by which to designate them, it was suggested that their differences in color might be used, but the writer preferred to record some of the poetic words from the language of the aboriginal inhabitants of the valley. On the larger island there are hot springs and orifices through which heated vapors escape, which are among the most interesting features of the basin. In the legends of the Pa-vi-o-osi people, who still inhabit the region in scattered bands, there is a story about diminutive spirits, having long, wavy hair, that are sometimes seen in the vapor wreaths ascending from hot springs. The word Pa-o-ha, by which these spirits are known, is also used to designate hot springs in general. We

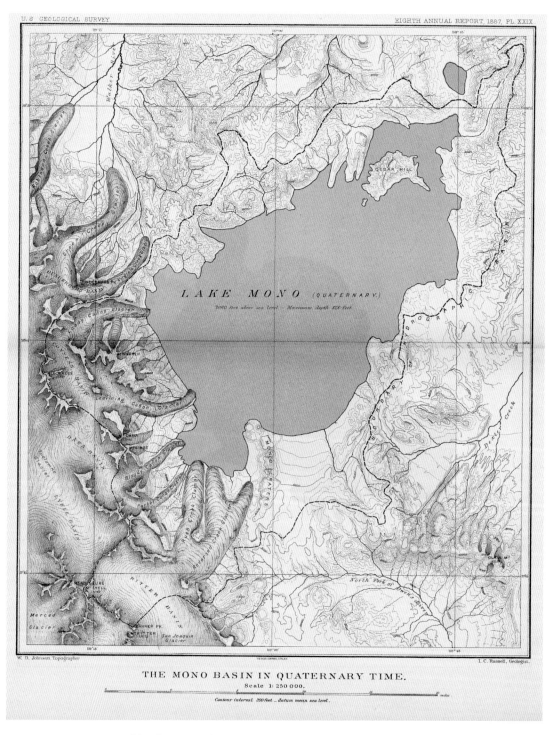

THE MONO BASIN IN QUATERNARY TIME.

Scale 1: 250 000.

Contour interval. 200 feet _ datum. mean. sea. level.

A map of the Pleistocene, showing Sierran glaciers and ancient Mono Lake (later named Lake Russell). (From Russell 1889)

may therefore name the larger island Paoha Island, in remembrance, perhaps, of the children of the mist that held their revels there on moonlit nights in times long past.

Russell was clearly enchanted by the Mono Basin and its inhabitants. He established the relationship between Sierra glaciers and desert lakes and portrayed a lost landscape of frigid rivers, overflowing basins, and endless sandy beaches. Although he could imagine the dancing spirits of Indian children, he did not know the antiquity of their presence. Subsequent work by archeologists in other desert locations provided evidence for that antiquity. Elizabeth and William Campbell wrote in 1937:

In brief, Lake Mohave was selected for study because so many noted students of geology had characterized it as a Pleistocene body of water. When its fossil shore features yielded archeological material not elsewhere found, it seemed definitely established that man lived here when the lake overflowed. A study of this material also disclosed great age. Its dissimilarity to recent cultures, its more primitive technique, its resemblance to relatively ancient forms, and its extreme weathering, not only placed it in a class apart, but pointed to a very remote origin. The discovery of the cut in the outlet channel and finding of worked flints beneath the surface of the beaches at Soda Station, prove that human beings occupied Mohave's shores at its high-water stage.

The evidence of an inhabited [lake] on an extinct river system indeed turns back a page on man's antiquity in the Mojave Desert region.

If these scientists rediscovered the desert's ancient wetness, others sought an understanding of its recent dryness. Weather stations were not established here until 1885 (at Camp Independence), so little was known about the intensity and duration of drought, much less its effects on plants and animals. During his famous surveys between 1860 and 1864, naturalist William Brewer recorded this very early remark:

Doctor Horn, of Camp Independence, in Owens Valley, a perfectly reliable man, was stationed in that valley last August. He has kept a rain gauge, and from that time to this [mid-May], *the rainy season, there has fallen in the aggregate less than a quarter of an inch of rain!* [italics his] None can fall now until next winter, and possibly not then, and yet these shrubs can live in such a climate, if they get a good wetting every two or three years. A view, comprising a field as large, or nearly as large, as the state of Connecticut, *has not a single tree in sight.* Such are the Californian deserts.

But facts and firsthand accounts were rare, often mixed with bizarre speculations and homespun anecdotes. Little could be done to disabuse the public of desert distortions, some of which originated with the tragedy of the Death Valley '49ers. Even *Scientific American* (1885) perpetuated the notion that the "climatic violence" of the region would itself impede objective inquiry because

. . . it is certain that no man could survive there long enough to secure continuous observations of any kind. [The existence of resident Indians and borax miners notwithstanding.]   (Chalfant 1930)

Chautauquan magazine (1891) summarized the popular impression of the deserts as uninhabited wastelands:

Animal life is confined to the most repulsive forms, such as the lizard and rattlesnake, scorpion and tarantula, the horned toad, and in some months, gnats. Occasionally a few blackbirds and crows hover about, but usually only in the train of the traveler in the hope of finding food in the scraps left behind. [Despite the fact that explorers, immigrants, and miners had long hunted quail, jackrabbit, desert bighorn sheep, and pronghorn.]   (Chalfant 1930)

Although scientists had been sent on every topographic survey since Frémont's, their writings were presented as supplements to technical reports on railroad routes, border alignments, and military missions. They collected a myriad of specimens, eventually described in obscure and arcane journals, but could not capture the context of, or relationships among, desert organisms. It would have been impossible to imagine the biological diversity and abundance of California's arid lands from this first generation of pressed plants and mounted skins.

The U.S. Congress recognized the need for a comprehensive scientific survey, which was finally authorized and funded by 1890. Launched from Washington, D.C., the Death Valley Expedition was ordered "to study the geographical distribution of plants and animals" of the region and report back to the Department of Agriculture and the Smithsonian Institution. Renowned naturalist and ethnographer Clinton Hart Merriam was appointed expedition head. He assembled a team of eight young scientists, including six zoologists and two botanists, along with nine assistants, teamsters, and packers. They descended from Cajon Pass on January 3, 1891, and followed the trails of Garcés, Frémont, and Manley across the Mojave. Heading north from Daggett, they eventually crossed the Panamint Range and set up a base camp at Bennett Wells. Nearly six months were spent exploring basins and ranges throughout the region, taking extensive notes, making collections and photographs, mapping terrain, and talking to the Timbishu Shoshone about life in the valley.

The sheer volume and quality of material gathered by this expedition is remarkable and much remains to be examined. Leonhard Stejneger, a curator for the Smithsonian, wrote (1893):

No collection of North American reptiles and batrachians [frogs and toads] has been made equaling or even approaching that brought home by the Death Valley Expedition. In the extent of the series of many species it stands unrivaled, and in the accuracy and detail of its labeling it surpasses them all. . . . Many of the specimens of the older collections have localities very vaguely

Members of the Death Valley Expedition of 1891—Vernon Bailey, C. Hart Merriam, T. S. Palmer, and
A. K. Fisher—take a rest in Lone Pine. Bailey, Palmer, Coville and Funston were in their twenties.
(William C. Burnett, Huntington Library)

indicated, as "California"; "From San Diego to El Paso"; in others, detailed localities are given, but
in such a way that in many cases it is impossible to identify them. . . . In the collection of the
Death Valley Expedition all the nine hundred specimens are individually and fully labeled;
altitudes are frequently given, and there is not the slightest doubt as to the correctness of the
statement attached to each and every specimen. . . .

It is the first attempt in this country on a similar scale to gather the herpetological material
together according to a rational plan and with a definite purpose in view. The result is a fine
series of specimens, unique in its completeness with respect to geographical localities within the
area explored by the expedition, a tract of almost 100,000 square miles, comprising a number of
nearly parallel desert valleys separated by intervening barren mountain ranges. . . . It has been
possible in many instances to follow the geographic variation in its various directions. The
present report does not pretend to exhaust this material, which will yield more definite results
when the adjoining territory shall have been searched as thoroughly and as intelligently as that
covered by the present expedition.

Virtually all organisms encountered received the same careful treatment, and many
new species and genera were eventually described. Beetles were most abundantly collected
(258 species, 19 new with two new genera), followed by moths and butterflies (85 species,
six new with three new genera). Bees, flies, grasshoppers, and even lice ("from a child's
ear, Lone Pine") were catalogued with thousands of specimens. At least 16 species of mol-

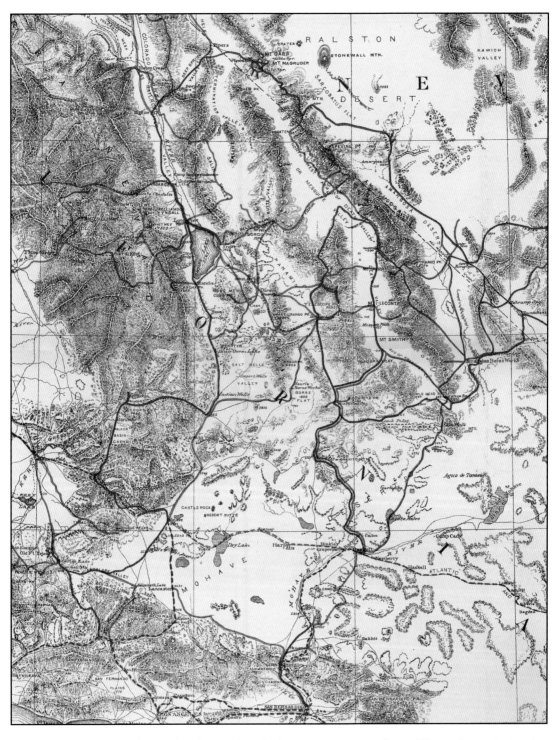

Routes of the Death Valley Expedition led by C. Hart Merriam in 1891. Red line marks Merriam's path, while blue line marks paths of others in the expedition. (From Fitch 1892)

lusks, four fish, 12 amphibians, and 44 reptiles from the desert were included in the final report, with more than 150 species new to science. Interestingly, the account of mammals was never published, but several members of the expedition would make disproportionate contributions to our understanding of the biota.

Ornithologist Albert K. Fisher compiled a list of 290 species and subspecies of birds for the entire expedition, 78 specifically observed in Death Valley and 137 in Owens Valley. Such impressive numbers dispelled the view that desert birds consisted of "a few blackbirds and crows," but even more remarkable was the attention paid to exact distribution and life history. Writing about Costa's Hummingbird *(Calypte costae)*:

At Coso the species was very abundant and several of its nests were found. Various kinds of plants were used as nesting sites, though the branching cactus *(Opuntia echinocarpa)* was most commonly chosen. Usually the structure was placed on the top of a lower branch, a foot or so from the ground, and under an overhanging mass of thick spiny branches, which formed a protection for the parent bird from the sun and weather, as well as its enemies. At Coso one of

(text continues on page 52)

Costa's Hummingbird nests in a silver cholla, as also observed by A. K. Fisher near Coso in 1891. (Angela Hyder)

REDISCOVERY: DESERT FISHES

European explorers had no reason to believe that the Great American Desert was teeming with native fish. Along the wide and deep Colorado River, fish would be expected, and indeed there were big fish—species of Razorback Sucker *(Xyrauchen texanus)*, Bonytail *(Gila elegans)*, and Bull Salmon *(Ptychocheilus lucius)* that routinely achieved 20 pounds. They were a staple food of Mojave people, who also used the remains to fertilize floodplain gardens of corn and beans. The Chemehuevis have a tribal name that literally translates as "those who work with fish." But expectations for finding fish within the dry interior were indeed low. Just before they entered Death Valley by way of Furnace Creek, the '49ers spent several December days at Ash Meadows. Staying near Fairbanks Springs, the immigrants gratefully drank the abundant, pure water and grazed their exhausted animals on the marsh vegetation. And during these restful days, William Manley recorded in his memoir the first sighting of a desert pupfish (the Ash Meadows Pupfish *[Cyprinodon nevadensis mionectes]*) in its spring-fed habitat:

Bull Salmon, also known as Colorado Pikeminnow, grew up to five feet long in the lower Colorado River. It is presumed extinct in California. (Sam McGinnis)

Lower Colorado River looking east to Fort Yuma, with ocotillo in the foreground. (Unknown artist, California Historical Society)

One night we had a fair camp, as we were close to the base of the snow butte [Telescope Peak?], and found a hole of clear or what seemed to be living water. There were a few minnows in it not much more than an inch long. This was among in a big pile of rocks, and around these the oxen found some grass.

Ash Meadows Pupfish is confined to springs. (D. W. Sada)

Others began to notice the splendid anomaly of fish in desert waters. Traveling along the Mojave River, Gwynne Heap was journalist for Lt. Edward Beale on the railroad expedition of 1853. They followed the Garcés route in midsummer but were delighted to find running water, abundant grass, grape vines, and shady groves of cottonwood. Near the Upper Narrows of present day Victorville, Heap was surprised by what he saw:

August 19. We encamped at noon near a large and deep pond of very cool and clear water, alive with fish, principally mullets, some of which were large.

This is the first description of the Mojave Tui Chub *(Siphateles mojavensis)*, endemic to this single desert drainage and long isolated from its relatives in the Central Valley and the northern Great Basin. Fossil evidence from the beds of Pleistocene Lake Manix suggests that great numbers of these large minnows (up to seven inches) were an important food source for many shorebirds, waders, diving birds, and raptors, some now extinct or absent from the modern landscape. These included two species of flamingo, a stork, a cormorant, and both extant eagles (bald and golden). As the desert lake receded, Mojave Tui Chub were confined to river and spring habitats that were less favorable in terms of water temperature (higher), oxygen content (low if stagnant), and quality (high salinity). Consequently, these remnant lakefish were historically found only in deep pools and sloughlike marshes that best resembled the ancient habitat.

The Mojave Tui Chub is now listed as endangered and no longer can be found in the Mojave River. The natural populations observed by Heap were genetically polluted after hybridizing with Arroyo Chub *(S. orcutti)*, which someone introduced to the river in the 1930s. Arroyo Chub were also better competitors, having evolved in coastal rivers that selected for greater tolerance to variations in water tempera-

➤

Mojave Tui Chub is the only native fish of the Mojave River.
(Steve Parmenter)

ture, oxygen, and quality. Only a single natural population of Mojave Tui Chub persists in Soda Springs at the Desert Studies Center in Zzyzx. To lessen the chance of extinction, fish from this population have been relocated to artificial habitats near China Lake, Barstow (once called "Fishpond"), and Camp Cady. But without a healthy, flowing, and protected Mojave River, this relict species has an uncertain and tenuous future.

these hummers was seen on a bright moonlight evening hovering about a bunch of flowers, and was heard again later in the same night. During our last trip to Death Valley Mr. Bailey saw one at Furnace Creek June 19, and the species was abundant all through the Panamint Mountains.

Botanists Frederick V. Coville and Frederick Funston compiled the first comprehensive flora from the Death Valley region, documenting 305 species from four categories of distribution (aquatic, wet soil, dry rock slope, and dry valley soil). They demonstrated that the native flora was exceedingly diverse by collecting 25 species of buckwheat *(Eriogonum)*, 18 species of milkvetch *(Astragalus)*, and 12 species of saltbush *(Atriplex)*, along with 42 new species and two new genera. They also documented that human-caused change had already begun, even in the most remote places. Eighteen species of European weeds had already become established along trails and at campsites, with six known from the recently plowed fields at Furnace Creek Ranch. Perhaps the most remarkable aspect of the Coville and Funston flora was its modern, ecological approach, recognizing assemblages of species that shared habitats across the landscape.

But it was Merriam that formalized the concept of ecological groupings of species from his observations in Death Valley and throughout the American West.

Most of the desert shrubs are social plants and are distributed in well-marked belts or zones, the vertical limits of which are fixed by the temperature during the period of growth and reproduc-

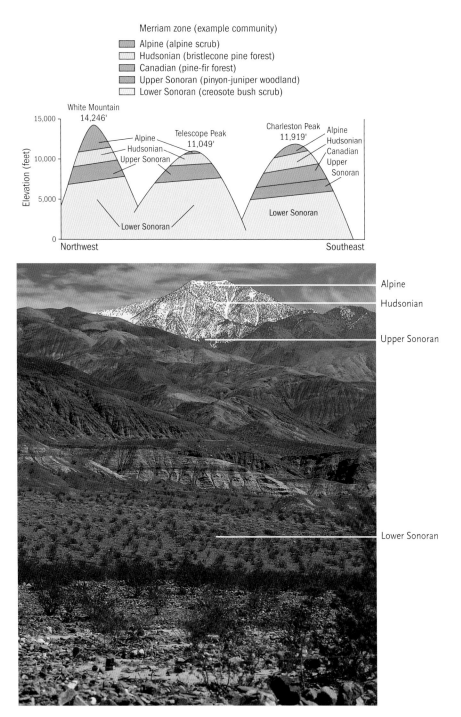

Merriam zone (example community)
- Alpine (alpine scrub)
- Hudsonian (bristlecone pine forest)
- Canadian (pine-fir forest)
- Upper Sonoran (pinyon-juniper woodland)
- Lower Sonoran (creosote bush scrub)

Upper   Merriam's life zones applied to three desert peaks. Only Charleston Peak has all five zones, an unresolved mystery. (Based on Kurzius 1981)

Lower   Merriam's life zones on Telescope Peak, viewed from Panamint Valley. (Author)

tion. Since the temperature at this season in places of the same latitude depends mainly on altitude, base level, and slope exposure, it follows that the boundaries of the several belts conform largely to the contours of altitude. . . .

The principal plant zones conform also to the animal zones, as defined by the limits of distribution of terrestrial mammals, birds and reptiles.

He goes on to propose the first system of community classification in North America based upon observations of plant, bird, and mammal distribution in relation to temperature. Although we now recognize the overwhelming importance of water availability, as well as the influence of many other environmental factors, Merriam's system of life zones (Sonoran, Upper Sonoran, Canadian, Hudsonian, and Alpine/Arctic) is still used by naturalists to describe the general effects of elevation and latitude on the biota. His perspective, forged in the heat and aridity of California's deserts, established the conceptual framework for understanding natural communities (species that occur together in space and time) and ecosystems (interactions between living entities and the nonliving environment). The Death Valley Expedition led by C. H. Merriam did nothing short of preparing the world for a new understanding of this place and its many remarkable inhabitants.

COMING TO CHERISH

Perhaps exploration, exploitation, and understanding are necessary before we can cherish a land. When a society is newly immersed in wilderness, the bravery and cruelty of the pioneer, the necessary emphasis on survival and the strong focus required for scientific inquiry simply forestall contemplation and artistic rediscovery. Footprints, flags, furrowed soil, and dead machinery become welcome signs that others have gone before, whether in the desert or on the moon. In California, the final rediscovery began when it was clear that the deserts had been subdued by roads, railroads, and reservations and deemed safe for all to come.

The reporter Charles Lummis sent dispatches from his desert wanderings to the *Los Angeles Times,* portraying himself as the last explorer of a disappearing frontier. He walked from Ohio to California, a journey of more than 3,500 miles in six months, to make a name for himself and the American West. His adventures often reinforced perceptions of danger and desperation that echoed those of the pioneers, including death at the hands of bandits, hunger, and unbearable thirst. But Lummis also saw something different in the land, something benign that had yet to be expressed in the journals and papers of the day—beauty. On his "tramp across the continent" in 1884–1885 he wrote:

On over the sandy, volcanic wastes, past the barren, contorted ranges of savage ruggedness and wonderful color, I trudged rapidly as possible; and still neither too hurried nor too beset with discomfort to extract a great deal of interest and information from every cruel day. This is a country of strange things; but none stranger than the appearance of its mountains. They are the barest, barrenest, most inhospitable-looking peaks in the whole world; and they are as uncordial as they look. Many a good man has left his bones to bleach beside their cliffs or in their death-trap valleys. They are peculiar in the abrupt fashion in which they rise from the plain, and more so in their utter destitution of vegetable life in any form. But strangest of all is their color. The prevailing hue is a soft, dark, red brown, or occasionally a tender purple; but here and there upon this deep background are curious light patches, where the fine sand of the desert has been whirled aloft and swept along by the mighty winds so common there, and rained down upon the mountain slopes where it forms deposits scores of feet in depth, and acres in extent. The rock bases of the mountains are completely buried in gentle acclivities of sand, while the cream or fawn-colored patches are often to be seen many hundreds of feet above the surrounding level. These mountains are not very high—none, I should judge, over 5,000 or 6,000 feet—but very vigorous in outline, and, at certain stages of the daylight, very beautiful in color.

Charles Lummis, flamboyant reporter for the *Los Angeles Times,* on his tramp in 1884. (Unknown photographer, Autry National Center, Southwest Museum)

Could the desert be more than cruel? Could it be pleasant and wondrous, a land of "fantasticalities" worth seeing despite the risks?

If Lummis was the first desert tourist in California, then John Van Dyke was the first desert philosopher. Van Dyke was a professor of art at Rutgers who traveled across portions of southeastern California at the turn of the century. He saw the desert as a metaphor for pure beauty and the ultimate destiny of the planet. He believed that long after humans and their meaningless civilization had been destroyed, all would be transformed into a shimmering, lovely landscape. In 1902 he wrote:

The desert has gone a-begging for a word of praise these many years. It never had a sacred poet; it has in me only a lover.

Is then this great expanse of sand and rock the beginning of the end? Is that the way our globe shall perish? Who can say? Nature plans the life, she plans the death; it must be that she plans aright. For death may be the culmination of all character; and life but the process of its development. If so, then not in vain these wastes of sand. The harsh destiny, the life-long struggle which

John Van Dyke, perhaps the first philosopher of the California deserts. (Unknown photographer, Rutgers University Libraries)

they have imposed upon all the plants and birds, and animals have been but as the stepping-stones of character. . . .

Not in vain these wastes of sand. And this time not because they develop character in desert life, but simply because they are beautiful in themselves and good to look upon whether they be life or death. In sublimity—the superlative degree of beauty—what land can equal the desert with its wide plains, its grim mountains, and its expanding canopy of sky! You shall never see elsewhere as here the dome, the pinnacle, the minaret fretted with golden fire at sunrise and sunset; you shall never see elsewhere as here the sunset valleys swimming in a pink and lilac haze, the great mesas and plateaus fading into blue distance, the gorges and canyons banked full of purple shadow. Never again shall you see such light and air and color; never such opaline mirage, such rosy dawn, such fiery twilight. And wherever you go, by land or by sea, you shall not forget that which you saw not but rather felt—the desolation and the silence of the desert. . . .

The deserts are not worthless wastes. You cannot crop all creation with wheat and alfalfa. Some sections must lie fallow that other sections may produce. . . . The deserts should never be reclaimed. They are the breathing-spaces of the west and should be preserved forever.

Far to the north, Mary Austin was writing similar prose about the lands east of the Sierra Nevada. Among the basins and ranges she did not see the end of civilization, but its origins and salvation. Only a few decades after the Owens Valley "wars," she acknowledged the special relationship between Indian people and the desert and invited the reader to transcend prejudice and rediscover what could still be learned. In 1903 she wrote:

So one comes to the country of the painted hills—old red cones of craters, wasteful beds of mineral earths, hot, acrid springs, and steam jets issuing from a leprous soil. After the hills the black rock, after the craters the spewed lava, ash strewn, of incredible thickness, and full of sharp, winding rifts. There are picture writings carved deep in the face of the cliffs to mark the way for those who do not know it. On the very edge of the black rock the earth falls away in a wide sweeping hollow, which is Shoshone Land.

It is the country of the bighorn, the wapiti, and the wolf, nesting place of buzzards, land of cloud-nourished trees and wild things that live without drink. Above all, it is the land of the creosote and the mesquite. The mesquite is God's best thought in all this desertness. It grows in the open, is thorny, stocky, close grown, and iron rooted. Long winds move in the draughty valleys, blown sand fills and fills about the lower branches, piling pyramidal dunes, from the top of which the mesquite twigs flourish greenly. Fifteen or twenty feet under the drift, where it seems no rain could penetrate, the main trunk grows, attaining often a yard's thickness, resistant as oak. In Shoshone Land one digs for large timber; that is in the southerly, sandy exposures. Higher on the table-topped ranges low trees of juniper and pinon stand each apart, rounded and spreading heaps of greenness. Between them, but each to itself in smooth clear spaces, tufts of tall feathered grass.

Mary Austin invited America back into the desert by providing a counterpoint to the stories of the '49ers. (Unknown photographer, Bancroft Library)

This is the sense of the desert hills, that there is room enough and time enough. Trees grow to consummate domes; every plant has its perfect work. Noxious weeds such as come up thickly in crowded fields do not flourish in the free spaces. Live long enough with an Indian, and he or the wild things will show you a use for everything that grows in these borders.

Hers was the first female voice that beckoned from the desert, a gentle voice of celebration rather than fear. She provided a counterpoint to the national disdain for arid lands and their native people. Her serene and lucid words were a welcome invitation to the very place that nearly destroyed parties of immigrants some 50 years before.

Responding to that invitation, Edna Brush Perkins and her friend Charlotte Hannahs Jordan traveled to Death Valley by horse-drawn wagon in 1920. Living in Cleveland, these early feminists could not imagine the vast, treeless expanses of the arid West. From Beatty, Nevada, a reluctant driver took their steamer trunks and camping supplies over the narrow trail through Daylight Pass:

Opposite Corkscrew Mountain the road turned abruptly around a point of rock. Charlotte and I were walking ahead of the wagon, we went gaily to the end of the promontory and were brought to a sudden stop by what we saw. There, without any warning of its nearness, like an unexpected crash of orchestral music, lay the terrible valley, the beautiful, the overwhelming valley.

We all stood silent then. We were about three thousand feet above the bottom of the valley looking down from the north over its whole length, an immense oblong, glistening with white,

View of Death Valley from Daylight Pass, "the beautiful, the overwhelming valley" witnessed by Edna Brush Perkins. (Larry Sansone)

alkali deposits, deep between high mountain walls. We knew that men had died down there in the shimmering heat of that white floor, we knew that the valley was sterile and dead, and yet we saw it covered with a mantle of such strange beauty that we felt it was the noblest thing we had ever imagined. Only a poet could hope to express the emotion of beauty stronger than fear and death which held us silent moment after moment by the point of rock. Perhaps some day a supreme singer will come around that point and adequately interpret that thrilling repose, that patience, that terror and beauty as part of the impassive, splendid life that always encompasses our turbulent littleness around. Before terror and beauty like that, something inside you, your own very self, stands still; for a while you rest in the companionship of greatness.

That sense of greatness in the landscape led to the establishment of Death Valley National Monument in 1933. The nation's largest state park, Anza-Borrego, was formed the year before, after the renowned landscape architect Frederick Law Olmsted had argued on behalf of a sanctuary:

Certain desert areas have a distinctive and subtle charm, in part dependent on spaciousness, solitude, and escape from the evidence of human control and manipulation of the earth, a charm of constantly growing value as the rest of the earth becomes more completely dominated by man's activities. This quality is a very vulnerable one. . . . Nowhere else are casual thoughtless human changes in the landscape so irreparable, and nowhere else is it so important to control and completely protect wide areas.

Edmund Jaeger in Death Valley, 1965. (Tom G. Murray, Riverside Metropolitan Museum)

The zoologist Edmund Jaeger not only saw greatness in the California deserts, he also saw the remarkable diversity of desert life. Unlike Merriam, his books appealed to a general audience of "so many travelers, vacationists and students of nature" coming to see for themselves in the 1930s and 1940s. Jaeger was very modern in his presentation of the desert, not only describing its plants and animals but also portraying their ecological interactions within the landscape. He knew that people must learn to *see* the desert to understand and cherish it. Seeing was more than looking out a car window; it was an active process of observation and interpretation. Toward that end, he took students into the Mojave, along some narrow, sandy track, stopping near a strikingly tall Joshua tree in the middle of wilderness:

We walked around to view the tree from many angles and to learn what curious desert wonders could be found near it. We were soon rewarded with so many sights of unusual interest that we decided to draw an imaginary circle, with the Joshua tree as its center and with a radius of a hundred feet, and then to list all the things we saw within what we decided to call our "Magic Circle." Let those who think that desert areas are places of desolation and just so much gray-green brush, sand, and gravel read now an account of our census.

(Jaeger 1961)

Jaeger's census (see sidebar) gives equal weight to slime mold, millipede, cactus, and rabbit, noting only that they occupied the same envelope of space and time. This view of biological diversity as place-based, as comprehensive, as the intersection of science and magic would strengthen during this phase of rediscovery. Others had acknowledged diversity among desert organisms. Frémont first noted that plants of the Mojave had "greater variety than we had been accustomed to see in the most luxuriant prairie countries; this was a peculiarity of *this* desert." But Jaeger pointed out that a tally of all forms of life would lead to an even greater appreciation of evolutionary origins and ecological process in what many had judged to be a "wasteland." His magic circle forced a new view, one born from actually seeing a place and its inhabitants before pronouncing vacancy or declaring minimal value. And, as John Muir view's had done for the Sierra Nevada, this view would lead to an urgent call for conservation and better management of public lands in arid California.

Jaeger invited us to look for the inhabitants of the desert, and John Steinbeck asked us to consider their importance to the nation. Later in life he took a journey in search of America with his dog, Charley. They camped and fished and rambled the continent, eventually crossing California on Route 66 through Needles. Steinbeck met the people, collected the stories, and saw the relationships between landscapes and life. He also echoed the premonitions of John Van Dyke within a modern, cold war context:

The Mojave is a big desert and a frightening one. It's as though nature tested a man for endurance and constancy to prove whether he was good enough to get to California. The shimmer-

WITHIN THE MAGIC CIRCLE

The account of objects within the Magic Circle, extracted from Dr. Jaeger's elegant text:

"A black meteoric stone over an inch and a half long . . . Two cactus wren's nests . . . made of the stems of wild buckwheat and vinegarweed, and decorated and lined with bits of woolly filago . . . [A cholla cactus with] some seldom-seen fleshy, ephemeral leaves, no doubt vestiges of organs much better developed in some ancestral cacti . . . [Another Joshua tree with] most of its long, spine-tipped leaves . . . twisted into a Turkish scimitar or into a corkscrew . . . On a creosote bush . . . the small, dark-brown nest of a potter bee, with its water-proof protective cover of bits of gravel set in hardened wax to form an intricate mosaic . . . A little *Trombidium* crawling over the sand . . . a handsome, harmless harvest mite . . . in search of food . . . A plump, brown millipede . . . The entrances to the subterranean homes of white-footed mice, kangaroo rats, and antelope ground squirrels . . . Scorpions . . . ground spiders . . . harvester [ants] and the honey ants . . . A brush rabbit's shallow burrow . . . [containing] the gray proprietor all hunched up . . . [Inside a] dead Joshua tree trunk, we discovered a four-inch *Xantusia*, or desert night lizard, . . . feeding upon termites . . . Flattish lumps of dried, white froth . . . [composed of] millions of microscopic gray-black spores . . . of slime molds or Mycetozoa . . . An abandoned badger's den . . . Cocoons of a case-bearer moth, as well as the 'robin's pin-cushion' or fuzzy creosote gall . . . A small green creosote

ing dry heat made visions of water on the flat plain. And even when you drive a high speed, the hills that mark the boundaries recede before you. . . .

I have driven through the Southwest many times, and even more often have flown over it—a great and mysterious wasteland, a sun-punished place. It is a mystery, something concealed and waiting. It seems deserted, free of parasitic man, but this is not entirely so. Follow the double line of wheel tracks through sand and rock and you will find a habitation somewhere huddled in a protected place, with a few trees pointing their roots at under-earth water, a patch of starveling corn and squash, and strips of jerky hanging on a string. There is a breed of desert men, not hiding exactly but gone to sanctuary from the sins of confusion.

At night in this waterless air the stars come down just out of reach of your fingers. In such a place the hermits of the early church piercing to infinity with unlettered minds. The great

grasshopper . . . [The songs of a thrasher and a cactus wren and] the pungent scent of creosote bush.

"All these things and more we saw or heard within our Magic Circle of a hundred-foot radius. And in the center stood our tall, long-trunked Joshua tree with its crown of four branches and its basketlike hawk's nest of creosote twigs.

"In the evening against the silhouette of the rocky hills surrounding the valley and the colorful clouds, small pipistrellid bats darted overhead. The last notes of the thrasher were heard far away. As the sky grew darker, bringing out the stars, we looked beyond our Magic Circle to that larger circle, the rim of the horizon."

Joshua tree at the center of a magic circle. (Angela Hyder)

This cactus-rich view of Mount San Jacinto was named "Devil's Garden" in the 1930s. Note the steam train crossing the pass at the foot of the hills. (Stephen H. Willard)

Similar view of Devil's Garden, 2006. The cacti were removed by collectors, the pass filled with highways and windmills, and the vegetation invaded by weeds. (Author)

concepts of oneness and of majestic order seem always to be born in the desert. The quiet counting of the stars, and observation of their movements, came first from desert places. I have known desert men who chose their places with quiet and slow passion, rejecting the nervousness of a watered world. These men have not changed with the exploding times except to die and be replaced by others like them.

In the war of sun and dryness against living things, life has its secrets of survival. Life, no matter on what level, must be moist or it will disappear. I find most interesting the conspiracy of life in the desert to circumvent the death rays of the all-conquering sun. The beaten earth appears defeated and dead, but it only appears so. A vast and inventive organization of living matter survives. . . .

The desert, being an unwanted place, might well be the last stand of life against unlife. For in the rich and moist and wanted areas of the world, life pyramids against itself and in its confusion has finally allied itself with the enemy non-life. And what the scorching, searing, freezing, poisoning weapons of non-life have failed to do may be accomplished to the end of its destruction and extinction by the tactics of survival gone sour. If the most versatile of living forms, the human, now fights for survival as it always has, it can eliminate not only itself but all other life. And if that should transpire, unwanted places like the desert might be the harsh mother of repopulation. For the inhabitants of the desert are well trained and well armed against desolation. Even our own misguided species might re-emerge from the desert. The lone man and his sun-toughened wife who cling to the shade in an unfruitful and uncoveted place might, with their brothers in arms—the coyote, the jackrabbit, the horned toad, the rattlesnake, together with a host of armored insects—these trained and tested fragments of life might well be the last hope of life against non-life. The desert has mothered magic things before this.

But Steinbeck could not have imagined the crush of humanity that would arrive at the doorstep of the California deserts by the end of the twentieth century. The military would claim areas large enough to conduct mock wars with battalions, heavy artillery, and jet bombers. Coastal cities would overflow the windy passes, spreading freeways, houses, and malls into the dry solitude. The land beneath the desert would finally become wanted, scraped clean of its life and watered into monotonous oblivion using distant rivers and ancient aquifers. Yet millions come each year to see and perhaps surrender themselves to the teeming, rugged vastness. Will these arid lands be cherished before irreversible degradation or meaningless consumption? Is American society capable of sustaining rediscovery, or will it be over after a few hundred years?

To cherish something with the heart is to live in fear of its demise. But our rediscovery must balance a fear for the future with the joy of today and an appreciation of the past. Our rediscovery must develop a healthy blend of human tendencies to explore, conquer, understand, and cherish. All are important, but none should be the only path available to all people and all corners of the landscape. People will decide the fate of the California deserts, people who speak, listen, see, and learn across boundaries of ignorance.

REQUIEM FOR SONORA

by *Richard Shelton*

1

a small child of a wind
stumbles toward me down the arroyo
lost and carrying no light
tearing its sleeves
on thorns of the palo verde
talking to itself
and to the dark shapes it touches
searching for what it has not lost
and will never find
searching
and lonelier
than even I can imagine

the moon sleeps
with her head on the buttocks of a
    young hill
and you lie before me
under moonlight as if under water
on my desert
the coolness of your face

2

men are coming inland to you
soon they will make you the last resort
for tourists who have
nowhere else to go

what will become of the coyote
with eyes of topaz
moving silently to his undoing

the ocotillo
flagellant of the wind
the deer climbing with dignity
further into the mountains
the huge and delicate saguaro
what will become of those who cannot
    learn
the terrible knowledge of cities

3

years ago I came to you as a stranger
and have never been worthy
to be called your lover or to speak your
    name
loveliest
most silent sanctuary
more fragile than forests
more beautiful than water

I am older and uglier
and full of the knowledge
that I do not belong to beauty
and beauty does not belong to me
I have learned to accept whatever men
    choose to give me
or whatever they choose to withhold
but oh my desert
yours is the only death I cannot bear

A Conspiracy of Extremes

Deserts in California can be defined as a conspiracy of extremes. There are extremes of geography, including mountains 14,000 feet above, and basins more than 200 feet below sea level. There are extremes of geology, the land having been built from ocean sediments more than 500 million years old, or from windswept sands that in this moment have started to form a dune. There are extremes of climate, from hottest and driest to most frigid in winter, with long periods of uncertainty as to what is coming next. Desert soils can be extremely thin, rocky, laden with salts, and nearly devoid of nutrients for plant growth. And nothing is more extreme than the long, changing history of this region, which has, during the last 12,000 years, included glacial-fed lakes resembling inland seas that were surrounded by rich, wooded savannas grazed by camels and mastodon. These extremes challenge the current occupants of California's deserts to persist, if not thrive, in a land of rock, sun, and endless blue sky.

To understand how desert plants and animals cope with such extremes requires knowledge of the land, especially its geography, climate, geology, soils, and waters. Such foundations of the physical environment set the ultimate limits for living systems and thus determine where certain organisms reside (their distribution) and how many can be supported (their abundance) by the available resources (water, food, minerals). When analyzed in this way, arid land in California can be ecologically divided into three deserts, each with its own defining physical environment (abiotic or nonliving components) and distinctive assemblage of organisms (biotic or living components). The deserts, known as the Great Basin, Mojave, and Sonoran, are thus defined by a combination of geographic,

A desert bajada is formed by flow of rock, sand, and gravel from a mountain. (Marli Bryant Miller)

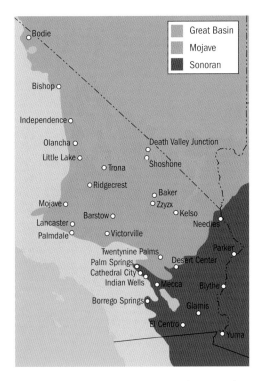

The Great Basin, Mojave, and Sonoran deserts, with ecotones at their boundaries. (Based on Bender 1982)

climatic, geologic, and soil features (table 1), but recognized by the presence and interactions of characteristic plants and animals. Collectively, the three comprise the California desert bioregion, an area of roughly 25 million acres from Bodie to the Mexican border. This chapter describes the abiotic foundations of the bioregion as a basis for understanding its origins, operation, and remarkable biota.

GEOGRAPHY OF A BIOREGION

The Great Basin is the northernmost and largest of the three deserts, although only a small fraction extends into eastern California. The Great Basin stretches from the Sierra Nevada to the Wasatch Front of central Utah and from the Columbia Plateau of Oregon and Idaho into north-central Arizona, an area totaling at least 157,900 square miles. The name refers to the fact that all river systems in this desert flow internally and not to the sea, a fact noted by John Frémont. California rivers, such as the Truckee, Walker, and Owens, are good examples.The Great Basin is not just one large basin. It is a collection of more than 150 "minibasins" separated by mountain ranges arranged as "an army of caterpillars marching to Mexico," according to the geologist Charles Dutton. Elevations are typically between 3,800 and 6,000 feet, while the surrounding mountains commonly exceed 8,000 feet. Death Valley is the lowest of the minibasins, with its elevation of 282 feet below sea level forming the terminus of the Amargosa River. Portions of the nearby White Mountains rise as high as 14,246 feet, creating dramatic relief and impressive environmental gradients. On a clear day it is possible to view smoldering desert from a snowy observation point surrounded by subalpine forests.

The southern Great Basin of eastern California and western Nevada reaches a critical, low-elevation edge between 3,000 and 4,900 feet, depending on longitude. Below this critical elevation it is displaced by another desert: the Mojave. The transition is easiest to detect while driving south along Highway 395 in the Owens Valley between Olancha and Little Lake. The elevation drop along this road is only a few hundred feet, but its effect on the desert is revealed here by the presence of Joshua trees *(Yucca brevifolia)*. Woodlands of these strange, shaggy prophets mark the otherwise imperceptible boundary between the Great Basin and Mojave deserts as an indicator and integrator of environmental changes over the land. Some elevation changes are related to rainfall, others to temperature (see the section "Climate"), both of which impose limits on the natural occurrence

TABLE 1 Abiotic Characteristics of California Deserts

	Great Basin	Mojave	Sonoran
Geography			
Size			
In North America (sq mi)	157,900	54,100	106,200
In California (sq mi)	6,900	27,400	11,300
States	CA, NV, UT, OR, WA, ID, AZ	CA, NV, AZ	CA, AZ
Elevation Ranges			
Basins (ft)	3,800 to 6,000	−280 to 4,500	−228 to 1,000
Mountains (ft)	to 14,246 (White Mountain)	to 11,049 (Telescope Peak)	to 4,150 (Pilot Mountain)
Drainage			
Rivers	Owens, Truckee, Walker	Amargosa, Mojave	Colorado
Contemporary lakes	Crowley, Mono, Owens	Coyote, Grimshaw, Soda	Salton Sea
Pleistocene lakes	Adobe, Long, Owens, Russell	Manley, Mojave, Panamint, Searles	Cahuilla (?)
Climate			
Precipitation			
Mean annual (inch)	6 to 16	2 to 10	2 to 10
Falling in summer (%)	13	9	24
Falling as snow (%)	60	20	< 2
ET/P Ratio	1 to 7	3 to 32	2 to 32
Air Temperature			
Mean annual (°F)	52 to 60	60 to 68	68 to 76
Mean annual range (°F)	36 to 44	36 to 44	36 to 44
Extreme highs (°F)	98 to 105	104 to 121	112 to 120
Days below freezing (number)	88 to 155	33 to 101	5 to 29
Geology			
Basins			
Alluvium (%)	28	51	60
Sand (%)	1	2	4
Glacial debris (%)	3	0	0
Bedrock			
Cenzoic volcanic (%)	30	11	5
Mesozoic volcanic (%)	3	1	0
Mesozoic granites (%)	21	11	13
Mesozoic sandstones (%)	< 1	< 1	1
Paleozoic shales (%)	3	3	< 1
Paleozoic sandstones (%)	1	3	< 1
Paleozoic limestones (%)	1	2	0
Cambrian/Precambrian mix (%)	7	14	8

NOTE: Ranges or mean values shown. Size in California estimated from vegetation types of Kuchler (1976). Geology percentages are for the California land surface, estimated from Jennings et al. (1977). ET/P is evapotranspiration-to-precipitation ratio.

Basin and range topography east of the Sierra. The pinyon pines and big sagebrush *(Artemisia tridentata)* are typical of the Great Basin Desert. (Author)

of sensitive, and therefore characteristic, plants and animals. Rivers still drain internally, the basin and range topography continues to dominate the landscape, but one community of inhabitants is gradually replaced by another. This transition zone, or ecotone, between deserts is difficult to map precisely, in part because of complex environmental gradients across a complex landscape, but also because of how much the gradients have fluctuated over long periods of time.

The Mojave is the smallest of the North American deserts (54,100 square miles), but it is the largest of the California deserts (27,400 square miles). Stretching east from the Tehachapi Mountains into southern Nevada and adjacent parts of Arizona, the region still drains internally and is considered by hydrologists to be part of the Great Basin. Again, it was Frémont who assigned the name Mojave, first to the river that guided immigrants along the Old Spanish Trail, and then to the desert as a whole. The word itself may have been derived from the word for bighorn sheep *(moha)*, which the Mojave people had already applied to themselves.

The Mojave Desert has an open, continuous quality as basins coalesce into broad, arid valleys, and the ranges appear distant, worn, and much lower in elevation than the ranges farther north. The Antelope, Lucerne, and Apple valleys lie between 1,900 and 2,500 feet elevation, while farther east, the Devils Playground is closer to 1,000 feet. The nearby New York and Providence mountains are between 6,800 and 7,400 feet, providing enough relief to support remnant conifer forests as well as woodlands of Joshua trees and pockets of marooned Great Basin species. Farther east the elevations drop off even more, until the Colorado River is crossed at about 800 feet and the landscape begins climbing back up toward 5,000 feet in western Arizona. Given the proximity to Los Angeles, Mojave landscapes have been used as backdrops for countless films and videos as the quintessential "desert" that both haunts and inspires humanity.

A very subtle ecotone exists between the Mojave and Sonoran deserts. Again, the difference in elevation is measured in only a few hundred feet, typically between 700 and 900 feet above sea level. If you drew a line from Needles to Amboy, and continued it south along the base of the San Bernardino, Santa Rosa, and Vallecitos mountains to the border with Mexico, you would roughly delineate the northwestern, California portion of this transition. It is a subtle transition because many of the same plants and animals are found on both sides of the line; however, a few characteristic species, again sensitive to gradients of rainfall and temperature, provide clues as to when that line has been crossed. The best indicators again fall into the category of "strange treelike plants," such as ocotillo *(Fouquieria splendens)* and palo verde *(Cercidium floridum* subsp. *floridum)*. Unlike Joshua trees, these species are sensitive to freezing temperatures during the winter months, temperatures that become common to the north and rare to the south of the ecotone.

The Sonoran desert covers about 106,200 square miles, but most of it lies in southern Arizona, Baja California, and northwest Mexico. California's piece, about 11,304 square miles, extends from the ecotone mentioned above, east and south to the lower Colorado River and toward the Sea of Cortez. Valleys are broad, usually below 800 feet, and can dip below sea level. The only significant mountain ranges, the Chocolate and Chuckwalla, barely exceed 4,000 feet. This low, hot, and very dry expanse is often referred to as a separate "Colorado Desert" because it bears only a slight resemblance to the relatively lush Sonoran uplands and Baja woodlands that are better sustained by summer rainfall. In the past the southern portion of this desert was essentially created by the rage and load of the Colorado River. Flooding could carve new channels through old landscapes, deposit mountains of sediment, and rework the entire coastal geography of the northern Gulf. Although Hoover Dam put a temporary end to the river's creativity, the extensive dunes, deep soils, wide delta, and the Salton Sea are remnants of its once great influence.

Upper   An ecotone will have a mixture of species from adjacent communities, here with pinyon pines of the Great Basin and Joshua trees of the Mojave. (Robert Thomas and Margaret Orr)

Lower   Mojave Desert landscape of broad basins and low mountains. Typical vegetation has an overstory of creosote bush *(Larrea)* and a low understory of desert dandelion and other herbs. (Robert Thomas and Margaret Orr)

CLIMATE

Deserts are places on the planet where the air is warm and dry enough to evaporate all of the meager precipitation that reaches the ground. For this reason, river runoff is rare and there can be very little water storage in the soil or in the bodies of living organisms. Experts still argue, however, about the exact climatic definition because there are so many kinds of deserts. In general, average annual precipitation in true desert is below six inches,

Sonoran Desert vegetation with tall ocotillo and shrubby creosote bush, and here with four species of stem-succulent cacti in the understory.
(Stephen H. Willard)

while extreme deserts receive less than three inches, and semideserts receive six to 12 inches or slightly more. Typical average air temperatures are harder to choose because even in the hottest areas, with daytime highs above 100°F, it is still possible to have freezing nighttime lows. Similarly, winter and summer temperatures can vary wildly. More importantly, the desert air mass itself, regardless of temperature, contains very little water vapor (humidity), so it constantly and quickly absorbs whatever moisture is found in lakes, leaves, and lungs. This idea of the strong evaporative power of the atmosphere in relation to the amount of water falling as precipitation is embodied in the evapotranspiration-to-precipitation ratio (ET/P). By this measure, true desert has an average ET/P range of five to 33, which means that the air has the power to evaporate from five to 33 times more water than falls as precipitation. In extreme deserts the ratio can greatly exceed 33, while in semideserts the ratio can be as low as two.

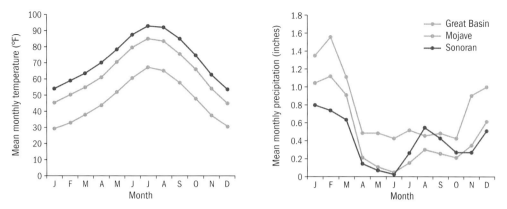

Monthly air temperatures and precipitation in the Great Basin, Mojave, and Sonoran deserts of California. (Data from NOAA 1971–2000)

But averages of annual precipitation, air temperature, and ET/P are not enough to characterize desert climates and understand their effects on plants and animals. Timing, the occurrence of stressful extremes, and uncertainty are crucial and more difficult to measure. Timing refers to the seasonal pattern of climate and is especially important because it controls plant activity, which in turn controls food availability for animals. Precipitation that falls predominately during the summer or winter or both can determine much about the species composition of deserts within the bioregion. Stressful extremes—whether they be periods of very low rainfall (dry decades in Death Valley may have average precipitation of less than .83 inches per year), of incredibly hot afternoons (up to 134°F), or of freezing temperatures that last for more than 36 hours—are probably the back-breaking straws for many desert species. But even the plant or animal best equipped for parching drought, searing air, or hard frost can be sorely tested by the uncertainty that accompanies these extremes. It turns out that extreme deserts are more likely than true deserts to have years without any precipitation, as was observed in Death Valley during 1929 and 1954. And true deserts at the lower end of the precipitation range (two to four inches per year) are more likely to have greater year-to-year differences than those on the higher end (four to six inches). The inherent uncertainty of such extremes makes biological tolerance mechanisms less effective and creates unpredictable patterns of plant productivity, animal reproduction, and persistence of species through time.

The climates of the California desert bioregion (the low precipitation, yearly patterns, temperature extremes, and uncertainty) are produced by three geographical factors: proximity to tall mountains, latitude, and elevation. A continuous chain of tall mountains, running more than 700 miles from Oregon into the Baja peninsula, creates a rainshadow that extends east from the crest. Rainshadow is created when moisture-laden air masses sweep out of the Pacific and are forced to rise, expand, and cool as they traverse the mountain barrier. The western slopes are drenched with rain and snow and support lush forests

A storm front dissipates as it passes from the Sierra to the Owens Valley. (Steve Matson)

between 3,000 and 10,000 feet above sea level. By the time the air masses cross the crest, they have been purged of humidity and begin a descent with compression and consequent heating. Thus, at similar elevations and latitude, Yosemite Valley receives about 50 inches of annual precipitation, while Bishop receives about eight inches. Additionally, every successive range east of the Cascade-Sierra-Peninsular chain purges and heats the air masses even more, further removing the chance of any possible maritime moderation. This not only creates drought, it creates extremes of temperature on a daily and seasonal basis. The California deserts are therefore interior, as well as rain-shadow, deserts.

Latitude is also a factor, especially with respect to yearly patterns and forms of precipitation. The Great Basin, which largely lies north of 36°N latitude, receives more than 70 percent of its water from Pacific storms during the cooler months of the year (September to May), with nearly 40 percent falling during a winter peak (November to February). Up to 60 percent of the annual precipitation falls as snow. Winter temperatures can be as low as −48°F, with several months averaging below freezing and isolated frosts occurring from September to May. Farther south (roughly 37° to 34°N latitude) the Mojave has a similar winter peak in precipitation (44 percent falling from November to February) and occasional snows (frequent in the Joshua tree transition zone), but the intensity and duration of freezing temperatures are less than in the Great Basin. Summer temperatures, however, are higher and get progressively more so toward the Sonoran Desert

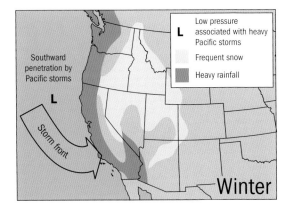

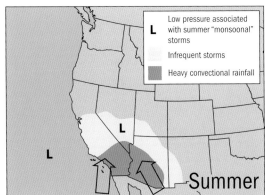

(south of 34°N). In the Sonoran, however, another moisture source becomes important during the hot summer months. Moist subtropical air masses push north from the Gulf of Mexico and the Sea of Cortez, meeting very few mountain barriers. Spectacular thunderstorms, accentuated by rising columns of cooling air, can drop more than 50 percent of the year's precipitation on the desert surrounding Tucson between June and September. Although this summer rainfall peak is diminished in California's portion of this desert, some areas (for example, Twentynine Palms) can receive 36 percent of their annual precipitation during this time. Pacific storms resume their dominance during the winter, but snows and hard frosts (freezing temperatures lasting more than 18 consecutive hours) are extremely rare, perhaps one event every decade or two.

Local variations in elevation can greatly modify the general patterns created by mountain chains and latitude. Low elevation means hotter and drier, with "lapse rates" of roughly +5°F and −1 inch of precipitation for every 1,000 feet of descent. Places such as Death Valley have so much topographic relief that it is possible to find elements of all three deserts within a single, short transect. Driving east only 20 miles from the crest of the Panamint Range (at 6,000 feet), you can descend from Great Basin woodlands of pinyon pine *(Pinus mono-*

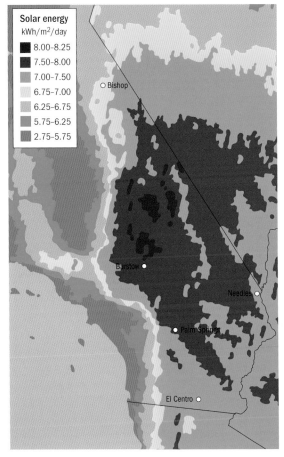

Upper Seasonal shifts in the positions of atmospheric pressure cells determine the patterns of annual precipitation in the California deserts. (Based on Harvey et al. 1999)

Lower Distribution of solar radiation over the California deserts. (Based on NREL 2003)

phylla) that receive snow almost every year, through droughted Mojave shrublands, and on into outposts of hot and frostless Sonoran desert below sea level. The same ecological span on a north-south transect from Bishop to Indio requires about 290 miles. Driving uphill toward high elevations means cooler and wetter climates. The ghost town of Bodie, near 8,000 feet, experiences the coldest winters in the state, if not the nation, because of its dry, interior, upslope location. And outposts of Great Basin species can be found in mountain ranges within and adjacent to parts of the Sonoran desert, far from the current ecotone.

To some extent, the air mass itself contributes to climatic extremes. On the lee side of the Cascade-Sierra-Peninsular ranges, the low atmospheric humidity results in few clouds and high exposure to solar radiation. The full spectrum and intensity of sunlight falls on rocky earth, where it is reflected by light-colored surfaces and absorbed by dark-colored ones. Reflection can be so pronounced on sand dunes that the total energy avail-

RAIN SHADOW AND WIND MACHINE

As the geography of the American West became known to explorers and pioneers, a scientific understanding of the arid interior began to emerge. Rather than wastelands forsaken by God, deserts were a predictable consequence of high mountains, atmospheric circulation patterns, and the physics of air parcels and water vapor.

William Manley, leader of the infamous Death Valley '49ers, struggled across successive ranges in eastern California in desperate search for water and safe passage. As if to taunt the unfortunate party, snow had topped high peaks to the west while drought dominated the low valleys of the path. He later recalled the deadly irony of rainshadow:

> In those days we got no rain, see no living animals of any kind except these of our train, see not a bird nor insect, see nothing green except a very stunted sage, and some dwarf bushes. We now know that the winter of 1849–1850 was one of the wettest ever seen in California, but for some reason or other none of the wet clouds ever came to this portion of the State to deposit the most scattering drops of moisture.

The experience would soon be understood as one of mechanism rather than providence. Mountains simply parch the water from storm fronts, and the resultant dry air is easier to heat as it slides down the eastern escarpment. Lack of condensation (clouds) also permits more solar energy to fall upon the desert soil and, therefore, to reheat the desert air. The hot desert air rises and leaves behind a low-pressure sink

able to drive photosynthesis, or to raise skin temperature, is greater than that coming from the sun alone. When absorbed by the soil, this energy is stored as heat and reradiated back to the air mass. The air mass temperature increases (especially because the air contains little moisture), expands, and begins moving upward as a local wind. Conversely, the same process of reradiation into the dry night sky produces rapid cooling of surface temperatures, the development of cold air pools, and downslope movement of the relatively dense air mass. Such cold air drainage can accentuate the difference between day and night temperatures as much as 60°F, especially during the winter. In the Great Basin, cold air drainage can significantly shorten the growing season in valley bottoms, producing plant and animal communities that are very different from those on nearby slopes.

As surfaces in the desert heat and reradiate their energy, several desert phenomena are created. Near the ground, perhaps only a few inches up, the air is still and searing as mid-

into which cool air flows from other parts of the state. This wind machine, a product of rainshadow and the desert itself, was first proposed by geologist William P. Blake as the railroad survey of 1853 rode through San Gorgonio Pass near Banning:

Ventifacts along the east side of Death Valley. Moving sand cuts grooves into basalt rock. (Marli Bryant Miller)

A deep bank of drifted sand has accumulated on the east side of this point of rocks, it having been blown over by the wind. The wind which thus transports the sand is not an ordinary shifting breeze, but is a constant and powerful current of air sweeping thorough the pass from the west. It pours in from the Pacific in an apparently unbroken, unvarying stream, passing over the surface with such violence that all the fine grains of sand are lifted from the dry channels of the streams, and are driven along the descending slope until they find a final resting place to the leeward of the projecting spurs of San Gorgonio. In respect to this prevailing current of air flowing inland from the Pacific, the pass appears to have the same relation to the interior valley of the Colorado that is held by the Golden Gate at San Francisco to the interior valley of the

➤

day soil temperatures exceed 122°F. Variations in these high temperatures lead to variations in air density, which in turn produce heat waves of refracted (bent) light. Under some conditions, these variations produce the puddle mirage, an illusion of light and dark air just beyond the reach of a thirsty human mind. Further rise of heated air masses causes objects to shimmer in the distance, and eventually the masses coalesce into thermals. Thermals can form over hot spots on the desert floor, with air that spirals around a low-velocity eye. Fine sands and clays are lofted, creating mischievous dust devils that appear, wander across the valley, and disappear during the midday heat. They move large amounts of clay, calcium carbonate, and other minerals from place to place, contributing to soil-building processes over thousands of years. Thermals can also coalesce over an entire desert landscape, creating regional uprisings into very high altitudes. With rapid ascent, the air mass expands and cools, allowing the formation of impressive thunderheads from relatively little water vapor. If conditions are right, a summer cloudburst can ensue or, more often in our deserts, a short but welcome break from the intense midday sun.

> Sacramento and San Joaquin. They both appear to be great draught-channels from the ocean to the interior, through which the air flows with peculiar uniformity and persistence, thus supplying the partial vacuum caused by the ascent of heated air from the surface of the parched plains and deserts.

He goes on to describe the geological evidence for this wind machine: the gouging of rock surfaces by moving sands:

> I had before me remarkable and interesting proofs of the persistence and direction of this air-current, not only in the fact that the deep sand-drift was on the east side of the spur, but in the record which the grains of sand engrave on the rocks in their transit from one side to the other. It would be difficult to find a place where the cutting poser of drifting sand is more beautifully and clearly exhibited than it is at this point. The whole surface of the rocks was smooth and polished, and even the limestone had a peculiar, rounded and smooth surface, which resembled that of partly dissolved crystals, or deliquescent specimens of rock salt. Long parallel grooves, deep enough to receive a lead-pencil, were cut on the surface of the hard and homogenous granite.

The grooved and pitted rocks (ventifacts) were eventually bulldozed and paved over, but the winds of San Gorgonio Pass still pour into the desert. A forest of turbines, the third-largest in the world, uses the wind machine to generate electrical power for about 100,000 homes.

Dust devils move tons of fine soil particles across the desert, seen here in Death Valley. They may also be a way for seeds to disperse. (Marli Bryant Miller)

Winds removed soil from around the base of these arrow weed *(Pluchea sericea)* shrubs, creating "Devil's Cornfield" in Death Valley. (Sherry Ballard)

GEOLOGY

The California desert bioregion is built from rocks of all ages and compositions. Precambrian and Paleozoic rocks (more than 505 million years old) are often carbonates of calcium (limestone) or magnesium (dolomite), with origins in ancient, warm seas. The seas came and went many times, producing waters so dense with shelled animals that remnant carcasses and precipitating lime settled into layers we now measure as 20,000 to 30,000 feet thick. Such sedimentary rocks can be loaded with fossils and embossed with shoreline wave patterns arrested in time. They can also be transformed by heat and pressure (metamorphosed) into translucent marble. In some cases, the earliest rocks are crystalline gneisses, formed by slowly cooling magmas that rose beneath the land surface, metamorphosed, and were finally uncovered by faulting, uplift, and erosion.

Mesozoic rocks (65 to 245 million years old) reflect cataclysms associated with continental drift, either as rising masses of granite or basalt heated by subduction along the western edge of the North American plate. The granitic masses, especially in the western Mojave, foreshadowed the rise of the 400-mile-long batholith (deep rock) that later became the Sierra Nevada. In addition, basalt was violently extruded by volcanoes that literally cooked the older rocks over which it flowed. The land flexed upward, building low hills with wide, intervening basins. Erosion of the hills filled the basins with great heaps of sandy sediments that rusted under the influence of rain and sun. These reddish or orange-brown sands became heaped into spectacular dunes that congealed into the characteristic sandstones of the desert southwest. Where they had once been associated with ancient beaches and muddy shorelines, these rocks abound with fossil plants and invertebrates.

During the Cenozoic (up to 65 million years ago) a new, violent wave of volcanic eruptions spread across the Great Basin region, spewing so much hot ash and lava that the

Upper   These tilted and warped beds of limestone in the Inyo Mountains were ocean sediments more than 500 million years ago. (Joseph Dougherty)

Lower   Volcanic cone and basalt flow in the southern Owens Valley near Little Lake. (Charles Webber)

landscape was nearly buried. The ash fused together into what is called a welded tuff, while the lava was an extruded form of granite called rhyolite. In other regions, erosion of older, uplifted rocks created featureless plains, while sediments were recycled into deep strata containing mastodon, camel, and horse fossils. These youngest layers, eventually battered by a great glacial epoch, can also act as a veneer that shields older underlying bedrock layers and keeps them from disappearing. Indeed, a geological map from almost anywhere in the California deserts is a kaleidoscope of bedrock colors, made elaborate, intricate, and complex by titanic processes over incredible periods of time.

What are those processes that built desert topography from this kaleidoscope of bedrock? Mountain building, or orogeny, was the result of collisions between land and sea plates, aided by batholith intrusions from below. Fractures in the bedrock itself, extending miles deep and miles long, are the faults along which mountains are uplifted and basins are dropped. Tectonic forces generated by the movement of crustal plates ruptured the base of nearly every mountain range in the desert, creating steep escarpments and exposing millions of years of subterranean structure. Some faults are large enough to define an entire region. The Garlock Fault, for example, runs west and east between Gorman and the Avawatz Mountains, a distance of about 150 miles. It forms the northern boundary of the Mojave's geological basement and is responsible for almost 500 feet of elevation difference and as much as 40 miles of lateral displacement. The San Andreas Fault cuts northwest across the Coachella Valley, eventually joining the Garlock Fault on its western end. Displacement along the San Andreas has been about 180 miles over the last 50 million years, creating the Sea of Cortez and the Salton Basin.

Desert topography has also been created by tectonic folding of bedrock layers rather than rupture along faults. Sandstones and limestones are partic-

Granite tors in Joshua Tree National Park are remnants of a Mesozoic batholith exposed by slow erosion of the surrounding plain. (Stephen H. Willard)

ularly plastic and can be scrunched and buckled into wavy, usually low hills. The Indio and Mecca hills adjacent to the Coachella Valley, for example, may be folding as a prelude to rupture by movements along the San Andreas Fault.

Finally, in many places significant relief was added by volcanic eruptions, as molten magma forced its way through the bedrock crust. In the vicinity of Little Lake, near the Great Basin–Mojave boundary, fluid lavas formed basaltic cliffs and canyons several hundred feet thick. Nearby are many scattered cinder cones, often circular at the base and perfectly symmetrical, formed from violent ejection of hot ash. Amboy Crater in the central Mojave rises 300 feet and is composed of both lava and ash ejected less than 2,000 years ago. In some places the volcanic deposits are so fresh they appear to cover ancient granites and limestones like a new overcoat. During the Cenozoic, there was enough ash and lava flow to cover thousands of square miles. The empty subterranean chambers left behind collapsed into calderas. Calderas, such as the one east of Mammoth Mountain, are depressions in the land that can be miles across and thousands of feet deep.

Although faulting, folding, and volcanic eruption are largely responsible for the topography of the California deserts, the surface features are the work of water, gravity, and wind. Ironically, water is the principal agent affecting desert landforms. With so little plant

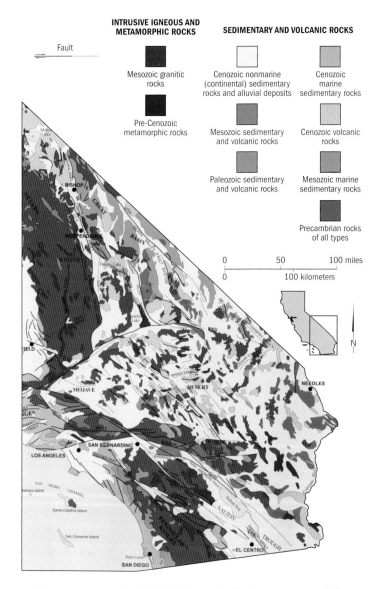

INTRUSIVE IGNEOUS AND METAMORPHIC ROCKS

Fault

Mesozoic granitic rocks

Pre-Cenozoic metamorphic rocks

SEDIMENTARY AND VOLCANIC ROCKS

Cenozoic nonmarine (continental) sedimentary rocks and alluvial deposits

Cenozoic marine sedimentary rocks

Mesozoic sedimentary and volcanic rocks

Cenozoic volcanic rocks

Paleozoic sedimentary and volcanic rocks

Mesozoic marine sedimentary rocks

Precambrian rocks of all types

Geological overview of the California deserts. Each color represents a different unit of material: tan is playa or bajada alluvium of the Cenozoic, pink is volcanic (Cenozoic), bright red is granite (Mesozoic), blue is sedimentary (Paleozoic sandstone and carbonate) and brown represents the most ancient rocks of all types (Precambrian). Faults are solid lines where visible, dotted where concealed by overlying rock. (From California Geological Survey 2006)

cover, the ground is exposed to the full force of infrequent, high-intensity storms. Such storms can drop an inch or more of precipitation as a cloudburst, especially during the summer when moist subtropical air moves north, or when thermals create thunderheads. Splashing hard against rock with little or no soil, the water begins to run off in torrents,

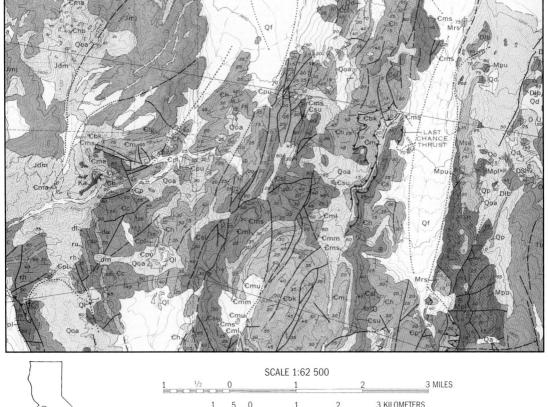

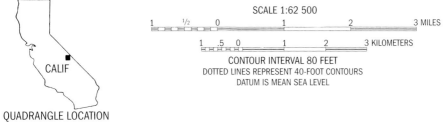

SCALE 1:62 500

1   1/2   0   1   2   3 MILES

1   .5   0   1   2   3 KILOMETERS

CONTOUR INTERVAL 80 FEET
DOTTED LINES REPRESENT 40-FOOT CONTOURS
DATUM IS MEAN SEA LEVEL

CALIF

QUADRANGLE LOCATION

Complex geology of eastern Inyo County (Waucoba Spring quadrangle). Each color represents a different unit of material: yellows are bajada or playa alluvia, pink and orange are volcanics of different ages,
reds are granite bedrock, greens and blues are sedimentary (usually sandstones and carbonate rocks,
respectively), and purples are intrusive igneous rocks (such as serpentinite). (From Nelson 1971)

with steep slopes funneling into steeper canyons. Ridges are shattered, channels are cut,
and waterfalls form within minutes. Soon these flash floods begin to carry away clays,
sands, gravels, and eventually boulders that wash down into the valleys. Great triangular
fans of these alluvial materials are built up at the mouths of canyons, often a thousand
feet high, spreading out widely as the slope diminishes. Only the finest suspended clays
and sands, along with dissolved minerals, wash into the center of the valley, where they
form flat, saline deposits over long periods of time. Water also helps erode desert mountains when it freezes in bedrock cracks, expands, and separates blocks of stone from each
other. Ultimately, such blocks may be brought down by the constant pull of gravity,

Upper left   Looking southwest along the Garlock Fault *(center)* with the Tehachapi Mountains on the right and Antelope Valley on the left. (NASA)

Upper right   A fault ruptures the ground surface in Anza-Borrego Desert State Park. (USGS)

Lower   Folded sedimentary rocks of the Mecca Hills east of Indio reveal intense pressures generated along nearby faults. (Author)

Desert landforms: faultblock mountain, cañon, bajada, and playa, all in one view of the Grapevine Mountains in Death Valley. (Marli Bryant Miller)

forming messy piles of mixed colluvial materials on the sides and along the bases of the steepest slopes. Erosion by wind is yet another landform agent in the California desert bioregion. Where the fetch is long and the rock particles small (for example, clays and sands), wind can remove the surface layers, propel them with scouring force, and eventually drop them at the foot of some fixed obstruction, such as a shrub or boulder. Sorting by grain size occurs during the process, with larger sands dropping during any reduction in wind speed and finer sands and clays transported much farther. Sand dunes can thus accumulate in one end of a valley while dust storms rise in the other.

Desert landforms are thus the products of bedrock geology, uplift by faulting, folding, and volcanic eruption, and surface erosion by water, gravity, and wind. Characteristic features are often given names that reflect a southwestern heritage. *Cañons* are the steep-sided cracks in the mountains carved by faults and raging waters. Their tortuous paths are stair-stepped by waterfalls, floored with polished rock slabs, filled with gutters of coarse gravel, and overhung by sheer walls undercut by the last good flood. Cañon mouths spill alluvium into the valley, forming a gentle, coalescing slope, or *bajada,* at the base of the mountain. Cut into the upper bajada surface are *arroyos,* or channels, that carry tons of debris-laden water into the basin. Coarse debris, such as boulders and large gravels, are common in this portion of the watercourse. As the slope of the bajada diminishes, an arroyo turns into a wide, braided wash filled with small gravels, sand, and other fine debris.

(text continues on page 88)

MUD VOLCANOES OF THE SALTON TROUGH

The movement of landmasses along the San Andreas Fault is evidence of plate tectonics. As the Pacific plate slipped past the North American plate over the last 60 million years, Baja California was separated from the Mexican mainland, and much of coastal California rafted to the northwest. This slowly opened a great rift, filled by ocean waters in the south (the Sea of Cortez) and flooded by the Colorado River in the north (the Salton Trough). The river mouth moved across this region like a pressurized hose, spewing Grand Canyon sediments across the rift. A vast delta was built at the mouth of the Colorado, and the fault-formed depression was alternately filled by riverine and marine materials. The basement of the Coachella and Imperial valleys and ancient Lake Cahuilla is, therefore, layers of soft muds and weak siltstones an astonishing 4,000 to 21,000 feet thick.

The burden of these sediments is still no match for the forces of plate tectonics. Movements along faults continue, revealed by strong earthquakes, offset stream channels, and a string of pumice domes, sulfurous vents, and hot springs along the eastern edge of the Salton Sea. These features reveal the underlying presence of magma in contact with surface waters and deep, muddy sediments.

Perhaps the most unusual expression of tectonic activity in the region is the occurrence of mud volcanoes. They were first recorded in 1853 by geologist William P. Blake, more than a century before the theory of plate tectonics would be advanced. A powerful earthquake shook Fort Yuma in 1852, where Blake rested after crossing the Cahuilla lakebed. After the quake,

> Major Heintzelman, the commanding officer of the post, observed a column of steam rising from the Desert, in a southwesterly direction, at the distance of about forty miles. Several weeks afterwards, he visited and examined the locality, and found a small mud volcano, in an active state. Puffs and jets of steam, mingled with large masses of black mud, were being constantly ejected to the height of thirty or forty feet. The orifice was in a shallow basin, partly filled with water, covering a surface of several acres. This was violently thrown outwards, in waves, at the time of each explosion; its temperature was found by

Eruption of mud volcanoes in the Salton Trough, 1857. Note human figure. (W. A. A. Veatch, Bancroft Library)

Major H. to be 108°. Numerous little cones were puffing out steam, like the exhaust of a small high-pressure steam engine; and in one of these, where gas and steam were issuing, the thermometer indicated a temperature of 170°F.

Another mud volcano was found about the same time, in the northwestern part of the Desert, northeast from Salt Creek, and probably near the lowest point of the ancient lake [Cahuilla]. Clouds of dust were thrown up from various parts of the Desert at the time of the principal shock, and the probability is, that there were many small openings and vents for subterranean gasses, that have never been found, or that have since been entirely obliterated.

The wonder of the mud volcanoes, captured in a fantastic lithograph published in 1857, would be temporarily lost. Land speculation and agricultural development had created a great demand for Colorado River water in the Imperial Valley. Engineers built nearly 400 miles of canals that carried between 16 and 100 percent of the river's flow by October 1905, allowing irrigation of almost 100,000 acres. But flash flooding in the Colorado drainage, evidently unexpected or underestimated, breached the canal system in February 1906. Vast quantities of water raged into the Cahuilla lakebed, carving two large rivers (Alamo and New) from once dry meandering washes. A new shoreline quickly rose in the basin, achieving its highest level by 1907 (−198 feet) and thus drowning the mud volcanoes. The volcanoes reappeared on a water supply map published in 1925, probably exposed by high

rates of evaporation and shoreline recession. Ongoing runoff from intensive agriculture has again elevated the water level, but the mud volcanoes reformed in the middle of a large, barren field. Most are four to seven feet tall, ooze clay lava, and pulse with deep, steady rhythms that resonate from within. In the temporary absence of movement along the fault, the muddy magma is cool and benign. But tectonic activity will renew contact with hot, deep waters, and the mud volcanoes will erupt again.

A mud volcano, five feet tall, erupting in the Salton Trough, 2006. (Author)

A bajada in spring, with creosote bush (dark green) and burrobush (light green). (Author)

At the foot of the bajadas, near the center of the basin, are *playa* surfaces that form a dusty flat when dry and a muddy lakebed when wet. Playas are concretions of clay and salts that have been liberated and transported from the mountain bedrock. The chemicals contained in the playa thus reflect local geology and can be economically important. Some playas contain large amounts of alkali, borate, gypsum, potash, and other "evaporite minerals" left behind when floodwaters are dissipated by the sun and mud shrinks into salt-encrusted polygons. Sand particles at the playa edge are swept up by wind into *arenas,* or sand sheets, that can eventually accumulate into dunes. It is these surface features, the cañons, bajadas, arroyos, washes, playas, and arenas, that provide the geological basis for desert soils.

SOILS

The gravel, sands, clays, and dissolved minerals that blanket the surface of desert landforms are parent materials for the formation of soils. These soils are never dark, humid, or thick like those of wetter, more biologically productive bioregions. Instead, desert soils reflect the climatic and geological extremes of arid lands, with less influence by plants and ground-dwelling animals. The lack of rain, combined with high evaporation and low runoff, means that little water is available to infiltrate the ground. Without infiltration, the downward movement of small clay particles and dissolved chemicals is restricted to the top few feet or so of parent material. Only over thousands of years can

Dunes form where sand-laden winds slow down and drop their suspended loads. The sculpting of giant crests and small surface ripples is accomplished by bouncing, colliding, and cascading grains. (Martin V. Covington)

desert soils develop greater thicknesses. Long periods of drought also reduce the amount of biological activity in the soil, restricting plant growth, and force dormancy on resident populations of invertebrates, bacteria, and fungi. Consequently, relatively little leaf, root, and carcass matter is added to the parent material from year to year, decomposition is slow, and critical nutrients such as nitrogen and phosphorus are in short supply. Layering of the soil is, therefore, weak, and colored profiles (indicating leaching and deposition zones for organic and mineral materials) are not readily apparent. Calcium carbonate can accumulate to very high levels even when parent material is not limestone, producing whitish concretions or cemented layers known as *caliche*. These characteristics cause all desert soils to be broadly classified as aridisols, but there are many local variations (18 soil types in the Mojave alone) that affect the distribution and abundance of desert plants and animals.

An important source of variation in desert soils comes from the grain size of the parent material. Coarse-grained gravels and large sands tend to be deposited near canyon mouths, at the tops of bajadas, and along arroyo bottoms as the speed of floodwaters begins to diminish (and these heavier particles settle out). Fine-grained clays, silts, and small sands, however, are lighter and can be carried by slower waters to the lower bajadas and playas. This gradient determines much about the interaction between local soil texture and the infiltration of rainfall or runoff. For example, a tablespoon of water can wet a coarse-textured soil of gravel and sand to a depth of 30 inches, but only to a depth of five inches in a loamy mix of clay, silt, and fine sand. Shallow storage results in three times more water loss due to evaporation than deep storage, so that less water is available for organisms to use. It is not surprising, then, to find productive, deep-rooted trees and shrubs associated with the coarse soils of arroyos and upper bajadas, while more drought-tolerant, shallow-rooted perennials dominate the fine soils of playas and lower bajadas. Burrowing animals, such as the Desert Tortoise *(Gopherus agassizii)*, tend to prefer lower bajadas with loamy soils that are easily excavated, yet strong enough to resist collapse.

Another source of local variation in desert soils comes from variations in chemistry. Calcium and carbonate dominate the soluble minerals, causing the soil pH to vary widely. Bajada soils can range from slightly acidic (pH 5.5) to moderately alkaline (pH 9.0), while playa soils range much higher (pH 8.2 to 10.9). Soil pH limits the availability of nutrients to plants, especially phosphorus, accentuating deficits caused by other processes. For example, nutrients that are soluble in water can be flushed from bajada soils during floods and deposited on the playa. But these are largely unavailable or mixed with such high concentrations of sodium and chloride that only a select few species can take them up through their root systems and utilize them for growth. These select species, called halophytes, have special physiological adaptations that allow them to extract water from brine and to cope with the nutrient deficits that result from high pH, inhibition of nutrient-producing microbes, and the extreme accumulation of sodium and chloride. Species that are sensitive are called glycophytes, and these require low-salt, low-alkaline soils typical of upland slopes. Salt accumulations in soil are second only to drought in limiting the activities of desert plants and are often responsible for distinctive distributions across the landscape.

Playa of fine alkaline clays carried to the bottom of a desert basin by water. This is the Racetrack in Death Valley. (Gary Jensen)

Processes that create the surface characteristics of desert soils are also important. Surfaces of bajadas and other alluvial slopes are especially influenced by the wind. Winds can deposit fine silts and clays between coarse gravels and small rocks that sift down, accumulate, and eventually lift the stones into place. Winds also do the opposite: they remove finer particles from bajada slopes, leaving behind gravels and small rocks. In either case, over long periods of time, the stones come to rest in the same, flat plane. The soil surface thus becomes armored with a desert pavement and can be further cemented together by carbonates of calcium and sodium. An additional, dark brown, glossy varnish is often added by bacteria. The microbes, living between the varnish and the rock, produce a slurry of minute clay particles mixed with manganese and iron oxides from their own metabolism. The varnish may trap windborne materials that bacteria consume and may act as a sunscreen that offers protection from high levels of ultraviolet radiation. Varnished pavements shed water, accentuating both flash floods and soil drought because infiltration is only one-tenth of what it is on unvarnished, less-consolidated surfaces. Instead, infiltration depends entirely on animal burrows to provide subterranean plumbing or on absorptive accumulations of fine particles and leaf litter protected beneath the canopies of long-lived shrubs. Plants tend to then grow around other plants, excluded from the dry, saline expanses of pavement between shrubs.

Lakebed polygons near Badwater, Death Valley. They form as salt-infused clay swells and shrinks in response to seasonal wetting and drying over many years. (Author)

Cryptogamic crusts are soil surface features that can also be found between shrubs and grasses in desert regions. Cyanobacteria, algae, and fungi form a living, photosynthetic layer, especially on basin soils with a shallow water table. They become physiologically active during brief, rainy periods and secrete a gelatinous coating that traps windblown clay and silt. Over many years a tangled, circular mat of filaments can form a smooth or rough, lichenlike growth when soil pH is slightly alkaline (7.5 to 8.5). The crusts can be black, brown, orange, or yellow in color and often become perched on stalks of soil if winds erode particles from around their base. The significance of cryptogamic crusts to desert soil is still emerging in the scientific literature, but evidence suggests they improve water infiltration, increase nitrogen, carbon, and overall nutrient levels, promote seed germination, and retard erosion. Consequently, the crusts are considered important soil builders and surface stabilizers in desert ecosystems.

Given the overall restrictions on biological activity in the desert bioregion, soils and soil surfaces form very slowly and can be preserved for incredible lengths of time. The oldest deposits of alluvial materials are generally found on bajadas near the base of adjacent mountains. If they have not been destroyed by flash floods and marauding arroyos, these deposits can be 100,000 to 500,000 years old. Such areas can be searched for pockets of well-developed, old soils that may have been produced during wetter, more vegetated periods in desert history. These old soils, or paleosols, take tens of thousands of years to form and are identified by their buildup of calcium carbonate below, and varnish above, the surface. The calcium collects as an impenetrable, cemented caliche layer up to three feet thick at a depth of three to six feet. It is so hard that the downward movements of water, roots, and burrowing animals are stopped. Pavements also take tens of thousands of years to form, and thick coatings of varnish may exceed 100,000 years. Needless to say, such surface antiquities repair themselves very slowly, if at all, once disturbed by human activity.

WATERS

Desert waters are rare and precious. Most of what falls as rain returns immediately to the atmosphere, except when strong storms breach the mountains or well up from rising, moisture-laden air masses. Floods that crash out of adjacent hills or shed from pavements provide short-lived opportunities for infiltration into rocky soil, groundwater recharge, or playa wetting. Nevertheless, there are such things as desert rivers, lakes, salt ponds, springs, and seeps. Some of these waters result from the proximity to extensive, high-elevation watersheds in adjacent mountain ranges. Others are the result of ancient precipitation and groundwater recharge occurring during the cold, wet Pleistocene Era (two million to 12,000 years ago). In either case, desert waters are centers of great biological activity, allowing non-

Upper   Desert pavement in the Salton Basin. (Author)

Lower   The dark ground surface in this creosote bush community is composed of cryptogamic crust. (Lloyd Stark)

Canyon of the Amargosa River south of Shoshone, with a dense riparian vegetation of willow (Salix). The terrace is the abandoned railbed of the Tonopah and Tidewater Railroad. (Thomas A. Schweich)

desert plants and animals to thrive and providing yet another set of physical features that produce diversity and beauty in the bioregion.

Rivers and lakes in the desert contain freshwater derived from adjacent watersheds. The Mojave River, for example, flows for more than 100 miles through bone-dry landscapes but originates in the San Bernardino Mountains. Similarly, the Amargosa drains the Spring Mountains of western Nevada, joins the course of the Mojave near Silver Lake, and terminates in Death Valley. The Owens is fed by many tributaries emanating from the east slope of the Sierra Nevada. Desert rivers flow slowly during the winter, peak during the spring melt, and may stagnate or disappear completely over the summer months. Along its way the water carries salt and sediment, evaporates, enters roots, infiltrates the porous valley alluvium, and builds groundwater reservoirs. Greatly diminished by these processes, the remainder flows gently into a brackish basin that often contains the shallow remnant of an ice age lake.

Mono Lake is the modern remnant of Pleistocene Lake Russell. (The names of Pleistocene water bodies are preceded by the term "Lake," while the names of modern water bodies are followed by it.) Once fed by glaciers descending from the Sierra, Lake Russell

READING THE LANDSCAPE

Processes that shape the earth are readily observed in the desert. These photos from southern Death Valley reveal the actions of faulting, alluvial deposition, and erosion by waves from Pleistocene Lake Manley.

Shoreline Butte is an ancient volcano whose dark, basaltic mass has been split in two by the Death Valley Fault system. In the aerial photo, the fault runs diagonally from upper left to bottom right. Lateral movement separated the main part of the butte (in the center) from the remnant at the bottom of the image (north). The Amargosa River flows along the fault line and has eroded away much of the base of the volcano.

To the right (west) of the butte are the coarse, stony materials that have been washed from the Panamint Range, just out of view. These alluvial deposits coalesce like rivers of rock, forming the gently sloping bajadas of the valley itself.

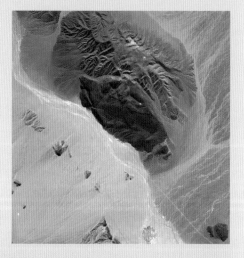

Careful examination of the north-facing slope of Shoreline Butte, in the very center of the image, shows a series of parallel lines. These can also be seen from the ground. Each line marks a shoreline that was cut by wave action during the gradual recession of Lake Manley between 12,000 and 8,000 years BP (before present). Prevailing winds made the waves powerful in this portion of the valley, as they rushed from north to south over the surface of the once vast lake.

Upper Aerial view of Shoreline Butte in Death Valley. (USGS)

Lower Ground view of Shoreline Butte, horizontally striped by ancient waves. (Marli Bryant Miller)

Fish Slough is a spring-fed wetland that provides refuge for the Owens Pupfish (Cyprinodon radiosus) north of Bishop. (Larry Blakely)

was more than 800 feet deep and 32 miles long. Death Valley was filled by Lake Manley, which at its high stand was 600 feet deep and 96 miles long. Connected by ancient rivers, many other basins in the region contained freshwater lakes and formed a continuous hydrographic system. That system affected the distribution of fish and other forms of aquatic life before global climate change produced the modern, arid landscapes we see today.

As evaporation and infiltration exceed river flow, the waters of these desert lakes become decidedly saline and ephemeral. Some lakes have dessicated completely, leaving behind a clay-bottomed playa surface as a memorial. But depending on the integrity of the basin's bottom, two types of playas commonly form. If the bottom sediments are rup-tured by deep, leaky cracks, then water continues to seep downward, taking the salts with it. The surface of this type of playa, called a recharge playa, is usually dry, sandy, and non-saline. But if the bottom sediments are intact and hold the water, then a discharge playa forms. A discharge playa is usually wet, muddy, and encrusted with salt left behind by evaporation. Salt ponds and streams can persist during most of the year on this type of playa, forming the so-called bitter springs that deceived and killed lost emigrants.

Springs and seeps are fed by groundwater that pushes to the surface where imper-meable rock or clay layers prevent deeper infiltration. The famous Palm Springs of south-ern California are in fact seepages of local groundwater that flow from faults exposed in canyons. The results of isotope-dating techniques show that the waters of the Death Val-ley Aquifer are known to have fallen during the Pleistocene and are, therefore, more than 10,000 years in transit. Stored in gravelly reservoirs that form the basement of desert basins, such fossil waters come to the surface at Ash Meadows as cool, sky-blue pools with billowing bottom sediments. Fossil waters that infiltrate to great depths encounter hot magma left over from one of many volcanic events in the desert's history. Under pres-sure the water can be heated beyond its boiling point (superheated) or turned into steam. This water gushes back to the surface along faults or fractures, creating geothermal springs and geysers.

Regardless of source, water controls the deserts. Its complete absence can lead to the death of individuals, the extirpation of populations, and the extinction of species. When in short supply over long periods of time, it can cause migration, shift the distribution limits of entire natural communities, and promote the evolution of drought-adapted or-ganisms. The periodic deluge will tear down mountains and spread them over the low-lands, providing materials for building bajadas and playas. Successive years of ample rain-fall will fill rivers, expand lakes, rejuvenate springs, and invite the return of drought-sensitive species. A climate shift that brings reliable patterns and greater amounts of precipitation will ultimately destroy deserts by removing a characteristic and extreme constraint on the biota. Deserts originate, operate, and persist within this continuum between water's ab-sence and water's abundance.

Operations and Origins

The abiotic extremes of the desert bioregion set the stage for how the biotic components live and interact. Each species is governed by its genetic inheritance, its abilities, and its limitations, given the resources made available by geography, geology, climate, and soils. With adequate water and soil, plants grow up to cast shade and make seeds. Herbivores will hide, browse leaves, store seeds in burrows, and defecate beneath plant canopies. Carnivores chase herbivores from the shrubs and dig into burrows to seize and devour their prey. These interactions create ecosystems within the bioregion—species that influence each other while coping with drought, heat, low nutrient availability, high salinity, and uncertainty. But the opposite is also true: species influence their immediate abiotic environment. The shade is cooler than the air, the fecal matter enriches the soil, and the enlarged burrow will allow floodwaters to infiltrate the pavement for deep storage. This influence is on a smaller, life-sized scale that ameliorates the regional extremes and promotes new biotic possibilities. The species and their interactions with each other and the abiotic environment define how desert ecosystems operate.

But when did these operations commence? The paradox of the California desert bioregion is that it contains very young ecosystems assembled from very ancient species. Many of its characteristic plants and animals originated millions of years ago under conditions that were warm and relatively wet, resembling subtropical environments now found in central and southern Mexico. Their long history may have preadapted them to conditions of high temperature and drought that did not completely develop until the end of the ice ages, only 10,000 or 12,000 years ago. Dramatic changes in climate and species composition, including the arrival of humans, were driving forces that shaped the modern deserts of today. And much of this story of origins and change is written on the landscape itself, etched into rocks and stored as fossils, and preserved over the millennia by aridity itself.

A Desert Tortoise grazes in a spring mix of native herbs, beginning energy flow at the base of the food web. (Gerald and Buff Corsi)

ECOSYSTEM OPERATIONS IN THE DESERT BIOREGION

In scientific terms, desert ecosystems operate by harvesting and storing solar energy as plant food (primary productivity), transferring food materials between species (energy flow), moving mineral nutrients between abiotic and biotic reservoirs (nutrient cycling), and affecting the small-scale, local climate. During these processes, individuals of each species strive to obtain a disproportionate share of limited resources (competition), devour each other (predation), and thereby change the array of species that occupy the landscape (succession). Any examination of how ecosystems operate within a bioregion must, therefore, examine these fundamental interactions between species and their environment.

PRIMARY PRODUCTIVITY

The world's deserts are found in latitudes that receive large amounts of solar energy. Between 10° and 30° north and south of the equator, cloud cover is minimized by dry, descending air masses, and the sun remains nearly overhead during much of the year. In eastern California, the number of cloudless days can exceed 340 days each year, allowing more than 4,182 kilocalories (calories times 1,000) to fall on each square inch of land surface. This represents the maximum potential energy for biological harvest. That harvest, known as primary productivity, is performed by plants conducting photosynthesis, and the amount they produce depends on the type of photosynthetic machinery they possess, the amount and type of leaf area in a given area of land, and the availability of limiting resources, especially water.

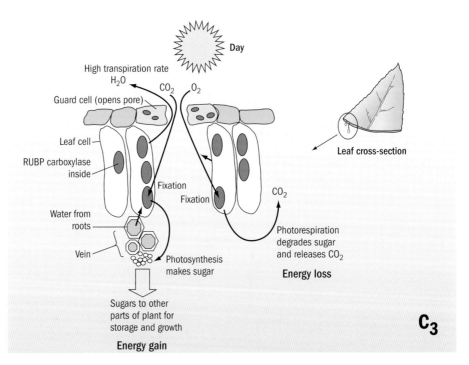

A leaf with C_3 photosynthesis. Carbon dioxide enters between wide-open guard cells (while water exits), is fixed, and is made into sugar by chloroplasts (dark green bodies). The sugar, exported through veins, represents an energy gain. Photorespiration can also occur in chloroplasts, resulting in energy loss.

Types of Photosynthesis

California desert plants can possess any one of the three known types of photosynthetic machinery (Table 2). The first type, called C_3 photosynthesis, is most common among all plants and algae. In C_3 photosynthesis the leaf cells contain an enzyme (RUBP carboxylase) that binds carbon dioxide (CO_2) from the atmosphere. This binding is called carbon fixation. The carbon compound is simultaneously activated and enriched using solar energy that has been captured by the same sunlit cells (light harvest). Thus, the activated and enriched molecules contain stored solar energy and can be used to make carbohydrates (food) or just about any carbon-containing compound the plant requires for growing and maintaining itself. This type of photosynthesis evolved first among bacteria and was subsequently inherited by the majority of sun-harvesting species over the course of earth's history.

But also inherited along with the C_3 machinery was a significant inefficiency; the enzyme also binds oxygen (O_2), which is a much more abundant gas than CO_2. This oxygen binding begins a process of photorespiration, rather than photosynthesis, a process that releases CO_2 to the atmosphere. The energy gain of the leaf is reduced by as much as 40 percent in C_3 plants, especially at higher temperatures (above 80°F). Higher temperatures stimulate photorespiration, so that more and more carbon is lost instead of sup-

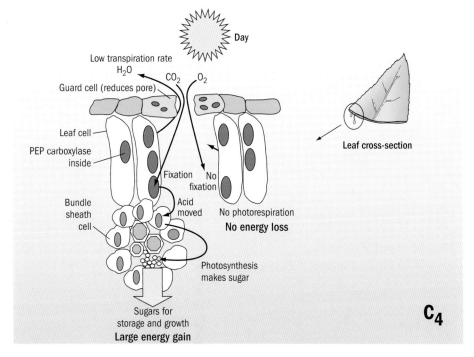

A leaf with C_4 photosynthesis. Carbon dioxide enters between partially open guard cells (low water loss), is fixed, and is shuttled into bundle sheath cells where it is made into sugar by chloroplasts. Photorespiration does not occur because the principal fixation enzyme does not bind oxygen. The gain of energy-rich carbon per unit of water loss is, therefore, much higher in C_4 than C_3 species.

porting plant growth. But at low air temperatures (40 to 80°F) or when ample water is available for evaporative cooling of the leaves, the C_3 type of photosynthesis is more than adequate. In fact, almost all desert plants in California active during winter and spring, including some of the most common and widespread species, are C_3, such as sagebrush *(Artemisia)*, pinyon pine *(Pinus monophylla)*, Joshua tree *(Yucca brevifolia)*, and creosote bush *(Larrea tridentata)*.

A second type of photosynthesis evolved in response to higher leaf temperatures. C_4 photosynthesis begins with a different carbon fixation enzyme (PEP carboxylase). This enzyme binds CO_2 in fully sunlit leaves, eventually making glucose and other food molecules; however, unlike the C_3 enzyme, PEP carboxylase cannot bind O_2. Every time fixation occurs in a C_4 leaf, there is only photosynthesis, not photorespiration. Without photorespiration the process can gain more carbon and store more of the sun's energy, even if leaf temperatures are in the range of 80 to 100°F or higher. At lower temperatures or under low-light conditions, there is less of a carbon-gain advantage, so C_4 plants tend not to be winter-active or found growing in a shady understory. Not surprisingly, this type of photosynthesis evolved in tropical grasses (such as corn *[Zea mays]* and sugarcane *[Saccharum]*), amaranths *(Amaranthus)*, saltbushes *(Atriplex)*, and in many other advanced flowering plants from warm, open, sunny habitats. Summer-active plants in the Mojave and Sonoran deserts usually possess the C_4 machinery.

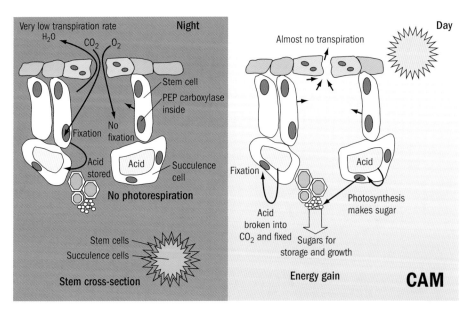

Stem of a cactus with CAM photosynthesis. Carbon dioxide enters at night (very low water loss), is fixed, and is shuttled into bundle sheath cells where it is stored as an acid. Photorespiration does not occur. During the day, solar energy is used to make the acid into sugar while guard cells are completely closed. The gain of energy-rich carbon per unit of water loss is, therefore, highest in CAM species.

TABLE 2 Comparison of the Three Known Types of Photosynthesis
Found in California Desert Plants

	C_3	C_4	CAM
Main fixation enzyme	RUBP carboxylase	PEP carboxylase	PEP carboxylase
Binds to . . .	Carbon dioxide or oxygen	Carbon dioxide	Carbon dioxide
Results in . . .	Photosynthesis or photorespiration	Photosynthesis	Acids that are stored
During . . .	Day	Day	Night
In cells of . . .	Leaf mesophyll	Leaf mesophyll	Stem or leaf mesophyll
Products	Made into sugar (energy gain) or broken down (energy loss) using light	Moved to leaf bundle sheath cells, fixed again and made into sugar (energy gain) using light	Fixed again during the day and made into sugar (energy gain) using light.
Advantages	High fixation rates at cool leaf temperatures	High fixation rates at high leaf temperatures (no photorespiration)	No photorespiration at high stem or leaf temperatures
	Rapid growth at cool temps	Rapid growth at high temps	Stomata closed during day, low transpiration rates
Disadvantages	Photorespiration at high leaf temperatures reduces energy gain	Low fixation rates at cool leaf temperatures	Limited acid storage capacity, low fixation rates, low growth rate
Water use efficiency	One gram carbon dioxide per 1,000 grams water	Two to three grams carbon dioxide per 1,000 grams water	Fourteen to 40 grams carbon dioxide per 1,000 grams water
Optimum leaf temperature	60 to 78°F	86 to 116°F	Cool nights
Types of plants	Algae, ferns, conifers, most flowering plants	Flowering plants only: summer annuals, some grasses, some sun-flowers, saltbushes	Cacti and succulents
Examples of California desert plants	Brown-eyed primrose (Camissonia claviformis), creosote bush (Larrea), Joshua tree (Yucca brevi-folia), pinyon pine (Pinus monophylla)	Cinchweed (Pectis papposa), desert holly (Atriplex hymenelytra) Eureka dunegrass (Swallenia alexandrae), four-wing saltbush (A. canescens)	Beavertail cactus (Opuntia basilaris), California barrel cactus (Ferocactus cylin-draceus), desert agave (Agave deserti), silver cholla (O. echinocarpa)

The third type of photosynthesis is a complex amalgam of C_3 and C_4 that, uniquely and remarkably, uses conditions at night to perform some of the carbon-gaining tasks. Air humidity is much higher at this time, so that less water is lost from tissues when the CO_2 is absorbed. The C_4 enzyme, PEP carboxylase, binds CO_2 in the dark, so that less water is lost and no photorespiration takes place. The four-carbon product is an acid that is shuttled into watery cells in succulent tissues for overnight storage. After sunrise, CO_2 is stripped from the acid and bound again with the C_3 enzyme, RUBP carboxylase. In the presence of light the products are activated and energized to make all necessary compounds. This type of photosynthesis, called crassulacean acid metabolism, or CAM, has the greatest carbon (and energy) gain per unit of water lost and is very advantageous in deserts with low rainfall, cool evenings, and coarse soil. Its principal disadvantage is that CAM plants are very slow growing because the storage capacity of succulent tissues limits the amount of acid (therefore, carbon) that can accumulate and be made into energy-rich compounds. Cacti, iceplants, and stonecrops are succulents that possess CAM and are usually found in dry, open, and rocky habitats where there is little competing plant cover.

Leaf Area

A unit of leaf area, such as one square inch of green tissue, is used to measure the rate of photosynthesis conducted by a single plant. Primary productivity, however, is measured per unit of ground surface area, say the 100 square feet of a 10 by 10 foot plot. When we measure this way, we are estimating the carbon gain of an entire ecosystem as contributed by all plants of all species in that plot. It is as if we treated all the live green leaves and stems collectively as one large photosynthetic surface. The area of that collective surface in a plot of known area is called the leaf area index of that ecosystem. Mathemati-

Upper Brown-eyed primrose *(Camissonia claviformis)*, a Mojave winter annual possessing C_3 photosynthesis. (Author)

Lower Torrey's amaranth, a Sonoran summer annual possessing C_4 photosynthesis. (James M. Andre)

cally, it is the ratio of live leaf area (square feet) to land area (square feet), and it is a useful way to compare how plants contribute to differences between ecosystems.

In shrub-dominated desert ecosystems, such as those found in the Mojave and Sonoran deserts, the leaf area index has been estimated to be between .7 and 1.0. This means there is about one square foot of leaf surface for each square foot of ground. In the Great Basin, the ratio can approach 2 where large, leafy shrubs such as big sagebrush *(Artemisia tridentata)* come to dominate. In contrast, a tropical rainforest can have an index of 11, and a cultivated field of corn can have an

Beavertail cactus *(Opuntia basilaris)*, a stem-succulent possessing CAM photosynthesis. (Author)

index of 4. This tells us that primary productivity in deserts is limited by the amount of leaf area, which in turn is limited by the availability of resources that produce leaf area, especially water and nitrogen.

Resource Limitations

Water is the resource that most limits primary productivity in deserts. This is because demand is high—plant bodies are 90 percent water by weight. Photosynthesis demands water. Each molecule of carbon dioxide taken up by leaves requires that several thousand molecules of water be lost in a process of gas exchange. And as already discussed in the previous chapter, the supply of water to arid lands is very low. Without water, photosynthesis is slowed or stopped, causing carbohydrate synthesis and plant growth to stop as well. The ratio of carbon gained to water lost is called water use efficiency, and it reflects the relative ability of plants with different types of photosynthesis to overcome this limitation. Because of high photorespiration, the leaves of C_3 plants have the lowest water use efficiency, about one gram CO_2 per 1,000 grams of water. C_4 plants are two or three times more efficient because they do not photorespire. CAM plants are the most efficient, gaining 14 to 40 grams CO_2 per 1,000 grams of water, because they open their stomata at night and, therefore, lose a lot less water when taking up carbon.

Given a high-demand and low-supply economy, competition for water becomes very intense. Overlapping root systems explore the same soil volumes, attempting to extract small amounts of available soil moisture. Plant species that quickly initiate root growth and draw water ahead of the roots of other species will be able to sustain photosynthesis

(text continues on page 108)

MEASURING PHOTOSYNTHESIS IN DEATH VALLEY

Technology is one element that drives discovery. Ancient irrigation and cropping technologies allowed native plants to be grown and selected for efficient food production along floodplains of the Colorado River and among meadows of the Owens Valley. Each species responded differently to cultivation, and this knowledge was used by Indians to determine which would provide reliable, nutritious harvests and which would not. In more recent times, field-portable instrumentation has allowed native plants to be physiologically examined under natural conditions almost anywhere in the desert. The responses of each plant species to light, water, temperature, and other environmental factors provide valuable insights into productivity, stress tolerance, and adaptation. Much of what we have discovered about photosynthesis in plants has come from using remarkable technology to study California desert species.

When an intact leaf is carefully sealed in a chamber with a translucent lid, it will immediately begin to absorb CO_2 (photosynthesis) and release water vapor (transpiration). The concentrations of CO_2 and water will fall and rise, respectively, at rates that depend on whether stomata are open, the area of the leaf, the type of photosynthesis (for example, C_3 or C_4), and the environment in the chamber. An infrared gas analyzer is used to precisely measure the CO_2 decrease while environmental conditions in the chamber are varied one at a time. If, for example, the amount of light in the chamber is varied from dark to full-sun intensity (while holding leaf temperature constant), the rate of photosynthesis will correspondingly increase until the biochemical machinery is running at maximum. The data are graph-

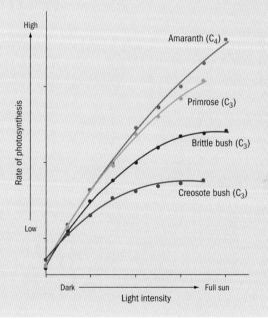

Responses of photosynthesis to increasing light intensity in Death Valley. C_4 and C_3 annuals, such as Torrey amaranth and brown-eyed primrose, achieve the highest rates of carbon dioxide fixation. Creosote bush, a C_3 shrub, has low rates because its waxy, evergreen leaves are less permeable to carbon dioxide. (Redrawn from Ehleringer 1985)

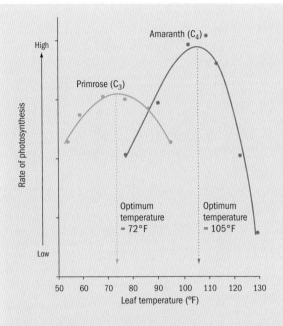

Amaranth (C$_4$) •

Primrose (C$_3$)

High

Rate of photosynthesis

Low

Optimum
temperature
= 72°F

Optimum
temperature
= 105°F

50   60   70   80   90   100   110   120   130
Leaf temperature (°F)

Responses of photosynthesis
to changes in leaf temperature. C$_3$ species have a much
lower optimum temperature
(arrow) than C$_4$ species and
are active during the cool
seasons of the year. (Redrawn
from Ehleringer 1985)

ically expressed as "light curves," allowing comparison of leaves from different species under different conditions. Simultaneous measurement of transpiration (increases in water vapor in the chamber) allow calculation of water use efficiency (the ratio of photosynthesis to transpiration rates) and even the degree to which stomata are open. The first infrared gas analyzer arrived in Death Valley during the 1960s as part of a mobile laboratory program funded by the National Science Foundation. Subsequent improvements included computerized controls, chambers for whole plants, and the creature comforts of a recreational vehicle.

Left   A leaf of desert holly *(Atriplex hymenelytra)* sealed in a chamber that measures photosynthesis under field conditions. (Harold Mooney)

Right   The Carnegie Institute Mobile Laboratory in Death Valley, July 1970. (Harold Mooney)

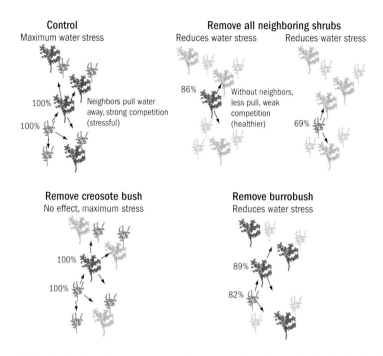

Control
Maximum water stress

100%

100%

Neighbors pull water away, strong competition (stressful)

Remove all neighboring shrubs
Reduces water stress   Reduces water stress

86%

Without neighbors, less pull, weak competition (healthier)

69%

Remove creosote bush
No effect, maximum stress

100%

100%

Remove burrobush
Reduces water stress

89%

82%

Removing neighboring shrubs reduces water stress (percentage of maximum levels), indicating that competition for soil water is strong. Removing burrobush (yellow) is especially effective, as it competes with itself and with creosote bush (green). (Based on Fonteyn and Mahall 1978)

and growth longer, thus gaining even more extraction capacity. As water moves through the soil and into the root system of one plant, it can pull the water away from, and out of, the roots of another. Below ground, the soil water is thus stretched like a web of rubber bands between competing root systems. The strongest competitors are those species that can generate and withstand the greatest pull (actually a suction force). This was elegantly demonstrated in the Mojave by an experiment that removed burrobush shrubs *(Ambrosia dumosa)* from around a single creosote bush. With removal, the water content of the creosote bush significantly increased, as though the rubber bands of water moving away had suddenly been cut. Similarly, experimental removal of big sagebrush allowed the surrounding perennial grasses to stay green longer and grow more vigorously. Ultimately, belowground competition for water contributes to the characteristic regular spacing between mature shrubs so commonly observed across desert landscapes.

Nitrogen is probably the next most limiting resource in desert environments. Again, demand is high, as it is an essential component in the machinery of life, required to construct enzymes and genetic material. Green plant tissues are two to three percent nitrogen by weight, mostly in the form of proteins such as RUBP carboxylase (the CO_2 fixation enzyme). Without nitrogen, the ability of leaves to fix carbon is extremely limited, even if moisture is abundant after winter storms. Consequently, competition for nitrogen among plants can be intense. Soil nitrogen comes from the decomposition of leaf litter in upper soil layers, supplemented by bacterial fixation and, more recently, deposition from air pollution. When fertilizers are experimentally applied, the growth of deserts plants is increased severalfold if water is not also limiting. Additional nitrogen also improves the protein content of young tissues, a change that leaf-eating insects can detect and profit from.

Estimates of Primary Productivity

Primary productivity represents the amount of energy that plants make available to other organisms. Water, nitrogen, carbon dioxide, and other resources are combined by photosynthesis into the carbohydrates, proteins, and fats that compose plant bodies, including those of progeny contained in seeds. Measuring the production of these life-giving materials is difficult, in part because they often end up below ground as roots, incorporated into small, ephemeral structures (for example, bud scales or root hairs), dedicated to mobile offspring (seeds), or degraded by plant respiration. Nevertheless, 10 square feet (about one square meter) of Great Basin has been shown to typically produce about 250 grams per year (186 grams of shoot and 64 grams of root dry matter). By comparison, 10 square feet of temperate deciduous forest consistently produces 600 to 1,500 grams per year, and the same amount of tropical rain forest between 1,000 and 3,500 grams per year. The difference is water, not temperature. Where groundwater is available and reliable, desert productivity can be much higher. Arroyos and basins in the sweltering Sonoran Desert support dense, productive stands of honey mesquite *(Prosopis glandulosa* var. *torreyana)*. Aboveground primary productivity can achieve 2,300 grams per 10 square feet per year (averaging 365 grams), half of which is turned into wood, a third into leaves, and the rest into energy-rich flowers, seeds, and fruit. The success of desert agriculture depends entirely on irrigation to achieve similar levels of productivity.

But most of the desert does not have reliable and available water. On stony bajadas of the Mojave dominated by creosote bush, primary productivity above and below ground is very low (a range of 60 to 120 grams per 10 square feet per year), and strongly correlated with precipitation received during the September to March growing season. An understory of herbaceous plants, perhaps as many as 20 species, produces only .5 grams of shoot per 10 square feet in a dry year (four inches of precipitation), but 2.5 grams in an average year (six inches). Adjacent shrubs, belonging to 12 species, collectively make 31 and 49 grams of leaves and fruits, respectively. The shrubs maintain some leaf area all year long and thus take advantage of weak

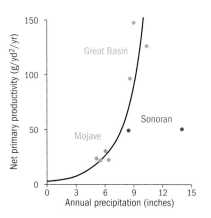

Primary productivity in the Great Basin, Mojave, and Sonoran deserts depends almost completely on annual precipitation. (Redrawn from Smith et al. 1997)

A showy display of winter annuals, such as sand verbena *(Abronia villosa)*, is a pulse of primary productivity triggered by ample rainfall. (Charles E. Jones)

storms with short bursts of photosynthesis. But successive drought years can reduce leaf area, photosynthetic rates, and primary productivity to near zero. Thus, the availability of soft, succulent, energy-rich tissues for grasshoppers, tortoises, and ground squirrels fluctuates greatly between years and over vast areas. Low, variable primary productivity constrains animal abundance, resilience, and complexity within desert ecosystems because it limits energy flow.

ENERGY FLOW

Primary production is first turned into secondary production by the consumption of plant parts or the resources they contain. Herbivores obtain their nutrition directly from materials assembled by photosynthesis, thus extending the process of energy flow from the sun through the ecosystem. Consumption of these organisms by carnivores is the next stage of secondary production, while carnivores preying on carnivores adds yet another. Thus, energy flows from one feeding tier to another: primary producer to herbivore (plant consumption), herbivore to carnivore (animal consumption), carnivore to carnivore (animal consumption), and so on. The complexity of feeding relationships in an ecosystem is often expressed as a food web. A food web is an ecological model that arranges species in tiers to illustrate energy flow.

But even the simplest desert community has a complex food web. Dunes and sand sheets in the Coachella Valley support about 175 species of plants, 96 species of vertebrates, and thousands of invertebrates and soil microorganisms—the number of possible feeding relationships is astronomical. Detailed studies have shown these species to occupy at least six tiers connected by multiple feeding chains and loops (feeding within a tier, as in the case of cannibalism). Simple chains between tiers (for example, plant-jackrabbit-coyote) are less common than long, branching chains that might span all tiers and include up to 11 species (especially when the belowground tiers are included). Omnivores themselves add complexity, feeding at multiple tiers. Top predators, those that supposedly have no predators themselves, may not exist in the real desert of the Coachella Valley because even the largest carnivores (such as Coyote *[Canis latrans]*) are known to fall as prey to another. Therefore, only the broad categories of plant consumption and animal consumption will be used to examine feeding and energy flow in California desert communities.

Plant Consumption

There are many types of desert herbivores and many responses of desert plants to herbivory. Browsers, such as Desert Bighorn *(Ovis canadensis nelsoni),* eat shrubs, clipping twigs with their associated leaves but leaving behind the majority of woody stems and roots. Their clipping activity often increases shrub growth by stimulating dormant buds to make new, leafy branches and by increasing the amount of light penetrating into the canopy. Grazers, such as Desert Tortoise *(Gopherus agassizii),* prefer soft, green tissues of herbs and grasses that are voraciously consumed during spring. Attached but partially eaten leaves are still active and can compensate for such loses. In fact, they achieve higher rates of photosynthesis after grazing because the smaller canopy has more water and light available. Sucking insects, such as aphids and scales (Homoptera), insert mouthparts into food-conducting tissues (phloem) to harvest carbohydrates and other valuable materials. The plants are thus parasitized but able to redirect food resources to new growing points on roots and shoots. Granivores consume entire plants as embryos, allowing application of the term "seed predators." A single kangaroo rat *(Dipodomys)* may devour thousands of plant progeny, but at the same time it disperses the uneaten seeds into new, potentially beneficial habitats. Each type of herbivore has unique effects on the plant life of the desert, and each has a different ability to assimilate plant productivity into its own energy-rich tissues.

Generalist herbivores may have strong preferences, but overall they eat a wide variety of plants. The choice may be made on the basis of water as well as energy content. For example, the Black-tailed Jackrabbit *(Lepus californicus)* is probably the most abundant mammalian herbivore native to the desert bioregion of North America. It is a generalist that

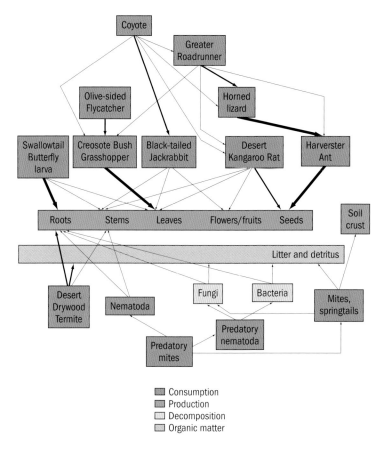

A simplified and incomplete California desert food web, above and below ground. Primary producers are in green, consumers in brown, decomposers in pink, and dead organic matter in gray. Bold arrows indicate a trophic specificity or strong preference.

prefers to graze on green, succulent tissues of many herb and grass species during winter and spring. As spring turns into summer, these hares become browsers of new twigs on creosote bush and are the only mammal that tolerates resins that permeate the shrub's tissues. (The resins are phenols that congeal plant proteins and starches, greatly reducing digestibility.) Jackrabbits often stand high on their haunches to sample many stems, preferring those with the highest water and lowest resin content. The rejected stems are scattered about like a sloppy pruning performed on thousands of shrubs. During a dry winter jackrabbits browse creosote bush, mesquite, snakeweed *(Gutierrezia sarothrae)*, Mormon tea *(Ephedra)*, big sagebrush, rabbitbrush *(Chrysothamnus)*, and even cacti (for example, *Opuntia*).

Granivores are often generalists that take advantage of the most abundant seed sources at a given moment during the growing season. A lush patch of seed-producing lupines *(Lupinus)* is an early-spring opportunity too good to be ignored by foraging kangaroo rats.

They stop chewing whatever is in their mouths and immediately begin stuffing fur-lined cheek pouches with seeds liberated from the legume. These are returned to storage rooms in burrows and cached for use at a later date. Foraging a few weeks later, the same animals find mesquite pods or saltbush fruits, so they harvest, stuff, and cache those species as well. Harvester ants (species of *Pogonomyrmex, Messor,* and *Veromessor*) also use underground storage to provide food for their larvae, preferring the small but carbohydrate-rich seeds of abundant annual herbs. Large-bodied granivores, such as the Desert Kangaroo Rat *(Dipodomys deserti)*, tend to select large, moist seeds when they have a choice. Similarly, small-bodied granivores, such as the Pale Kangaroo Mouse *(Microdipodops pallidus),* tend to collect from small-seeded, perennial species. Specialization does evolve, but it is unusual; Bailey's Pocket Mouse *(Chaetodipus baileyi)* has the unique ability to digest the toxic seeds of jojoba *(Simmondsia chinensis)*. But these patterns are not rigid and are often overruled by an animals' energy and water needs that arise during the course of a desert year.

Specialist herbivores obtain energy from one or just a few plant species or genera. Approximately 70 percent of all herbivorous insects fall into this category. The Creosote Bush Grasshopper *(Bootettix argentatus)* feeds exclusively on the resinous leaves of its namesake, never having to forage beyond the boundaries of a single, perennial canopy. More than 20 species of bees completely rely upon the pollen and nectar of creosote bush flowers for their nutrition. Larvae of metalmark butterflies (for example, *Apodemia*) feed on the roots of several buckwheat *(Eriogonum)* species, while the adults rely upon floral nectar. But insects are not the only specialists. Chisel-tooth Kangaroo Rats *(Dipodomys microps)* use

Upper Black-tailed Jackrabbit, a generalist herbivore, browsing the spring foliage of wishbone bush *(Mirabilis bigelovii)*. (Ron Niebrugge)

Lower The Creosote Bush Grasshopper, a specialist herbivore, never leaves the canopy of its food-source namesake. (Ryan Sawby)

flattened incisors to remove the salt-encrusted epidermis that covers leaves of desert shadscale *(Atriplex confertifolia)* and eat the succulent inner tissues. They are one of a few mammals that can obtain nutrition from foliage that would normally upset the ionic balance of bodily fluids. It's probably not surprising that specialists depend on widespread, abun-

Left Harvester ant moving the fruit and seed of desert mistletoe *(Phoradendron californicum)* back to an underground nest. (E. S. Ross)

Right A floral display of desert pepper weed from seeds that were carried back to the nest of harvester ants at Ash Meadows. (Author)

dant, and long-lived plant species, rather than unreliable ephemeral or rare plants, even if it means overcoming or tolerating harmful chemistry or poor-quality food content (for example, low protein).

Plant consumption also takes place below ground, but we know a lot less about it. Roots provide food for fungi, bacteria, nematodes, and termites. Members of the legume family, such as mesquite, produce root nodules that house nitrogen-fixing bacteria (see the section "Nutrient Cycling"). New, soft roots of grasses exude small amounts of carbohydrate into the soil and become surrounded by a crusty tube (rhizosheath). The roots of the perennial Indian ricegrass *(Achnatherum hymenoides)* have whitish rhizosheaths of sand and clay particles that create an ideal habitat for bacteria and fungi. The fungi (mycorrhizae) form a network through the soil that facilitates seedling establishment and shrub growth by acting as an extended root system. Nearly all dominant species in the desert have roots associated with mycorrhizal fungi. Although plants lose some hard-won photosynthetic resources, these microorganisms supply roots with valuable nitrogen fixed from the atmosphere or gathered from other places in the soil environment. Microscopic roundworms known as nematodes swarm around sheathed and unsheathed roots in great numbers, with some species feeding directly on root exudates. Others prey upon the root-feeding microorganisms, extending the underground food web. Finally, termites are very important underground plant consumers in all warm, arid regions of the world, and the Mojave and Sonoran deserts of California are no exception. At least 40 species of desert termite consume the cellulose of woody roots (and shoots), a very abundant resource associated with all shrubs and trees. Some termites are specialists, such as the Desert Drywood Termite *(Pterotermes occidentalis)* of the Sonoran Desert, which prefers blue palo verde *(Cercidium floridum)*. Others are generalists, devouring any persistent plant parts they come across. Cellulose digestion is actually performed by a diverse microbial community that symbiotically resides in the hindgut of each insect. Water is liberated in the process, and a small branch of ocotillo *(Fouquieria splendens)* will lose half of its weight in 17 years instead of 29 years. All forms of plant consumption allow the sun's energy to flow into, and be assimilated by, another set of bodies for other, predatory organisms to consume.

Animal Consumption

Desert carnivores come in all shapes, sizes and types, but strict dietary specialists are almost unknown. This is because predators must be opportunistic—they must eat any species of available prey if it can be captured and is palatable. In all food webs, predators need to eat many prey species, but herbivore prey are much less abundant than the plant life they depend on because of inefficiencies during energy flow. If 100 grams of consumable, energy-rich plant material is produced in a desert year, only 10 grams becomes part of the herbivore body because the other 90 grams is burned in respiration, is undigested and defecated, or is simply left underground or in the canopy. When a carnivore devours that 10 grams of herbivore body, only one gram becomes part of the carnivore body, because the other nine are respired, defecated, or left with the carcass. If the carnivore were about the same size as the herbivore it consumed, it would need to kill and eat at least 10 for self-maintenance. Consequently, the predator will always be much less abundant than its prey because of the inefficiencies imposed by respiration, digestion, and harvest. And, if the predator

Upper Desert Kangaroo Rat, a generalist granivore, that fills its cheek pouches with seeds of many plant species. (Lloyd Glenn Ingles)

Center Bailey's Pocket Mouse, a specialist granivore that prefers the seeds of jojoba. (Roger W. Barbour)

Lower Seed-containing fruits of jojoba, a shrub of the Sonoran Desert. (Charles Webber)

The Arid Land Termite, an important decomposer of desert woods. (E. S. Ross)

Ants are the main food of the Desert Horned Lizard, a "sit and wait" predator. (Dee E. Warenycia)

itself becomes prey to another carnivore in the food web (thus adding another feeding tier), this same reduction in abundance will be repeated. Food webs are often visualized as a pyramid of abundance, with progressively smaller numbers of consumers as the number of feeding tiers increases.

In California's deserts, lizards are the most abundant vertebrate predators, consuming very large quantities of ants, termites, grasshoppers, and other insects. A single Desert Horned Lizard *(Phrynosoma platyrhinos)* can eat 70 to 100 harvester ants in a day, constituting 50 to 90 percent of its diet. It is a slow-moving predator that remains still while lapping up individual workers that forage in the vicinity. A flashing, moist tongue delivers the morsel to the back of the mouth, where it is swallowed without chewing. If too much time elapses between wandering ants, the horned lizard plods to another patch of ground to wait again, or retires beneath a shady shrub to digest its chitinous load. Termites make up 17 percent of the stomach contents of Side-blotched Lizards *(Uta stansburiana)*, which stalk their prey and then leap forward to grab, chew, and swallow. This species will forage far and wide to come across a colony, stopping to ambush workers that leave the underground nest. Zebra-tailed Lizards *(Callisaurus draconoides)*, on the other

hand, are active, fast-moving predators that can lift their front legs off the ground during a sprint. Across the sandy surface of a dune, they appear as a blur of black and white stripes that snatches beetles and even small lizards while on the run. These various types of predatory lizards, the "sit and wait," "stalking," and "rapid attack" types, have different energy requirements and, therefore, tend to prefer the different food sources that fulfill those requirements.

Snakes are also common desert predators, but as a group, they consume a broader array of prey animals than do the lizards. Smaller, nonvenomous species rely mostly on the same abundant, herbivorous insects. The Western Blind Snake *(Leptotyphlops humilus)* uses its sense of smell to follow the pheromone trails of ants and termites back to the nest. Adults, pupae, larvae, and eggs are all on its

Upper   The Zebra-tailed Lizard is a rapid attack predator, often found on sand dunes. (Daniel L. Geiger)

Lower   A Western Blind Snake uses smell to find its insect prey. (William C. Flaxington)

menu, as are millipedes and centipedes. Another small desert hunter is the Western Shovelnose Snake *(Chionactis occipitalis)*, which emerges at night from beneath the sand sur-

Upper Mojave Desert variant (subspecies *occipitalis*) of the Western Shovelnose, a nocturnal predator. (William C. Flaxington)

Lower Colorado Desert variant (subspecies *annulata*) of the Western Shovelnose. (William C. Flaxington)

face to feed on almost any ambling insect, as well as spiders, scorpions, and centipedes. The Mojave Patchnose Snake *(Salvadora hexalepis mohavensis)* finds and unearths the eggs of other reptiles using its enlarged "nose," but it will also eat grasshoppers, lizards, and small mammals. Larger snakes, such as constrictors and the venomous rattlesnakes, forgo the insects in favor of rodents, with a few rabbits, lizards, and ground-dwelling birds thrown in the mix. Overall, the abundance of snakes and lizards in the desert is restricted by the abundance of their prey but promoted by the lower energy requirements of their ectothermic metabolism. Conforming to the environmental temperature, or adjusting for it by basking, burrowing, or aestivating, greatly decreases the amount of food required for small carnivores to survive long periods of low productivity in the desert.

Large, warm-blooded predators are much less common than reptiles and have very general diets and wide geographic and ecological distributions. As a matter of fact, no species of canines, raccoons, weasels, skunks, or cats are endemic, or even limited to, any of the California deserts. The top tier of the food web pyramid is so small that higher-level carnivores can use the desert to hunt but cannot live there full time. Instead, it seems that these predators are commuters, able to travel long distances between desert lowlands and forested uplands in search of prey. Packs of Coyote *(Canis latrans)* can be heard barking and yelping on the floor of a warm desert valley, but they have been known to make a 30-mile roundtrip in a single night, following canyon trails down and up the side of an adjacent mountain range. When hungry they will eat almost anything, from carrion to grasshoppers, in addition to the preferred diet of fresh meat and fruits. Despite this mobility, at least one desert subspecies, the Desert Coyote *(C. l. mearnsi),* has evolved as a small-bodied version with paler, gray fur. The Gray Fox *(Urocyon cinereoargenteus)* prefers to live in chaparral and pinyon pine woodlands but occurs across all deserts of North America as the subspecies *U. c. scottii.* They prefer small rodents and birds but have been known to eat insects, berries, and even fungi. Adult Mountain Lions *(Puma concolor)* travel about six miles per night while hunting deer and Desert

Bighorn in uplands and adjacent mountains. They require a kill every six to 10 days to meet their energy requirements, even more if supplying kittens. Perhaps the one exception to the lack of large, resident predators is the Desert Kit Fox *(Vulpes macrotis)*, which tends to locate its burrows near those of its favorite food, kangaroo rats. Nevertheless, they have been known to eat any rodent, as well as rabbits, lizards, insects, and berries.

Left Desert Kit Fox, a top predator that establishes burrows near its primary food source, kangaroo rats. (Larry Sansone)

Right Coyote, a top predator that forages widely within and beyond the desert. (Lloyd Glenn Ingles)

Microscopic carnivores extend the belowground food web. Soil mites (Acari, a type of arthropod), are probably the most abundant predators in desert soils, feeding on the nematodes and fungi associated with root systems. There are also predatory nematodes and amoebae, which are abundant only when soils are moist. Although many other, larger predators live in burrows (for example, tarantulas, sun spiders, centipedes, and desert shrews), they actually hunt on the surface and are not a part of the belowground flow of energy.

NUTRIENT CYCLING

The flow of materials in an ecosystem is called nutrient cycling. Materials are stored in reservoirs and moved between reservoirs by fluxes. Reservoirs can include rocks, the atmosphere, soil, bodies of live organisms, dead leaf litter, wood, and carcasses. The fluxes are transfer processes, such as weathering, fixation, uptake, and decomposition. Gases, liquids, and solids are stored and moved, while the time it takes to move from one reservoir to another can vary from seconds to eons.

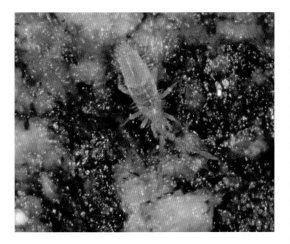

Upper Springtails are part of the decomposition process that recycles nutrients in desert soils. (Ryan Sawby)

Lower Red mites may be the most abundant predators in the underground food web. (Ryan Sawby)

Given the great geological diversity found within the California desert bioregion, we might expect that bedrocks are a primary source for many minerals with biological importance. Limestones are high in calcium, dolomites in magnesium; granites have potassium, aluminum, and silicon, and volcanics can contain sodium, sulfur, potassium, and many other minerals. The varnishes found on desert pavement have high concentrations of iron and manganese, while lakebed deposits are rich in sodium, chloride, and borates. But until eroded and dissolved in water, the components of rocks are unavailable to plants and other organisms. Thus, rainfall and runoff control the flux of these materials into a desert basin, and distribution across the landscape is very uneven. Patches of high and low mineral concentrations are strewn across bajadas, depending on the duration and intensity of erosion and transport during flood events. And highly soluble materials, such as sodium and chloride, are flushed into playas, where they accumulate and become concentrated by evaporation.

Unlike other mineral nutrients that can originate from the weathering of rocks, nitrogen comes from the atmosphere and is made available by biological fixation. Nitrogen gas makes up more than 70 percent of the air at sea level but is so chemically stable that it does not react at temperatures and pressures conducive to life. Only the nitrogen-fixing bacteria are able to turn atmospheric nitrogen into forms that organisms can use, primarily nitrate (NO_3) and ammonium (NH_4). These symbiotic bacteria (for example, *Rhizobium*) obtain carbohydrate food from the roots of pea family plants, such as mesquite, milkvetch *(Astragalus)*, and lupine, but give back nitrogen. One common species, the smoke tree *(Psorothamnus spinosus)*, obtains a third of its required nitrogen from bacteria-harboring root nodules. Other nitrogen-fixing bacteria (for example, *Azotobacter*) inhabit the rhizosheaths of grasses, while blue-green cyanobacteria are an essential component of cryptogramic crusts that cover the soil surface. During a rain the crust leaks nitrogen, mostly in the form of ammonium, into the soil layers below. The presence of nitrogen-fixing organisms associated with plants or crusts accentuates the uneven distribution of nutrients in deserts.

Centipedes shelter underground but feed at night on the soil surface. (Ryan Sawby)

Nutrients weathered from rocks or fixed biologically become stuck to the surface of soil particles. Clays are especially important because they have a very high surface area per unit of volume and thus can store more nutrients than large sand particles (and more water). Owing to their chemical lattice structure, clay surfaces are dominated by negative charges and tend to attract positively charged nutrients. This creates a soil reservoir of calcium, sodium, potassium, and magnesium that plant roots can readily access. But negatively charged nutrients, such as nitrate and phosphorus, are not as readily held and become leached out if uptake by roots does not occur. Once incorporated into plants, some nutrients will remain below ground if they become a part of a live root system. When roots die, bound nutrients will again enrich the soil reservoir as part of the organic humus. Above ground, shed plant parts gather around the base of shrubs as a litter layer that can double soil nitrate and potassium levels compared to adjacent soils in the open.

Nutrient uptake by desert plants depends on fine feeder roots that actively grow through moist, enriched soil. These conditions are met only during some seasons of nondrought years. Therefore, water and nutrient acquisition are linked opportunities that require rapid responses when many organisms are simultaneously demanding these resources. Once released from dormancy, annual plants take advantage of nutrient-rich soils beneath the canopies of shrubs, developing a shallow, concentrated root system. Some soil bacteria not only compete with plants for nitrogen, they deplete the soil by taking up nitrates for conversion back into inert, useless gas (nitrifying bacteria). In light of such intense competition, it may not be surprising that desert shrubs have ways of storing and internally recycling nitrogen that minimize return to the soil and maximize tolerance of low availability during long, dry seasons. Storage proteins and sequestered amino acids can be held inside woody stems and roots and used sparingly to make more ephemeral parts or those more susceptible to ingestion by herbivores.

Finally, any nutrient held in the live tissues of plants or animals can be released back into the ecosystem by decomposition. The process begins when tissues are fragmented by wind, gravity, teeth, or digestive enzymes. The fragments fall to the ground as litter or fecal matter, or sometimes as a carcass left behind after the best parts have been consumed. Soil arthropods, such as springtails (Collembola), mites (Acari), and a wide variety of insect larvae, begin feeding on the fragments or inoculating them with the spores of fungi carried on their bodies. When moisture is available, fungi and bacteria emerge from spores and begin decomposing all dead tissues and fecal matter. Termites consume wood and dung in great quantities, releasing energy-rich glucose sugars from the inert polymer of cellulose. Surface litter in the Mojave loses about 55 percent of its weight in the first year of decomposition, while roots lose about 80 percent. The carbon-containing compounds are harvested for energy, but the associated minerals are either assimilated and used by the decomposers or released back into the soil for plant uptake (mineralization). In deserts, fragmentation and mineralization may be separated by months or even years because decomposition depends on water.

SUCCESSION

Most of us know succession as the process of species replacing one another over time. Competition, soil development, shading of short plants by tall ones, and other interactions allow self-perpetuating climax species to locally eliminate pioneer species, creating a stable ecosystem in decades or centuries. It is easily observed in humid climates as deciduous trees invade a fireless grassland, producing a woody forest where herbs once prevailed. As the overstory canopy structure becomes developed, it attracts forest-dwelling animals that do not frequent shorter, more open types of vegetation. Thus, succession has been described as a sequence of species replacements, usually leading to progressive, cumulative changes in the community of organisms and in the ecosystem of interacting abiotic and biotic components.

But does succession occur in California deserts? Are there separate pioneers and climax species, and if so, what is the nature of the interactions that drive replacement? The eminent ecologist Forrest Shreve postulated that succession did not occur in deserts, primarily because he thought that the pioneer species were the climax species and that drought imposed great limits on how much plants could modify the environment. However, more recent studies performed in California do establish that succession occurs in our deserts, but it is slow and subtle and not very predictable. Species replacement is not orderly, and stable climax communities can seldom be identified. Desert succession reflects the life histories of colonizing species and is very sensitive to geology, climate, and other localized conditions that affect the sequence and outcome. If it occurs on open ground that has never been vegetated before, the process (a primary succession) is very

The town of Skidoo near Death Valley, 1906.
(Yeager and Woodward)

Skidoo, 1999, has been used to study succession. Natural recovery of the native vegetation has been slow, especially on the compacted street soils. (Dominic Oldershaw)

slow for lack of soil and colonizers. If it occurs where disturbance has removed existing vegetation but not the soil, the process (a secondary succession) can be more rapid but still dependent upon climate extremes and soil damage.

Open, unvegetated ground in deserts is commonly created by wind erosion and dune formation. Fine grains of sand are swept from bajadas and washes, bouncing along for great distances in a windstorm. If a rocky outcrop interferes, the particles stop bouncing and aggregate as deep sand patches on the lee side. Such fresh deposits are not soil because they lack organic matter and microorganisms, and they may not hold water and mineral nutrients very well. Over time a primary succession begins on the nascent dunes. The sands are invaded by spores and seeds that disperse from soils of adjacent areas, but mortality after germination is high. Bacteria and fungi that depend on roots for carbohydrate or litter for cellulose and nitrogen find none, and so the underground food web and nutrient cycling are very slow to establish. Similarly, most seedlings find insufficient water and minerals to grow and reproduce. Annual plants stand the best chance because they can shift developmental gears rapidly when resources are lacking. Stressed, diminutive, but precocious herbs opt to produce flowers and seeds rather than an extensive root system or leafy canopy. New seeds will be produced in a month or two, just as the sands dry out. They fall back into the patch to wait for another year, having successfully established a pioneer generation. Perennial plants delay reproduction in favor of establishing a durable, woody presence but usually die trying. Even if they survive, perennials do not flower for several years and must endure the desert's uncertainties and extremes. Death without reproduction is likely, and so a new invasion must happen before such species have another chance. But as the withered bodies of annual and perennial plants accumulate, they slowly enrich the new sands with small quantities of organic material. Next

Blackbush takes many centuries to establish and develop during succession, especially in nearly pure stands. (William C. Flaxington)

Blackbush flowers reveal membership in the rose family. (James M. Andre)

year's wind will bring more spores and seeds to these "islands of fertility," and next year's rain will wet the mixture to begin another round of slow, progressive change. Annual plants will dominate this sandy ground for years, but eventually the modifications they produce will allow short-lived and then long-lived perennials to establish and flourish.

How long does primary succession take? Studies on alluvial fans at 5,000 feet in the Panamint Range near Death Valley have shown that massive, new layers of rocky debris tumble from granitic mountain slopes every few thousand years. Existing vegetation and soil are completely buried, unable to contribute to the new vegetation. Annuals, especially weedy filaree *(Erodium cicutarium)* and brome grasses *(Bromus)*, invade from the surrounding community within the first few years. Short-lived shrubs, such as grape soda lupine *(Lupinus excubitus)* and buckwheat arrive afterward, often brought in by migratory animals from beyond the immediate area. The lupine, which harbors nitrogen-fixing bacteria, slowly enriches the surface debris, enabling other species to become established. Desert peach *(Lycium andersonii)*, spiny hop-sage *(Grayia spinosa)*, and Nevada ephedra *(Ephedra nevadensis)* form a shrubby canopy that gradually dominates the slope, taking several thousand years to do so. This matrix of colonizers and shrubs may eventually be invaded by a few slow-growing individuals of blackbush *(Coleogyne ramosissima)*. After the passage of 5,000 to 10,000 years, long enough for global climate change to occur, an almost pure canopy of only one or two species forms, in a community known appropriately as blackbush scrub. This succession alters the rocky debris into a soil with carbonate deposits, modest enrichment by organic matter, and higher levels of nitrogen and phosphorus.

Secondary succession begins with a soil that has been denuded by disturbance. Nutrients and a seed bank are already in place, but compaction from vehicles, hoofs, and feet can prevent infiltration by water and inhibit penetration by roots. Compaction is slowly eased by wet-dry cycles, freeze-thaw heaving, animal burrowing, and root death. Secondary succession has been studied on the streets and lots of ghost towns in the Mojave, whose chronology and severity of disturbance are easy to document. Once abandoned, the succession begins with a progressive replacement of annuals by short-lived perennials. Weedy annuals establish in one or two years, while shrubs such as cheesebush *(Hymenoclea salsola)* and rubber rabbitbrush *(Chrysothamnus nauseosus)* form an intermittent canopy within one or two decades. These rapidly growing, often crown-sprouting shrubs provide protected, enriched sites for the germination of long-lived species. However, a century or more is required for creosote bush and California barrel cactus *(Ferocactus cylindraceus)* to produce their original cover and abundance.

Succession can be viewed as an ecosystem's response to disturbance. Some forms of disturbance have always been present in deserts: wind erosion, debris flow on bajadas, flooding in washes and rivers, lightning-set fires on high-mountain slopes. As succession occurs in areas disturbed at different times, the landscape becomes spatially diversified. Mosaics of recovering vegetation support a wider variety of organisms than do monotonous stands of the same dominant species. Even aquatic ecosystems are positively influenced by disturbance, with low levels promoting the maximum number of invertebrates in a particular desert spring. But the type of disturbance, its intensity, and how often it occurs are critical. Not all perturbations are beneficial, especially those that become too frequent or have no ancient history in a particular ecosystem. And context is very important; succession in the modern, weed-infested world can be very different from that which occurred prior to European settlement. But understanding the interaction between disturbance and succession in different desert ecosystems also gives clues to how human-caused damage can be healed.

ECOLOGICAL MODELS OF THE DESERT BIOREGION

When scientists have gathered sufficient evidence about how a small piece of nature works, they test their understanding by building a model. Models are built to integrate and synthesize the evidence and to make predictions about how that piece of nature would be expected to operate when current data are insufficient to tell us all we need to know. Models can be as simple as a hypothesis, or they can be complex mathematical expressions

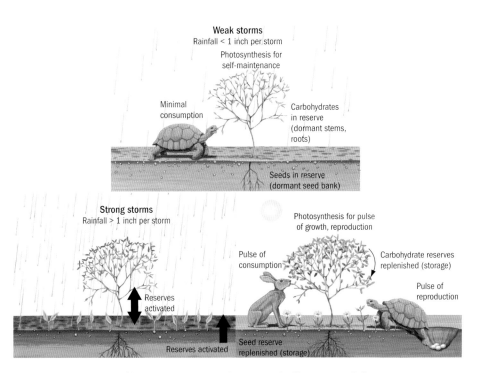

The pulse-reserve model of desert ecosystems. Weak storms only allow perennial plants to maintain themselves with meager photosynthesis, resulting in low availability of food for consumption by herbivores. Strong storms activate the carbohydrate and mineral reserves previously stored in dormant stems, roots, and seeds, triggering a pulse of plant growth and reproduction. The abundant new tissues (especially those of annual plants) support a large pulse of animal consumption and reproduction, as well as a pulse of storage to replenish reserves (especially seeds in the seed bank). The pulses help plant and animal populations renew themselves before the onset of the next drought. (Based on Noy Meir 1973)

used to manage or simulate a natural system. At present, our discoveries and rediscoveries about the California desert bioregion are enough to build ecological models that fall in between—more sophisticated than a hypothesis but still lacking many components that would allow accurate prediction or beneficial manipulation.

The operational model that best fits the arid regions of California has been called pulse-reserve. The name signifies two key concepts. The first is the dependence of desert ecosystem processes on intermittent, sometimes aseasonal pulses of available water. With water, plants conduct photosynthesis and begin the process of energy flow to all other organisms, which in turn enhances nutrient cycling and succession. In the absence of water, these processes slow and even stop, possibly for very long, uncertain periods of time. The second concept explains how life in deserts persists under these constraints. The response of the desert biota to pulses of water is the creation of reserves. Reserves can be the seeds of annual plants, the drought-resistant buds of shrubs, the spores of bacteria and fungi, the cysts of nematodes, the fat deposits of ground squirrels, or the food caches of tarantula hawks *(Pepsis)* or kangaroo rats. Each of these represents an energy or material investment in a long, uncertain future as an essential adjunct to the organism's genetic inheritance. In effect, the investment is used to keep genes intact while enduring the difficult conditions between unpredictable pulses.

In most other terrestrial ecosystems, control of biological activity seldom rests with a single, overriding environmental factor. Consequently, productivity, nutrient cycling, and succession fluctuate seasonally but are never absolute, on-off responses to pulses as they are in deserts. Reserves are created, but they span only relatively short, suboptimal seasons whose end is relatively predictable. Perhaps arctic and alpine ecosystems come closest to deserts, where extremely cold temperatures effectively arrest biological activity for most of the year. But a rain pulse in the desert can initiate a biological response, whereas a heat pulse in the alpine zone has no comparable effect.

The pulse-reserve model is used to explain how desert processes take place through time. Another model, the patch-mosaic model, is used to explain how those same processes occur across space. A patch is a piece of earth where a particular process is operating at a given moment in time. It can be

The patch model of succession in desert ecosystems. The development of perennial vegetation on a given patch of ground is not a predictable progression. It depends on which species arrive and dominate the conditions peculiar to that patch at a given time. An open patch may often be colonized by short-lived shrubs, such as burrobush (*Ambrosia*), that tolerate exposure to full sun. If the soil is deep, with adequate water-holding capacity, then seedlings of longer-lived species requiring nurse plants (for example, palo verde or saguaro [*Carnegia gigantea*]) can subsequently establish in the meager shade. Palo verde might also act as a nurse plant for saguaro. Patches with shallow, dry soils, however, will favor establishment of cholla cacti (*Opuntia*) and drought-deciduous species with shallow root systems. Death produces a transition back to open ground unless reestablishment occurs. (Redrawn from McAuliffe 1988)

small or large but usually repeats itself over a single bajada or an entire watershed. It may be dominated by one species of plant or animal, a distinctive assemblage of species, or distinctive features related to soil, water, or geology. Landscapes, which by definition are large-scale, are composed of dissimilar patches that form a regional mosaic.

One example of a patch may be that cluster of seed-producing lupines presented earlier in this chapter. It began long ago when some ancestral seeds came to rest on a streak of fine-textured sands and silts left behind by a flash flood that flowed down a bajada. The streak held water when it rained, allowing the lupines to germinate, grow large, and leave behind many progeny over the years. The litter from old shoots and the nitrogen from root nodules enriched the developing soil, providing even better lupine habitat. Kangaroo rats distributed some lupine seeds to other silty streaks in the vicinity, across intervening areas too rocky and dry to allow germination or successful establishment. Within each streak, the seeds become redistributed by the wind. Open, flat areas were swept clean while shallow, surface depressions gathered and harbored the bouncing seeds. The depressions produced another level of patchiness when plants were produced, but on a small scale that matters to mites and nematodes, not to widely foraging kangaroo rats.

Upper Small-scale resource patch, a cluster of seed-containing fruits of an annual lupine. (Larry Blakely)

Lower Mesoscale resource patch, a single seed-bearing lupine plant surrounded by open ground. (Richard Zmasek)

The mosaic created by the streaks of fine, water-holding soil is a dynamic and heterogeneous feature of this particular desert ecosystem. Lupine patches were created by deposition during flash floods along the foot of a mountain range, but only when accompanied by seed dispersal and followed by a rainfall event. Through time, lupine patches in the same mosaic disappear as the enriched soil becomes dominated by long-lived creosote bush shrubs. The persistence of lupine-using animals thus depends on how they respond to the patch creation and disappearance dynamic over the whole of the bajada.

Animals not only respond to patches, they often create them. Burrowing and colonial species, especially ants, termites, Desert Tortoise, and kangaroo rats, disturb the soil, add seeds and litter, and promote water infiltration. The extent of their digging, burrowing, and seed collection activities defines the size and characteristics of the patch. Close examination of a seed-harvester ant mound in the Great Basin shows that deep soil materials have been brought to the surface and distributed in a low, round cone more than a yard in diameter. White powders from the caliche layer mix with discarded seed chaffs and fruit walls, enriching the surface soil with calcium, nitrogen, phosphorus, and potassium. Total organic matter is also greater and more rainfall can be absorbed and held. Seeds of annual plants that escaped being carried into the colony entrance can germinate and grow profusely around the base of the mound, taking advantage of this fertile, moist "island." These plants add even more organic matter, providing a productive underground habitat for bacteria and fungi that associate with roots. The flowery shoots redirect pollinator flights in spring and waylay seed foragers in summer. Because ant colonies space themselves out to minimize competition, these patches appear like stepping-stones across the desert, transforming the spatial distribution and activity of the biota.

Landscape-scale resource patch, a population of annual lupines that is separated from other populations by intervening vegetation. (Richard Zmasek)

ORIGINS OF THE DESERT BIOREGION

How and when were the deserts of California created? Given the importance of rainshadow and elevation to the development of arid, hot climates, it is not surprising that the origins of the desert bioregion are related to the uplift of the Cascade-Sierra-Peninsular mountain chain. Of course, this was not a single abrupt event, but an irregular process of mountain building over the last 11 or 12 million years. The stage was set for this orogeny when the earth was still transitioning from a Mesozoic Era of reptiles, conifers, and widespread tropical climates to a Cenozoic Era of mammals, flowering plants, and less predictable temperate and arctic climates. Geologists divide the Cenozoic into the Tertiary (about 65 to two million years ago) and Quaternary (the last two million years) periods. The Tertiary was characterized by progressive climatic changes, from wet to dry and mild to extreme. The Quaternary was (and is) a period of wide oscillations between frigid, wet climates and hot, dry climates over the planet's mid- and high latitudes. With respect to the evolution of desert species, many of their lineages arose during the Tertiary and subsequently diversified. But it turns out that desert ecosystems are somewhat younger than their species, originating in the late Tertiary and developing their modern form and operation during the Quaternary.

Desert Events

Era	Period	Epoch	Time	Climate	Geological	Biotic	Human
Cenozoic	Quaternary	Holocene — now / late / mid / early	< 1 kya / 1-5 kya / 5-8 kya / 8-11 kya	Little ice age, then warming / Neopluvial / Altithermal / Slow warming, drying	↑ Volcanism / Rivers and lakes recede	Europeans fragment landscape / Modern deserts in place / Great Basin desert retreats north / Mojave desert forms, desert fishes isolated / Megafaunal extinction (terrestrial)	Europeans arrive / Diverse diet, agriculture / Seed gathering expands / Diet from hunting
		Pleistocene — late / mid / early	11-12.5 kya / 12.5-800 kya / 0.8-2 mya	Cool, wet to warm, dry / Pluvial cycles / Cool, wet winters	Last glacial retreat / Glacial cycles, lakes ↑	Creosote bush arrives / Juniper-sage woodlands in So. Cal. / Large and small mammals arrive	First people arrive
	Tertiary	Pliocene / Miocene / Oligocene / Eocene / Paleocene	2-5 mya / 5-24 mya / 24-37 mya / 37-58 mya / 58-65 mya	Summer drought begins / Temperate forming / Shift to winter rain begins / Summer and winter rain	Volcanism / Sierran uplift begins	Subtropical iguanas arrive / Sonoran desert forms / Thornscrub plants evolving / Subtropical woodland and grasslands	
Mesozoic	Cretaceous / Jurassic / Triassic		65-245 mya	Tropical and subtropical	Granite batholith forms / Volcanism	Mass extinction (aquatic and terrestrial) / Mass extinction (aquatic and terrestrial)	
Paleozoic	Permian / Carboniferous / Devonian / Silurian / Orodivician / Cambrian / Pre-Cambrian		245-570 mya / >570 mya	Tropical and subtropical	Continental drift / Sedimentary rocks / Warm seas, carbonate	Mass extinction (aquatic and terrestrial) / Mass extinction (aquatic) / Mass extinction (aquatic)	

Geological time and major events in the deserts of North America. Note that time units change from thousands to millions of years ago (kya to mya). Arrows indicate ongoing events.
(Based on Van Devender 2000 and Hill 2006)

THE LATE TERTIARY

Prior to the rise of the Cascade-Sierra-Peninsular chain, western North America was a low, undulating plain dominated by forests of conifers and broad-leaved hardwoods. Twenty-five million years ago, the coast ranges did not exist, and the ancient Pacific Ocean lapped a continental edge along the east side of what is now the Central Valley. The Nevadan Hills ran north to south along this coast, eroded remnants of a once-high range of sedimentary mountains. With an estimated elevation of only 3,500 feet, the hills were too low to block storm fronts, and rainfall was abundant, reliable, and evenly distributed across the continental interior. To the south, the influence of subtropical climates created oak and palm forests, rich pine and juniper woodlands, and thorny shrublands with exposure to seasonal drought and high temperatures, but there were no desert ecosystems at this time. The ancestors of modern desert species were, however, already establishing lineages under these semiarid conditions, including pinyon pine, cacti, ocotillo *(Fouquieria)*, acacia *(Acacia)*, palo verde, grasses, sunflowers, tortoise, boas, skinks, and other small reptiles.

Uplift of the modern, granitic Sierra started slowly as the crystalline batholith ruptured the older sedimentary layers of the Nevadan Hills from beneath. The south of the range rose more than the north, accompanied by the rise of other fault-block and volcanic mountains throughout the region. Elevations of this new landscape steadily increased, accelerating sometime after 11 million years ago, and began to obstruct the flow of Pacific frontal storms as they moved east. Summer drought intensified, and temperatures became more extreme (both hot and cold), leading to the extinction and geographical redistribution of plants and animals. Forests were confined to higher elevations or along river channels, woodlands were transformed into grasslands by the loss of trees, and thorny shrublands were teased apart into chaparral or semiarid steppe according to how different species of perennial plants were able to withstand prolonged, intensifying drought. Development of the Sonoran Desert was well underway by eight million years ago, as some of its most characteristic plants were derived or had evolved from the thorny shrublands, including

DESERT FOSSILS

An Ammonoid fossil from the early Triassic Union Wash Formation, about two inches in diameter. (Waucoba4)

Desert fossils are remnants of ancient, non-desert environments. They document the existence of vanished seas, shorelines, and landscapes that once supported productive and complex webs of life. Those webs were composed of many species known only from impressions in sediments or body parts turned to stone. As those fossils are now unearthed, dated, and identified, we develop an undisputable record of change in these now arid lands. That record is used to understand the evolution of the planet and its remarkable biota.

The first reef-forming animals on earth are found in the Poleta Formation limestones of the Inyo Mountains. Archeocyathids were spongelike invertebrates that secreted calcareous shells in the warm waters of a Precambrian ocean, some 575 to 550 million years ago. They were discovered in the 1890s by Charles Doolittle Walcott (of Burgess Shale fame), along with a rich assemblage of brachiopods, worm tracks, and trilobites. In the same vicinity is Mule Springs limestone, which contains the greatest concentration of fossil algae of any Cambrian rocks in the Great Basin. A single blue-green alga, known as *Girvanella*, may comprise some 40 percent of the rock volume, often appearing as nickel-sized, black blobs embedded in the bluish-gray rock.

At least two dozen, and possibly three dozen, species of extinct Ceratitic ammonoids have been found in early Triassic rocks (240 million years old) of the Union Wash Formation near Lone Pine. The ammonoids (cephalopods, relatives of octopi, nautilus, and cuttlefish) were marine swimmers (rather than bottom-dwellers) that rapidly diversified after the world's worst mass extinction event. The Permian-

➤

desert ironwood *(Olneya tesota)* and saguaro. This subtropical "protodesert" probably spread north and west across eastern California and the newly separated Baja peninsula, bringing the ancient relatives of fan palms *(Palmoxylodon mohavensis)* to Red Rock Canyon and iguanas *(Pumilia* and *Iguana)* to the Los Angeles Basin.

THE QUATERNARY

The warmth of the late Tertiary came to an abrupt ending about two million years ago, marking the transition into the Quaternary Period. Temperatures across the continent

Triassic extinction (251 million years ago) eliminated 95 percent of the planet's species, including 84 percent of all marine genera. It may have been caused by comet or asteroid impact, or by volcanism on a scale we cannot imagine. The oceans were infused with sulfur and purged of oxygen, leading to seafloor burial under thick layers of carbonate. These events have been recorded in the Union Wash limestones, as well as the subsequent diversification of the ammonoids.

Dinosaur fossils from the Mesozoic are almost unknown from California deserts. Rocks of this age (235 to 65 million years ago) are relatively common, but evidence of a spectacular reptilian fauna is absent. Much of what was to become the state was beneath the western ocean at this time, leading to sedimentary formations devoid of terrestrial creatures. To the east, in what is now Arizona, Utah, and Colorado, wind-deposited sandstones contain rich deposits of fossil dinosaurs, including those of sauropods (four-legged herbivores) and theropods (the bipedal carnivores). Some must have also roamed along the ancient continental shore because California's only known dinosaur tracks are found in the Mescal Range east of Baker. The Aztec Sandstone records the footprints of four species of quadruped reptiles and three species of ostrichlike dinosaurs from this era.

In contrast, fossils of extinct mammals, birds, and fish are very abundant in the rocks and sediments of the Cenozoic. Titanothere Canyon in Death Valley was named after the 1933 discovery of a massive, knobbed skull that dated back to about 30 million years ago. This rhinoceroslike herbivore was 16 feet long and stood eight feet tall at the shoulder. The sediments of Pleistocene Lake

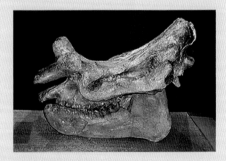

Skull of a Titanothere, a mammalian herbivore that roamed the Death Valley region 30 million years ago. (Waucoba4)

plummeted and rainfall increased, gradually at first, and then catastrophically as snow-packs hundreds or thousands of feet thick began to accumulate at higher elevations and latitudes. This was the beginning of the Pleistocene Epoch, a time of great climatic fluctuation during the Quaternary. At least four intervals of glacier building and advance are known from the Pleistocene of the Sierra, separated by warmer, drier intervals of glacial retreat. The last major retreat began about 23,000 years before present (BP), leading to the arid and hot Holocene Epoch (11,000 years BP until today). The ancestors of desert mammals first appeared during the early Pleistocene, including those of jackrabbits, kangaroo rats, and bighorn sheep. But the deserts of California, particularly the Mojave and

A mastodon tusk emerges near a creosote bush in 1937 from the Pleistocene sediments of Lake Rogers (Death Valley). (Thomas Clements)

Manix contain the remains of 21 species of mammals, 25 species of birds, and a vast array of aquatic organisms (including Mojave Tui Chub [Siphateles mojavensis]). The remains of saber-tooth cats, mammoths, dire wolves, ground sloths, storks, and flamingos comprise one of the richest fossil assemblages in western North America, second only to the tar pits of Rancho La Brea.

But in terms of providing a long, continuous record of life in a changing desert environment, the badlands of Anza-Borrego are unsurpassed in North America. A six-million-year sequence of eroded sediments, spanning the late Miocene, the Pliocene, and the Pleistocene, contain more than 550 types of fossil plants and animals. The earliest assemblages of marine fossils include everything from plankton, urchin, and shrimp to sea turtle, walrus, and dugong (sea cow). Millions of years of filling by the Colorado River eventually produced a Pliocene lake and stream system, surrounded by savannas and riparian woodlands of avocado *(Persea coalingensis)*, laurel *(Umbellularia salicifolia)*, walnut *(Juglans pseudomorpha)*, and buckeye *(Aesculus)*, as well as ancestral species of cottonwood *(Populus)* and willow *(Salix)*. Apparently, such ecosystems in the region were both productive and diverse because they could support three genera of bears, four species of camels, five species of ground sloths, six equines (horses and zebras), and six felids, including jaguar, cheetah, and sabertooth.

Great Basin, began to assume their modern species composition, ecosystem processes, and geography during the final transition between the Pleistocene and Holocene. This transition was marked not only by the development of drought and heat extremes, but also by the extinction of many large-bodied mammals and the arrival of people from across the Bering Sea.

Pleistocene Climates Foster Diversity and Abundance

It is hard to imagine the landscapes of Pleistocene California, so obscured by time and so altered by the crush of ice, the blast of wind, the erosive determination of water and gravity, and the inevitable flow and ebb of life. We get glimpses from the geological remnants of these landscapes, including U-shaped mountain valleys, moraines below the mouths of canyons, and ancient lakeshores carved high on the slopes of now-dry basins. The biological remnants are equally illustrative, providing direct evidence of dramatic change across space and time. Scientists continue to discover the remnants of Pleistocene landscapes, including fossils, pollen deposits, and live populations of plants and animals now stranded far from their closest relatives. When all of the evidence is considered, the climate of eastern California during the late Pleistocene had between 60 and 300 percent more precipitation and was 5 to 14°F cooler on average than today. These differences are enough to account for the rich and unusual assemblage of large-bodied mammals, the lowland forests, woodlands, and grasslands, extensive river and lake systems, productive wetlands, and the prosperity of indigenous human cultures.

The Pleistocene megafauna of the California deserts included abundant large-bodied herbivores. Giant Ground Sloth (*Nothrotheriops shastensis*) is known to have fed on the leaves, fruits, and seeds of Joshua trees (recorded from fossilized dung), while camels probably grazed on extensive stands of C_4 grasses. (From Martin and Klein 1984, used with permission)

The abundant fossil record in western North America tells us that the desert lands of today were not covered by desert ecosystems during periods of glacial advance. The Rancho La Brea fauna of Southern California was composed of an incredible array of large-bodied mammals. Some had arrived from the distant south and could thrive under the humid, almost subtropical conditions that persisted at low elevations. Giant anteaters, ground sloths, and capybara originated in South America, migrating across the Panamanian land bridge when sea level was at least 400 feet lower than today. Camels, llamas, tapirs, horses, and sabre-toothed cats were already here. Other mammals immigrated from the north and came to occupy a lush mosaic of grasslands, oak savanna, and juniper woodlands in Pleistocene California. These included mammoth, mastodon, hyena, wolf, and jaguar. Bones and teeth from the La Brea Tar Pits near Los Angeles, Lake Manix shorelines on the Mojave River, Gypsum and Pintwater caves near Las Vegas, and Colorado River deposits near

Upper   This woodrat midden contains a continuous 28,000-year record of change in the local desert vegetation. (Ken Cole)

Lower left   The Desert Woodrat uses locally collected plant materials to build long-lasting middens. (Lloyd Glenn Ingles)

Lower right   Cutting into the black concretion of plant materials and woodrat urine reveals a layer of pinyon pine needles from a woodland that disappeared thousands of years ago. (T. R. Van Devender)

El Golfo de Santa Clara suggest these animals were imbedded in a complex and extensive food web, supported by high levels of plant productivity.

Fossil plant assemblages extend our knowledge of the Pleistocene as far back as 45,000 years BP. But these fossils are not merely leaf impressions in mudstone; they are actual remains preserved under desert conditions, expertly collected and carefully archived over millennia by the Desert Woodrat (*Neotoma lepida*). These lowland rodents, also known as Packrats, forage for succulent food materials within acre-sized nesting territories, preferring new leaves in the winter and spring from every plant in the vicinity. Cactus stems and yucca leaves are harvested to meet the need for ingestible water later in the year. Invariably, extra leaves, stems, spines, twigs, fruits, and almost anything else of interest is brought back and incorporated into the nest itself. The woody, haphazard pile (midden) is often a yard or more in diameter and nestled among rocks, within a cave, or under some canopy of pungent branches. Each solitary animal lives in the fresh, upper layers, escaping from predators within spiny galleries, and discharging its concentrated urine into older, lower layers. New layers are sequentially added by succeeding generations, while old layers become cemented together by a dark, hardened shellac of crystallized uric acid. Over time the nest grows taller and taller and the order of layers from top to bottom represents a continuous record of climate-driven change in local plant life. The chronology can be firmly established when samples are removed from different layers, identified as to plant species, and radiocarbon dated. Woodrat middens found in some desert caves are more than 20 feet tall, each accounting for several thousand years of change in the local vegetation. Older nests can be linked to younger nests in the vicinity by finding layers with the same corresponding dates and fossil remains. Therefore, we can discover much about the Pleistocene history of the desert bioregion by exploiting the monumental byproducts of unwavering woodrat behavior.

The analysis of plant fossils in middens from across eastern California and southwestern Nevada has revealed that during the last glacial advance, the forests we now see at high and midslope elevations were more than 2,000 to 3,300 feet lower, driven downslope by frigid, ice-accumulating conditions. Middens that now are surrounded by woodlands of pinyon and juniper contained needles, cones, and twigs of bristlecone pine *(Pinus longaeva)*, limber pine *(P. flexilus)*, Jeffrey pine *(P. jeffreyi)*, and white fir *(Abies concolor)*, mixed with a number of species of montane shrubs. Some of these species were also displaced far to the south, reaching peaks of the Transverse Ranges in Southern California (for example, San Jacinto and San Gorgonio) and even a few isolated desert ranges (for example, New York and Providence mountains). Similarly, middens that are now surrounded by the shrub-dominated vegetation of the Mojave contained the fossil remains of pinyon pine, Utah juniper *(Juniperus osteosperma)*, big sagebrush, and other species of the modern Great Basin. Low-elevation middens in the central Mojave document that Utah juniper was 3,000 feet lower during periods of glacial advance. Thus, until about 12,000 years BP, most of eastern and southeastern California was cool and wet, dominated by forests and woodlands, and composed of species now confined to higher elevations and latitudes. Evidently, these areas were productive enough to support the rich and abundant Rancho La Brea food web of large-bodied mammals, many of which were herbivores. Desert species of plants and animals persisted in drier, warmer pockets of rainshadow east of the Transverse and Peninsular ranges into Nevada, and within the lowest reaches of the Colorado River drainage. But only in southernmost Arizona and Mexico did the prehistoric Sonoran Desert resemble its modern, arid self.

With high precipitation and extensive glaciers over the Sierra and the highest peaks of Southern California, the runoff of rivers must have been impressive. After fault slippage blocked the course of the Mojave River about 15,000 years ago, the raging overflow rapidly carved Afton Canyon into solid rock, creating a steep-walled gorge 150 feet deep and five miles long. Its waters had long flowed into the central Mojave, creating an interconnected series of placid blue lakes. During decades or centuries with consistent rainfall and snowpack, cool temperatures, and low evaporation, these pluvial lakes would grow to immense sizes and overflow their basins. Lake Manix, for example, covered about 124 square miles and drained eastward into Lakes Cronise, Soda, and Silver. This Mojave River system connected with the Amargosa River system, which then flowed north into Death Valley to form Lake Manley. Lake Manley also received water from Lake Russell (the modern Mono Lake) that flowed south

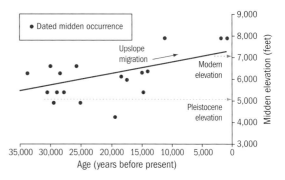

Upslope migration of white fir in the Mojave Desert over time, based upon Packrat midden records from different elevations. White fir needles, twigs, and cones found in low-elevation middens dated back to the late Pleistocene (30,000 to 12,000 years BP) and were absent from more recent layers. Those found in high-elevation middens, however, dated back to different ages in the Holocene, including the most recent layers. (Redrawn from Wigand and Rhode 2002, with conversion of radiocarbon dates to calendar age using the Fairbanks program)

to Lake Owens, southeast to Lake Panamint, and out through Wingate Pass. Other systems flowed through the ancient desert bioregion, including the vast Lake Lahontan, which covered much of western Nevada and included the Truckee, Walker, Carson, Susan, and Humboldt rivers. Although much of this story is told by reading the geological evidence etched into the landscape, other parts have been revealed by the modern distributions of desert pupfishes *(Cyprinodon)*, whose ancestors once roamed these lakes and rivers.

Surrounding these pluvial lakes were extensive freshwater wetlands. We know this from taking sediment cores at the edges of modern basins and extracting microscopic deposits of pollen from different depths. The deposit at each depth is from a mixture of species, most of which release their pollen to the wind rather than to insects. When the mixture is analyzed according to the proportion contributed by each species and radiocarbon dated, it can be used as part of a chronological reconstruction similar to that derived from woodrat middens. At Tule Springs near Las Vegas, buried lake sediments from 30,000 to 16,000 years BP are dominated by cattails *(Typha latifolia* or *T. angustifolia)*, grasses *(Distichlis* and *Phragmites)*, and bulrushes or tules (probably *Scirpus americanus* or *S. acutus* var. *occidentalis*, respectively) that were part of a shallow, freshwater marsh. A woody riparian vegetation thrived nearby, with birch *(Betula)*, ash *(Fraxinus)*, willow, and cottonwood. Mixed into the samples was the abundant pollen of pine, fir, and sagebrush, suggesting a forest or woodland setting similar to that of modern Mono Lake, rather than the scrubby Mojave Desert. As warmer, drier conditions periodically returned, pines and firs retreated upslope, while junipers and grasses spread across low-elevation plains. But with sustained

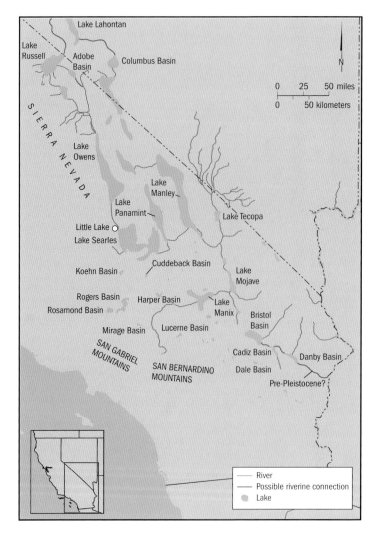

A map of the Pleistocene lake and river systems of eastern California, shown
with highest water levels and possible overflows between basins. (Based on
Norris and Webb 1976)

river runoff, the lakes and their wetlands persisted even as distant glaciers shrank. Sediment samples near the contemporary, saline playas of Panamint Valley show an abundance of cattails and tules dated as late as 10,435 years BP. Today the nearest cattail populations reside only at freshwater springs upslope in adjacent mountains.

Into this cool, wet Pleistocene landscape of large mammals, rich woodlands, extensive lakes, and productive wetlands, the humans first wandered. From across the Bering land bridge that connected Siberia and Alaska, their generations survived passage among continental ice sheets and beneath mountain glaciers, over tundra and through boreal forests. These skilled, meat-seeking hunters followed the abundance of mammalian prey into the Great Plains, rapidly spreading in all directions once the ice obstacles had been passed. The earliest confirmed artifacts, five-inch-long spearheads of flint with grooved (fluted) sides, were discovered in 1932 near Clovis, New Mexico. Some of these elegant projectiles were still imbedded between the ribs of mammoths, horses, and camels, confirming the place of people in the Pleistocene food web. Evidence of a similar cultural tradition in the California desert bioregion has been excavated near Lake Hill above the ancient marshes of Panamint Valley. A three-inch-long knifepoint and a crescent-shaped blade made from heat-treated chalcedony were found just above layers of burned reeds dated to 11,400 years BP. Nearly as old are numerous long-stemmed points, borers, and scrapers of the Lake Mojave tradition known from farther south. These people hunted a wide variety of large game across the region but also collected important plant materials to supplement their diets. They camped around the edges of Lake Panamint in small groups, perhaps 10 to 20 people, moving frequently to follow prey and to avoid extremes of weather. But shortly after their arrival, drastic changes would take place in the lives and traditions of these first Americans, as the lush, productive Pleistocene gave birth to the sparse, droughted Holocene and the final establishment of the modern desert bioregion.

Holocene Trends Shape the Modern Desert Bioregion

The climate gradually warmed between 12,000 and 8,000 years BP, as shown by woodrat middens that record a progressive replacement of pine and fir forests with woodlands of juniper and sagebrush. Subalpine trees (such as limber pine) began retreating from 5,900 feet toward 9,000 feet (limber pine's modern lower limit in the northern Mojave). Similarly, the lower elevational limit of forest trees such as white fir rose from 5,200 feet toward 7,200 feet. There may have been some short intervals of cooler and wetter conditions, but overall the trend toward aridity had begun. At low elevations in the Mojave,

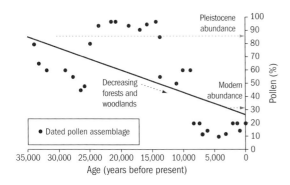

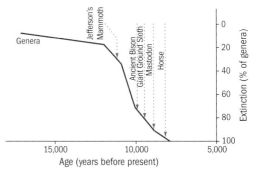

Reductions in the abundance of conifer pollen from cores taken across the Great Basin show the retreat of woodlands and forests during the Holocene. (Redrawn from Wigand and Rhode 2002, with conversion of radiocarbon dates to calendar age using the Fairbanks program)

The time of extinction of Pleistocene mammals, including the last known occurrences of several large-bodied species from the California deserts. (Redrawn from Mead and Meltzer 1984, with conversion of radiocarbon dates to calendar age using the Fairbanks program)

A bedrock mortar used to process desert seeds in Anza-Borrego Desert State Park. (Author)

woodlands of juniper and oak mixed with grasses were invaded by cacti, Joshua tree, and drought-tolerant shrubs that had previously been confined to exposed, south-facing sites with shallow soils. These mixtures of migrating species resulted in temporary, rich assemblages of plants supporting a food web that initially included large-bodied mammals. Fossilized dung from the Giant Ground Sloth found in caves throughout the desert contain the roots, stems, seeds, and flowers of many lowland plants, including Mormon tea, Joshua tree, mesquite, and saltbush.

Yet, despite this gradual shift in climate and vegetation, at least 31 species of large herbivores went extinct during a 4,000-year period. Jefferson's Mammoth *(Mammuthus jeffersonii)* was essentially gone by 11,000 years BP, Ancient Bison *(Bison bison antiquus)* by 10,000 BP, ground sloth (species of *Nothrotheriops, Mylodon*) by 9,400 BP, Mastodon *(Mammut americanum)* by 9,000 BP, and horse *(Equus occidentalis)* by 8,000 BP. Ecologists cannot explain this progression by changes in climate and vegetation alone, in part because there is no indication that overall productivity of these lands had been significantly diminished. Larger fluctuations in climate had already taken place throughout the Pleistocene without a comparable loss of animal species. Besides, the lowland plants commonly eaten by these herbivores were abundant, even expanding their ranges, as glaciers receded for the last time (for example, the plants found in Giant Ground Sloth dung). And modern camels and horses are certainly able to fare well in deserts with greater aridity than that of the early Holocene. Such ecological arguments, combined with archeological discoveries of flutes lodged in the butchered remains of these species, suggest that early human populations must have contributed to the extinctions. Some archeologists have argued that Indians could not have been so efficient and would have switched to other prey or greater use of plant resources before the brink had been reached. Others point to the fact that each species would have its own response to the end of the Pleistocene, and therefore, each would meet its own unique fate. Indeed, some megafaunal species lived on elsewhere (for example, horses, tapirs, camels, and capybara), refusing to participate in a global mass extinction. In all likelihood, a combination of climate change, vegetation response, and human predation brought this last, great period of animal diversity to an end.

There is evidence that Indian diets developed a greater reliance on small mammals

The wetlands of Saratoga Springs, Death Valley, have a long prehistory of human occupation. (Author)

and a much greater variety of plants during the early Holocene. Undisturbed camps on the grounds of Fort Irwin in the central Mojave contain the burned bones of jackrabbits, rabbits *(Sylvilagus)*, woodrats, deer mice *(Peromyscus)*, and kangaroo rats, in addition to those of Pronghorn *(Antilocapra americana)*, deer *(Odocoileus)*, and bighorn sheep. Other sites also include small numbers of reptile and bird bones, as well as insect parts. Kitchens, hearths, and fossilized human dung (coprolites) preserved in caves demonstrate that large amounts of locally collected plant materials were processed, cooked, and eaten. Great Basin caves that once overlooked lakes and marshes contain remnant seeds of tules, sedges (Cyperaceae), and cattails, as well as cones and seeds of pines collected from the surrounding woodlands. In areas that were drier, the ancient diet was derived from playa and bajada plants, including seeds of iodine bush *(Allenrolfea occidentalis)*, many types of grasses, fruits of cacti, and herbs such as buckwheat, phlox *(Phlox)*, and bedstraw *(Galium)*. Technologies for grinding seeds and making baskets had their desert origins around 10,000 years BP, becoming more common in the archeological record as environmental changes required humans to use a more diversified resource base.

Climate change accelerated during the mid-Holocene, with higher temperatures and lower precipitation across all of western North America. Eastern California became even drier and warmer than it is today, causing major shifts in plant and animal distribution that led directly to formation of the modern desert bioregion. The interval between 8,000 to 5,500 years BP has been called the Altithermal, and it had a multitude of impacts on

Joshua trees near Tejon Pass, beyond the desert edge, in 1854. (C. Koppel, Bancroft Library)

the landscape and its inhabitants. Montane conifers were pushed even farther upslope than they are today, as evidenced by a forest of standing, dead trunks of bristlecone pine among stands of younger, live trees in the White Mountains. At lower elevations in the Great Basin, Utah juniper was eliminated from woodlands, leaving behind vast, treeless oceans of big sagebrush. Woodrat middens indicate that junipers receded at least 1,000 feet above where we find them today. Grass pollen that had once been abundant in core records was virtually eliminated and replaced by pollen of drought- and salt-loving chenopods, such as saltbushes. And toward the south, shrubs we now associate with the driest bajadas of the Mojave and Sonoran regions finally arrived in abundance. These included the two most dominant and characteristic warm-desert species of today, creosote bush and burrobush. There is also evidence that Mojave plants climbed west and north over the Transverse Ranges, spilling into the southern San Joaquin Valley. Isolated stands of Joshua tree still persist in the vicinity of Tejon Pass, and populations of creosote bush and saltbush can be found around the western edges of the Tulare Lake basin.

Increasing evaporation and decreasing precipitation during the Altithermal had desiccated entire lake and river systems, confining fish and amphibian populations to permanent trickles and isolated springs. Marshes, composed of drought-susceptible plants with little or no tolerance of salt, became progressively less productive and as geographically restricted as the fish. Lakebeds were transformed into playas, as slurries of mud and evaporite minerals hardened into thick, crystalline polygons. Vast quantities of fine sand exposed along hundreds of miles of shoreline were lofted by strong prevailing winds,

The Joshua trees of Tejon Pass, east of Interstate 5, in 2006. (Author)

scouring basins and dry riverbeds until reaching the mountainous ends of valleys. Dunes and deep sheets began to form wherever the winds were slowed and sand fell from the sky. These new, mobile, and abrasive landforms probably had very little vegetation, preventing stabilization for thousands of years.

Less is known about the responses of animals to the impacts of the Altithermal. Fossils from this period are rare, so inferences are usually made from modern ecological limits. Large, mobile herbivores probably headed north and upslope, where plant productivity was greater and more reliable. Pronghorn and Mule Deer *(Odocoileus hemionus)* would have abandoned lowland areas of the developing Mojave and Sonoran deserts, finding adequate browse in the Great Basin (where both thrive today). Species with a heavy dependency on drinking water and steep landscapes, such as Desert Bighorn, became confined to a few tall mountain ranges with permanent springs or runoff. And as the herbivores went, so did their predators, thereby decreasing the complexity of food webs during the mid-Holocene. In addition, very few woodrat middens were occupied during this interval, suggesting these and other rodents were greatly reduced in numbers at low elevations.

With such reductions in plant productivity and food web complexity, these must have been difficult times for Indian people. Archeological sites from this period are as rare as middens, which could indicate reductions in human population size, geography, and cultural activity. Not only would water have been less available, but so would fish, watering mammals, marsh plants, insect larvae, and waterfowl. There was probably a major shift from lowland to upland resources, with less emphasis on occupying permanent villages. Frequent movements among ecosystems became the way of life, exploiting an even greater variety of food plants. Long-distance hunting trips probably required greater planning and division of labor to minimize risk and ensure that every effort produced a net gain in food calories for the group as a whole. Perhaps it is not surprising that new tool technologies for improving success and economy of the hunt also appeared around this time. Stemmed, rather than fluted, projectile points were innovative and effective weapons for piercing a tough, moving hide. More importantly, they could be reshaped and reused if broken and did minimum damage to wooden shafts on impact. Grinding rocks and pestles were used extensively for processing seeds and were often left at the campsite rather than carried. But like all drought-susceptible organisms, Indians were tethered to fewer, more widely spaced, reliable sources of water during the Altithermal and could venture only as far as their physiological limits would allow.

The extreme drought ended about 5,500 years BP, marking the beginning of the late Holocene. Oscillations, rather than progressive trends, characterize subsequent changes in desert climate, vegetation, and animal life up to the present time. Midden and pollen data from across the West demonstrate that temperatures initially remained warm, but annual precipitation and the frequency of strong frontal storms increased. Many of the Altithermal trends in desert vegetation had been reversed within 1,000 to 1,500 years; montane treelines descended, juniper woodlands expanded, lakes refilled, marshes reestablished, and grasses again became dominant components of the shrubby vegetation. And as if the shift back toward wetter, productive conditions had some sort of internal momentum, the climate slid into a neopluvial period. Temperatures become cool, winter precipitation increased relative to summer precipitation, and remnant glaciers expanded. The nosedive ended after 2,000 years BP with a rapid return (in one or two decades) to warm, dry conditions accompanied by the ebb and flow of vegetation. Cores from the upper layers of lake sediments demonstrate that junipers had subsided, shrubs increased relative to grasses, and fires were more frequent as evidenced by bands of fine charcoal. Drought and fires continued to diminish the woodlands, although a shift back toward summer rainfall oc-

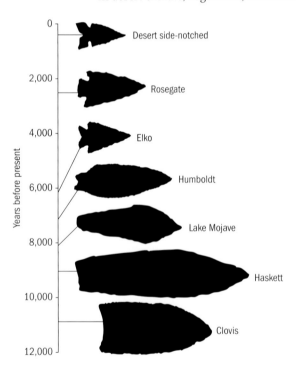

Changes in projectile point technology in the Great Basin reflect changes in the diversity, size, and abundance of available prey. The progression from spearheads toward smaller points mounted on arrow shafts reflects a shift toward swift, small-bodied prey after extinction of the Pleistocene megafauna. (Redrawn from Jennings 1986)

Petroglyphs of Desert Bighorn, Wildrose Canyon, Death Valley National Park. (Author)

curred between 1,600 and 900 years BP, encouraging the northward and downslope expansion of pinyon pine. But another oscillation back toward cold, wet winters and drier summers led to the Little Ice Age about 350 years BP, with corresponding increases in glaciers, junipers, desert lakes, and marshes.

The last thousand or so years of Indian culture in the desert bioregion were supported by these essentially modern ecological conditions. Lakes and marshes were still important, reliable sources of plant and animal foods in all desert areas with internal drainage. But the burgeoning indigenous population in these lowlands probably made the use of upland resources more attractive. Large game animals were largely confined to higher elevations and subject to climate-driven fluctuations in abundance. Bow hunting with arrows having small, notched points traces back to this period, particularly in the central and northern Mojave. Throughout the Coso, Saline, Panamint, and Newberry ranges was a hunting "cult" dedicated to Desert Bighorn. Rock outcrops record hunting scene petroglyphs, while caves have preserved sheep figurines carefully fashioned from split twigs. But Black-tailed Jackrabbits may have been the most reliable source of meat for most desert people, and the skins were widely used to make warm blankets and clothing. The use of plant resources became even more diversified as hunters and their families moved between drainage basins. Groups foraged over vast areas, timing their arrivals to correspond with the ripening of food crops, including pine nuts (mostly pinyon), starchy agave root (for example, *Agave deserti*), beans of mesquite, and grains of Indian ricegrass. Their travels put them in contact with very different cultures, allowing trade to flourish (for example, playa salt was commonly exchanged for shells and acorns from the coast). New technologies for basket making and pottery were also imported from the southwest, becoming very well developed during prehistoric times.

There is evidence that a few desert groups came to practice forms of agriculture, especially during periods with increased summer precipitation (for example, 1,500 to 500 years BP). The Owens Valley Paiute began irrigating wild food plants long ago by digging ditches and diverting water from Rock, Bishop, and Independence creeks. They created or supplemented marshy conditions that supported wild populations of wild hyacinth *(Dichelostemma capitatum)* and yellow nut sedge *(Cyperus esculentus)*. Both species produce starchy, nutritious underground stems that were dug out with sticks when needed. In addition, an array of useful native grasses, edible herbs, and seed-producing plants also benefited from water supplements and the tending of plots. Similar irrigation technologies were also used by the Cahuilla of the lower Colorado River to grow wild food plants, medicinal herbs, and tobacco. Domesticated crops such as maize, beans, squash, and melons were also raised, the seeds obtained by trade with tribes in Arizona and northern Mexico.

European people arrived in California during the Little Ice Age. The first crossing of the Great Basin in 1776 was made possible by a flowing Mojave River and a series of reliable desert springs. Friar Garcés rejoiced at the life-giving waters and easy passage provided by his "Arroyo de los Martires." Along the way Garcés encountered a multitude of Indian people whose long-established trade routes had already linked the Colorado River with coastal California. In effect, Garcés had only to rediscover what the Mojave people had learned over the millennia. Although he pioneered the Old Spanish Trail and began rumors of mythical rivers that would lead others across the Great Basin, Garcés had no idea of the long, varied history of these desert lands and their remarkable biota.

Remarkable Biota

The desert's conspiracy of extremes, so recently developed in its present form, has fostered the evolution of biological diversity. Ancestral species arrived in the late Tertiary and early Quaternary and were exposed to unprecedented oscillations in climate and landscape. Pleistocene glaciers advanced, retreated, and advanced again. The lowland biota was pushed and pulled from one basin to another, forming complex and productive communities typical of cooler northern latitudes. As glaciers finally receded, higher temperatures and lower precipitation progressively spread north from the lower Colorado River basin and west toward the Cascade-Sierra-Peninsular mountain chain. A blanket of new climates was laid across the kaleidoscopic land surface, withering the trees and lush grass, arresting soil development, and beginning the formation of varnish, pavement, and crusts. Rivers slowed and eventually stopped flowing, vast lakes began to desiccate into playas, and dry winds gathered the sandy shores into shifting dunes. Arid habitats with new conditions for life were formed.

The tolerance limits of some species were exceeded by elevated heat and prolonged drought. Physiological stress made them less likely to reproduce, so populations became smaller and fragmented into isolated pockets of favorable habitat. If those pockets resis-

Desert Bighorn seldom venture far from rocky terrain in their search for water and browse.
(Christopher L. Christie)

Unique relicts of the California deserts are also referred to as paleoendemics. Ancient species that have persisted in western North America include (clockwise from upper left): Eureka dunegrass *(Swallenia alexandrae)* (Author), Desert Iguana *(Dipsosaurus dorsalis)* (Larry Blakely), Giant Palm Borer *(Dinapate wrightii)* (Arthur V. Evans and James N. Hogue), and Pale Kangaroo Mouse *(Microdipodops pallidus)* (Lloyd Glenn Ingles).

ted further, drastic changes, then small groups of individuals of such species could persist and carry forward a biased fraction of their genetic inheritance. In this way, one evolutionary lineage became several, each with a unique gene pool exposed to new, subtly different conditions during natural selection. Today we see evidence of this kind of diversification in many desert organisms, from butterflies to snails, poppies to pupfishes, and lizards to bighorn.

To be sure, all of these new, stressful conditions also took their toll on the biota of the predesert regions of California. Cool, moist, productive landscapes grazed by mastodons, horses, sloths, and tapirs rapidly disappeared. The rate of change was so great that whole-sale extinction, rather than persistence in unchanging pockets, became the fate of many species. Newly arrived, burgeoning human populations may have contributed to extinction with intensive hunting or gathering. Drought-susceptible but widespread plants and animals, such as pinyon pine *(Pinus monophylla)* and Pronghorn *(Antilocapra americana)*, contracted northward and upslope into whatever tall mountains may have been locally available. Drought-tolerant plants and animals, such as creosote bush *(Larrea)* and leopard lizards *(Gambelia)*, expanded from lowland strongholds in Arizona and Mexico that were barely affected by the glacial epoch. Over time these contractions and expansions would appear as slow-motion migrations as dispersing seeds or individuals happened to find appropriate habitat in one direction but not another.

Yet, as the desert expanded, one other category of species did none or little of the above. When fragmented into isolated populations and exposed to new conditions, these species didn't evolve. When faced with rapidly developing, often-harsh extremes, they didn't go extinct. And when species around them migrated beyond the horizon, they persisted in little pockets of preferred habitat, as though home was home regardless of how the neighborhood was changing. These species, among the great mysteries of biology, are called relicts. The deserts of California support many relicts—ancient, unyielding, and often the only remnant of an evolutionary lineage or long-gone ecosystem to make it into the modern world. Relicts, by their stubborn and singular nature, are often the most interesting and unusual species in the biota.

BIOLOGICAL DIVERSITY: THE RICHNESS OF SPECIES

Today's biota of the California desert bioregion is the sum of its complicated past. Evolutionary diversification, extinction, migration, and persistence of relicts all contribute to the tally of living things we find in the Great Basin, Mojave, and Sonoran deserts. The most recent, comprehensive tally of biological diversity in the California deserts (table 3) was completed in 1980 by the Desert Plan Staff of the Bureau of Land Management ("The Future of This Arid Bioregion"), but new species are constantly being discovered.

Contrary to popular belief, the deserts are teeming with life. Nearly 2,500 species of native plants and vertebrate animals have been documented on the arid lands of eastern California. This number, called species richness, would increase by a factor of 10 or more if native species of soil bacteria, fungi, protozoans, insects, algae, lichens, and mosses were included in the tally. Insects alone number in the thousands, with 1,425 species known from a single 14,000 acre preserve (Deep Canyon) near the Salton Basin. Estimates of species richness in the desert will require constant updating, due to evolution, extinction, discovery, and rediscovery.

Many desert species are endemic, that is, found only on these lands and nowhere else

TABLE 3 Tally of Native Plant and Animal Species in the
California Desert Bioregion

Vascular Plants	1,836
Fish	43
Amphibians	16
Reptiles	56
Birds	425
Mammals	97

NOTE: The total of 2,473 species does not include bacteria, fungi, algae, mosses, protists, or invertebrates, nor does it account for subspecies or varieties. (Based on BLM 1980, updated in Latting and Rowlands 1995)

in the world. Endemics either evolved here or were marooned as relicts, and are among the most important living elements in the bioregion. In fact, they are *of the bioregion*, organic expressions of this extreme landscape and its unique history. The California deserts have produced more endemic plant species per square mile than the fertile grasslands of the Great Central Valley or the montane forests of the Sierra Nevada. At least 72 species and subspecies are known only from the California desert bioregion. Most (40) are associated with the Mojave, especially carbonate mountain ranges in the Death Valley region. Insects and fishes also have a high degree of endemism, with many unique species and subspecies to be found on particular dunes, in isolated springs, or in other islandlike habitats.

With so many species it is not possible to write an account of each one, especially when emphasizing the evolutionary processes and ecological interactions of the desert bioregion. Instead, this chapter examines the lives of a few characteristic plants and animals, lives that evolved under extreme conditions. As such they are used to illustrate how biological material of any kind, whether it be flower, feather, or flesh, responds to a minimal and uncertain supply of water. The response could be something structural, physiological, or behavioral, that is, how this particular organism operates under these conditions — or it could be something evolutionary, that is, how a lineage changes through time when exposed to the forces of natural selection and isolation. The framework for examining the remarkable biota of the California deserts will be how vastly different species tolerate, avoid, or succumb to drought.

EVOLVING WITH DROUGHT

Drought is more than the absence of rainfall; it is an extreme depletion of soil moisture that can last for long, uncertain periods of time. The extreme depletion of soil moisture means that plant growth stops, and little or no new, succulent material is available for animal consumption. Even if rain comes, there may be no biological benefit unless significant moisture is stored and prevented from evaporating before organisms can find and consume it. Thus, a drought may extend through periods of light rain as though water had never touched the ground. As previously discussed, whole years have gone by without measurable accumulations, but there may be consecutive years with measurable but biologically impotent rainfall. Desert organisms must persist regardless of how little water is available and how uncertain their next opportunity for rehydration will be. Drought is, therefore, a major evolutionary force in deserts that shapes and creates diversity in a wide variety of organisms.

Yet not all desert organisms have the same level of drought tolerance. In fact, some species have no tolerance at all. Drought-susceptible species can exist only in habitats that never run out of ample, persistent water. Their physiological activity is possible only when they constantly use as much water as they need. They have no mechanisms for enduring tissue dehydration and generally cannot enter into a state of dormancy until more water is available. A good example is a desert pupfish *(Cyprinodon)*, which out of water, promptly dies. Desert fan palms *(Washingtonia)*, with their giant water-releasing leaves, must be rooted in permanently wet soil. They are "all or none" and can persist only where the water supply is assured or accessible after a short, easy journey. Such species are either very mobile (for example, birds) or confined to springs, seeps, riversides, or other wet habitats for some or all of their lives.

On the other end of the spectrum are drought tolerators. Drought tolerators have the greatest ability to maintain some low level of physiological activity even when it has been months or years since moisture was available. They can endure with very little water in their tissues and in some cases have evolved ways to internally recycle the water they use. Cacti that have crassulacean acid metabolism (CAM) photosynthesis are able to remain green and harvest light energy while completely shut off from the soil and atmosphere to conserve water. Their growth at this time is negligible, but they maintain a slow metabolic idle, just in case a few drops of rain become available for uptake. Tolerators can withstand tissue dehydration and may never enter into a true state of dormancy or hibernation.

In between the susceptibles and the tolerators are the avoiders. Drought avoiders have dormancy mechanisms that allow complete suspension of physiological activity rather than tolerance mechanisms that adjust their cells to progressively lower levels of hydration. They may use one part of their life cycle, such as an encysted egg or a quiescent adult, to patiently wait for their next opportunity. Terrestrial desert snails in the genus *Micrarionta* retreat into their shells, secrete a seal around the opening, and wait for years before eating or drinking again. Drought-avoiding plants may be reduced to brown, dry sticks that come to life a week or so after significant rains have fallen and dampened the soil. Of course, with protracted drought the dream state of dormancy can effortlessly transition into the silent state of death.

Above Open guard cells on the leaf epidermis allow carbon dioxide to enter as water exits. (Author)

Right Fronds of California fan palms regulate their temperature by transpiring large amounts of water. (Dee E. Warenycia)

DROUGHT-SUSCEPTIBLE SPECIES

Phreatophytic Trees

The leafy canopy of a desert tree can lose 60 to 100 gallons of water to the atmosphere in a single summer day. Imbedded in its green epidermis are millions of stomata, each a pore surrounded by two guard cells. The guard cells swell open or shrink shut, thus adjusting the size of the pore. This is the mechanism for regulating the diffusion of water vapor out of the leaf (transpiration), while permitting gaseous carbon dioxide to diffuse into the leaf. Carbon dioxide uptake by the moist, green cells inside (the mesophyll) is the beginning of photosynthesis, which supplies all organic molecules the plant needs for growth. If the supply of water is limited by drought, the soil's storage capacity, or competition among root systems, then tissue dehydration (water stress) causes wilting, and the guard cells immediately close their pores. Without the exchange of water vapor for carbon dioxide, photosynthesis and growth cease, thus compounding the water stress problem because new roots will not be added to permeate unexplored, moister areas of the soil. Therefore, most desert trees persist only where permanent, reliable sources of groundwater can be exploited to support gas exchange. Species that routinely tap into these sources, whether from surface springs or deep water tables, are called phreatophytes, and they are always long-lived, woody trees or shrubs.

California fan palm (*Washingtonia filifera*) is a relict phreatophyte of an ancient tropical past, with most of its close relatives found farther south in Mexico and Central America. Fossil impressions of its huge fronds are known from rocks well beyond its current range in the Sonoran Desert of California and northern Baja, with ages exceeding 20 million years. At present it is found only where groundwater is forced to the surface by faults or an impermeable rock layer, often at the base of hills or within a canyon or arroyo. Fan palm roots are like those of any typical monocot (such as grasses or lilies): numerous, small in diameter, fibrous, and shallow. They completely permeate the wet soil layers and are so effective at water uptake that other plant species are at a competitive disadvantage.

The water absorbed by fan palm roots is transported upward by numerous vascular bundles in the massive, fibrous trunk. A single growing point (meristem) at the end of the stem grows upward at a maximum rate of two feet per year, producing a dense sphere of pleated fronds up to 96 feet above the ground. Each frond has a surface area of over 20 square feet (upper and lower sides combined) and transpires enough water to keep its mesophyll 10 to 30°F cooler than the air temperature. Similar to the function of sweating in mammals, this profligate use of water maintains the fronds near the optimum temperature for conducting photosynthesis. Even the tearing of the frond into narrow strips by the wind facilitates the dissipation of water and heat while simultaneously promoting carbon dioxide uptake. With high rates of gas exchange and ideal mesophyll temperatures, the rapid growth of leaves, stems, and roots is sustained during the hottest and

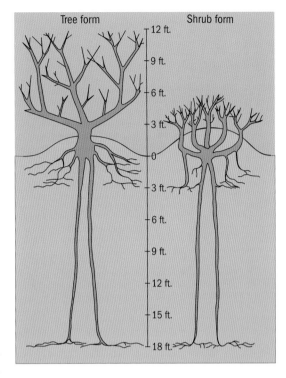

The architecture of honey mesquite varies with site conditions and possibly genes. Where there is constant, plentiful moisture (for example, near springs), phreatophytic trees develop a single trunk and large leafy canopy. Less reliable moisture produces a highly branched shrub form that devotes more resources to reproduction. When planted together in a garden, however, some of the architectural differences are retained, suggesting a genetic, rather than environmental basis. (Redrawn from Sharifi et al. 1982)

driest times of the year. Old, shaded fronds are quickly replaced by new, fully illuminated ones with greater photosynthetic capacity. Dead fronds are not shed, instead they hang down and form a skirt that protects the stem when ground fires sweep through the oasis. Crowded together along the drainage, a vigorous stand of fan palms effectively reduces canopy space and light for other plants, further dominating the supply of water.

Honey mesquite *(Prosopis glandulosa* var. *torreyana)* has very different ways of being a phreatophytic tree. Instead of growing tall like the fan palm, it grows down. The root system is woody and stout like that of most dicot trees (such as oak *[Quercus]*) but has an architecture reflecting two strategies for growth. One strategy is to send a few roots deep into the water table near arroyos or streambeds. Mesquite roots have been found at depths between 160 and 200 feet and are essential for supplying water during prolonged drought. The second strategy is to have many shallow roots (up to 90 percent of the to-tal root mass) in the top three feet of soil, where recent precipitation is stored. This root system is very diffuse and positioned to make maximum use of meager storms that barely wet the ground. Sands are most effective at absorbing light rains, and mesquite trees are often associated with low dunes (such as near Stovepipe Wells in Death Valley) that read-ily surrender stored water. Growth during the spring and early summer is relatively fast as the soft, delicate leaves maximize their carbon dioxide gain. As summer progresses, the stomata close during the hot, dry midday but remain open in early mornings and late afternoons. It is somewhat surprising to see that mesquite drops its leaves in fall when air temperatures moderate and rains return. However, phreatophytes can be independ-ent of seasonal water availability as long as they are tapped into constant and reliable un-derground sources.

Upper The Powdered Dancer is found near or below sea level in the Sonoran Desert. (Ryan Sawby)

Lower Male Mexican Amberwings lead females to oviposition sites at the water surface. (Ryan Sawby)

Dragonflies

Although adult dragonflies soar across large stretches of arid ground, they can complete their life cycle only in the presence of persistent pools of water. This is because the eggs, which are laid in or on algal mats, have no defense against desiccation. In addition, the larval stages are aquatic nymphs that must pump oxygenated water across their rectal gills to breathe. The nymphs are predators that feed ex-clusively on other water-dependent insects, includ-ing many that must in turn feed on algae. Even the final transition in life relies upon water pressure to burst the last nymphal skin prior to emergence of the winged, fully formed adult. In this sense, drag-onflies are as much amphibian as frogs and sala-manders and must have reliable aquatic habitat.

As an adult, the Powdered Dancer (*Argia moesta*) has a pale, silvery or bluish body more than an inch long and a wingspan of almost 2.5 inches. (Inter-estingly, the reflective blue color intensifies at higher air temperatures and becomes gray and even tan at lower temperatures). It is frequently seen flying just above the surface of an alkali-encrusted shoreline or sandy beach. A dancer might perch on the ground or in the low branches of a shrub, waiting for prey insects to fly by. The same agile flight skills that al-low snatching prey in midair also provide avoidance of bird and insect predators. Searching for food and escaping from predators may take a dancer a few miles from water, but it usually returns to search for a mate. Flowing water is preferred for egg deposition, so issuing springs and rivers make the best natural habitat. A male darts from its perch and pounces on a female in midair, sometimes knocking her to the ground. Attaching to her thorax with special appendages on his abdomen, the male becomes physically linked to a female for copulation. The process can take minutes or hours while sperm fertilize many eggs. Still in tandem, the pair completely submerge themselves in water until she deposits all eggs into the algal mat. Adults live their lives during the warmer months of the year (April to October), while the eggs and larvae complete the aquatic phases of the cycle during the cooler, wet months.

Similar to other dragonflies, the Mexican Amberwing *(Perithemis intensa)* is not only drought susceptible, it is also sensitive to high air temperatures. Although active during the day (diurnal), the golden yellow adults do most of their foraging for food and mates in the mornings and late afternoons of spring and summer. But intense middays with soaring temperatures require finding shade or assuming a distinctive body position called the obelisk. The still, perching amberwing will point its abdomen directly toward the sun, thus minimizing exposure of body surfaces to intense, direct rays. At noon it will sit still and erect, casting no shadow, to avoid lethal doses of heat and rapid loss of precious body water.

Desert Pupfish

The existence of fishes in the desert is testimony to the long and varied history of this land; however, the existence of endemic species and subspecies of fishes in the desert is testimony to the creative powers of evolution. Often compared to Darwin's finches on the Galapagos Islands, the evolution of pupfishes *(Cyprinodon)*, poolfishes *(Empetrichythys)*, dace *(Rhinichthys)*, chubs *(Siphateles)*, and suckers *(Catostomus, Xyrauchen)* in eastern California and adjacent Nevada is just as compelling and enlightening.

Permanent springs in the vicinity of Death Valley may each harbor a different species or subspecies of pupfish, depending on how spatially or temporally isolated they are from each other. The extreme case is a cavernous spring known as Devils Hole, sunk into the side of a limestone hill in Ash Meadows. The hole is more than 450 feet deep and was probably formed after an ancient earthquake collapsed the roof of a water-filled cave. Perhaps a million or more years ago the hole had a watery connection to a fish-filled lake or river that receded, stranding an ancestral population of what we now call the Devils Hole Pupfish *(C. diabolis)*. This small (an inch or less long) but very distinct species (no pelvic fins or territorial behavior) is entirely dependent upon a sunlit shelf of rock, roughly 10 square feet in size, that is submerged be-

The Devils Hole Pupfish rarely exceeds an inch in length. (Unknown photographer, U.S. Fish and Wildlife Service)

Devils Hole is a limestone cavern with a roof that collapsed thousands of years ago. Once inundated by a Pleistocene lake, its water now wells up from the Death Valley Aquifer. (Author)

The food web of the Devils Hole ecosystem takes place on this shallow, sunlit shelf of rock submerged below one foot of water. The endlessly deep connection to the aquifer is further back. (Author)

low a foot of fresh, ancient water from the Death Valley Aquifer. The shelf provides a surface for spawning and an algal-based food web but is susceptible to water table fluctuations, invasion by poisonous cyanobacteria, and human disturbance. Nevertheless, the Devils Hole Pupfish has persisted for untold centuries, diverging in its solitude as a relict of the distant past.

The closest relative to the Devils Hole Pupfish lives less than a mile away. The Amargosa Pupfish *(C. nevadensis)* is large bodied (up to 2.5 inches), has pelvic fins, and displays aggressive, territorial behaviors. It occupies springs, pools, and intermittent rivers in the Ash Meadows–Death Valley region. These aquatic habitats were connected when the Amargosa River was a tributary to Lake Manley some 20,000 years ago. As watery connections were severed by climate change, ancestral populations diverged to form an impressive array of variable subspecies. The variations are now confined to certain springs and drainages, such that each isolated system supports one of six different subspecies (Amargosa River Pupfish *[C. n. amargosae]*, Tecopa Pupfish *[C. n. calidae]*, Ash Meadows Pupfish *[C. n. mionectes]*, Saratoga Springs Pupfish *[C. n. nevadensis]*, Warm Springs Pupfish *[C. n. pectoralis]*, Shoshone Pupfish *[C. n. shoshone]*). The Ash Meadows version (Ash

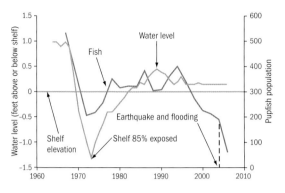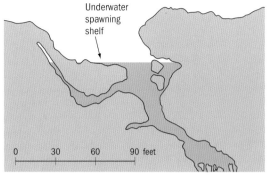

Decline of the Devils Hole Pupfish began with the lowering of the water level in Devils Hole by local pumping for agriculture. By 1973 the feeding and spawning shelf was 85 percent exposed, and the population was reduced to a third of its prepumping size. With the 1976 Supreme Court decision upholding water rights for the refuge, water and fish rebounded. But a mysterious decline, unrelated to water level, began in the late 1990s and was accelerated by earthquake and flash flood disturbance. (Left, redrawn from Wullschleger and Van Liew 2006; right, redrawn from Soltz and Naiman 1978)

Meadows Pupfish) occupies only warm springs near Devils Hole, while the Amargosa River version (Amargosa River Pupfish) is found between Shoshone and Badwater in remnant stretches of that Death Valley tributary. An inverse of the Galapagos, these desert waters are aqueous islands in a terrestrial sea, whose riverine archipelago flowed during the last glacial period.

Unlike true seas, however, these small bodies of water can vary greatly in temperature. Typical groundwater springs, those usually associated with desert wetlands and oases, discharge cool water that can be warmed in the sun or chilled by frigid air. In a single day, temperatures can fluctuate by 27 to 36°F, compared to just 2 or 3°F in a mountain stream or lake. Pupfishes may be the most thermally tolerant of all fishes on the planet, capable of making unique adjustments in the short term with their behavior, and in the long term with physiological acclimation. On the floor of Death Valley, the Cottonball Marsh Pupfish *(C. salinus milleri)* seeks out shallow waters in the early morning because of maximal overnight cooling. But shallows also warm up the most during the afternoon, so the fish returns to deeper waters near the spring source. But progressive heating during the spring and summer requires an acclimation of the cellular machinery itself. Over days and weeks, new genes are expressed that code for enzymes capable of optimal operation at higher and higher temperatures. The enzymes catalyze the basic metabolic reactions the pupfish needs to take up oxygen, digest food, energize muscles, and expel waste. Ultimately, this desert pupfish is capable of withstanding short exposures in the range of 104 to 111°F and can comfortably live and reproduce between 90 and 97°F. This remarkable ability also allows some species to live in thermal springs that discharge very hot water. Steep gradients in water temperature are the result of cooling downstream and along the shallows. Amargosa River Pupfish must confine themselves to stream edges, where the

Upper   Cottonball Marsh is a salt-encrusted, spring-fed remnant of Lake Manley, some 240 feet below sea level. (D. W. Sada)

Lower   The Cottonball Marsh Pupfish tolerates salinities up to 2.5 times that of seawater. (D. W. Sada)

temperature can still be as high as 107°F. If startled by a shoreline threat, however, they may panic into the hot current and instantly die. Life in these extreme waters exists on an invisible edge.

Materials dissolved in the waters pose other problems for pupfishes. Salts that accumulate in basins and the lower drainages of streams are concentrated by high rates of evaporation. Aptly named, Salt Creek flows through a moonscape of salt-encrusted clay lakebeds, a remnant of ancient Lake Manley in the Death Valley basin. Its slow, shallow waters vary in salinity from .5 to 1.6 times that of seawater (roughly 35 parts of salt per thousand parts of water), depending on flow and season. There can be so much salt that in some places the bank is overhung by crystals, rather than leafy canopies. Yet this is the home of the endemic Salt Creek Pupfish *(C. salinus salinus),* which must actively drink the brine, extract water, and excrete salts from its kidneys and gills. The species is capable of biological reverse osmosis but must constantly expend energy to balance its internal chemistry. As salinity increases, this fish takes less than eight hours to increase its blood serum concentrations while maintaining a constant percentage of total body water.

Other species that move between fresh- and salt-water (such as Steelhead *[Oncorhynchus mykiss]*) require 50 to 170 hours to make the same adjustment. All of these physiological adaptations allow this pupfish to tolerate salinities that are two or three times that of seawater, well beyond the limits of most fishes. They also exhibit a remarkable tolerance to low levels of dissolved oxygen and can even survive a long winter under anaerobic conditions while buried in muddy bottom sediments. The underlying biology of these tolerance mechanisms is largely unknown, and consequently, we have much to discover about animal evolution under extreme desert conditions.

But our understanding of these rare and endemic fishes is even more profound when we learn

Upper Salt Creek stops flowing in summer and is reduced to a series of isolated ponds and marshes. (D. W. Sada)

Lower The Salt Creek Pupfish experiences wide fluctuations in water temperature and salinity. (D. W. Sada)

that the waters upon which they depend fell upon the land 8,000 to 12,000 years ago. Those ancient rains and snows began their slow percolation on a cool, wooded, Pleistocene savanna, only to emerge from springs in a hot, scrubby, modern desert. This subterranean system, called the Death Valley Aquifer, is a vast, interconnected labyrinth of carbonate rocks, caves, and corridors. Permeable ground is found beneath 4,400 square miles of

The daily movement of Salt Creek Pupfishes is predictably controlled by water temperature gradients. At dawn the surface waters have cooled overnight, and fishes have moved into lower, warmer depths. The cool water sinks and fish rise in the morning, only to go back into lower and now cooler levels as the afternoon heats the surface. By evening the fishes begin to rise into cooler, upper layers that cool throughout the night. (Redrawn from Soltz and Naiman 1978)

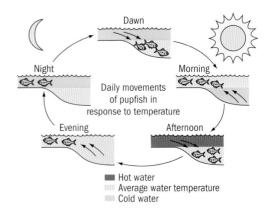

this region, including two mountain ranges over 10,000 feet (Spring Mountains and Sheep Range) and 10 intermountain basins. The sheer volume of water moving through the aquifer is enormous, with major springs in Ash Meadows alone discharging over 10,000 gallons per minute. However, the great age of the water (determined by oxygen isotope ratios) suggests that the aquifer is not being replenished by the meager precipitation of today. This fossil water simply lags behind the progressive march of climate, providing an essential gift from the past to the aquatic creatures of today, including these remarkable species of pupfish.

Birds

Flight liberates birds from drought. Most of the 420 species of native birds in the California deserts are capable of simply leaving when water and food resources become scarce. They can leave by going upslope into adjacent mountains, where snows fall and pines, firs, and other nondesert species provide the necessary resources. They can also leave by passing through, going north, south, east, or west for hundreds or thousands of miles where drought effects are mild. Consequently, the vast majority of birds have not evolved physiological or behavioral mechanisms that allow drought avoidance or confer drought tolerance (with a few, interesting exceptions such as the Greater Roadrunner *[Geococcyx californianus]* and the Verdin *[Auriparus flaviceps]*).

An example of a typical, drought-susceptible bird of arid lands is the Pinyon Jay *(Gymnorhinus cyanocephalus)*. This is a gregarious, crowlike inhabitant of lowland pine and Joshua tree woodlands near and adjacent to the Great Basin. Water sources must be visited nearly every day, in part because this bird loses much water from its body by simply breathing and cooling itself by evaporation. When a flock approaches a pool or stream, most of the jays act as noisy sentries while at any one time only a few take the risk to drink. Pine nuts are the preferred food when available in late summer and fall. During a year with good cone production (which depends, in part, on precipitation), the plentiful seeds are extracted and stored for consumption during the following winter and spring. Breeding occurs early in a spring supplied with stored pine nuts, and nestlings are fed a regurgitated, energy- and water-rich slurry. In a year with poor cone production, the jay must switch to insects and the seeds of other species. Breeding is delayed until August, but reproduction may fail completely if the cone crop fails or falls short.

Desert Bighorn

Bighorn sheep in North America are found from the Yukon to northern Mexico, occupying the steepest terrain and highest elevations west of the Mississippi. Desert Bighorn (*Ovis canadensis nelsoni*) is the only one of three subspecies that thrives in the Great Basin, Mojave, and Sonoran deserts. It is the largest native vertebrate in the bioregion and is most limited by the availability of water.

Winter water, in the form of snow or puddles, can be distributed over large areas of desert mountains and uplands. Bighorn have been observed eating frozen water and well-hydrated plant material and can thus be independent of permanent sources at this time of year. Cool temperatures and ample forage mean the sheep near Death Valley may drink only once in 10 to 14 days. Summer water, however, can be confined to a very few canyons and sheltered locations. Ephemeral waters from precipitation and runoff can be trapped in a bedrock pothole or tank *(tinaja)* that sheep use opportunistically. Permanent waters from discharging springs are more reliable and thus an extremely important feature in a Bighorn's landscape. Other habitat requirements must of course be met, including ample forage, rocky cliffs for escaping from predators (for example, Mountain Lion *[Puma concolor]*), open vegetation structure (vision is this species' most important sense for detecting predators), and refuge from climatic extremes. High air temperatures, low humidity, and intense solar radiation can lead to heat stress, a major source of mortality during the summer. These animals compensate by spending up to seven hours per day bedding down on shady ledges or beneath a lone, cliff-hanging tree. But water—drinking water—must eventually be consumed to regulate the composition and density of body fluids within a narrow range, despite inevitable loss through breath, urine, and feces.

Pound for pound the adult male and female drink about the same amount, but the record gulp was 4.9 gallons at a single visit to a watering hole by a ram (23 percent of his body weight). The longer the interval between visits the more water will be consumed, and an average minimum of four percent of body weight per day must be taken in during the summer. There is no evidence to suggest that water derived from ingested food (including cacti) or from dew collecting on plant surfaces (extremely rare in California deserts) is at all significant in maintaining a positive water balance. For these reasons, wildlife conservationists often install "guzzlers," holding tanks, and other developed sources to provide large amounts of reliable water.

To drink at a watering hole in the desert is not without risk. The spring, seep, tank, or pothole is a magnet for all kinds of animals, including those in search of a meal. Wary Desert Bighorn require that the hole be positioned in a canyon with steep sides, or water-

Wary bighorn approach a spring in the Cuddleback Mountains, only to be surprised by the remote camera. (Unknown photographer, U.S. National Park Service)

hewn from solid rock, thus providing escape terrain. But the area cannot have too many large boulders, overhangs, or dense thickets of riparian vegetation that could harbor a Coyote *(Canis latrans)* or Mountain Lion ready to pounce. The imperative to replenish body fluids is tempered by skittish, alert behaviors and a group sensitivity to alarm postures and snorted warnings. Drinking can be a rapid, fleeting activity, with rates as high as three quarts per minute. Two or three minutes may elapse before the animal rises from a crouch to scan the dangerous surroundings. The ground around permanent sources is usually littered with the bones and carcasses of weak, thirsty, and otherwise debilitated Bighorn that had to return for just one more drink.

When a drought occurs, the sheep must respond to several, compounded problems. A lack of green leaves, stems, and other nutritious (protein-containing) plant parts can force a wide-ranging search in terms of area and elevation. Along the way Desert Bighorn will take advantage of many species (more than 470 have been documented), preferring broad-leaved forbs to grasses, and both of those over small-twigged woody plants. This kind of dietary flexibility is required when food resources among habitats can vary so widely. But during the summer, the search is tethered to reliable water sources, with overall movements generally less than six miles (often less than two). Limited forage and water availability usually take their toll on the lambs, and population sizes can fall precipitously.

If the drought is severe enough to dry up a once reliable water source, the animals reluctantly move on. High mortality is usually associated with these movements because chances of finding another, underutilized spring are low. Springs that remain dry and abandoned for several years are usually not reclaimed when flow returns. Thus, severe drought can both cause direct mortality and lead to the loss of habitat and a contraction in the overall range of Desert Bighorn.

Humans

At best, humans *(Homo sapiens)* can tolerate a 10 percent loss of body fluids before delirium, debilitation, and death. We discharge water in sweat, urine, and breath and must drink frequently in order to replenish. Native people of the Mojave were justifiably proud of their ability to endure four days of thirst, but even they did not stray from rivers and reliable springs along their routes across the desert. Immigrants preferred to drag wagons and weary bodies up into high, steep mountains with snow patches, rather than follow an easy, lowland route that was dry or carved by salty water. The writer Charles Lummis came dangerously close to learning the physiological limit imposed by dehydration:

On my tramp in 1884 I had been three days without water when I reached the clear shallow Mojave River near where Victorville stands today [1925]. My tongue was an inch out of my mouth, hard and dry, and so swollen that my teeth could not close by half an inch. I rushed into that blessed stream, which is about one hundred feet wide and six inches deep, and fell on my face, broken arm and all, and *soaked*. It was more than an hour before I could get a drop down; and the first swallow gave me excruciating pain. The horrors of death by thirst have never been exaggerated in any description that has come under my notice. Hunger is not in comparison—it is in a way its own anesthetic. I have been eight days in the wilderness without food, in bitter cold, with no greater discomfort than faintness; with no pangs and no delirium; and when at last I got a handful of birch buds, they did not distress me in the least. But thirst is torture—madness—illusion—delirium; and the desert seems to mock the hallucinations of the mind. The mirage showed them glittering cities—trains of horsemen—above all, water!   (Lummis 1925)

During the peopling of these lands at the end of the Pleistocene, vast lakes, marshes, and powerful rivers were fed by runoff from well-watered, if not glaciated, uplands. The Indians of this ancient Great Basin were not limited by drought. They lived in relatively permanent villages on the edges of productive marsh systems (*toiwaitu* or "cattail-place"), with plenty of wetland foods (shoots, waterfowl eggs, and fish). Summertime hunting in adjacent mountains provided meat for drying and seeds for storage. But during the Holocene development of the modern deserts, mobility was essential for most desert people. Hunting and gathering would be done at great distances from the villages, now beside desiccated lakebeds or moved near springs. Thus, foragers had to know where reliable sources of water could be found, or how to make them more reliable by excavation (as the Cahuilla did) or the construction of pottery reservoirs to detain a slow trickle (as the Death Valley Shoshone did). Aboriginal agriculture also developed in the Owens Valley and in the Salton Basin, where ample runoff or groundwater were available.

DROUGHT-AVOIDING SPECIES

Annual Herbs

In the plant world, drought has its greatest impact on the soft, moist, herbaceous tissues of the shoot and root. Annual plants, those which germinate, grow, flower, set seed, and die in less than one year, are composed only of herbaceous tissues (hence the plants are called herbs), with none of the woody, durable tissues found in shrubs and trees. The green leaves and branching roots of annuals can perform well only if soil water is readily available after they emerge from seeds during winter and early spring. The roots extract water from between sand and clay particles with a suction force that originates in the cell walls of leaves and is transmitted through the water-conducting tissues (xylem) of the stem. If the soil contains sufficient water, or if root growth keeps finding wet layers, leaves will remain hydrated, with open guard cells and active photosynthesis. The photosynthesis provides materials for more root and shoot growth, and ultimately for flower and seed production. But after sparse winter rains, droughted soils bind small amounts of water very tightly, requiring a suction force so great that herbaceous tissues dehydrate, collapse, and eventually die. The cell walls of the xylem itself can collapse, similar to a flimsy straw when the milk shake is too thick and hard to draw. The consequences of drought are great in annual herbs, including the complete failure of reproduction in species that must make seeds to persist.

Despite the prevalence of drought in this bioregion, the California desert flora has hundreds of annual herbs, including many endemic species. Clearly, the consequences of being so susceptible must be offset by the evolution of mechanisms that prevent those consequences. In the case of annuals, the mechanisms usually involve strict control over

Variety (species richness) of annual plants with short, drought-avoiding life cycles is greatest where precipitation is least predictable. Seven times more annual species are associated with low-elevation saltbush scrub than with alpine scrub on a transect from the Owens Valley into the White Mountains. (Redrawn from Spira 1987)

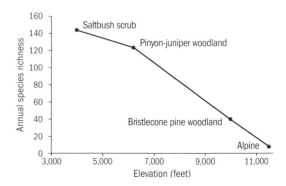

Upper   Desert sunflower, a C_3 winter annual, emerges from the seed bank en masse to flower, set seed, and die by May. (Larry Blakely)

Left   The headlike cluster of flowers in a desert sunflower. (Larry Blakely)

germination in long-lived, deeply dormant seeds. Dormancy during drought can be enforced by chemical or mechanical means. Chemicals inhibiting the plant embryo must sometimes be leached from the surrounding seed coats by successive percolating fronts of soil water during a cool rainy season. Once removed (and once the soil has been sufficiently soaked), germination proceeds and success of the seedling (growth and reproduction) has been assured. Other species, such as Fremont's milkvetch (*Astragalus lentiginosus* var. *fremontii*), have seeds with a thick, hard, waxy exterior coat that mechanically inhibit germination. The seeds resist taking up water that barely wets the surrounding soil after a summer cloudburst or during a winter with few, weak storms. Doing otherwise would mean germinating during hot, dry, or inhospitable times, when death of the seedling would be certain. If, however, an inch or more of precipitation soaks the soil between September and January, the coat will imbibe enough water to expand and rupture, allowing germination to proceed. Chemical and mechanical dormancy work by cutting the embryo off from inadequate but deceptive amounts of water, doing so for years or even decades. Only wind

Left Cinchweed also has headlike clusters of flowers, as a member of the sunflower family. (James M. Andre)

Right Cinchweed, a C_4 summer annual, emerges from the seed bank en masse to flower, set seed, and die by late October. Here is the September 1988 bloom. (James M. Andre)

abrasion, attack by microbes, or passage through the gut of some granivore can weaken the coat of old seeds over long periods of time.

The great majority of annual, drought-avoiding plants in the desert bioregion are winter annuals possessing C_3 photosynthesis. Desert sunflower *(Geraea canescens)* and sand verbena *(Abronia villosa)* are among dozens of such species responsible for spectacular wildflower displays in spring. They germinate in response to strong storms and cool, even cold, air temperatures that occur from November to February. As seedlings they often produce low, circular rosettes of leaves that lie flat and take advantage of the warm soil surface. Under these conditions, the brown-eyed primrose *(Camissonia claviformis)* is capable of photosynthetic rates higher than those of our best, irrigated crops. Growth is rapid, and only one or two months are required for stems to elongate, branch, form flowers, and begin seed production. As long as soil water can be extracted by low levels of suction, the leaves continue to supply food for more roots and shoots, the latter making more and more flowers, seeds, and fruit. Each robust plant, looking more like a small shrub than an herb, produces thousands or tens of thousands of progeny. But as the soil dries and high summer temperatures develop, these plants will senesce, die, and release their copious seeds to the soil.

A small subset of species comprises summer annuals that grow and flower from June to September after germinating when soils still hold winter water (March) or are wetted by strong summer storms (especially in the Sonoran Desert). Summer annuals such as cinchweed *(Pectis papposa)* possess C_4 photosynthesis and can perform well in air temperatures that inhibit C_3 species. As a result, summer annuals take advantage of water that is "off limits" to many winter annuals, even though they are just as drought susceptible and prone to dormancy if the right conditions do not arise. There are a few C_3 summer annuals, such as Clark's bugseed *(Dicoria canescens* subsp. *clarkiae),* but these usually grow in deep sand and must produce an extensive root system to tap water that is stored several feet below the surface. Regardless of their type of photosynthetic system, summer annuals might not flower until July, set seed in August, and die by late September.

Over many years the dormant seeds of annual herbs accumulate in the soil's hidden reserve of life, known as the seed bank. This is because even in a good rainfall year, not all will find themselves under optimal conditions and not all will overcome internal controls that enforce dormancy. In years with barely sufficient rainfall, a small fraction of each species in the seed bank (perhaps the oldest, most worn down seeds) will still germinate, grow to a small size, produce two or three flowers, and perhaps provide a dozen seeds (instead of thousands). Consequently, the seed bank is composed not only of the seeds of many species, but also of many generations of each species, generations that experienced different environmental conditions during growth and different mates during reproduction. And the numbers can be phenomenal: a square yard of Mojave Desert soil may hold 25,000 or more live seeds from 20 different species of annual herbs. It is from such seed banks that spectacular floral displays are borne, such as those seen in Death Valley and Anza-Borrego during wet, cool winters. But more importantly, it is the seed bank that is every annual plant's hedge against the uncertainties of desert drought.

Drought-Deciduous Shrubs

Weak storms that drop small amounts of rain do not end drought. The seeds of annual plants remain dormant if a fourth to a half inch of precipitation reaches the ground, especially when air temperatures are high. The soil may wet to a depth of a few inches, but annuals won't take a chance and germinate. A few woody perennials, however, will "jump" at the opportunity to use this ignored form of transient water before slipping back into a drought-induced dormancy. This is a form of avoidance that quickly and efficiently produces frail, productive tissues, uses the transient water, and jettisons those tissues as the soil returns to dryness. There are many species of such drought-deciduous woody plants in the desert, and one of the best

Ocotillo is a treelike, drought-deciduous perennial of the Sonoran Desert. (Glenn and Martha Vargas)

A rain-triggered flush of ocotillo leaves achieves high rates of photosynthesis before withering. The spines, however, persist. (James M. Andre)

examples is a tall, treelike (arborescent) shrub called ocotillo *(Fouquieria splendens)*.

Ocotillo is a relict species from a relict family (Fouquieriaceae) with subtropical origins during the Miocene (24 to five million years ago). Apparently intolerant of prolonged freezing temperatures, this species is common in the Sonoran Desert and reaches a northern limit at the ecotone to the Mojave. Seed germination requires summer rather than winter rains, with a "trigger" storm that drops at least an inch of water to wet the soil. Seedlings are vulnerable to the quick return of drought, frosts, and voracious herbivores (for example, jackrabbits *[Lepus]*) and rarely survive the slow transition to woody adult. The few that do grow and branch produce long, coachwhip stems covered with stiff spines, the dried remnants of the first leaves. These leaves, which possess C_3 photosynthesis, are active when rains have been ample and, therefore, stems can elongate and flowers can form and open. After leaf fall, the younger, bare stems are capable of conducting photosynthesis themselves because they have guard cells to permit carbon dioxide entry and chlorophyll-containing cells just below the waxy surface. Stem photosynthesis can be sustained for some of the year, but usually as short bursts in early morning and late afternoon. Enough carbohydrate is made to maintain, but not grow, the stems, and even this eventually is halted by drought. Active young roots, most of which reside a few inches below the surface, are shed to prevent water flow from the live plant into the dry soil. This is the dormant state of the ocotillo — leafless, no growth, no reproduction, little or no stem photosynthesis, no water loss to the parched atmosphere, and no water uptake for lack of active roots.

Yet, millions of live cells are inside, waiting for the next pulse of rain. If the pulse is enough to perceptibly wet the soil, the woody old roots immediately produce soft, new, shallow roots. Water uptake begins, sending relief throughout the vascular tissues and stimulating physiological activity in the stems. Some of the awaking cells form growing points (meristems) at the base of each spine. Hundreds of meristems start to divide, each a very short shoot that produces a cluster of new green tissues within three or four days of the rainfall. Soon the brown, dry, spiny stems are covered by expanding, rapidly photosynthesizing leaves. The leaves are paper thin, soft, and very leaky. There is no metabolically expensive wax to inhibit carbon dioxide absorption (thus maximizing photosynthetic gain), but consequently there is no cuticle to prevent water loss. Nor is there any ability of leaf cells to tolerate dehydration—they can remain active only as long as water uptake continues. Such leaves are "cheap" to produce, and therefore, their disposal in the face of drought represents only a small cost to the overall economy of the plant. So, there is a frenzy of physiological activity, but no expectation that these soft root and leaf tissues will be used for more than a few weeks. Once the soil water runs out, the cheap parts are shed and life recedes into the persistent, woody skeleton. Other weak storms in the same year can elicit other such frenzies, but an inch or so of rain is required for new stem growth and production of the bright profusion of tubular, red flowers.

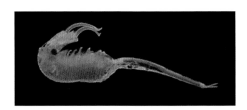

An adult Alkali Fairy Shrimp, almost half an inch long, swims in the ephemeral waters that collect on a playa. (Hugh Clifford)

Alkali Fairy Shrimp

Embedded within the alkaline surface of the driest, dustiest playas of the central Mojave Desert are billions of eggs of Alkali Fairy Shrimp *(Branchinecta mackini)*. The eggs, only 1/125 of an inch across but numbering 50 to 600 per square foot, are dormant and waiting for the next good storm. The storm must produce enough standing water to last at least a week for the eggs to begin hatching. The "trigger " mechanism is unknown but could involve sensing oxygen, salinity, or temperature within the top inch of wetted sediment. It is known, however, that the duration of hatching is tightly controlled by the rate of increase in pond salinity—more and more eggs remain dormant as salts are concentrated by evaporation and lack of rain. But once stimulated to hatch, the shrimp grow rapidly (up to one inch) and become reproductive within one or two weeks, depending on temperature. During that time they establish a miniature food web of ephemeral organisms, including bacteria (feeding on clay particles and bits of organic matter), green and blue-green algae (primary producers), herbivores (the Alkali Fairy Shrimp), aquatic predators (*B. gigas,* the largest known fairy shrimp, three inches long), and migratory birds. Each female shrimp becomes an egg-laying machine, continuously laying up to 2,000 new eggs that settle into the drying but life-filled playa.

The Desert Tortoise will drink from winter puddles and eat succulent native annuals to rehydrate. (Gerald and Buff Corsi)

Desert Tortoise

As they emerge from burrows in early spring, Desert Tortoises *(Gopherus agassizii)* learn if the winter has been wet or dry. A wet winter in the Mojave Desert produces a bumper crop of lush, green annual herbs to eat and leaves behind small puddles of water to drink. The herbs, especially native buckwheats

(*Eriogonum*), lupines (*Lupinus*), marigolds (*Baileya*), and gilia (*Gilia*) replenish the long-hibernating animals with carbohydrates, fats, and proteins. New leaves, almost bursting with succulence, also supply water that toothless jaws squeeze from the tissues. The lumbering animals complete hydration by lapping at local puddles, when available. Uric acid crystals and potassium salts that have accumulated in bladders over the winter are finally flushed out, probably with great relief. From February to April or May, the primary activity of Desert Tortoises is grazing native annuals to obtain the fuel and water needed for mating, egg laying, hiding from predators, and improving their burrows. A full state of hydration allows them to extend their activities into the summer (including two or possibly three clutches of eggs until July) by browsing dead leaves and stems.

After a dry winter, emerging animals learn how little their replenishment will be. Instead of native annuals (which remain dormant in the seedbank), much of the green material is composed of opportunistic, nonnative weeds. The Desert Tortoise will eat these unpalatable species, often low in protein and tough to chew, but the energy required for growth and reproduction may not be obtained. Native shrubs and cacti are the next preferred sources, but even new leaves and stems may not contain much water under drought conditions. These foods also contain large amounts of potassium, which become concentrated in blood plasma when urination does not occur. The water conserved in the bladder (up to 40 percent of body weight) is not used to flush uric acid and salts but kept as a reserve to allow further precipitation of metabolic waste. The tortoise must then tolerate the buildup of minerals because it lacks the nasal salt glands of chuckwallas and roadrunners that would allow excretion. Thus, water conservation becomes critical to sustaining the search for more plant resources. Travel outside of the burrow becomes confined to early morning and early evening. Shade cast by shrubs is used as temporary refuge from high temperatures and predators. The scale-covered shell and horny skin lose no water to the hot, dry wind, but refuge is frequently taken in burrows, where temperatures are 20 to 30°F cooler and the humidity is three or four times higher. If the spring remains dry, plants will "brown up" early and become indigestible to a dehydrated animal. Mating activities are then suspended, but some hard-shelled, waterproof eggs may be fertilized using one- or two-year-old sperm stored in the female cloaca (reproductive and excretory tract) since the last good spring. The eggs won't start hatching for another three or four months, but adults must still avoid the year's worst drought and heat. They are forced to retreat into burrows and enter into a state of summer hibernation (sometimes called aestivation). Heart rate, breathing, digestion, and waste disposal are all reduced in favor of minimizing water loss and maximizing the chances of surviving until the next good rain.

The Desert Tortoise is widely distributed across deserts in North America. A southern race of solitary, bajada-dwelling animals digs shallow burrows in rocky soils of the Sonoran Desert in Arizona and Northern Mexico. A northern race of communal, basin-dwelling animals digs extensive burrows (up to 35 feet long) in loamy soils of the Mojave Desert of California, southern Nevada, and southwestern Utah. Perhaps these races represent two lineages that were affected in different ways by climate change during and after the Pleistocene. The southern race would have been minimally affected by distant glacial environments and thus remained similar to ancestral tortoises in its behaviors. The northern race, however, would have been exposed to the full brunt of changes in climate, hydrology, soils, and biotic communities. Vast areas of once suitable habitat became too cold, wet, and dominated by large, dangerous predators. Populations of tortoises shrank or were extirpated, leaving behind those that could endure Pleistocene conditions by sharing deep burrows at the lowest available elevations. Male aggressiveness would have been selected against, while fast and tenacious digging favored escape from predators and extreme temperatures. In the modern Mojave Desert, these same behaviors allow persistence under hot and dry environments at the northern edge of their range. Although speculative, this scenario explains much about the current distribution of the Desert Tortoise in California, where populations reach the highest densities known for the species — up to 578 per square mile.

Costa's Hummingbird

Many hummingbirds are capable of long-distance migration, but Costa's Hummingbird *(Calypte costae)* resides in the lower-elevation deserts of southern California, southern Nevada, Arizona, and northern Mexico. It is strongly attracted to tubular, red flowers that produce large amounts of nectar — the complex, watery, energy-rich reward produced by glands at the base of petals of beardtongues *(Penstemon)*, ocotillo, chuparosa *(Justicia)*, and boxthorn *(Lycium)*. Nectar and small insects comprise a high-octane diet that supports a supercharged metabolism and extraordinary flight capabilities. During their peak of spring activity, they daily consume 70

Costa's Hummingbird depends on nectar-producing flowers to meet its metabolic energy requirements. (Stephen Dowlan)

percent of their body weight in food and four to eight times their body weight in water. But how do these requirements relate to drought avoidance?

The energy requirements of these hummingbirds are best met during the spring and early summer, when nectar flowers are open and insects are most active and abundant. A food-producing window of five or six weeks is necessary to lay and incubate eggs, hatch and feed nestlings, and finally fledge the young. After the window closes, both adults and youth must take advantage of whatever meager resources are available during the rest of the year. Late-flowering plants and summer cohorts of insects provide less abundant and nutritious foods, but energy demands of the hummingbird body may greatly exceed the total energy supplied. Cold nights and long-distance flights are especially draining, so Costa's may enter a state of torpor. Torpor in a hummingbird is a temporary, nighttime reduction of metabolic activity. Body temperature drops 20 to 30°F (from 105°F), heart

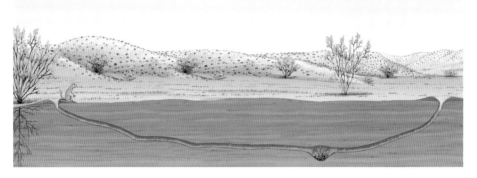

The extensive and deep burrow system of Mojave Ground Squirrels provides a refuge from summer drought, high temperatures, and predators. This one is 18 feet long, three feet deep, and dug into soft sand. (Redrawn from Bartholomew and Hudson 1961)

and breathing rates slow, and the bird appears lifeless as it clings to a branch, bill pointing straight upward. And with the reduction in breathing, a great source of water loss in birds, torpor achieves a significant level of water conservation. This form of summer dormancy is rare in birds, known only from other hummingbirds and the White-throated Swift *(Aeronautes saxatalis)*.

Mojave Ground Squirrel

Even if trees were abundant in the desert, they would not provide the right kind of shelter for squirrels. High air temperatures and dry winds would permeate the canopies, causing unrelenting and lethal exposure. Desert squirrels are, therefore, ground squirrels, capable of digging burrows into sandy or gravelly alluvial soils. The burrows can be 18 to 20 feet long and extend three or more feet below the bajada surface. The sheer mass of soil surrounding the burrow can store vast amounts of solar energy and reradiate it back into the cool night sky. Consequently, burrow temperatures can be 20 to 40°F cooler than aboveground temperatures, with correspondingly higher humidity. In California, several species of ground squirrel take advantage of these moderated, subterranean conditions. All have cylindrical bodies with well-developed claws for digging, all use burrows to shelter themselves from predators as well as the desert's climatic extremes. But unlike other burrowing desert animals, such as the Desert Tortoise and the Pinyon Mouse *(Peromyscus truei)*, the Mojave Ground Squirrel *(Spermophilus mohavensis)* is active throughout the day. Despite high temperatures this squirrel is constantly in motion, foraging for food, searching for mates, and excavating new burrows in a frenzy of activity between sunrise and sunset. It is an especially good example of a drought-avoiding rodent that uses every waking hour to accumulate the succulent, energy-rich resources necessary for persistence. When those resources can no longer be found, a ground squirrel enters a long, uncertain sleep beneath a blanket of insulating, sheltering soil.

In late February the desert shrubs provide the Mojave Ground Squirrel with its most important dietary item—fresh, green foliage. New leaves of burrobush (*Ambrosia dumosa*), saltbush (*Atriplex*), cheesebush (*Hymenoclea salsola*), and spiny hop-sage (*Grayia spinosa*) are laden with protein, starch, and water. After a good, wet winter, this squirrel emerges from hibernation to find new shrub growth forming a lush *palapa* above its burrow entrance. Standing on hind legs it listens and scans for hawks, coyotes, and other predators. The squirrel appears thin, weighing only about 100 to 150 grams, and will begin browsing its palapa immediately if there is no sign of danger. It scurries from shrub to shrub, consuming large amounts of foliage to break the fast and rehydrate its body. Other plants, especially annual forbs, are

Mojave Ground Squirrels forage on new, succulent leaves from shrubs and herbs after emergence from winter hibernation. (Alison M. Sheehey)

also voraciously consumed during a wet, productive spring, but these often grow out in the open, more dangerous spaces between shrubs, where fast-moving predators can strike. Later in the season, both forbs and shrubs produce seeds the squirrel gathers and eats in great quantities. If the opportunity arises, it will also eat insects, fungi, and roadkill carcasses; however, there is no evidence that these foods are stored by the Mojave Ground Squirrel in its burrow for use during leaner times of the year. Instead, the squirrel will feed intensively for as long as the foods are available, and convert what it eats into body fat. It is the accumulation of fat that enables the Mojave Ground Squirrel to hibernate for such long periods of time. With a wet winter and productive spring, more than 100 grams of fat are usually added to an adult male between February and late July, enough to meet the energy requirements of hibernation for more than a year.

But in drought years, the squirrel has fewer options. Sparse winter rains, especially if accompanied by warm, windy conditions, prevent soils from saturating and seeds from germinating. Annual forbs might not appear at all, and stressed shrubs may produce only a few, meager leaves. Such conditions require the animal to take more risks after it emerges from hibernation. As in wet years, the male begins its search for a mate almost immediately, even though the female may take a few more days or weeks to become receptive. Copulation happens underground to avoid being lethally preoccupied while predators roam. But once mating is over, the search for food becomes all consuming, especially for the pregnant female. Greater distances are crossed to gather the available food, with greater expo-

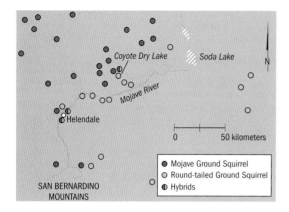

The Mojave River has long separated the Mojave Ground Squirrel from its close relative the Round-tailed Ground Squirrel. Hybrids of the two species are known only from the contact zone along the river. (Based on Hafner 1992)

sure to drought-desperate predators. Home ranges more than double and can exceed an acre for a single female. If, however, there is not enough shrub foliage during the first week or two of pregnancy, the developing embryos are aborted, and reproduction fails. The adult squirrel will continue to search for food in order to add to its fat reserves, but after a particularly dry winter it may return to its burrow and begin hibernating as early as April. This drought-avoiding rodent thus "opts out" of reproduction in favor of surviving until the next rainy season suspended in a deep state of torpor.

Torpor in a Mojave Ground Squirrel is a continuous, long-term state of physiological depression that conserves the energy stored as fat. Body temperatures, normally maintained in the range of 90 to 100°F, slowly drop to within a degree of the burrow temperature. Temperature-regulating responses, such as shivering, are deactivated, and brainwave activity is immeasurably low. The heart rate and overall metabolic rate drop to about one percent of normal, and shallow breaths become spaced about a minute apart. Thus, oxygen consumption is lowered (as is the loss of water), and energy consumption drops 87 percent compared to an active animal. The 3.5 ounces of fat accumulated during a year with average rainfall and food availability can, in theory, provide energy for about 340 days in torpor. Less fat would mean fewer days before recharge becomes necessary, and successive drought years can result in high rates of mortality, especially for smaller, juvenile animals.

The Mojave Ground Squirrel is endemic to California, wedged between the east slope of the Sierra and the northern bank of the Mojave River system. This distribution includes much of the Antelope Valley, China Lake, and Barstow areas, reaching into the southern Inyo region near Little Lake and Searles Lake, but still only covering about 10,000 square miles. The nearest relative is the Round-tailed Ground Squirrel *(S. tereticaudus)*, which is widespread through the southeastern Mojave

Round-tailed Ground Squirrels are found south and east of the Mojave-Amargosa river systems. (Lloyd Glenn Ingles)

and Sonoran deserts into Mexico, an area more than 10 times larger. These two species are very distinctive yet produce live offspring if they come in contact and mate. The potential zone of contact is hundreds of miles long, but such hybrids are rare and confined to a few disturbed areas. There seems to be an ancient and rather effective physical barrier that keeps the two species apart—the Mojave River and its associated lakes and playas. Apparently, waters flowing through this drainage system formed a boundary that isolated the two ground squirrels from each other during the Pleistocene, allowing the Mojave Ground Squirrel to develop a larger head, shorter tail, unique fur coloration, and a novel number of chromosomes. Even though the watery barriers disappeared or became intermittent about 6,000 years ago, the two species have remained geographically separated and biologically distinct.

DROUGHT-TOLERANT SPECIES

Desert Mosses

Living cells depend on water to maintain structure, dissolve and transport materials, and perform all biochemistry. As the water content of cells declines, cells shrink and lose membrane integrity, and their components begin to clump and congeal. The intricate arrangements of organelles (nuclei, mitochondria, and so forth) collapse, and the essential reactions of life come to a halt during desiccation, the ultimate death knell of drought. Only a handful of the earth's 1.75 million species can recover from the loss of all cellular water, among them the mosses.

Mosses are ancient plants, among the first organisms to colonize the dry land surface more than 400 million years ago. They lack roots, xylem and phloem vascular tissues, and stomata for regulating photosynthesis and transpiration. Water is intercepted from rain or absorbed from the soil or rock surface and redistributed across a moss's diminutive, spongelike body. Only a fraction of an inch of rain is needed to wet the tissues and begin cellular repair processes (which are poorly understood at present). Within hours the photosynthetic activity of shoots is restored, allowing growth and even reproduction. These activities are sustained, however, only if the moss body remains hydrated. During a year that Las Vegas received 4.7 inches of of precipitation, bodies of species of *Crossidium* were saturated for 31 days, partially hydrated for 35 days, and desiccated for 299 days. Two months of physiological activity, comparable to some desert annuals, is enough to permit 125 species of these plants to reside in the Mojave Desert.

Desiccation tolerance in desert mosses comes with significant constraints. In the absence of roots for tapping soil water or stomata to retard transpiration, the duration of physiological activity is entirely at the mercy of the environment. Hot, dry air and direct sun accelerate desiccation and truncate rare, unpredictable opportunities for growth. Consequently, mosses are confined to shady, cooler microhabitats within any desert community, such as north-facing slopes or the base of an overhanging boulder. Optimal temperatures for photosynthesis are 60 to 70°F, a rather narrow and surprisingly moderate range for a region of extremes. A summer Sonoran Desert cloudburst, combined with 90 to 110°F

Left This green mat of *Crossidium* shoots grows at the base of its own rocky watershed (about one foot in elevation), becoming active within a few hours of runoff from the surface above. (Lloyd Stark)

Right Spore-producing individuals of *Crossidium*, which each grow from a shoot tip of the green mat after a wet year (scale is in millimeters). Each is formed when the green mat is wet enough to allow a moss sperm to swim and fertilize a moss egg on a shoot tip. (Lloyd Stark)

air temperatures, causes irreversible tissue damage. A series of light rains in the Mojave (each less than .14 inches) causes mosses to partially hydrate, rapidly desiccate, and lose their chlorophyll. The young shoots of a mat or crust become bleached and cease growth. So strictly bracketed in space and time, desert mosses grow slowly, compete poorly, live long, and are easily damaged by natural and human-caused disturbances.

Evergreen Shrubs

Evergreen shrubs are caught between the parched earth and a scorching sky. Droughted soil pulls water out of root systems, while hot, dry air exerts great evaporative power on leaves, stems, and flowers. Live, active tissues must maintain a critical minimum level of hydration despite the inevitable exit of water. Dormancy and thus avoidance might be an easier evolutionary option, except that they preclude an opportunistic response to light storms that bring transient moisture. Evergreen shrubs have evolved features that conserve and gather water while tolerating the effects of dehydration during the most challenging drought. Tolerance is costly in terms of energy and material, but it allows rapid responses to small amounts of available water. That water is ultimately exchanged for carbon dioxide by photosynthesis, thus providing more food for further resistance, as well as growth and reproduction.

Creosote bush *(Larrea tridentata)* may be the most successful evergreen shrub in the deserts of North America. Success is measured in terms of geographic range (central Mex-

ico and northern Baja to California, Nevada, Arizona, Utah, Texas, and New Mexico), total area covered (149 million square miles), elevation range (−235 to 5,072 feet), abundance (densities up to 390 plants per acre), longevity (a single individual may exceed 11,000 years), insect associates (at least 60 species, including 22 species of flower-feeding bees), dominance among associated plants (highest total shoot weight and canopy area per unit of ground area), and value to humans. It is the principal and characteristic plant of the Mojave and Sonoran deserts, able to persist where rainfall dwindles to an average of three inches per year, and tolerant of consecutive years with none at all. What are the structural and physiological features that bring success to this species?

Leaves of creosote bush excel at conserving water. They are displayed at a steep angle relative to the horizon (more than 70°) to minimize the interception of solar radiation during the intense midday hours.

Upper Evergreen and drought tolerant, creosote bush is the dominant shrub of the Mojave and Sonoran deserts. (Charles Webber)

Lower The waxy, persistent leaves and hairy, spherical fruits of creosote bush. (Charles Webber)

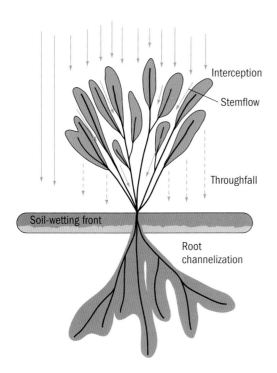

Rain is intercepted and guided to the soil by funnel-shaped shrub canopies with grooved stems. (Redrawn from Whitford 2002)

Interception

Stemflow

Throughfall

Soil-wetting front

Root channelization

Their small size (less than half an inch long) makes them effective dissipaters of heat to the wind (convectors), rather than using transpired water for the same purpose (see "Phreatophytic Trees" for a contrast). With stomata closed on a hot, almost still day, leaf temperatures remain below the lethal limit (about 115°F) even as the surrounding soil surface exceeds 130°F. A thick, resinous cuticle seals the epidermis from the atmosphere, producing a shiny, slightly reflective surface (which also reduces heat from sunlight). Stomata are sunk into deep pits below the epidermal plane, which slows the rate of transpiration by humidifying the sheltered depression. Transpiration is also minimized by confining stomatal opening to the cooler, slightly more humid hours of the morning and late afternoon. These features maximize the ratio of carbon gained from photosynthesis to the water lost through transpiration (the leaf's water use efficiency), an essential trade of one precious resource for another.

But having water-conserving leaves is only part of the adaptive equation for evergreen shrubs; water-gathering structures are of equal importance. Creosote bush has a canopy of steeply angled stems (often more than 50° from the horizon) that intercept rainfall and guide it downward as stemflow. Approximately 30 percent of any significant precipitation becomes narrowly focused toward the base of the shrub. The conical shape of the canopy becomes more pronounced in young plants and in plants from the driest parts of Death Valley. Creosote bush also has a tiered root system that can take advantage of different forms and quantities of soil water. A shallow tier of fine roots permeates the upper eight inches of loose soil, poised to immediately extract water from light summer storms or the first rains of the growing season. These radiate out laterally from the root crown for more than three feet, forming a circular zone that well exceeds the reach of the canopy. Fine roots may also collect condensation from the underside of shallow rocks that cool more than the surrounding soil during a cold night. A second tier of larger, woody roots angles down from the crown, providing anchorage against the wind and surfaces that channel stemflow into deeper soil layers. A third tier of narrow, woody roots extends three to 10 feet deep, reaching water that is necessary for sustaining life during the longest of droughts. Building an extensive, tiered root system requires twice as much material to be allocated below ground compared to the shoot system, and desert shrubs often have root to shoot ratios that exceed a value of two.

Even with such elegant water conservation and gathering features, creosote bush must still tolerate and survive the stress of dehydration. Dehydration robs living cells of internal water pressure (turgor) that powers tissue expansion and growth. Turgor in leaves is also essential for stomatal opening and sustaining basic metabolism—its prolonged absence results in wilting, overheating, and death. Evergreen shrubs maintain leaf turgor by dissolving more solutes (such as sugar) in their mesophyll, thus prompting more water to flow into the cells (by osmosis) from the water-conducting tissues of the xylem. This inflates the mesophyll with additional turgor at a cost of the solutes (that might otherwise be used for more root growth) and the water that was once held in the xylem of the stems. Suction causes water in the stem xylem to be replaced with water from the root xylem, and suction again causes water in the soil to be extracted and funneled to the root xylem. But the parched soil holds its scant water very tightly, bound up in the smallest of capillaries between clay particles. This binding by capillaries generates another suction force, one that works in opposition to the suction forces generated within the shrub. It can be overcome only if exceeded, and only if the xylem tissues do not collapse in the attempt (also see "Annual Herbs"). The xylem tissue of creosote bush resists collapse by adding woody reinforcement to its thick-walled plumbing. Again, this investment is costly in terms of materials, but it pays off in terms of consistent, opportunistic gains in an uncertain and variable environment. These gains allow some amount of flowering and seed production in every year, regardless of rainfall.

The ancestor of our creosote bush is found in the arid regions of southern Argentina. The two are so similar in appearance that for years only one name applied to both species (L. divaricata). We now recognize that the ancestor arrived in the deserts of northern Mexico some 10,000 to 15,000 years ago after an amazing, unknown dispersal event across thousands of miles of intervening tropics. Divergence of our species (L. tridentata) from the ancestral species (L. divaricata) began as deserts spread northward after the Pleistocene. The species apparently evolved in spurts, each spurt representing an increase in the number of chromosome sets of the nucleus, accompanied by a dramatic expansion of distribution. The race in central Mexico has the ancestral two sets (diploid), while the Sonoran race has four sets (tetraploid), and the Mojave race six sets (hexaploid). Chromosomal evolution is common in plants subjected to environmental extremes, producing hardy and distinctive forms of biological diversity within different populations of a single species.

Stem-Succulent Cacti

Cacti possess crassulacean acid metabolism (CAM), which requires succulent tissues for storing the products of nighttime carbon dioxide fixation. A layer of green cells just below the stem's epidermis does all of the photosynthesis, while the thick mass of whitish cells that occupies most of the stem's interior contains watery vacuoles that do the storage. The vacuoles become progressively more acidified with organic acids that accumulate during a long, cool night when the stomata are open and carbon dioxide is being fixed. But this capacity for accumulating carbon-rich acids appears to be at odds with the aridity of the surroundings. How is succulence maintained in these stem tissues when the surrounding soil and atmosphere are so dry?

(text continues on page 185)

DEALING WITH HEAT

Plants and animals of the desert live within an extreme energy environment. If not used for photosynthesis, sunlight falling onto an organism can be transformed into heat. The heat makes all molecules move faster, thus raising internal temperature and potentially causing cell structures and processes to run amok. Unlike pavement, which simply sizzles, living systems must maintain temperatures within a relatively narrow range

Panting and posture promote heat loss in a Desert Horned Lizard. (Gerald and Buff Corsi)

that is readily exceeded on most desert days. What features allow desert organisms to deal with excess energy?

The evaporation of water, as transpiration from leaves, sweat from skin, or breath from lungs, is the most effective dissipater of excess energy. Every gram of liquid that is converted to vapor expends 590 calories that would otherwise cause thermal havoc. The Desert Horned Lizard (*Phyrnosoma platyrhinos*) resorts to panting, mouth agape, and covering itself with bodily wastes when evaporative cooling is required. But this mechanism requires expendable moisture that is rarely available. Consequently, most desert organisms possess other mechanisms that minimize exposure or maximize dissipation.

Behaviors that minimize exposure are common among animals. Unlike any other canine in North America, the Desert Kit Fox (*Vulpes macrotis*) uses burrows all year long and can thus occupy some of the hottest, driest valleys. The Prairie Falcon (*Falco mexicanus*) usually builds its nest on north-facing cliffs to avoid direct sun. But being nocturnal, like most desert rodents, some reptiles, and a wide variety of insects, provides significant advantages in terms of body temperature, water use, and metabolism. The Sidewinder (*Crotalus cerastes*) emerges from winter hibernation as a diurnal hunter, its body tracking the cool temperatures of spring (60 to 70°F). This rattlesnake is a "sit and wait" predator, coiling on or within the sand and ambushing prey that wander into striking range. As the seasons progress, sand temperatures become lethally high (above 130°F), but the snake maintains an average body temperature of only 77°F by retreating into rodent burrows and becoming a nocturnal hunter. During the same time, in the same habitat, the strictly diurnal Coach-

The Sidewinder is a nocturnal predator. (William C. Flaxington)

The Coachwhip is a diurnal predator. (William C. Flaxington)

whip *(Masticophis flagellum)* has a higher average body temperature (86°F), uses 2.6 times more water, and requires 2.1 times more food. To meet these demands the Coachwhip must actively search burrows and plant canopies for its prey, while having to spend a lot of time cooling off in the shade.

Perennial plants don't have the option of behavioral avoidance, yet are bathed in far more irradiance than can possibly be used for photosynthesis. Consequently, the surfaces of leaves and stems heat up rapidly after sunrise, especially when the soil is drying and stomata begin to close. New shoots that develop under hotter, drier conditions become progressively modified to minimize exposure to, and absorption of, solar energy. For example, spring leaves of desert holly *(Atriplex hymenelytra)* in Death Valley tend to be displayed horizontally to ensure the warm temperatures (80 to 100°F) optimal for C_4 photosynthesis during the cool season.

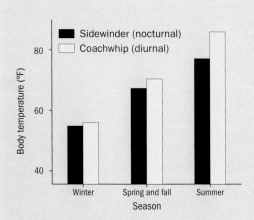

Small differences in the body temperatures of diurnal and nocturnal snakes make a big difference in their food requirements, especially during summer months. (Data from Secor and Nagy 1994)

But leaves that complete development during the hot summer (for example, 100 to 110°F), however, are displayed at angles up to 70° from the horizon, enough to lower temperatures by 5.4°F and transpiration by 15 percent. They also develop a thick coating of white, salt-filled epidermal hairs that increase the reflection of light (albedo) and minimize absorption of solar energy. High albedo reduces leaf temperature another 7.2°F and transpiration another 14 percent. The dense coverings of spines on cacti, the pewter-colored

➤

waxes on tenebrionid beetles, and the ash-white fur of Mojave Ground Squirrels serve the same purpose.

In the absence of evaporative cooling or enhanced albedo, the dissipation of absorbed energy requires an organism to transfer heat to a cooler material in the environment. An Antelope Ground Squirrel *(Ammospermophilus leucurus)* will flatten itself against a shady patch of soil or burrow wall. A small body (compared to nondesert ground squirrels) is particularly effective, given its higher surface-to-volume ratio. The dilation of blood vessels in the legs of birds and ears of jackrabbits can also promote heat transfer to the air, but this can be tricky. Unless the wind blows, a stationary organism becomes surrounded by a layer of still air (the boundary layer) that quickly achieves the same, high tem-

Upper left Leaves of desert holly vary in display angle and reflectance as the dry season progresses. (Author)

Upper right The leaf hairs of white bear poppy *(Arctomecon merriamii)* exceed a quarter of an inch in length. (Author)

Lower left The ashen epidermis of the Desert Ironclad Beetle *(Asbolus verrucosus)* increases its reflectance, thus decreasing its heat load. (Arthur V. Evans and James N. Hogue)

perature and cannot, therefore, remove heat. Larger body parts have a thicker boundary layer and require higher wind velocities before the heated air is moved along and replaced by slightly cooler air. Therefore, smaller body parts, including leaves, are better able to dissipate heat with less wind. This helps explain the predominance of small leaves in desert plants and the prevalence of compound leaves (with small leaflets) at lower latitudes in North America.

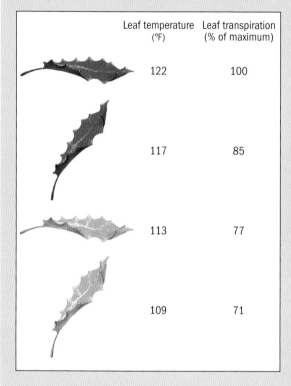

Leaf temperature (°F)	Leaf transpiration (% of maximum)
122	100
117	85
113	77
109	71

The temperature and transpiration rate of desert holly leaves depends on hairiness (more hairs means lighter color and more reflection of solar energy) and angle of display (higher angle means less interception of solar energy). The air temperature (113°F) and humidity were held constant. (Redrawn from Mooney, et al. 1977)

The root system of a silver cholla *(Opuntia echinocarpa)* radiates out a distance of several yards from the main stem, perhaps two to five times its height. The vast majority of the woody, anchoring roots are less than 2.5 inches deep while most of the soft, permeable feeder roots are within less than an inch of the soil surface. It's the feeder roots that can absorb the available water, especially light rains that barely wet the soil. Such roots proliferate within days of a downpour and immediately transfer the shoot's water deficit to the soil as a suction force. The force is generated within the capillaries of cell walls that fill and expand as water is drawn from the soil. The hydrating stem itself, which is ribbed like an accordion, will also expand in volume. A wet soil, especially if its texture is coarse (gravelly or sandy with large pore spaces between particles), readily releases the water to the feeder roots. But when the soil begins to dry, water is not so easily extracted. In fact,

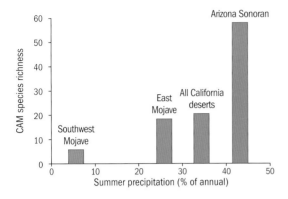

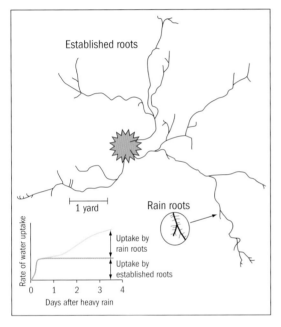

Upper The species richness of succulents with CAM photosynthesis is greatest in deserts with summer rainfall. The ephemeral water is rapidly taken up and stored, thus restoring nocturnal fixation and growth before other species can respond. (Redrawn from Rowlands 1995)

Lower Rapid response of a California barrel cactus to a soil-wetting rain. New rain roots arise from an extensive, dormant root system and increase water uptake within a day. The rain roots mostly die back as the soil dries up. (Redrawn from Nobel 1988)

the drying soil pores can generate a suction force of their own that begins to exceed the force that pulls water into the cactus. Stomata on the stem begin to stay closed at night, as well as during the day, for lack of water and turgor. Under these conditions, the soil could cause stored water to reverse itself and lethally flow out of the plant. Just before this happens, however, the cholla abscises all of its feeder roots and seals the scars with a layer of corky, waterproof cells. This prevents stored water from flowing back into the bone-dry soil, while retaining a permanent system of anchoring roots. The anchoring roots have the ability to produce new feeder roots within days of a new, soil-wetting rain. As little as a fourth of an inch falling on sandy soil can initiate root formation within 24 hours and restore nocturnal stomatal opening and carbon dioxide uptake 24 hours later.

Once the storage tissues of the cholla stem are recharged, the rate of water loss to the atmosphere is kept very low by nocturnal stomatal opening, waxy cuticles, and reflection of solar heat by dense, whitish spines. Nocturnal, rather than diurnal, stomatal opening reduces the water concentration gradient between stems and the atmosphere, thereby lowering transpiration rates by a factor of five or six. When stomata are forced to stay closed during prolonged drought, the thick cuticle is very effective at retaining stored moisture. Even flowers and fruit feel like they have been dipped in wax. But such effective ways of slowing transpiration also allow daytime stem temperatures to soar for lack of evaporative cooling. The shear mass of a water-filled stem can retard the rate of temperature change, but young plants and growing tissues require additional protection. Spines and dense epidermal hairs form a shade-producing lattice above the stem apices, their light color reflecting the intense, midday sun. Young plants of barrel cactus (*Echinocactus polycephalus*) are nearly obscured by a cage of long, tusklike spines that also deter water-seeking herbivores. But cacti

and other stem-succulent species (such as desert agave) can tolerate much higher temperatures than other plant species. With a gradual rise in air temperatures, stomatal opening, nighttime acid accumulation, and enzyme functions become progressively more tolerant of higher tissue temperatures. This ability to acclimate is not well understood, but it allows cacti to grow at 136°F and survive 143°F.

During prolonged drought, cacti are cut off from the soil by root abscission and cut off from the atmosphere by closed stomata and a waxy epidermis. Carbon uptake stops, so no new materials are available to sustain growth. Live tissues keep respiring, using up stored starch to maintain basic structures and functions. The photosynthetic machinery remains fully illuminated, and chlorophyll molecules cannot stop intercepting photons during the day. In the absence of new carbon from the atmosphere,

Upper left   A young barrel cactus is obscured by its own cage of overarching spines. (Author)

Upper right   Each rosette of desert agave *(Agave deserti)* can flower only once in its life, but branching keeps the individual plant alive. It has CAM and is a member of the lily family. (Robert Potts)

Lower right   The silver of silver cholla results from reflectance of solar energy by dense spines. (Author)

these pigment molecules would rapidly degrade (photo-oxidize) if the products of light harvest could not be used to complete carbohydrate synthesis. It appears that carbon dioxide released by respiration and trapped inside stem tissues is fixed again by photosynthesis. Such carbon recycling thus prevents photo-oxidation of chlorophyll by allowing the light and carbon harvesting machinery to idle until the next rain.

So, if CAM and its associated traits are so remarkable, why don't all desert plants possess them? The succulence required for acid storage may make some cacti species susceptible to freezing damage. Low temperatures cause water in succulent tissues to form ice crystals, which in turn causes cellular dehydration and membrane destruction. The northern geographic limit of saguaro *(Carnegia gigantea)*, which barely enters southeastern California, is where freezing temperatures are sustained for 24 or more hours. Other cacti are not as sensitive and can survive Great Basin winters. But even with optimal temperatures and water availability, CAM plants are very slow growing. A California barrel cactus that is 14 inches tall grows only half to three quarters of an inch in a wet year and not at all in a dry year. Besides the constraints imposed by lack of water, the CAM mechanism is internally constrained by the acid storage capacity of the tissues. And those light-starved storage tissues use much of the carbohydrate for respiration without contributing to photosynthesis themselves. Slow growth makes stem succulents weak competitors with more drought-tolerant perennials, such as creosote bush, that can extract water from finer, drier soils. Consequently, cacti and other succulents are usually confined to coarse bajada soils or rocky mountain slopes that tend to hydrate and drain rapidly and have low cover by shrubs. They are seldom found in basin bottoms with clay soils (also where cold air drainage promotes freezing) and never on dunes where rates of sand deposition can exceed rates of stem growth. And in the lowest, hottest valleys where warm, dry nights are the rule, cacti lose their nocturnal gas exchange advantage and are virtually absent. Thus, succulent species have traded competitive ability for tolerance of extreme conditions, keeping them confined to the sparsest of desert habitats.

Nematodes

No form of drought tolerance in animals is more remarkable than the ability of nematodes to withstand desiccation. (There are probably hundreds of nematode species in the desert bioregion, but they are so poorly known that we speak of them collectively). Nematodes inhabit the microscopic spaces between soil particles and are active when those spaces are filled with water. At this time they are busy eating, swarming around young plant roots, and laying large numbers of tiny eggs. But as the soil dries and the spaces become filled with air and dying roots, the nematodes lose water from all cells in their bodies. Like the mosses, nematodes lose so much water that cells actually collapse and organelles become flaccid. Metabolism comes to a complete halt (as far as we can determine), and the bodies assume a coiled, dehydrated form. But when these coiled forms are placed back in water, their cells rehydrate and resume all aspects of their lives within an hour, including movement, feeding, and reproduction. This is not the same as dormancy within a hard-walled cyst or impenetrable seed coat; it is nothing short of the re-animation of biological dust.

Most nematodes are predatory, consuming bacteria, fungi, protists, and other tiny organisms. Others are parasites of plants, collecting the carbohydrate-rich leakage from young epidermal and vascular tissues of roots. Nematodes, in turn are often prey for predaceous mites and other soil-dwelling insects. They are extremely abundant, even under desert conditions: one square yard of Mojave Desert soil to a depth of one foot was estimated to contain more than one million nematodes. Although a million nematodes weigh less than .1 gram, they join the microscopic arthropods (mites, springtails, and so forth) to form a drought-tolerant, abundant, and essential component of the food chain in desert soils.

Greater Roadrunner

If drought tolerance evolved in any bird, it would probably be in a diurnal, flightless, territorial inhabitant of arid lands. The Greater Roadrunner *(Geococcyx californianus)* is such a candidate, but complete studies of its water economy are lacking. We do know this bird is commonly found in open desert and pinyon woodlands, often sprinting along paths

The Greater Roadrunner secretes salt from glands on its bill, one way of regulating water balance.
(Lloyd Glenn Ingles)

between shrubs in search of prey. The diet is varied according to seasonal availability, usually consisting of lizards, snakes, insects, mice, and young rabbits. Succulent plant materials, such as cactus fruits and sumac berries, are also important, but rarely are dry grains or seeds. These materials, especially those with blood and other bodily fluids, are a primary source of moisture for the Greater Roadrunner. But these fluids also contain excessive amounts of sodium, potassium, and chloride ions that could upset the predator's salt balance if not excreted. Excretion in urine requires the loss of large amounts of water. Instead, the bird has a pair of nasal glands that secrete tiny droplets of extremely concentrated salt. Crystals collect near the junction of bill and face, just below the eyes, essentially filtered from the juices of its prey. This leaves more water for evaporative cooling by breathing. Other flightless birds from arid lands around the globe also possess nasal salt glands, such as Ostrich *(Struthio camelus)*, Sand Partridge *(Ammoperoix heyi)*, and the Australian Dotterel *(Peltohyas australis)*.

Recent studies of three small-bodied desert birds suggest that their exclusive diet of insects allows them to live independent of liquid water. Unlike most other species, the Black-tailed Gnatcatcher *(Polioptila melanura)*, Lucy's Warbler *(Vermivora luciae)*, and Verdin *(Auriparus flaviceps)* are able to balance moisture loss with moisture gained from breakdown of food molecules. The exclusive use of this metabolic water was first known from a few small mammals (see below) as the ultimate drought-tolerance mechanism.

Desert Kangaroo Rat

Few mammals on the planet do not require drinking water at regular intervals. Even Camels *(Camelus dromedarius)*, which can tolerate a 30 percent loss of body fluids (compared to 10 percent in humans), must replenish themselves by drinking or at least by eat-

The burrow of a Desert Kangaroo Rat provides a cool, humid refuge from drought. Seeds provide its only source of water. (Glenn and Martha Vargas)

ing succulent, green plant material after a few weeks. Kangaroo rats *(Dipodomys)*, of which there are more than 30 species and subspecies in California, have the ability to live their entire lives without drinking or eating water. These burrowing, nonhibernating rodents are able to break down carbohydrates and fats, extracting metabolic water from the carbon skeletons of its food, even if bone dry. A gram of carbohydrate, such as the starch stored throughout plant herbage, yields more than .5 gram of water from the process of respiration. A gram of fat yields a full gram of water, but plants consign much of what they manufacture to seeds. Seeds are understandably prized when available in spring and summer. They are gathered, hulled, and stuffed into fur-lined cheek pouches at a maximum rate of nine per second! Filled pouches can contain several hundred seeds, which are stored in underground chambers as reserves of both food and water.

But relying exclusively on food metabolism for producing water also requires adaptations that conserve it under arid conditions. Very little water is lost during excretion because the Desert Kangaroo Rat *(Dipodomys deserti)* is able to concentrate nitrogenous wastes as urea in very dense urine. Their kidney tissues are highly specialized compared to rodent species from moist habitats, with elongated loops of Henle, a thick medulla, and an extended renal papilla that permit more water to be reabsorbed before the urine is passed to the bladder. "K-rats" also lack particular protein-lined channels (aquaporin channels) in certain kidney cell membranes that would otherwise allow water to flow back into the collected urine. Consequently, k-rat kidneys use a quarter of the water that a human kidney would use to excrete the same amount of urea, making their urine more than 14 times more concentrated with solutes than their blood plasma. These kidney features also allow k-rats to drink standing water with salt concentrations as high as seawater. The large intestines of k-rats may also be specialized because the water content of their fecal material is a third of that produced by laboratory rats.

Perhaps the most important adaptations for water conservation are behavioral, rather than anatomical or physiological. This is because k-rats must compensate for being small and having a relatively high rate of metabolism and internal heat production per unit of body size. In general, small-bodied mammals must dissipate more internal heat than large-bodied mammals to keep a steady body temperature. Ultimately, this results in small mammals losing much more water per unit of body weight by evaporative cooling (through breath or sweating) than large mammals. The loss is accentuated under hot desert conditions and by relatively small differences in body size. For example, a Cactus Mouse *(Peromyscus eremicus)* weighing 25 grams would lose water at a rate of 20 percent of its body

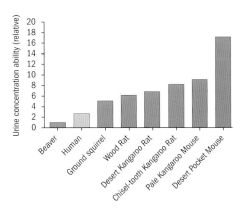

Comparison of urine concentrating–water conserving abilities of mammal kidneys. The ability to concentrate urine has been correlated with the thickness of the renal medullary, where reabsorption of water takes place. Comparing desert to nondesert rodents (for example, Desert Kangaroo Rat to Beaver) reveals an eight- to 12-fold increase in the thickness of the medullary, corrected for differences in body size. (Based on Al-kahtani et al. 2004)

weight per hour if active under hot, sunny conditions. A Desert Kangaroo Rat weighing 100 grams would lose about 13 percent per hour. In contrast, a large Burro *(Equus asinus)* or Desert Bighorn weighing 440 pounds would lose only one percent per hour. Because a 10 to 15 percent loss is lethal, the mouse would die in about a half hour, the rat in an hour, and the Burro or Bighorn in a long day of constant dehydration. Therefore, it would be impossible for either rodent species to be day-active under desert conditions—both must confine the majority of their activities to the night, when the air is cooler and more humid. Foraging, mate searching, territory defense, and digging may thus be nocturnal behaviors mandated by body size. Burrows are underground refuges from the high temperatures and low humidity that would lethally undermine all other water-gaining and water-conserving adaptations.

Desert k-rats have an affinity for sandy, loose soils near valley bottoms and dunes. Sandy soils allow construction of deep, complex burrows, with long runways (30 to 100 or more feet long), multiple entrances, storerooms, and a spherical nest chamber. A main entrance is often dug beneath the canopy of a creosote bush, providing some cover from predators and a reliable seed source for food and metabolic water. But nighttime forays can take these bold, rapidly bouncing animals hundreds of yards away from their homes in search of seeds during spring and summer, or fresh, green leaves during a wet winter. Ingestion of fresh leaves appears to be requisite for successful reproduction, but cached seeds insure survival if the rains don't come.

The Desert Kangaroo Rat is one species with four subspecies found in the desert bioregion from northeastern California to northern Mexico (ours is *D. d. deserti*). It is among the largest k-rats in North America, an adult male having a body five inches long, a tail eight inches long, and a total weight up to 148 grams. The Giant Kangaroo Rat *(D. ingens)* weighs up to 195 grams and is endemic to relict desert vegetation in the southwestern San Joaquin Valley.

Greater Than the Sum of the Parts

Desert species are interwoven like the twine of a living basket. Plants with different life histories and physiologies are the primary strands that form vegetation, which covers the land surface. The vegetation is a resource providing varied foods and is a multilayered weave that supports the activities of hundreds of other entwined species. Bacteria swarm around root systems that leak carbohydrates, scale insects attach to bark and suck sap, horned lizards seek refuge beneath shady canopies, birds nest in woody stem crotches, and "robber" bees rob flowers of nectar and pollen. The spaces between thorny shrubs determine how fast predators can chase their prey, while the height of uppermost branches can limit how far baby spiders disperse when wafting away on balloons of silk. All such interactions in a given place, at the same time, under a certain set of conditions, comprise the splendid basketry of a biological community.

Communities of plants and animals are usually defined first by their vegetation, then by the animal species most dependent on that particular vegetation. In some cases we see very high fidelity, meaning that if you find species X then there is a high probability of finding species Y and Z, and perhaps even A, B, and C. For example, the Creosote Bush Grasshopper *(Bootettix argentatus)* never sets a tarsus on other shrubs or even the ground. But in many cases the relationships are rather general, so that the species composition of communities can be much less predictable. Highly mobile or generalist species, such as deer or jackrabbits *(Lepus)*, don't have strict requirements for particular plants

Community-level interactions: canopy cover of creosote bush nurses a barrel cactus, shades a jackrabbit, and captures the seeds of dispersing annuals. (Glenn and Martha Vargas)

TABLE 4 Tally of Vegetation Communities in the California Desert
Bioregion (California Department of Fish and Game 2003)

Forest	8
Woodland	43
Riparian (includes scrub, woodland, and forest types of riparian)	52
Scrub	239
Grassland	23
Wetland	13

NOTE: The total of 378 types is about one fifth of the total communities found in California as a whole. The tally does not include underwater communities, nor does it take into account the contributions of animal species to creating biological diversity at the community level.

or community types. Ecologists keep this range of interdependencies in mind, allowing the concept of communities to be applied in useful yet fluid ways.

Humans have been one species among many in the communities of the desert. At first their interactions may have been characterized as being that of a "supreme predator," overwhelming certain animals with superior hunting skills. Over time and with the continued development of extreme conditions, the human species may have been forced to moderate its behaviors, restricted by the lack of large game mammals and subject to the uncertainties of drought. Knowing plant species may have become as important as hunting, so that crops of pinyon nuts, grass grains, tule roots, and onion bulbs could be reliably predicted and gathered. The arrival of other races soon altered the nature of interaction between humans and the desert, a topic to be covered in the next chapter. Regardless, it is important to include humans in any discussion of biological communities, especially when their influence has been established for thousands of years.

How many communities are there in the California desert bioregion? Given the fluid nature of species composition and the long-standing effects of humans, this question has yet to be answered with scientific certainty. In an attempt to delineate and tally communities in California in the same way as species, a first approximation suggested 378 native desert communities in the bioregion and another eight that have originated from recent human activity (table 4).

The categories used to tally communities reflect the growth forms and ecological preferences of the most common or characteristic plant species in each vegetation type. "Scrub" is a term applied to vegetation dominated by shrubs. As such, it is usually woody and open with one or two canopy layers less than six feet tall. Scrub communities tend to be found on lower-elevation bajadas, dunes, and mountainsides. Grasslands, which are rare in California deserts, are dominated by species of perennial bunchgrasses that have clusters of stem-producing buds at the base. The bunchgrasses form a single canopy layer

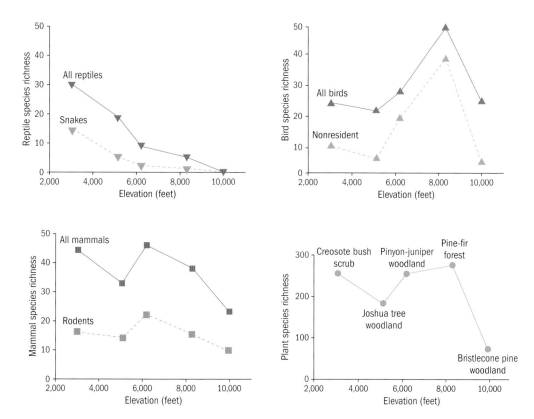

The patterns of species richness along an elevation gradient. Mammals are relatively diverse at all elevations, but birds are more varied at higher elevations (with conifer forests) and reptiles at lower elevations (with warmer temperatures). (Based on Bradley and Deacon 1967)

less than three feet tall, often interrupted by a smattering of shrubs. Although grasses can occur in many desert community types, they come to dominate (as steppe vegetation) only in the wetter, cooler Great Basin or at midelevation sites with deeper soils. Wetland vegetation is confined to permanent sources of fresh or saline water that support the growth of drought-susceptible marsh plants. The marsh plants are often grasses or grasslike plants that emerge from underground stems (rhizomes), such as cattail *(Typha)* or tule *(Scirpus acutus)* and form a single, dense herbaceous canopy layer. Riparian communities are confined to the banks of flowing watercourses. The watercourses may be ephemeral, such as arroyos, usually holding moisture below the surface, or they can be year-round rivers or spring-fed streams. Unlike marshes, riparian communities have woody vegetation composed of deep-rooted trees and/or shrubs and consisting of two or three canopy layers that may exceed six feet in height. Woodlands are dominated by widely spaced trees whose canopies do not overlap (as they do in a forest). Between the trees are numerous shrubs forming a dense, lower understory, and there is usually another, shorter canopy layer of herbs and grasses. Forests have overlapping tree canopies that form an overstory layer dominating the entire community. Shrubs and herbs may form additional canopy layers, but trees determine most of the characteristics of these higher-elevation community types that require cold, wet winters.

It is the structural complexity and food production by vegetation that provide resources for animal populations. The number and arrangement of canopy layers form the nooks, crannies, and perches essential for regulating body temperature, nesting, roosting, and escaping from predators. The vegetation also produces the primary energy sources for all food webs in the form of roots, stems, leaves, sap, pollen, nectar, seeds, and fruits. Although we know quite a lot about the community requirements and affinities of individual animal species, we have yet to comprehend the full array of interactions and dependencies that exists in the simplest assemblages of plants and animals. However, our rudimentary knowledge does not prevent describing desert communities and using the descriptions to better understand the future of biological diversity in arid California.

GREAT BASIN COMMUNITIES

At the highest latitudes and elevations in eastern California, the Great Basin supports productive and structurally diverse communities. Higher precipitation and lower temperature, proximity to mountain runoff, and extensive distribution during the Pleistocene have produced communities that are at or beyond the edge of aridity. Basins between Modoc and Inyo counties support woodland and grassy scrub vegetation (steppe), with lush wetlands and riparian forests wherever freshwater accumulates or flows. Mountain peaks above 8,000 feet regularly receive summer precipitation and winter snows, with cool temperatures that blunt evaporation and support the growth of forests. Consequently, many Great Basin communities are semiarid rather than arid desert communities, but their distribution and proximity to the drought-stricken lowlands make them an integral part of the overall landscape.

FORESTS AND WOODLANDS

Bristlecone Pine Forest
High peaks along the California-Nevada border often support forests or woodlands of bristlecone pine *(Pinus longaeva)*. Above 8,500 feet in the White, Inyo, Panamint, and Last Chance mountains, slow-growing trees form an open, parklike overstory that often contains limber pine *(Pinus flexilis)*. Bristlecone pines are slow growing because of the short, cool summer and long, frigid winter. Low temperatures lock up soil water as ice, producing droughtlike stress in the leaves. But, more importantly, slow growth results from a strong preference for sinking roots into dolomite bedrock. Rocks of the 600-million-year-old Reed Formation are shell white and contain some of the oldest mollusk fossils on the continent. Weathering produces an alkaline, nutrient-poor soil that many plant species cannot tolerate. Consequently, the annual rings of bristlecone trunks are crowded

together (at least 25 to the inch), with almost no separation during a drought. Stems appear like bottlebrushes because live needles are retained for 20 to 30 years (compared to three to 10 years in most other pines). The dense, resinous wood resists high winds and attack by fungi and insects and can support a canopy for thousands of years. Bristlecone pine is especially well known for responding to adversity with longevity, and several individuals in the White Mountains exceed 4,600 years in age.

Upper   Bristlecone pine populations depend on mountaintop conditions in the Great Basin. (Christopher L. Christie)

Lower   Only soils derived from Reed Formation dolomite (right) support bristlecone pine in the White Mountains. Note the sharp ecotone. (Author)

Beneath the overstory of ancient, gnarled trees is a sparse understory of low shrubs, grasses, and herbs. Some species spread upslope from the Great Basin, such as little-leaf mahogany *(Cercocarpus intricatus)*, yellow rabbitbrush *(Chrysothamnus viscidiflorus)*, spiny phlox *(Leptodactylon pungens)*, Richardson's mulygrass *(Muhlenbergia richardsonis)*, and squirreltail grass *(Elymus elymoides)*. Other species reach down from timberline to inhabit this subalpine forest. Moundlike canopies of limestone aster *(Erigeron uncialis)* and mountain milkvetch *(Astragalus kentrophyta)* resemble alpine shrubs that take advantage of warmer temperatures near the soil surface to extend the growing season. Showy floral

The Pygmy Nuthatch forages on tree trunks and nests in desert-edge forests, especially those of bristlecone pine. (Herbert Clarke)

displays by silver lupine *(Lupinus argenteus* var. *tenellus)* and Clokey paintbrush *(Castilleja applegatei* subsp. *martinii)* provide ample pollen and nectar resources for frenzied bees, hummingbirds, and other pollinators that gather during the short summer.

The presence of cone-bearing trees at high altitudes increases the variety of birds that can frequent desert mountains. Boreal species usually associated with northern, cool, and moist environments can find plentiful food and nesting sites while surrounded by otherwise unsuitable conditions. In the White Mountains at least 40 species of boreal birds breed in these forests, some with a strong affinity for bristlecone pine. Usually confined to lower-elevation stands of ponderosa pine *(Pinus ponderosa)*, the Pygmy Nuthatch *(Sitta pygmaea)* nests exclusively in these desert-edge bristlecones, thereby extending their range well beyond the Sierra Nevada. The Olive-sided Flycatcher *(Cotonopus cooperi)*, Red-breasted Nuthatch *(S. canadensis)*, and Golden-crowned Kinglet *(Regulus satrapa)* also build nests where tree cover and other factors are favorable. But not all bristlecone forests are alike; these three species have not been found in similar habitat just 25 to 100 miles to the south for reasons that are not yet clear. It may have to do with the absence of other essential community types in the overall landscape. Without other kinds of forest (for example, riparian) supplying resources, only 29 boreal bird species breed in the bristlecone forests of the Inyo Mountains and just 16 species in the Panamint Mountains on the western edge of Death Valley.

Montane and Desert Riparian Forest
Riparian forests flank streams that wind down from the high country, connecting montane and desert communities and providing resources that would otherwise be absent from the transition. Along the eastern slopes of the Sierra Nevada, deciduous thickets of quaking aspen *(Populus tremuloides)* form a tall overstory at the bottom of nearly every canyon or wherever the water table is just below the soil surface. The thickets are the result of lateral roots producing upright "branches" that look like separate, densely packed trees. This vegetative growth has largely taken the place of sexual reproduction in aspen stands across the West, and thickets (clones) may be thousands of years old. At elevations between 6,000 and 10,000 feet aspen is joined by several species of montane pine (for example, lodgepole pine *[Pinus contorta* subsp. *murrayana]* and Jeffrey pine *[P. jeffreyi]*), as well as black cottonwood *(Populus balsamifera* subsp. *trichocarpa)* and mountain alder *(Alnus incana* subsp. *tenuifolia)*. Beneath these trees is an understory of tall, deciduous shrubs such as water birch *(Betula occidentalis)* and several species of willow *(Salix)*. Where

A riparian forest of quaking aspen and Jeffrey pine descends from the Sierra into the big sagebrush of Lee Vining Canyon. (Charles Webber)

sediments accumulate and waters move slowly, a meadowy ground layer of rushes *(Juncus)*, sedges, and grasses may form, punctuated by a wide variety of showy herbs. This kind of riparian forest is also found at higher elevations in the White Mountains where streamflows are permanent.

As mountain canyons spill into the Owens Valley, a desert riparian woodland replaces this montane riparian forest. Aspen and pines give way to open stands of black cottonwood, Fremont cottonwood *(P. fremontii)*, and arroyo willow *(Salix lasiolepis)*, with smaller shrubs of wild rose *(Rosa woodsii* var. *ultramontana)* and pink currant *(Ribes nevadense)* in the understory. Fingers of sagebrush scrub invade from the surrounding woodlands and desert, and the meadowy layer of sedges and rushes is confined to wet banks and small depressions immediately along the watercourse. The juxtaposition of productive trees, multilayered canopies, and flowing water allows nondesert species to inhabit desert landscapes. In the White Mountains, for example, the overstory of riparian forests and woodlands provide specific feeding and nesting resources for Red-naped Sapsuckers *(Sphyrapicus nuchalis)* and Western Wood-Peewees *(Contopus sordidulus)*. Sapsuckers use their stout, strong bills to probe pine and cottonwood bark for ants and wood-boring beetles. They relish sap, the sugary exudate of the tree's phloem tissues, extracted from holes drilled around trunks in rows or checkerboard patterns. Holes in large, dead trunks become cozy nesting chambers when excavated to a depth of 15 inches. Trees are also essential for nesting Peewees, which seem to require horizontal branches at least 20

feet above the ground. They prefer the outer edges of desert riparian vegetation, giving them open air-space to dart out and grab insects in flight. Beneath the tree overstory, a dense willow understory supports Calliope Hummingbirds *(Stellula calliope)* and MacGillivray's Warblers *(Oporornis tolmiei)*. The hummingbirds sip sap out of sapsucker holes and weave tiny nests from spider silk and sprigs of moss, bark, and lichen. Lower, dense canopy layers attract warblers because they harbor insects that hide in the humid, streamside leaf litter and meadow peat. Such requirements could never be met in the sunny, arid conditions that prevail in the surrounding desert scrub.

The watercourse itself can provide essential habitat for Great Basin fishes. As adults, Lahontan Cutthroat Trout *(Oncorhynchus clarki henshawi)* live in large, remnant Pleistocene lakes as predators of other, smaller fishes. The warm, alkaline waters of Pyramid and Walker lakes in western Nevada allow the fishes to grow large (more than 40 pounds) and live up to 10 years. But spawning, embryo development, and hatching require fresh, cold, oxygen-rich water that meanders through higher-elevation riparian forests and meadows. Historically, adults in Pyramid Lake would migrate more than 60 miles up the Truckee River to spawn in the eastern tributaries of Lake Tahoe. While searching for optimal gravel beds for depositing eggs, they feed on aquatic insects and larvae floating downstream toward the desert and the lake beyond.

Pinyon and Juniper Woodland

The upper, semi-arid edge of Great Basin Desert is defined by woodlands of pinyon pine *(Pinus monophylla)* and Utah juniper *(Juniperus osteosperma)*. Widely spaced, snow-cone canopies of these two diminutive conifers are usually surrounded by a pale green matrix of big sagebrush *(Artemisia tridentata)*, antelope bitterbrush *(Purshia tridentata)*, and rubber rabbitbrush *(Chrysothamnus nauseosus)*. Na-

Upper   The Red-naped Sapsucker uses aspen trunks for foraging and sheltering. (Tim Zurowski)

Lower   Lahontan Cutthroat Trout is threatened with extinction by hybridization with introduced trout. (D. W. Sada)

Upper A spacious woodland of pinyon pine and Utah juniper approaches the north shore of Mono Lake. (Author)

Lower Woody seed cone of pinyon pine, an important food source for Great Basin granivores. (Author)

tive bunchgrasses, a few cacti (for example, old man cactus *[Opuntia erinacea]*), and some pincushion perennials (for example, cold desert phlox *[Phlox stansburyi]* and sulfur-flowered buckwheat *[Eriogonum ovalifolium]*) often join this shrubby understory as they do in sagebrush scrub (see below). Hugging the surface of the ground are dense cryptogamic crusts, some dark green, others orange or black, whose algal and fungal components become activated by rain or snowmelt.

Covering more than 3.3 million acres of California and represented in some of the earliest Pleistocene packrat middens, pinyon and juniper woodlands are known to vary greatly across space and through time. In colder and drier regions to the north and at low-elevation ecotones with desert scrub, juniper tends to dominate or take the place of pinyon. It is western juniper *(Juniperus occidentalis)*, rather than Utah juniper, that is found on

Upper   An old Utah juniper near the summit of Tin Mountain, Death Valley. (Author)

Lower   Fleshy seed cones of Utah juniper are eaten by animals despite their high resin content. (Author)

volcanic soils of the Modoc Plateau and in the rain shadow of Mount Lassen (and into eastern Oregon and Washington). Similarly, California juniper *(J. californica)* is most often associated with desert-edge woodlands of southern California, including those in the Tehachapi, San Gabriel, Little San Bernardino, Coxcomb, and Santa Rosa mountains. These woodlands are complex mixtures of Great Basin and Mojave species, which can include big sagebrush, Joshua tree *(Yucca brevifolia)*, and creosote bush *(Larrea tridentata)* within a stone's throw of each other. Oaks *(Quercus)* and chaparral shrubs may also join as inland extensions of coastal communities. The mixture probably reflects a coincidence of steep gradients in precipitation and temperature where mountains and deserts meet, but it also reflects the complicated history of plant migration since the Pleistocene. Utah juniper dominated desert lands during much of the last glacial period but began to shift rapidly northward and upslope during the early Holocene (12,500 to 8,000 years BP). Pinyon pine did the same but was not widespread or common until summer rains and milder winters returned to these mountainous regions a few thousand years ago. Other Great Basin species (for example, big sagebrush) became confined to north-facing slopes and basins with cold air drainage and snow accumulation. Conversely, Mojave species overran the dry and warm margins of these marching woodlands during the Altithermal, becoming confined to south-facing, well-drained bajadas. The remnant, almost swirling patterns of vegetation over the landscape illustrate the climatic sensitivity of this woodland to scrub ecotone.

Pinyon and juniper woodlands are also as productive as they are widespread and complex. The large, protein-rich seeds of pinyon pine are readily removed from open cones by Pinyon Jays (*Gymnorhinus cyanocephalus*) and Clark's Nutcrackers (*Nucifraga columbiana*). Strong, sharp-edged bills tear cones apart, crack the thick seed coat, and remove nutritious tissues in a noisy frenzy of feeding during fall. Each bird will also cache thousands of whole seeds beneath shrubs and within rotting logs for winter and spring consumption. Forgotten caches often produce seedlings, making these birds effective, long-distance pinyon dispersers. Juniper berries (actually fleshy cones containing seeds) are collected by mammals as well as birds. On a single foray from a laden tree, a Round-tailed Ground Squirrel (*Spermophilus tereticaudus*) can stuff its cheek pouches with a hundred or so husked seeds ready for winter storage. Agile Kangaroo Rats (*Dipodomys agilis*), Mule Deer (*Odocoileus hemionus*), and even Desert Bighorn (*Ovis canadensis nelsoni*) eat the berries despite the resinous, aromatic flavor.

Upper   The Clark's Nutcracker uses seeds of several conifer species as food. (Brian Small)

Lower   The Pinyon Jay has a strong preference for pinyon seeds. (Tim Zurowski)

Humans relied heavily on pinyon and juniper woodlands throughout their long history in the Great Basin. Pinyon seeds were the most important plant food of the Owens

Minnie Williams, an Owens Valley Paiute, collects and winnows pinyon nuts in the Inyo Mountains. (John and Nancy Peterson Walter)

Valley Paiute, inspiring collection technologies, social covenants, and spiritual ceremonies that are still practiced today. Green, unopened cones were pulled from the trees in late summer, roasted over sagebrush coals, and shaken to release the seeds onto a woven mat. Hulls were broken by rolling a *mano* (hand stone) over the nuts on a *metate* (grinding slab), and winnowing the pieces away with a shallow basket until the kernels were clean. During fall the brown, open cones could be knocked from the branches with long wooden poles so that seeds fell out onto mats placed beneath the canopy. At the end of the harvest, poles were used to strike the branch ends, a form of pruning that favors cone formation in subsequent years. Working their own tracts of woodlands, a family group could collect 30 to 40 bushels of nuts (more than 300 pounds) before the first snows fell. Groups from different villages would share productive tracts if a local crop failed during a particular year, and trespassing was rare. Men, women, and children participated in the harvest, which was celebrated with feasting, dancing, gaming, courting, and trading. An overall blessing fell upon the camps, bestowed by sacred smoke from fragrant, sagebrush-fed fires.

SCRUB

Big Sagebrush Scrub

The most characteristic and widespread community of the Great Basin is the one dominated by big sagebrush. Dominance in this case means that one species contributes 70 percent of the ground cover and 90 percent of the plant material (by weight) in a given stand, with a smattering of other shrubs, grasses, and herbs. Sagebrush scrub occupies more than 1.8 million acres in California, with nearly 44 million acres across the American West. The community commonly spans an elevation zone between 4,000 and 9,000 feet on a very wide variety of soils, including well-drained gravels and dense clays or silts. Climate regimes are also varied but always include cold, snowy winters and hot, dry summers with less than 15 inches of annual precipitation. Wetter and cooler climates at higher elevations or latitudes support other communities with a considerable sagebrush component, such as steppe (grassy) or savanna (woody with scattered pinyons, junipers, or other conifers). Drier and warmer climates at lower elevations have sagebrush ecotones that mix with woodlands of Joshua tree and scrub communities dominated by blackbush

Big sagebrush scrub in the Mono Lake Basin. The dark shrubs are antelope bitterbrush. (Author)

(Coleogyne ramosissima) on well-drained bajadas, or saltbush *(Atriplex)* on clay soils or near saline basins.

Despite the abundance of big sagebrush, many plant species share the remaining resources of the community—it just doesn't seem so. Sharing the shrub canopy layer are other pale green or gray green species with gnarled stems and narrow leaves whose growth form and general appearance closely resemble big sagebrush. Some, such as rubber rabbitbrush or black sagebrush *(Artemisia nova)* are members of the same plant family as big sagebrush (sunflower family [Asteraceae]) and possess similarities as part of a common evolutionary heritage. Others belong to very different, unrelated families with little common inheritance. Antelope bitterbrush of the rose family (Rosaceae), hop-sage *(Grayia)* of the goosefoot family (Chenopodiaceae) and Nevada ephedra *(Ephedra nevadensis)*, a gymnosperm (Ephedraceae), hide among the sagebrush and do little to counteract an impression of monotony. The similar appearance of these species is evidence for convergence, or the evolution of the same characteristics in different lineages in response to strong environmental selection. In the Great Basin, cold winters may select for dense, spherical canopies that resist wind and the crush of heavy snow. Hot, sunny summers may select for pale, filamentous foliage that reflects light and reduces heat load and transpiration rates.

The shrubs of big sagebrush scrub are productive suppliers of herbage and browse for an abundance and wide variety of native animals. Underground, the total living mass of root-associated nematodes is two to eight times that of any other desert community in North America, amounting to about .42 g of these microscopic worms in every square yard of soil surface. Caterpillars of the Hera Moth *(Hemileuca hera)* feed exclusively on leaves of big sagebrush, while those of the closely related Nuttall's Sheep Moth *(H. nuttalli)* avoid overlap by preferring antelope bitterbrush. The late summer flowers of rubber rabbitbrush attract large numbers of blister beetles (Meloidae) and longhorn beetles (Cerambycidae) in search of energy-rich pollen and nectar. Yellow rabbitbrush and winterfat *(Krascheninnikovia lanata)* are the winter targets of pruning jackrabbits *(Lepus)* that consume nearly the entire canopy. Even though herbivory is usual in birds, the Greater Sage-Grouse *(Centrocercus urophasianus)* obtains 75 percent of its diet from the leaves of big sagebrush. Pronghorn *(Antilocapra americana)*, Mule Deer, and Desert Bighorn have a much more varied diet but rely heavily on perennial grasses, antelope bitterbrush, and Nevada ephedra for browse.

But these same shrubs respond differently to herbivory; some thrive while others disappear or endure. A year after winterfat plants had seen intensive pruning by jackrabbits, the new growth was significantly greater than that of protected plants. Yellow rabbitbrush was also capable of this compensatory growth by supplying carbohydrates stored in the root system to surviving buds. The new shoots are lush and photosynthetically productive but must replenish carbohydrate reserves before the next pruning in order to respond again. Big sagebrush, however, does not exhibit compensatory growth and dies after several rounds of defoliation. Instead, chemical defenses are used to repulse generalist herbivores. The fragrant, essential oils so characteristic of big sagebrush create stomach problems for ruminant grazers

Upper   Hera Moth on the tridentate leaves of its larval food source, big sagebrush. (Christopher L. Christie)

Lower   Greater Sage-Grouse require large tracts of big sagebrush scrub, up to 2,500 square miles per population. (Ian Tait)

An outcrop of carbonate rock in the Last Chance Mountains has a sparse vegetation composed of many unusual plant species. (Author)

(for example, Pronghorn) by inhibiting microbial activity necessary for digestion. The oils also taste awful, at least to people. Another chemical, called methyl-jasmonate, is released by damaged foliage and wafts through the stand where it is absorbed by uneaten, "eavesdropping" plants. Field studies have demonstrated that this airborne warning induces the formation of more antiherbivore oils in big sagebrush to help endure, if not deter, a voracious onslaught.

Carbonate Scrub

Ancient limestone and dolomite rocks, spatially patchy and spanning a wide elevation range (2,500 to 14,000 feet), create a mosaic of unusual habitats in eastern California. These habitats straddle the Great Basin and Mojave deserts and are surrounded by the regional woodlands and scrub vegetation that are characteristic of both deserts. However, communities on carbonate rocks often have their own assemblages of plants, many of which are rare and endemic, and most have extremely restricted distributions. For these reasons, eminent botanists Peter Raven and Daniel Axelrod have called the plant

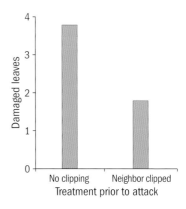

If neighboring shrubs of big sagebrush are clipped to simulate an herbivore attack, a nonclipped sagebrush will manufacture chemicals that reduce subsequent damage to leaves by insects (compared to a sagebrush with unclipped neighbors). This "eavesdropping" is also known from willows. (Redrawn from Karban et al. 2002)

ASSEMBLING RODENT COMMUNITIES

Analysis of biological communities includes structural and functional approaches. Plant species are often grouped together if they are found in the same canopy layers (for example, overstory trees or low-growing herbs). A description of the local vegetation by canopy layer can impart an image of how the plant biomass is arranged in three-dimensional space. A functional approach would group together species that perform the same tasks and make similar contributions to the community. Coexisting trees that produce large, energy-rich seeds or fruits (for example, pinyon pine, Utah juniper, and Sonoran scrub oak) might be considered one guild in a pinyon-juniper community, while animals that collect and consume them would constitute another (for example, Pinyon Jay, Panamint Chipmunk *(Tamias panamintinus)*, and Mule Deer). An analysis by function allows ecologists to ask what controls species richness, food web complexity, competition, and evolutionary processes in a given assemblage of organisms.

Our deserts are world renowned for studies conducted on the rodent granivore guild—native mice and rats (in the family Heteromyidae) that stuff cheek pouches with seeds at night to cache in burrows by morn. Live-trapping in low-elevation communities of the Great Basin, Mojave, and Sonoran deserts revealed the same strong pattern: there is but one heteromyid species of a given body size in any single location. More precisely, the ratio of body weights from one size rodent to another is between 2.0 and 3.1, and never less than 1.5. For example, the smallest rodent in a local patch of Great Basin scrub could be a pocket mouse *(Perognathus)*, with an average body weight of 6.8 grams, the next largest a kangaroo mouse *(Microdipodops)*, 14 grams, the next a Merriam Kan-

life of these habitats "the richest and most interesting in transmontane [desert] California." They determined that nearly 80 plant species are endemic to this complex landscape, largely because of evolution and persistence on carbonate rocks.

Most, if not all, carbonate-loving plants in the desert are perennials, growing as long-lived woody shrubs or herbs arising from rhizomes or root trunks. At lower elevations, these plants are commonly found on cliff faces or in deep canyons, surrounded by typical desert scrub vegetation. They are usually distinctive in their appearance, with showy flowers, and are often the only species in a unique genus. Examples include July gold *(Dedeckera eurekensis)* (a shrub restricted to Bonanza King Dolomite), naked-stemmed daisy *(Enceliopsis nudicaulis)*, rixford rockwort *(Scopulophila rixfordii)*, and prickle-leaf

garoo Rat *(Dipodomys merriami)*, 32 grams, and the largest a Desert Kangaroo rat *(D. deserti)*, 100 grams. The sequence of body weight ratios is then 2.1, 2.3, and 3.1, respectively. This observation is so consistent across habitats and geography that many ecologists regard the body ratio principle as a "rule of assembly" with respect to rodent communities in North America.

There is no consensus, however, among ecologists as to the mechanism that enforces this rule. The first hypothesis was that species with different body sizes gathered different-sized seeds, thus allowing coexistence with minimal competition. But large-bodied heteromyids will often gather small seeds if abundant in a patch. They will also supplement their diet with insects and green herbage when necessary, further eroding the argument that competition for seeds is always at work. A second hypothesis suggested that smaller mice and larger rats actually foraged in different microhabitats within the vegetation, using seed patches that are spatially separated. This was based on the observation that mice seldom ventured beyond the edge of shrub canopies, while kangaroo rats spend more time foraging in the open spaces between shrubs. This may have evolved in response to predators (kangaroo rats have large eyes, acute hearing, and bipedal jumping that facilitate escape) or as a result of thermal stress on cold nights (small-bodied mice would lose more body heat than large-bodied rats when exposed to the open sky). As is often the case in nature, simplistic explanations do not withstand prolonged scrutiny.

(Hecastocleis shockleyi). There are also carbonate endemics that have evolved from large, widespread genera, including napkinring buckwheat *(Eriogonum intrafractum)*, limestone monkeyflower *(Mimulus rupicola)*, and limestone penstemon *(Penstemon calcareus)*. They all take advantage of moisture stored deep within rock crevices, in an otherwise dry and hot landscape of bare rock.

Besides being composed of endemic species, the vegetation itself has a unique architecture that packs in more plant species per unit of ground area than adjacent communities found on other rock types. This difference in species richness and canopy structure is revealed by a species-area sampling technique. If a tape measure is anchored to a stake in the center of a carbonate community, it becomes the radius of an ever-widening, circular plot. Starting with a small radius, say one yard, it is easy to walk around the circumference and record the number of plant species rooted inside the three square yard area. The plot is enlarged with a new radius, the circumference is walked, and any additional species are added to the growing tally. This is repeated for a number of these nested, circular plots and plotted as a graph of cumulative species richness against community area. In the Inyo Mountains, communities on carbonate rocks have nearly twice as many plant species per unit of area as do adjacent communities on basalt rocks, some of which are endemics. It's likely that the additional species are accommodated because the nutrient-poor, alkaline carbonates inhibit plant growth (see "Bristlecone Pine Forest"), preventing any one species from dominating and usurping the available resources. Indeed, each shrub canopy growing on limestone is 20 to 40 percent smaller than those of the same species growing on basalt. Phosphorus may be particularly in short supply on these extreme soils, allowing a richness of species to take the place of productivity and dominance by a few. Whether animals, particularly insects, respond to the richness or productivity of these plant communities is not yet known.

MOJAVE COMMUNITIES

Communities of the Mojave Desert did not assume their modern composition until the mid-Holocene, some 8,000 to 5,500 years before present. Aridity spread and drought-tolerant species invaded, while semiarid Great Basin communities contracted upslope and northward. Consequently, most Mojave communities are youthful and share many of their dominant species with Great Basin and Sonoran communities that appear to be of much greater antiquity. There is also difficulty in geographically defining the Mojave's dynamic boundaries, especially when tallying species and describing natural communities. Some ecologists view the Mojave itself as an ecotone, drawing species from high and low elevations, from cold and hot climates, and from north and south into a recognizable, if not consistent, mix. However, plant endemism in the Mojave is similar to that of the California desert bioregion as a whole. Annuals show high levels, with nearly 80 percent of the 250 or so species having evolved only here. Combined with unique climatic and geological features, endemism provides a justification for recognizing the Mojave as a distinct desert with its own communities and biological indicators.

FORESTS AND WOODLANDS

White Fir Forest
High mountains rise above the eastern Mojave, as islands rise from the sea. Along the edge of Death Valley, the 11,049 foot summit of Telescope Peak supports isolated stands of bristlecone pine much like those described in the White and Inyo ranges, as well as extensive woodlands of pinyon and juniper (see above). Farther east and south are the Kingston (7,300 feet), New York (7,400 feet), and Providence (6,900 feet) mountains,

which also support remnants of Pleistocene woodlands, driven upslope during the Holocene spread
of lowland aridity. Persistent snows, scattered summer rain, and moderated air temperatures provide
refuge for the drought intolerant, stranded above a
hot, unforgiving sea of dry air. Climate change,
which landed the castaways in this precarious position, will ultimately determine their fate unless the
mountains themselves rise further and faster into
the cool sky.

Among the most precarious of castaways are
small stands of white fir *(Abies concolor)* found above
6,400 feet in the Kingston and New York mountains.
Located in steep, north-facing canyons of crumbling
granite, the two populations are composed of only
150 and 30 individuals covering 30 and two acres,
respectively. The largest trees exceed 50 feet in height
and 28 inches in trunk diameter, with leafy canopies
barely overlapping (and thus, forming a forest).
Seedlings are very rare, indicating that persistence
even under present conditions is not certain. A consistently reproducing population of at least 1,000
trees is known from north-facing, limestone slopes
of the Clark Mountains (above 6,250 feet). Careful
analysis has revealed that all three fir populations are
more closely related to those in the distant Rocky
Mountains *(A. c. concolor)*, rather than the nearby
Sierra Nevada *(A. c. lowiana)*. Perhaps a series of an-

Pollinators visit the New York Mountains cryptantha
(Cryptantha tumulosa), a rare and endemic borage.
(James M. Andre)

cient dispersal events, leapfrogging across an archipelago of desert mountains, has brought
this eastern tree to the edge of California.

Mountain leapfrogging is also revealed by the geographic distributions of other species
in these stranded forests, with paths emanating from nearly all directions. Rock spiraea
(Petrophyton caespitosum), desert ash *(Fraxinus anomala)*, Utah juniper, and two-leaf
pinyon *(Pinus edulis)* are probably ancient refugees from the continental divide. More recently arrived from the Sierra Nevada are varieties of Jaeger's mustard *(Halimolobos diffusa*
var. *jaegeri)* and red heuchera *(Heuchera rubescens* var. *pachypoda)*. At least four plants extend to the New York Mountains from the San Bernardino and San Gabriel ranges, including a drought-sensitive bedstraw (Parish's bedstraw [*Galium parishii*]) and a rock-loving
sedum *(Sedum niveum)*. Even two species of California oaks (canyon oak [*Quercus chrysolepis*]
and Sonoran scrub oak [*Q. turbinella*]), which spread north from central Mexico long ago,

(text continues on page 216)

BUTTERFLY ENDEMISM

Animals capable of traveling long distances are less likely to be stranded on habitat islands and, therefore, less likely to produce unique, endemic forms of biological diversity. A given species of bird or large mammal tends to be composed of similar-looking individuals across the desert bioregion due to a lack of reproductive isolation. Genetic novelties tend to be shared or lost, as mating occurs without regard for the geography of participants. Consequently, mobility and mixing discourage the evolution of subspecies or varieties in species that widely disperse, even if populations inhabit the most remote mountain ranges.

An interesting exception to this paradigm is observed in butterflies (and moths as well). Butterflies are strong fliers, capable of migrating over hundreds, if not thousands, of miles of extreme terrain (for example, the Monarchs *[Danaus plexippus]* that migrate between North America and Mexico). Even small-winged species can move considerable distances. Yet, desert mountains are replete with endemic subspecies from almost every lepidopteran lineage. How do butterfly populations become isolated as a prerequisite for evolutionary divergence?

Papilo indra calcicola

The life cycle of butterflies is a process of metamorphosis between distinct stages: egg to caterpillar (larva) to chrysalis (pupa) to adult. Whereas adults are fliers, the other stages are limited to habitats that support specific kinds of host plants that provide food and shelter. The degree of isolation and differentiation of butterfly populations depends on the specificity and geographic distribution of their host plants. In some cases hosts can be multiple species belonging to a widespread plant family, usually resulting in a large butterfly distribution. Larvae of the Desert Orangetip *(Anthocharis cethura)* feed on a number of native mustards (for example, jewelflower *[Caulanthus, Streptanthus]*, tansy mustard *[Descurainia]*, and thelypodium *[Thelypodium]*) that occur over vast areas. Consequently, the butterfly species is widespread (northwestern Nevada to Baja California), with subspecies corresponding to extensive desert regions (for example, *A. c. hadromarmorata* of the Great Basin, *A. c. mojavensis* of the Mojave, and *A. c. bajacalifornica* of the Sonoran). But if a butterfly's host is but a single plant species, the potential for isolation

and differentiation is much greater. For example, DeDecker's Blue Butterfly (*Icaricia acmon dedeckera*) feeds only on the buckwheat relative known as July gold (*Dedeckera eurekensis*). Both butterfly and host are entirely confined to a few canyons between 4,000 and 5,600 feet in eastern Inyo County. In this case, the persistence of a relict plant (a paleoendemic) has fostered the recent evolution of a specialist butterfly (a neoendemic) within just a small sliver of California desert.

Similar, extraordinary patterns of endemism result when butterfly populations have been geographically stranded by the patchy distribution of their host plants. Three different subspecies of Desert Swallowtail Butterfly (*Papilio indra*) are endemic to different limestone ranges of the eastern Mojave: *P. i. panamintensis* in the Panamint Mountains of Death Valley, *P. i. calcicola* scattered from the Grapevine to the Muddy Mountains in southern Nevada, and *P. i. martini* in

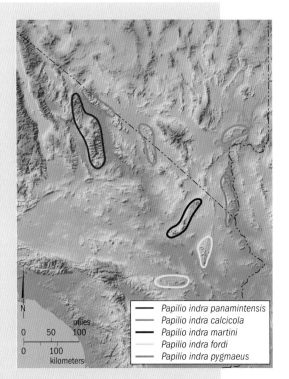

Evolution of subspecies of *Papilio indica* on isolated desert mountains. (Based on Emmel 1998)

the Providence Mountains east of Kelso. The larvae of all three feed on lomatiums (*Lomatium*, in the carrot family), which often prefer soils derived from carbonate rocks. On nearby granitic rocks, a related food plant, cymopterus (*Cymopterus*), hosts two additional subspecies: *P. i. pygmaeus* of the Dead Mountains northwest of Needles and *P. i. fordi* in the Old Woman Mountains near Essex. That's a total of five endemic forms of Desert Swallowtail within a 125 mile radius. The subspecies differ in size and coloration (especially of the hindwing), as well as the rate at which the larvae develop into pupae (more rapid at lower elevations). Such fine-scaled patterns of endemism are undoubtedly typical of other specialist herbivores that have yet to be discovered.

Upper The Panamint Chipmunk is found on mountains in eastern California. (Herbert Clarke)

Lower The Panamint Kangaroo Rat collects the seed cones of Utah juniper throughout its desert-edge range. (Lloyd Glenn Ingles)

have found a high-elevation home. Some of these populations probably deserve recognition as endemics, diverging through time as isolated pools of unique genes. A buckwheat (Hermann's buckwheat [*Eriogonum heermannii* var. *floccosum*]) and a potentilla (*Potentilla patellifera*) are known only from desert forests of white fir and pinyon pine.

With so many stranded plants on high Mojave ranges, we should not be surprised to find stranded animals as well. Many became known to science from collections made by the Death Valley Expedition, especially rodents first described by C. H. Merriam. The Panamint Chipmunk (*Tamias panamintensis panamintensis*), for example, is widely distributed along the eastern Sierra, the White-Inyo ranges, and the Panamint Mountains. But a separate subspecies (*T. p. acrus*) can be found only in about 40 square miles of the Kingston Range, a minimum of 60 unoccupied miles from relatives to the northwest and 25 miles from relatives in the New York Mountains. This mountaintop subspecies is distinctive; individuals have smaller bodies, shorter skulls, and darker fur than the widespread subspecies. Similarly, a hundred-mile stretch of the Mojave River separates a distinctive subspecies of Panamint Kangaroo Rat (*Dipodomys panamintinus leucogenys*) in the New York Mountains from its western ancestor (*D. p. panamintinus*). Probably a great number of other interesting disjunctions remain to be rediscovered by faunal surveys of these isolated habitat islands, each a steppingstone toward understanding the complex history of the bioregion.

Joshua Tree Woodland

The Great Basin–Mojave boundary is sinuous and intermittent, like the surface of boiling water. It sloshes upslope onto the sides of mountains and across midelevation bajadas where winter snows last a few days but cold temperatures persist. It is broken where hot summer winds and southern exposures accentuate soil drought. Isolated blurbs can be found farther north and west, remnants of the Altithermal "push" of hot desert as it boiled over into the land of sagebrush, junipers, oaks, bunchgrass, and chaparral. Many species of perennial plants occupy this dynamic boundary, but the most characteristic is the Joshua tree. Spacious woodlands of this giant lily (literally, Liliaceae) closely delineate the extent of the Mojave Desert at its upper, wetter edge. This transitional elevation is

Joshua tree woodland often has an understory containing many species of shrubs, herbs, and grasses. (Author)

around 2,500 feet in the western Mojave (near Palmdale), 3,000 feet in the northern Mojave (near Little Lake), and as high as 5,600 feet in the northeastern Mojave (near Death Valley), after rising from sea level 20,000 years ago (as revealed by packrat middens).

Joshua tree woodlands actually have very little Joshua tree in them, with typical stands supporting 50 individuals per acre that erect only .2 percent cover as a sparse overstory. The understory, however, is well developed from a variety of shrubs, including blackbush, desert shadscale *(Atriplex confertifolia)*, Nevada ephedra, and winterfat with a collective density of 2,930 per acre and about eight percent cover. Cacti (for example, silver cholla *[Opuntia echinocarpa]*, hedgehog cactus *[Echinocereus engelmannii]*) contribute another one to two percent cover, and perennial grasses (for example, big galleta grass *[Pleuraphis rigida]*, desert needlegrass *[Achnatherum speciosum]*) add as much as four percent. Perhaps the visual impact of this desert tree is simply overpowering, as branched and twisted canopies of dagger-shaped leaves offer somber, white bouquets to the sky in exchange for rain.

But many animal species interact with and depend on Joshua tree, ultimately determining its appearance, distribution, and abundance in the community. The number and position of branches is partly determined by larvae of the Yucca Weevil *(Scyphophorus yuccae)*. Apical meristems at the terminus of each branch are the preferred food. Feeding on these growing points stimulates lateral meristems along the length of the stem to grow out and produce more branches. Adult females of the Navaho Giant Yucca Skipper butterfly *(Megathymus yuccae navajo)* seek out Joshua sprouts arising from underground run-

Upper Visitors have long been fascinated by variations in the growth form of Joshua tree. (Unknown photographer, Bancroft Library)

Center Short, unbranched growth form creates a dwarf Joshua tree woodland. (Sam Stewart)

Lower Larvae of the Yucca Weevil browse the meristems of Joshua trees and affect the pattern of branching. (Arthur V. Evans and James N. Hogue)

ners (rhizomes) in which to lay eggs. Sprouts and rhizomes provide shelter and food, often becoming hollow, dead chambers as the caterpillars consume the soft, fibrous interiors. The decaying chambers may be colonized by termites or ants that, in turn, provide shelter and food for the Desert Night Lizard *(Xantusia vigilis).* This insectivore climbs around and through the gray brown stems, which its skin color closely matches, searching for prey and avoiding predators. Other vertebrates nest among or within the branches, including over 20 species of birds. Scott's Oriole *(Icterus parisorum)* weaves its hanging pouch with fibers pulled from stems and leaves and will supplement an insect diet with yucca nectar (similar to its tropical relatives). In the absence of rocky grottos, woodrats *(Neotoma)* build their middens around the base of large, spreading trees. They gnaw the dagger-shaped leaves from the canopy to incorporate into the pile, strip the sugary husk off swollen floral ovaries, and collect seeds released from the dry fruit. Rodents, in general, are probably the principle agents of dispersal and distribution. But long ago this function was undoubtedly performed by the Giant Ground Sloth *(Nothrotheriops shastensis)* prior to its early Holocene extinction, judging by the copious amount of Joshua tree seeds found in fossilized dung.

A symbiotic interaction evolved between Joshua tree and a small, white moth known as the Yucca Moth *(Tegeticula paradoxa).* Unlike most pollinators, Yucca Moth limits its use of floral resources by visiting only the open blooms of Joshua tree. This moth has specialized structures and behaviors that intentionally, rather than passively, collect pollen from the anthers of a flower and deposit it precisely on the stigma of another. A female uses her unique mouthparts to form a ball of yucca pollen that can be transported in flight. Landing among fleshy petals, she loads the ball into a stigmatic cavity where success of pollen tube growth and fertilization are assured. At the same time, she lays her eggs

at the base of the ovary so that hatching larvae find plenty of developing seeds to eat. The larvae eventually exit from the ripe fruit, burrow into the ground, and wait in dormancy before metamorphosis and emergence as adults. In this way, reproduction of moth and tree depend upon each other and upon feedbacks that balance the mutual advantages. Seeds are produced in abundance and can tolerate a small amount of feeding damage. Thus, a minimum level of sexual reproduction augments rhizomatous growth and longevity to ensure Joshua tree persistence. If too many eggs are deposited (potentially wiping out all seeds), the tree will abort the entire flower, killing larvae and constraining growth of the moth population. In years too dry or hot to promote flower production or metamorphosis, some larvae remain dormant in the soil like seeds, waiting to emerge as adults when favorable conditions return to the promised land.

SCRUB

Creosote Bush Scrub

The arrival and subsequent evolution of creosote bush transformed arid lands in North America after the Pleistocene. As the centuries became progressively drier and warmer, patches and wide arcs of lowland vegetation underwent an ominous succession; standing, dead pinyons and junipers first revealed where the rate of change was greatest. Soil for-

Upper left   Navaho Giant Yucca Skippers lay their eggs in Joshua tree rhizomes. (Gayle Strickland)

Upper right   The Desert Night Lizard is a common inhabitant of yucca stems and debris. (Jeff Lemm)

Lower   Scott's Orioles often build their pendulous nests in Joshua trees. (Ron Niebrugge)

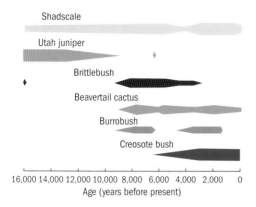

Shadscale

Utah juniper

Brittlebush

Beavertail cactus

Burrobush

Creosote bush

16,000 14,000 12,000 10,000 8,000 6,000 4,000 2,000 0
Age (years before present)

Fossils from a packrat midden in Eureka Valley demonstrate the arrival of creosote bush and other Mojave Desert shrubs near the northern limit of distribution. Utah juniper, typical of Great Basin woodlands, disappears from the midden at about the same time (6,400 years BP) during the Altithermal. The width of each bar indicates relative abundance of the species in the midden. (Redrawn from Spaulding 1985 with conversion of radiocarbon dates to calendar age using the Fairbanks program)

mation stopped, and many semi-arid shrubs and grasses no longer tolerated the sparse and uncertain rainfall. These too succumbed, and they left behind a more open landscape in which the drought tolerant could thrive. Spreading northwest from the Chihuahuan Desert of Mexico, the fuzzy, bouncing fruits of creosote bush eventually chased receding woodlands into eastern California. Crossing each desert produced a leap in chromosomal evolution, diploid to tetraploid to hexaploid, by the time the Mojave was reached. Widespread establishment must have come in waves, as genetically fortified seeds germinated in response to the last of the cold rains, perhaps sheltered by wooden skeletons of vanquished Great Basin species.

The dates of arrival are not well known. In the northern Sonoran Desert of Arizona, creosote bush twigs from packrat middens are not older than 10,580 years before present. Another 2,000 years were required before appearance in middens from the eastern Mojave near Las Vegas, along with its constant companion, burrobush

King Clone, a single individual of creosote bush, whose calculated age is 11,700 years. (Matt Weiser)

(Ambrosia dumosa). Death Valley was not reached until 5,000 years ago. But some areas of the western Mojave may have been colonized earlier, because the estimated ages of individual, living creosote bushes exceed 10,000 years. In the Lucerne Valley the oldest grow as broken, circular rings, dying at the center and expanding outward as stems root along the edge. The largest ring, dubbed "King Clone," is 62 feet in diameter and could be 11,700 years old because its rate of expansion averages only .026 inches per year. If so, these creosote bush rings are the original colonists of the warm Mojave, marking the exact spots that seeds first found the new, modern desert.

The most common form of creosote bush scrub is found on well-drained bajadas, below unstable mountain slopes and above the ancient shorelines of now dry lakes. The two-layered vegetation contains a mixture of long- and short-lived shrubs with low skirts of annual herbs. Creosote bush dominates the community by contributing 70 to 90 percent of the total plant cover on over three quarters of the Mojave. In addition, it is tall, evergreen, and exceedingly drought tolerant and can produce essential resources (root exudates, leaves, sap, nectar, pollen, and seeds) during almost every year of its long life. Consequently, the species is as ecologically reliable as it is widespread, supporting the

Upper Kite photo (from 50 feet above the ground) of the same bajada shown on page 88, revealing the downhill flow of rocky alluvium and the patterns of shrub distribution. Creosote bush is dark green; burrobush is light green. (Author)

Lower A Common Chuckwalla browses the spring foliage of brittlebush, common on rocky terrain in creosote bush scrub. (Jeff Lemm)

precarious lives of many desert animals. Creosote bush is usually joined by other, less stalwart perennials, depending on elevation, soil texture, and salinity. Small drought-deciduous shrubs, such as burrobush, cheesebush, and brittlebush *(Encelia farinosa)*, are common associates that intensively compete for soil water. In wet years they can be very productive, with nutritious leaves and flowers for grazing Chuckwallas *(Sauromalus obesus)* and Mojave Ground Squirrels *(Spermophilus mohavensis)*. Other plant life forms in the canopy layer include stem-succulent cacti (beavertail cactus *[Opuntia basilaris]*, silver cholla, teddy-bear cholla *[O. bigelovii]*, barrel cactus *[Echinocactus polycephalus]*), shrubby yuccas

After strong storms leave behind a few inches of winter precipitation, hundreds of species of annual plants may be found across the Mojave. They are often small in stature but can occur in great numbers. A few common species include these "bellyplants"; all are winter annuals (clockwise from upper left): *Linanthus parryi, Monoptilon belliforme, Nama demissum,* and *Eriophyllum wallacei.* (All photos by author)

(Mojave yucca *[Yucca schidigera],* Spanish bayonet *[Y. baccata]*), and perennial bunchgrasses (big galleta grass, Indian ricegrass *[Achnatherum hymenoides]*).

Annual herbs form another canopy layer, perhaps only a few inches tall and gathered like aprons beneath the shrubs. This layer is built from the seed bank, producing vast quantities of green, succulent shoots in response to optimal rainfall and temperature conditions. This is the principle source of water and food for desert tortoises after they emerge from hibernation. Densities of winter annuals, such as plantain *(Plantago insularis* var. *fastigiata),* can be in the range of 3,000 to 5,000 per square yard. Even if the spring turns hot and dry, most of these survive to flower and produce several viable seeds each. The seeds can be blown around until coming to rest in the leaf litter beneath shrubs, or be carried off by granivorous ants and rodents. Those collected by Desert Harvester Ants *(Veromessor pergandei)* travel distances up to 300 feet from their parent plant on route to being cached and eventually eaten. But many are inadvertently dropped along the way or accidentally end up in a pile of refuse outside the nest. Although death is a common outcome, sheer numerical abundance ensures that the herb layer of this community will persist as part of a large, dynamic seed bank.

On bajadas above 4,000 feet in the eastern Mojave Desert, creosote bush scrub blends into Joshua tree woodland. Precipitation is more reliable, with dustings of snow in winter, and soils are composed of well-drained gravels and sand. Shrub richness nearly doubles in a typical stand (for example, from 13 to 22 species), and total cover approaches 15 percent (up from 10 to 12 percent), as members of both communities mix. The vegetation is also structurally complex, with three canopy layers (Joshua tree, shrub, herb). A few Great Basin species even creep down from above, and cacti, grasses, and annual plants become particularly diverse. With the addition of carbonate rocks or clay particles, blackbush, desert shadscale, and wolfberry *(Lycium)* can dominate, along with more than 40 species of annuals. But surprisingly, a complex community that is rich in plant species does not support the largest number of vertebrate species. The total number of reptiles, birds, and mammals has two peaks, one in creosote bush scrub and the other in adjacent islands of remnant pine-fir forest. Ectothermic ("cold-blooded") reptiles prefer the lower, warmer, creosote bush scrub community, with 30 species tallied. This drops to 19 species in shrub-rich Joshua tree woodland and nine species in tree-dominated pinyon-juniper woodland. Snakes appear particularly sensitive, dropping from 15 species to five and then to two along the same gradient. But mammals, especially rodents, become most diverse in pinyon-juniper woodland, perhaps because of abundant and reliable nut resources. Birds, regardless of whether they are residents or migrants, are most diverse at high elevations among stranded, isolated stands of coniferous trees. Total species richness in the Mojave Desert, therefore, depends on having an array of communities along an elevation gradient, each with a distinctive set of ecological attributes and each supporting a distinctive assortment of organisms over the whole of the landscape.

Saltbush Scrub and Alkali Meadow

At their lower, basin-facing edge, the soils of bajadas become fine textured, salt affected, and nutrient poor. Runoff waters can temporarily saturate the impenetrable surface in and around playas, reducing soil oxygen levels and thus retarding root growth. In addition, cold air drains downhill from adjacent mountains, collecting as invisible, frigid pools that damage or kill sensitive, new leaves. Despite its remarkable tolerance of drought and heat, creosote bush surrenders to this array of basin conditions. The tolerance limits of drought-deciduous and succulent species (cacti) are also exceeded, in large part because salt reduces the ability of these plants to extract water from the soil. Consequently, the species of creosote bush scrub abdicate basin habitats to a host of specialists, the halophytes, which form their own unique, salt affected communities.

Walking downhill along a transect from creosote bajada to basin bottom, the first salt-affected community encountered has dry, well-drained soils. There is a gentle, almost imperceptible slope composed of porous gravel that allows clays, salts, and water to keep flowing, thus preventing accumulation to extreme levels. Nevertheless, creosote bush is

Xerophytic saltbush scrub dominated by desert holly below a creosote bush bajada in Death Valley. (Author)

rather abruptly replaced by shrubs with limited salt tolerance but remarkable drought and temperature tolerance. This community is sometimes called xerophytic saltbush scrub, in reference to its dry (xeric) and slightly salt-affected nature. Its shrubs are members of the same remarkable saltbush genus, *Atriplex,* that tend to be leafy evergreens with C_4 photosynthesis. In Death Valley, desert holly *(Atriplex hymenelytra)* may be the only perennial species found in salty soils (one to two percent salinity by volume) below creosote bush scrub, especially where the bajada gravels originated from the erosion of carbonate mountains. With lesser influence by carbonate, other saltbush species may dominate, including desert shadscale, allscale *(A. polycarpa),* and four-wing saltbush *(A. canescens)*. Annual herbs appear between the shrub canopies after a wet winter, but they tend to be small, short-lived, and few in number compared to upslope.

Continuing downhill, the transect inevitably comes to the edge of a playa. The edge and shallows support a second, distinctive salt-affected community called halophytic saltbush scrub. Accumulations of salt, alkali, and clay turn the soil surface creamy white and crusty. The playa floods with runoff during wet winters, and groundwater is only a few feet deep. But soil salts are 10 to 20 times more concentrated than found in areas of xerophytic saltbush scrub. In addition to one or more species of *Atriplex,* there are leaf succulent members of the same family (Chenopodiaceae) that are exceedingly salt tolerant. Playas at higher elevations (above 3,000 feet) often have greasewood *(Sarcobatus vermiculatus)* as a dominant shrub, while those at lower elevations have seepweed *(Suaeda moquinii)* and rusty molly *(Kochia californica)*. The most salt-tolerant chenopod is iodine bush *(Allenrolfea occidentalis),* a sprawling tangle of jointed, watery stems and woody scaffolding. The tangle often tops a soil mound, almost three feet tall and five feet in diameter, that forms as brine is wicked up by the root system to the soil surface and salt-laden dead shoots pile up beneath the canopy. Salinities in mound soil and groundwater range between three and six percent, which are near the upper limit of tolerance for higher plants. Encrusted mounds topped with live and dead shrubs dot the playa edge and often support salt-tolerant, perennial grasses. Thickets of desert saltgrass *(Distichlis spicata* subsp. *stricta)* arise from spreading rhizomes, while clumps of alkali sacaton *(Sporobolus airoides)* have buds clustered at the base of their stems. They frequently have roots in shallow lay-

Halophytic saltbush scrub dominated by greasewood and shadscale, as observed from 75 feet above the floor of Death Valley. (Author)

ers of wind-blown sand that collect in the lee of mounds. The sands are readily leached of salt by small amounts of rain, which provides the grasses some relief during the growing season.

These same grasses form an alkali meadow with more water than salt, but the soils are still fine grained and crusty. Flooding may be seasonal, reflecting the predominance of winter precipitation in the Mojave, but it is reliable because the meadow is in a low, flat basin fed by an upland watershed. Leaves and stems produce a deep green haze above the radiant, white ground surface. The canopy is supplemented by grasslike plants with erect, photosynthetic stems, such as rushes (for example, Baltic rush *[Juncus balticus]*), spikerushes (for example, *Eleocharis rostellata*), and sedges. Broad-leaved, herbaceous species are also common, and many have showy, insect-pollinated flowers. Wild iris *(Iris missouriensis)*, shooting star *(Dodecatheon pulchellum)*, Mojave thistle *(Cirsium mohavense)*, and alkali pink *(Nitrophila occidentalis)* provide a succession of pollen and nectar from May to October for the Alkali Bee *(Nomia melanderi)* and other burrowing pollinators. Finally, there is usually an assortment of shrubs invading from the adjacent halophytic scrub community that adds to already diverse flora. In the Owens Valley more than 60 plant species have been documented from alkali meadows, both common and rare. Almost all are perennials that propagate from rhizomes, indicating that seeds can germinate and establish only when the salty ground is sufficiently diluted by fresh, runoff waters.

Left   Alkali meadow in the Owens Valley, dominated by Baltic rush and alkali sacaton. Lavender blossoms are from the rare Owens Valley checkerbloom. (Larry Blakely)

Right   Owens Valley checkerbloom *(Sidalcea covillei)*, a relative of hibiscus. (Larry Blakely)

Surprisingly, other forms of biotic diversity are associated with the extreme soils of these salt-affected communities. The ecologist Charles Hunt collected a series of soil samples from 12 bajada-to-basin transects in Death Valley. The longest transects extended more than five miles, from creosote bush scrub down into xerophytic and halophytic saltbush communities, on through alkali meadow and out onto the barren saltpan left behind by Pleistocene Lake Manley. Samples were cultured in the laboratory under a wide variety of conditions to stimulate dormant spores and promote the growth of otherwise invisible organisms. Overall, 22 species of algae were tallied, including 18 blue-greens (some capable of nitrogen fixation) and four green algae, from salinities as high as eight percent (well beyond the six percent tolerated by higher plants). Even on the gravelly bajada, algae (for example, *Phormidium tenue, Chlorella vulgaris*) were found on the underside of translucent stones where dew accumulates after a cold night. These microgreenhouses are yet another source of primary productivity in the desert. More diverse were the soil fungi, with 48 species showing up under culture. Some species were common, others rare, and a few completely new to science. They lived in all communities along the transects and could extend out onto the playa where salinities ranged between 10 and 12 percent. Ecologically, these fungi decompose plant litter and soil humus (for example, *Botrytis carnea*), parasitize insects *(Beauveria densa)*, and form symbiotic relationships with the roots of higher plants. The latter are termed mycorrhizae, which are essential for the successful establishment growth of most desert plants. Hunt's study also found many unusual bacteria tolerant of salinities up to 15 percent, but these were not catalogued.

VARIATIONS IN RIPARIAN COMMUNITIES

Upper Riparian community dominated by Sonoran scrub oak at 5,700 feet in the New York Mountains. (Mark C. Hoshovsky)

Lower Riparian community dominated by black-stemmed rabbitbrush at 3,000 feet in the Dead Mountains. (David L. Magney)

Nothing about desert communities is simple to describe. A single type, such as "Mojave riparian," can have many variations across the landscape. Some variations are due to changes in species composition, others to the physical structure of the canopy(s). In turn, such variations affect how and which animals utilize available resources. Ecologists are only now developing sophisticated systems for classifying desert communities, those that recognize variations and reflect an understanding of the responsible environmental factors.

In the mountains of the eastern Mojave, for example, the composition and structure of riparian vegetation changes every few hundred yards along a single watercourse. Steep, narrow canyons cut into bedrock by relatively frequent stormwaters support the most riparian plant species and community types. With more available water, canyons contain forests and woodlands of pinyon pine, canyon oak, and Fremont cottonwood. Tall shrublands of desert baccharis *(Baccharis sergiloides)* and catclaw *(Acacia greggii)* are also present. If the bedrock is limestone, then desert sage *(Salvia dorrii)* and virgin brittlebush *(Encelia virginensis)* dominate the riparian scrub. As the same watercourse spills out of the canyon and cuts into the upper portions of an alluvial fan, several forms of arroyo riparian communities may be present. Arroyo riparian tends to be found on intermittently flooded gravels or bouldery materials. Here the communities tend to be dominated by tall shrubs such as desert willow *(Chilopsis linearis)* or desert almond *(Prunus fasciculata)*. Arroyo riparian grades into wash riparian on the lower, gentle portions of the same alluvial fan, as sandy and braided channels carry runoff into the terminal basin. Wash riparian is composed of low, widely spaced shrubs, such as cheesebush *(Hymenoclea salsola)*, black-stem rabbitbrush *(Chrysothamnus paniculatus)*, and smoke tree *(Psorothamnus spinosus)*, each of which can form a distinctive community type.

Expanded inventories of the microbiota from saltbush and meadow communities will add large numbers to the tally of species richness in the bioregion.

Freshwater Spring and Marsh

Freshwater springs that provide permanent and abundant water can harbor a wealth of drought-susceptible species in the desert bioregion. Native fishes (pupfishes *[Cyprinodon]*, poolfishes *[Empetrichythys]*, dace *[Rhinichthys]*, chubs *[Siphateles]*, and suckers *[Catostomus]*) are diverse and remarkably tolerant of fluctuations in temperature and salinity owing to their specialized physiology. But they are generalist feeders, able to take advantage of whatever is most abundant in any given season, whether plant or animal. During spring and summer, pupfishes graze on algae growing on submerged, well-lit surfaces. A pupfish rips up a mouthful, drops to the bottom, and swims in

Upper Ash Meadows Naucorid *(Ambrysys amargosus)*, a rare inhabitant of freshwater springs. It is about one quarter of an inch long and uses fanglike front legs to capture prey. (Shawn Goodchild)

Lower Springsnails *(Tryonia)* of Ash Meadows are less than one-sixteenth of an inch across. (D. W. Sada)

place to stir up a cloud of dislodged filaments and colonies (plowing). Turning around, it not only gobbles up the suspended salad, it also devours hapless, drifting insect larvae and crustaceans (for example, amphipods and ostracods) that once hid in the mat. Later in the year, after algal and animal production subside, the fish plows through decaying materials to harvest the rich coating of bacteria and aquatic fungi. When there is little else to eat in winter, a pupfish will take protein-rich snails despite their large, indigestible shells. For the Devils Hole Pupfish *(Cyprinodon diabolis)*, this entire food web is produced on a small shelf of limestone submerged at the mouth of an endless, underwater cavern. If the water level in the cavern drops just a couple of feet, the exposed shelf and its food will no longer be available to this ancient, precarious species.

Around the water's edge can be well-developed wetland vegetation, depending on the type of spring and its location in the landscape. At low, valley-bottom elevations in the Death Valley region, mineral springs with high salt content issue from mounds of ashy white deposits left behind by evaporation. Only tolerant plants, including iodine bush, desert saltgrass, and arrow weed *(Pluchea sericea)*, can use the available moisture, and they form a two-layered, open scrub blending into adjacent halo-

Point of Rocks Spring, Ash Meadows, receives its water from the Death Valley Aquifer. (Author)

phytic communities. However, moving upslope just beyond the basin floor can make a big difference in wetland vegetation. If springs flow through bajada or arroyo gravels instead of buried lakebeds, they contain much less salt. Woody, salt-sensitive phreatophytes, particularly honey mesquite *(Prosopis glandulosa* subsp. *torreyana)*, screwbean mesquite *(P. pubescens)*, and desert baccharis *(Baccharis sergiloides)* can then form a tall, often dense overstory above a mixture of other shrubs and meadow perennials. Dense thickets of cattail, tule *(Scirpus acutus* subsp. *occidentalis)*, and common reed *(Phragmites australis)* tolerate low oxygen levels in the permanently saturated soils and produce stable banks of coarse thatch and peat. Stable, vegetated banks appear to be essential for harboring certain invertebrates, including springsnails *(Pyrgulopsis carinifera, Tryonia clathrata)*, Moapa Riffle Beetles *(Stenelmis moapa)*, and naucorid beetles *(Ambrysus mormon, Pelocoris biimpressus)*. Large numbers of such invertebrates graze algae growing on the wet thatch or form a productive web of Lilliputian predators and prey among the reeds.

The marsh vegetation of Saratoga Springs is zoned, with cattail and tule near the water and saltgrass farther away. (D. W. Sada)

The spring-fed freshwater marsh, with its reliable water and food, can thus support drought-sensitive, terrestrial vertebrates that live in, or migrate through, the bioregion. Amphibians, such as the Black Toad *(Bufo exsul)*, Red-spotted Toad *(B. punctatus)*, and California Treefrog *(Hyla cadaverina)*, require water for their eggs, tadpoles, and porous skin. They consume invertebrate prey when air temperatures are moderated by nightfall, revealing their abundance by an almost deafening chorus of male calls during the summer mating season. Birds of all sorts are drawn to the springs. Waterfowl are attracted by tule and cattail seeds, shorebirds by bottom-dwelling invertebrates, herons by fish, and flycatchers by winged insects that emerge from aquatic larvae. The one square mile of marsh and open water at Saratoga Springs provides habitat for over 150 of the 332 bird species recorded from Death Valley National Park, an area of 5,200 square miles. Springs are, of course, also important watering holes for mammals. They will often be visited by Desert Bighorn if located near steep, rocky terrain and surrounded by open vegetation that is easily penetrated. Otherwise, the sheep can be so wary of hidden predators that they prefer other, distant water sources to meet their demands. The Coyote *(Canis latrans)* is the most abundant predator, and probably most successful when small groups (three

to seven) pursue ewes and lambs. But along the desert edge, Mountain Lions *(Puma concolor)* with their greater size and strength are better able to bring down mature sheep.

Permanent marshes were the habitat that supported the most native people throughout the desert bioregion. During the late Pleistocene and early Holocene, marshes were extensive and associated with vast lakes and riparian areas. Resources were abundant and reliable, and women foraged for seeds, rhizomes (especially those of cattail), eggs of waterfowl, and small animals, as each became available during the year. Men fished and hunted for animals attracted to the lake or seeking lowland shelter during harsh winter months. There was little reason to leave the basin for very long, except when harvesting pinyon nuts or pursuing migratory prey. But as the lakes, rivers, and marshes began their contractions during the mid-Holocene, the people shifted their activities to more reliable communities and less sedentary

A surprising number of amphibians dwell in the bioregion. Some are widespread species and others are endemics that are found only in isolated spring and riparian habitats. Clockwise from upper left: Black Toad, endemic to Deep Springs Valley; Inyo Slender Salamander *(Batrachoseps campi)*, endemic to the Panamint Mountains; and Red-spotted Toad, widespread in Mojave and Sonoran desert habitats with reliable water. (All photos by William C. Flaxington)

lifestyles. Small, ephemeral marshes were abandoned in favor of larger, spring- or river-fed marshes. Frequent moves to a wider variety of temporary homesites became necessary, and upland resources became relatively more important. But the reliance upon springs and marshes became more accentuated and precarious as the rigors of the Mojave became fully developed. Native people came to know every seep, every sign of hidden moisture as they traversed long distances in search of subsistence. This knowledge was given freely to gentle Friar Garcés and other respectful Europeans who entered the vast deserts without a clue.

Communities of the Sonoran Desert were least disturbed by the climatic fluctuations of the Pleistocene. It is true that pinyon-juniper woodlands, Joshua tree woodlands, and even California chaparral spread into central Arizona with a trend toward cool, wet winters and dry, warm summers. But at low elevations far to the south and east of the glaciated mountains, and closer to the influence of warmer, subtropical weather systems, there were refuges for desert communities. For example, below 1,100 feet along the lower Colorado River and surrounding the northern Sea of Cortez, creosote bush scrub persisted during the Pleistocene under hot, frost-free, summer-wet conditions. Lush riparian forests of Fremont cottonwood were home to boa constrictors and giant beavers, while desert grass-

Upper   Elephant tree is a tropical relict found in Anza-Borrego Desert State Park. Its Old World relatives include frankincense and myrrh. (Author)

Lower   Leaves and fruit. (Charles Webber)

lands and marshes supported camels, llamas, horses, and other remarkable animals. As arid conditions spread north during the Holocene, Sonoran communities expanded from the refugia, with extinction of the Pleistocene fauna but enrichment by frost-sensitive flora (for example, saguaro *[Carnegiea gigantea]*, blue palo verde *[Cercidium floridum]*, and desert ironwood *[Olneya tesota]*) that had been confined even further to the south. Some of these species made it into southeast California (for example, ocotillo *[Fouquieria splendens]*, elephant tree *[Bursera microphylla]* and palo verde into the Anza-Borrego region, saguaro to the Whipple Mountains), but the majority of the rich Sonoran flora and fauna was excluded by low or uncertain amounts of summer rainfall. Thus, the communities of California's Sonoran Desert are poorer in species and simpler in structure than those of Arizona and northern Mexico.

WOODLANDS

Arroyo Woodland

Phreatophytic trees use deep, woody roots to extract groundwater that has been gathered from uplands, transported by arroyos, and eventually stored in deep alluvium and basin sediments. Photosynthetic productivity is prolonged because stomata remain open and leaves are retained longer into the summer months. Consequently, a tall, sometimes dense overstory of smoke tree, desert willow, and blue palo verde follows the braided and stony watercourses that carve bajada surfaces. Often there's not much of an understory because small plants can be readily uprooted or buried by floods. Where arroyos have a low grade or flow into basins, thickets of arrow weed, chuparosa *(Justicia californica)*, and desert baccharis can raise total community cover above 20 percent.

The most widespread phreatophytic tree of the Sonoran Desert is honey mesquite. It may also be the most ecologically important in terms of supply-

Upper   Arroyo woodland in Anza-Borrego Desert State Park with blue palo verde (yellow flowers) and chuparosa (red flowers). (Aaron Schusteff)

Lower   Arroyo woodland dominated by smoke tree in the Marble Mountains. (James M. Andre)

ing resources to other creatures, including humans. Its deep
root system provides nodular homes for nitrogen-fixing bacteria, essential for maintaining primary productivity in many
southwestern desert ecosystems. The finest roots are colonized
by multiple species of mycorrhizal fungi, exchanging sugars and
other photosynthetic products for minerals gathered by the hy-
phae. Shed leaves, twigs, and fruits are so rich in nutrients that
soil fertility beneath the canopy is significantly elevated. With
age, the woody roots and stems capture mounds of wind-
blown sand that become riddled with burrows of native rodents.
Female Mesquite Borer beetles *(Megacyliene antennata)* lay eggs
beneath the bark into twig tips where the hatched larvae will
feed. Insectivorous birds are thus attracted to the canopy, including Black-tailed Gnatcatchers *(Polioptila melanura)* and
Verdins *(Auriparus flaviceps)*. From older branches protrude the
leafless stems of the parasitic desert mistletoe *(Phoradendron
californicum)*, whose red berries are the principle winter food
of the Phainopepla *(Phainopepla nitens)*. Wedged into forks,
drilled into trunks, hanging from branches, and even propped
behind shingles of bark are innumerable nests of many bird
species. Sweet-scented flowers attract more than 160 species
of solitary bees that collect the glowing, ultraviolet-reflecting
pollen. Male tarantula hawks (wasps of the genus *Pepsis*) stand
on the inflorescences, sustaining themselves with nectar while
females hunt for arachnid prey. The fruit pods (actually
legumes) harbor larvae of the Mesquite Beetle *(Bruchus deser-*

Upper Cahuilla people living and working in honey mesquite woodland near the Coachella Valley in the 1930s. (Stephen H. Willard)

Lower Bean-containing pods (legumes) of honey mesquite. (Robert Potts)

torum), which feed on the nutritious seeds (actually beans). In the Sonoran Desert, 29 species of insect granivores have been found burrowing within pods, of which 27 are specialists on mesquite. A great variety of mammals also ingest these hard-coated beans, including the Desert Pocket Mouse *(Chaetodipus penicillatus)*, Desert Bighorn, and Mule Deer. Along the Colorado River up to 90 percent of the Coyote's fall diet comes from mesquite pods. It appears that no other species of desert plant has as many associated and dependent animals as does mesquite.

Native desert people were also dependent on mesquite for subsistence. They lived among the dense arroyo woodlands, building houses, harvesting seeds, and burning fuels derived from these long-lived indicators of water. While scouting a rail-road route in 1853, Captain Blake traversed the ancient bed of Lake Cahuilla:

We passed several Indian trails, and about noon met an Indian family traveling in the opposite direction. The young men came

Storage basket for mesquite beans, often woven from arrow weed and willow, 1907. (Alfred Kroeber)

first, carrying bows and arrows and an old flint lock musketoon; an old Indian and squaw followed, bearing the burdens. They stopped with surprize [sic] as we came up, and unrolling some rags from a great yellow ball invited us to eat. This proved to be made of the pounded beans and pods of the mezquite [sic], which is an important article of food to them, but prepared in that way, and partly fermented, was not a very agreeable refreshment to us. . . . As we approached some of their villages, we passed several holes dug in the clay, two or three feet deep, that contained water, and were evidently springs that the Indians had enlarged. The largest and best of these springs were surrounded by extensive rancherias, or villages of huts, located in thick groves of mezquite trees, which were quite abundant, and grew so thickly together that the Indian huts were completely hid.

While surveying the same area in 1856, the botanist C. C. Parry observed how mesquite pods (and their inhabitants) were gathered and used:

A due mixture of animal and vegetable diet is also secured in the mesquite bean, the pods of which are largely occupied with a species of [bruchid beetle]. The whole pod and its contents are pounded into a fine powder, only the woody husk of the seed being rejected. The process of baking is equally primitive. A squaw takes, generally from her head, a cone-shaped basket of close texture; the meal, slightly sprinkled with water is packed in close layers into this hat or pot as the case may be; when full it is carefully smoothed off and then buried in the sand exposed to a hot sun. The baking process goes on for several hours, till the mass acquires the consistency of a soft brick, when it is turned out, and the hat resumes it proper position on the head. The solid cake so made . . . is sufficiently palatable, containing a gummy sugar which dissolves in the mouth and is unquestionably nutritious.

(Patencio 1943)

Subsequent chemical analysis confirmed Parry's assertion: the pods contain up to 31 percent sugar and 10 percent protein, nearly equal to cultivated barley and well exceeding the contents of acorns so important to nondesert tribes. Thus, the sun's energy captured by photosynthesis of the leaf mesophyll is stored as carbohydrate in the legumes. And, the fertility that originates with fixation by root nodule bacteria is stored as protein in the beans.

Such ecological blessings were recognized in a Cahuilla rite known as "feeding the house," a ceremonial meal of first beans that had to precede the fall harvest. Related families would then visit a particular, traditional grove, with each person gathering about 175 pounds in a long day. One acre of mesquite-dominated woodland reliably produced about 11 tons during the autumn month of *menukis-kwasva* ("ripening time of beans"). Summer rains were forestalled by shaman prayers until dry beans could be sealed into protective granaries woven of wickers of arrow weed and aromatic wormwood *(Artemisia)*. The shamans knew their beloved *ily* trees would, nevertheless, thrive without such rains because groundwater is what maintains phreatophytic woodlands.

Fan Palm Woodland

California fan palms *(Washingtonia filifera)* dominate their habitat by usurping the groundwater, maintaining high rates of photosynthesis and growth, and spreading their fronds wide and high. Thick trunks support a dense overstory above the oasis floor, while a variety of other plants contribute to an understory that reflects watercourse characteristics. If groundwater flows slowly but reliably from faulted bedrock, then a marsh thicket of tule or cattail develops among the trunks. Where runoff scours the canyon before sinking into deep gravels, mesquite, arroyo willow, black willow *(Salix gooddingii)*, cottonwood, velvet ash *(Fraxinus velutina)*, or even California sycamore *(Platanus racemosa)* form a tall riparian canopy. In the sunny ecotone between California fan palm groves and the surrounding desert, arroyo species (for example, arrow weed), alkali meadow species (for example, alkali sacaton, rushes), and saltbushes colonize soils impregnated with salts left behind by surface evaporation. But none of these species can displace fan palms from their enclaves as long as water remains abundant throughout the year.

Other characteristics of the California fan palm and its habitat help groves persist and thrive. An adult palm lives an average of 80 to 90 years, approaching 150 years where sheltered from flashfloods, tumbling boulders, and windstorms *(chubascos)*. A long life in a well-watered habitat allows hundreds of thousands, if not millions, of seeds to be left behind by each tree. Only Coyotes and humans are known to eat the seeds, and the most voracious palm herbivores became extinct after the Pleistocene (for example, camels, sloths, and mammoths). Chewing and sucking insects still take a toll but are kept under control by ground fires that occasionally sweep through the oasis. Adult palms are capable of surviving a fire because sensitive vascular tissues are scattered throughout the damp, massive trunk, rather than localized beneath the outermost bark. Dead fronds, hanging like a thick hula skirt, burn cool and slow if ignited and deflect the intense heat generated by rapid incineration of the understory. Only one in a hundred palms dies in a typical fire, while charred survivors sprout a leafy canopy within weeks. With competitors reduced to ashes, fan palms claim a larger share of the available water and light. The soft, mineralized soil promotes germination, especially if seeds had been eaten and defecated by Coyotes. Digestive acids break down the seed coat while in transit, allowing rapid absorption of water when in contact with wet soil. Recent surveys have confirmed that fan palms are expanding their range, with new groves reported in the Salton Basin, Anza-Borrego, and Death Valley.

Indians also spread the seeds of fan palms and actively managed the groves. The Cahuilla ethnographer Francisco Patencio recorded:

Aerial view of fan palm woodland near Palm Springs, with deciduous Fremont cottonwoods. (Charles Webber)

Now the people were settled all about the country in many places, but they all came to the Indian Well to eat of the fruit of the palm tree. The meat of the fruit was not large, but it was sweet like honey, and was enjoyed by everybody—animals and birds too. The people carried seeds to their homes, and palm trees grew from this seed in many places.

Larger oases, such as Thousand Palms and Andreas Canyon, hosted permanent villages with ample water, game animals, and useful plants. Houses woven from fronds were nestled in the shade, and dried fibers were used to make fire. Clusters of fruit were collected in fall using long poles of willow, with each tree producing up to 200 pounds of datelike flesh. But the size and reliability of the harvest depended on what other organisms were competing with the people. Patencio found:

It was the medicine men who burned the palm trees so that they could get good fruit. The bugs that hatched in the top of the palm trees they made the fruit sick, and no fruit came. After the trees were set afire and burned, the bugs were killed and the trees gave good fruit. Now that the medicine men are gone, the worms are taking the flower, the green fruit, and the ripe fruit.

Fan palm trunk riddled with the galleries of the Giant Palm Borer. (Author)

Among the insect competitors ("pests") that affect California fan palms are red spider mites, date scale, and the largest bostrychid beetle in the world, the Giant Palm Borer *(Dinapate wrightii)*. The borer's two-inch larvae spend up to six years prior to metamorphosis eating through and hollowing out the trunk. Adults are equally voracious, reducing the palm's infrastructure to powder. Such trees are more likely to be toppled by fire, flood, and wind. After extensive study, the U.S. Department of Agriculture rediscovered that periodic, low-intensity burns were the most effective means for controlling populations of these insects.

SCRUB

Arborescent Creosote Bush Scrub

Although dominance by creosote bush is a shared feature between the Mojave and Sonoran deserts, there are also many ecological distinctions. Winter storms that bring snow to the Antelope Valley drop only a cold rain at Indio. Summer thermals that stir up dust devils across Death Valley bring thunderheads and warm rain to Yuma. Crossing the transition zone from north to south (roughly defined by U.S. Interstate 10), summer and winter temperatures increase, winter frosts become rare, and total rainfall decreases and becomes more variable but the proportion falling in summer increases. This climatic extremism is accentuated at the lowest elevations in the Salton Basin and moderated from west to east as more humid conditions prevail toward Tucson. In response, other plants join the tetraploid (rather than hexaploid) race of creosote bush in Sonoran vegetation, many with distributions centered in Mexico. These species are often frost-susceptible, drought-deciduous, or succulent perennials that grow as small, upswept trees with bizarre patterns of branching and growth. California's version of this "arborescent creosote bush scrub" is a patchy mixture of sensitive species at the northern limits of the dry subtropics.

The structure of this community is similar to that of creosote bush scrub in the Mo-

Arborescent creosote bush scrub of the Sonoran Desert. (Author)

Desert ironwood often exceeds 30 feet in height and is the tallest tree in the Sonoran Desert. (Charles Webber)

jave Desert. Creosote bush is still dominant in the three- to six-foot-tall overstory, with scattered burrobush and brittlebush forming a lower, sparse understory where the shrubs gather their skirts of annuals around their bases. On rocky bajadas above the lowest basins these two species are joined by a long list of other shrubs that are most characteristic of northern Mexico and Arizona. These include bladderpod *(Isomeris arborea)* and California buckwheat *(Eriogonum fasciculatum)* bordering upslope chaparral, while jojoba *(Simmondsia chinensis)*, catclaw, and desert-lavender *(Hyptis emoryi)* are more typically desert plants. Cacti can be more diverse and abundant than in the Mojave, with a wider variety of growth forms. Sandy soils support a different assemblage rich in C_4 shrubs (for example, California croton *[Croton californicus]*) and grasses (for example, big galleta grass) that can also begin succession where flashfloods, wind storms, or human activities create a searing, unvegetated pavement. But protruding above all canopy layers are the characteristic, arborescent species of this desert. Ocotillo thrusts its spiny, coachwhip stems up to 30 feet above the ground. During spring its bright clusters of red, tubular flowers attract migrating hummingbirds that rely upon the rich nectar for a reliable food source. On thin soils with little water-holding capacity, individuals grow slowly and live for 100 to 200 years. Palo verde can reach 25 feet in height with its blue green photosynthetic stems. Like ocotillo, it is drought-deciduous but in the driest areas may be restricted to arroyos with coarse soils that collect and store runoff. Unlike ocotillo, it grows fast, dies young, and attracts a diverse array of bees (bumble *[Bombus]*, sweat [Halictidae], leaf-cutter [Megachilidae], and carpenter *[Xylocarpa]*) that gather pollen for nest-bound larvae. Desert ironwood grows very slowly to 35 feet, building a trunk so dense that it sinks in water. Consequently, individual trees probably exceed 200 years of age and remain standing for 1,000 years after death. Despite these remarkable feats of growth and longevity, all three are sensitive to frost and thereby excluded not only from the Mojave Desert, but also from Sonoran Desert basins that receive cold-air drainage from adjacent uplands.

Anna's Hummingbird *(Calypte anna)* visits ocotillo to obtain nectar and inadvertently carries large pollen loads between flowers. The yellow grains are visible on the face. (Ron Niebrugge)

Sensitive species near the limits of their distribution can be subjected to unpredictable, often catastrophic climatic events. Such events kill large numbers of individuals, reducing the spread and vigor of populations and confining the distribution of an entire community type. A southward shift in the position of the jet stream has brought the Mojave's freezing temperatures into the Sonoran Desert at least six times in the twentieth century (1913, 1937, 1949, 1962, 1971, and 1978). When air temperatures ranged from 10 to 21°F for a minimum of 18 consecutive hours, damage to Sonoran species was widely reported. Juvenile saguaros, barrel cacti, elephant trees, desert ironwoods, and palo verde were killed by the tens of thousands on each occasion, especially at their upper and northern distributional limits.

Interestingly, these same species are not catastrophically affected by prolonged drought and high temperatures. Compared to severe cold, these conditions are geologically ancient and widespread, allowing the slow, progressive evolution of physiological and structural tolerance mechanisms. The mechanisms permit perennial plants to capture sparse, unpredictable rainfall (for example, through drought-deciduous leaves and rapid root production), withstand dehydration (by solute adjustment and cell wall reinforcement), and prevent heat stress (through spine shading and stem-rib radiators).

A giant saguaro emerges from the shelter of its nurse plant. (Author)

Yet, such mechanisms meet their limitations in the most extreme portions of the Sonoran Desert. A barren slope of newly deposited alluvial gravels may remain essentially unvegetated for decades or centuries despite constant invasion by the bouncing fruits of creosote bush. Other, short-lived species dominate the early stages of succession before the long-lived, stress-tolerant perennials can gain a roothold. Such species provide certain, essential conditions that facilitate the establishment of others and lead to a patchy pattern of community development. For example, a low-growing canopy of burrobush is most often a prerequisite for the germination and growth of creosote bushes because it captures the moving fruits and provides a shady, enriched soil for young, vulnerable seedlings. Eventually, the two plants compete, and only the more stress tolerant, long-lived creosote bush will persist in that once-shared space. But the now large canopy of creosote bush can then serve as nursery for seedlings of palo verde and saguaro that join this unique vegetation in the Whipple Mountains. Desert ironwood is known to serve as nurse to 165 plant species in the lower Colorado River valley and is absolutely required by some to get established. Dependency on such a nurse plant may be a common phenomenon among arborescent species of the Sonoran Desert, and a fascinating demonstration of how diversity begets diversity in biological communities.

The processes of facilitation and competition in arborescent creosote bush scrub create patterns of plant distribution over the landscape. Patchiness would clearly result from the initial clumping of nurse plants and their young dependents. Bare zones that separate these patches are evidence that facilitation is required to provide a new, open alluvial surface with its own covering of desert vegetation. But the clumping pattern between associated species begins to disappear when competition takes its toll. As the dependents grow up, they erect light-grabbing canopies that reduce the photosynthetic gain of the nurses. As the dependents grow out and down, their root systems spread into the bare zones and throughout soil layers to usurp the available moisture. New, regularly spaced patches emerge as if greedy root systems of different shrubs hold each other at bay. The distances between individual creosote bushes increase with increasing canopy size, and as precipitation becomes sparser or less reliable. Both are indirect indicators that competition for water is a major determinant of how spatial patterns develop within the community. Direct indicators, such as the canopy removal experiments discussed previously, show that competition is initially very strong when it is between two different species (for example, burrobush and creosote bush), but becomes less intense once a single species, regularly spaced, comes to dominate.

The diversity of plant species found in arborescent creosote bush scrub can, therefore, be maintained over long periods of time only as a mosaic of patches at different stages of community development. Open, bare patches initially provide habitat for small annuals and short-lived perennials. Patches of short-lived species provide habitat for long-lived shrubs. Patches of long-lived shrubs provide habitat for the strange, arborescent species typical of this desert (for example, palo verde, desert ironwood, ocotillo, and the cacti). And finally, as competition thins the rich, mature patches, some come to support a single, dominant species while others revert to barrens as old plants eventually die.

Cactus Scrub

Cacti are prominent throughout the California desert bioregion. In pinyon-juniper woodlands of the Great Basin, old man cactus is most frequently encountered, with its flat stems and long, grayish spines. Creosote bush scrub and Joshua tree woodland of the Mojave

Cactus scrub dominated by teddy-bear cholla. The cholla propagates clonally as stems hitch a ride on hide, shoes, and other moving objects. (Author)

Desert are commonly interspersed with beavertail and California barrel *(Ferocactus cylindraceus)* cacti, the former lacking spines and the latter so densely armored that the stem can hardly be seen. But in the Sonoran Desert, the number of species and their ability to dominate a community are unsurpassed.

Usually imbedded in a matrix of creosote bush scrub, nearly pure and dense stands of teddy-bear cholla form on south-facing slopes with permeable soils. Warmer temperatures and higher rates of water infiltration (due to sand or uncemented gravels) would maximize the CAM advantage of stem-succulent species, especially where summer rain is infrequent. This particular species has a vertical trunk up to five feet tall that branches profusely. The branches, or "joints," are covered by a golden armor of barbed spines. If gently brushed by a passing animal, the easily detached joints appear to "jump" into the fur or cloth (hence the other common name "jumping cholla") for a long ride. After dislodging and falling to the ground, each joint can root and grow into a new clone. This species has lost the ability to reproduce sexually by making seeds, in part because many individuals appear to possess three, rather than two, sets of chromosomes. The extra set of chromosomes prevents normal sorting of genes during the formation of sex cells (such as those contained in pollen). Consequently, the entire hillside stand of teddy-bear cholla is likely to have originated from a single genetic individual.

In other stands of cactus scrub, dominance is shared by a host of species with large and small stature. The saguaro creates an intermittent canopy up to 30 feet tall on bajadas of the Whipple Mountains (eastern San Bernardino County). It can tower above other members of arborescent creosote bush scrub, including ocotillo, foothill palo verde *(Cercidium microphyllum)* and desert-lavender. But another, lower layer of diverse stem succulents is usually present, including pencil cactus *(Opuntia ramosissima)*, buckhorn cholla *(O. acanthocarpa)*, barrel cactus *(Echinocactus polycephalus)*, California barrel cactus, hedgehog cactus, and pincushion cactus *(Mammillaria)*. These cacti are often joined by the leaf-succulent agave *(Agave deserti)* throughout the Sonoran, but especially on rocky, well-drained slopes. This rich, arborescent cactus scrub is an outpost of the Arizona Sonoran Desert, confined to small, scattered stands in mountains just west of the Colorado River.

The Algodones Dunes are extensive accumulations of sand from the Colorado River. (Author)

Sand Dune Scrub

The desert's dunes originated in ancient, watery basins and floodplains. Sand particles of all sizes were carried from eroding uplands to form lakebeds, beaches, and berms during the Pleistocene. Succession led to vast tracts of shoreline vegetation, especially during periods with wetter, cooler climates. But regular flooding and ongoing deposition kept these sediments open and exposed to the wind. As Holocene aridity developed, the sands began to move en masse, lofted through canyons and into dead-end valleys. Sheets and patches moved like amoebae, coalescing, dividing, and flowing over the landscape. Dunes began to accumulate where air currents and topography conspired; winds were slowed by hillocks and outcrops, dropping their suspended loads one grain at a time. The fluvial sands of the ice age were thus transformed into the aeolian sands of today, moving over great distances and carrying the seeds, cysts, and eggs of a specialized biota.

Algodones Dunes are the most extensive in California, covering more than 230 square miles between the Colorado River delta and the Salton Basin. The river was the ultimate source of sand as it roared into the Gulf of California or intermittently spilled into ancient

(text continues on page 248)

THE SAND FOOD COMMUNITY

Life on a desert dune has intricate cross-linkages, like strands of a spider's web. Over evolutionary time the relationships among sand-loving plants and animals become silk strong and extensive, despite a barren, windswept appearance to the habitat. This is especially true on an old, large dune that, by its proximity to an ancient and reliable source of sand, could accumulate and support desert species as ice age conditions swirled across the landscape. Con-

Sand food, a flowering parasite limited to a few dunes in the Sonoran Desert. (R. Mitchel Beauchamp)

sider the example of sand food *(Pholisma sonorae)*, a plant endemic to dunes of the lower Colorado River. Descended from a family of subtropical parasites, the species is at the center of a rich assemblage of host plants, pollinating insects, seed predators, and herbivores.

On the Algodones Dunes, sand food parasitizes at least six species of host plants, including another rare and endemic plant, dune buckwheat. Its minute seeds, buried or carried deep beneath the sand surface, germinate in response to winter rains and the presence of chemicals released by the host's rhizosphere. The parasite root then grows toward the host root, fuses with it, and extracts water, minerals, and carbohydrates at an astonishing rate. Proliferating within the sand, the leafless, succulent stems can develop a hundred branches and eventually outweigh the entire host by 20 or 30 times. Mushroom-shaped stalks emerge from the dune surface in spring, each producing a multitude of tubular, purple flowers. The flowers open in a slow, spiral pattern, from center to edge of the stalk, offering a banquet of nectar and pollen over the next two months.

Insect pollinators are the principle guests at the banquet. In a single spring, in one location, 11 species of native butterflies, wasps, and flies have been collected from the flowers of sand food. Examination of captured specimens revealed that small-bodied sand flies (such as *Leptoconops californiensis*) had the greatest allegiance to (and dependence on) sand food pollen; perhaps because they were less capable of flying between widely spaced canopies of other plant species. Most hovered within three feet of the sand food, never venturing across the open dune. Each body carried relatively few grains (two to 50), which were probably redistributed among flowers of a single cluster. Adults must also feed on the blood of passing lizards before burrowing to lay eggs. More effective at moving pollen of sand food was the large-bodied Bembix Wasp *(Bembix rugosa)*. Its long, stout mouthparts hold up to 700

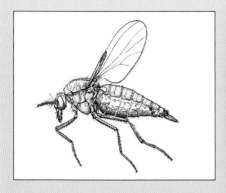

Sand fly *(Leptoconops),* a biting fly ("no-see-um") commonly associated with sand food plants on the Algodones Dunes. (Unknown artist, CSIRO)

The Bembix Wasp, a native that moves large quantities of sand food pollen over long distances. (Author)

pollen grains, including those of other species, gathered from long flights across the dune. Adult wasps must also capture flies to continually feed their ravenous, underground larvae. It is not yet known if seed production by sand food is promoted more by distant pollen (genetically distinct and carried by wasps) than local pollen (genetically similar, carried by sand flies), as it is in other rare plants.

Sand food also provides resources for seed predators and herbivores. Harvester ants are often found within the withering flowers, sometimes collecting seeds and sometimes tending mealybugs that tap into and exude the plant's sugary sap. Succulent stems and flower stalks are gnawed by jackrabbits, as much for precious water as nutrition when spring turns to summer. Such water, gathered from deep, moist sands by the host plant and stored by the parasite, would otherwise be unavailable to thirsty animals. Humans also valued the stems, which were eagerly gathered by the Cahuilla, Yuma, and Cocopa people. A Papago guide introduced Colonel Andrew Gray of the 1854 Railroad Expedition to roasted *biatatk* ("sand" plus "root"), which was described as "luscious, resembling the sweet potato in taste, only more delicate" (Ebeling 1986).

But there is a limit to the tensile strength of any web, and the biological community surrounding sand food has been torn apart across much of its original range. Flooding of the Cahuilla Basin destroyed the dune systems that supported these species in the north. To the south, agricultural development on sandy soils has been equally effective. And in between, especially on portions of the Algodones Dunes open for off-highway vehicles, host plants, burrowing pollinators, and herbivores have been obliterated by the crush and spin of wheels. It now takes the isolation of wilderness to ensure that modern life does not sweep away the flagging remnants.

Upper left Flat-tailed Horned Lizard *(Phrynosoma mcallii)*, another endemic to dunes built from Colorado River sands. (Wade C. Sherbrooke)

Lower left Colorado Fringe-toed Lizard can "swim" across a surface of unconsolidated sand. (William C. Flaxington)

Right Algodones Dune sunflower, a woody species endemic to the dune system. (Author)

Lake Cahuilla. The sheer volume of sand in this regional complex, perhaps as much as 11 billion cubic yards, forms longitudinal ridges and peaks rising up to 300 feet above the surrounding bajada. Most topographic features of the dune mass now only fluctuate in position, as winds shift direction between seasons. But giant crescents (barchans) still cross the creosote bush flats of the Imperial Valley at rates of 20 to 60 feet per year until they fuse with the dune mass, are recaptured by running waters, or are carted off from fields and roads.

Dunes that have not been disturbed by human activity have a sparse but unique vegetation dominated by sand-restricted plants (psammophytes). These species seldom venture onto stony bajadas or clayey playas. They take advantage of, and may in fact require, water stored in deep, permeable sands, while tolerating abrasion, burial, and deflation (having the ground blown away from the root system). Roughly half of these species are annuals, which can hide in the seed bank or tumble along with the moving dune surface. Most are low growing or have hardened tissues that resist blasting by high-velocity grains. Stems and flowering stalks have the ability to rapidly elongate and emerge above mounding sands. Main roots have high tensile strength and remain as functional conduits even if shoots spin wildly in the wind when dislodged. Typical psammophytes on Sonoran dunes include sand verbena *(Abronia villosa)*, bugseed *(Dicoria canescens)*, panic grass *(Panicum urvilleanum)*, and coldenia *(Tiquilia plicata)*. Slow-growing shrubs and cacti, typical of the surrounding bajada (for example, creosote bush and silver cholla), are excluded from unstable dune surfaces.

Old dune systems also support endemic and unusual species that form endemic and unusual communities. At least five plants are known only from the Algodones Dunes, perhaps relicts of the Colorado River delta. These include dune buckwheat *(Eriogonum deserticola)* and Wiggin's croton *(Croton wigginsii)*, both shrubs, and the herbaceous Algodones dune sunflower *(Helianthus niveus* subsp. *tephrodes)*, Peirson's milkvetch *(Astragalus magdalenae* var. *peirsonii)*, and Spanish needle *(Palafoxia arida* subsp. *gigantea)*. When protected from off-highway vehicles, these species form a psammophytic vegetation that supports a food web of specialized insects and reptiles. For example, milkvetch roots are the primary food source for larvae of the dune weevil *(Miloderes)*. The larvae are immune to chemical toxins that give these plants their other common name—locoweeds. Mammals in particular are sensitive to these grazing deterrents, becoming "loco" as alkaloids irreversibly damage the nervous system. However, the weevils feed with impunity beneath the sand until metamorphosis and emergence as adults. Adults tractor across the dune in search of mates and milkvetches to produce the next generation of eggs. Larvae and adults are prey for the Western Shovelnose Snake *(Chionactis occipitalis)* and Colorado Fringe-toed Lizard *(Uma notata)*. The snake is able to "swim" through the upper sand layers by virtue of its streamlined head and smooth body scales. The lizard is able to "hydroplane" on the dune surface with flattened scales on elongated rear toes. Both are swift predators that escape predation and high midday temperatures by diving down into the aeolian sand pool.

The Future of This Arid Bioregion

The California desert bioregion is fragile, despite its diversity and long history of incessant change. Hard-won resources cannot be lost or used extravagantly without consequence. A patch of clay soil formed during the Pleistocene is forever lost after its shield of pavement has been scraped away. The branch broken beneath a wheel contains carbon and nitrogen that would otherwise make seeds. Water diverted from a spring cannot provide habitat for algae, mollusks, dragonfly larvae, or pupfishes. A tortoise taken as a pet will not contribute genes to the next generation. Such small forms of squander have enormous, cumulative impacts when perpetrated in the modern world. Weeds invade, populations fade, ancient species fluctuate into oblivion, and entire communities are irreversibly degraded. All forms and linkages of desert life, even when shaped by extreme conditions, become easily frayed when stresses are novel or too suddenly applied.

How can the California deserts be conserved and ultimately restored? Scientific knowledge of biological diversity and ecological processes is essential, but insufficient. There must also be an honest assessment of how we, an imperfect but well-meaning species, threaten resources and compromise the future of an arid bioregion. Once the threats are known, science can be used to develop remedies that diminish the threats and heal the wounds we inflict. Ultimately, the future of this arid bioregion will depend on how discovery and rediscovery can be woven together, to restore mindful humans to a diverse, self-sustaining desert.

A lush resort with lawns and fountains, Palm Desert. (Cherie Northon)

Until the Garcés *entrada,* change came slowly to the California desert bioregion. Dramatic shifts in climate, from cold and wet to hot and dry, took place over hundreds, if not thousands, of years. This was also true for the extinction of the Pleistocene fauna, even if aided by a burgeoning population of native people. The replacement of pinyon-juniper woodland with creosote bush scrub was gradual, constrained by rates of seed dispersal and the short distances that individual ants, lizards, and rodents migrate. Generations were exposed to new, more extreme conditions, allowing some genes to leave behind more copies and some populations to flourish — to adapt and, therefore, to evolve. Even the final disappearance of ancient Lake Cahuilla took at least 60 years, slow enough to allow generations of fishermen to become obligate hunters — to adjust and, therefore, to persist.

Rapid change, on the order of years, rather than centuries, truncates the possibility of adaptation, adjustment, and persistence in nonhuman organisms. More often, it leads to small, unstable populations with a high probability of extinction. This is especially the case when the agent of change is novel, with no previous history in desert lands. For millennia, such agents were kept at bay by isolation, with oceans, mountain ranges, and continental distances impeding their progress. But with the *entrada* and all subsequent incursions, footpaths became highways, railways, and lines of flight. Species from elsewhere, including *Homo sapiens,* could arrive, establish themselves, and begin altering the landscape at unprecedented rates. Those new species also required the intensive use of limited resources, including water, soil, land, and other organisms to achieve their own population growth and persistence. Such resources become depleted, especially if they were also in short supply, with little possibility of replenishment under the modern tempo.

Understanding current threats to the diversity and integrity of the California desert bioregion can begin, therefore, by examining effects of losing isolation from the outside world, and the depletion of essential or rare resources that define life in these arid lands.

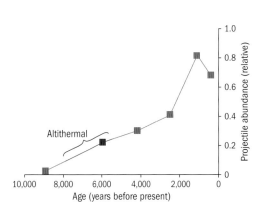

The growth of Indian populations in the Great Basin has been inferred from the relative abundance of projectile points found at archeological sites. Low growth is observed during the arid Altithermal and was highest prior to European contact. (Redrawn from Madsen 2002)

LOSS OF ISOLATION

Human Incursion: Rapid and Irreversible

No species brings change to a landscape like *Homo sapiens.* We live long, we have considerable resource needs, and we have a brain that can invent new ways to alter the environment in our favor. Technological thinking can compensate for the long time required to create, raise, and fledge offspring so that population growth rates are maximized under existing conditions. The more people, the more resource consumption and environmental alteration—which was as true for aboriginal Indians as it is for contemporary desert people.

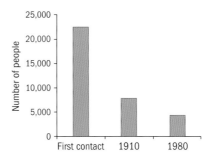

The decimation of Indian populations in the California deserts by disease, cultural disruption, and conflict after European contact. (Data from Kroeber 1925 and Leland 1986)

Arriving at the end of the Pleistocene, a relatively small number of aboriginal founders took advantage of the abundant game and wild plant foods supplied by moist, cool, predesert ecosystems. Population growth rates, estimated from counts of projectile points, achieved a maximum of three percent per decade during this early, favorable period. After desert conditions developed and the megafauna went extinct, growth rates declined to .8 to 1.6 percent per decade. In response the people built jackrabbit traps and fish traps, developed irrigation systems, and planted indigenous crops in highly managed "fields." By the time of first contact with Europeans (between 1770 and 1850, depending on cultural group), an estimated 21,000 to 24,000 Indians were living in the Great Basin, Mojave, and Sonoran deserts of California. They were scattered in family clusters (10 to 50 people) or among villages (several hundred people each) across vast desert territories, rarely gathering into throngs of one or two thousand (such as that which greeted Garcés along the Colorado). Etched into the bajada pavement were footpaths, no wider than a sandal, which connected villages, mesquite groves, favorite stands of pinyon pine, and reliable springs. Exchange with the world beyond brought seashells, corn, and pottery, but there is no evidence that imported materials caused detrimental or permanent change to the biota of the arid land.

Europeans opened the floodgates of change, forever connecting the California desert bioregion with the rest of the world. A trickle of explorers turned into a torrent of immigrants, bringing with them the agents of rapid and irreversible change. Disease organisms spread rapidly among native people who once had isolation as their only immunity. A single smallpox epidemic in 1863 reduced the Cahuilla population from 3,238 to 1,181 over a two-year period. Horses and iron weaponry enforced religious subjugation and colonization. The Serrano, Vanyume, and Kitanemuk were assimilated into missions by 1834 and extirpated within a few decades. All others had been moved onto reservations before 1880, including the Mojave, who dwindled to 1,050 souls by 1910. Lumber and hardware could then be imported to newly vacated tracts and fashioned into permanent settlements or boom-and-bust industries. Only a century after Garcés, the desert had been fully prepared for inundation by the modern world.

In that modern world, 40 times more people occupy the bioregion than at the time of first contact. The 2000 census found over 1.2 million residents from Bodie to the Mexi-

Subdivisions protrude into the rapidly growing Coachella Valley near Palm Springs, 1988. (Paul F. Starrs)

can border, gathered into nearly 100 towns and cities beneath the great rain shadow. More than 366,000 dwellings cover a total of 1,513 square miles of developed land. The two largest cities, Lancaster and Palmdale, share 235,000 people as they spread and merge across 200 square miles of the Antelope Valley. Equally impressive, and more prophetic, are the rates of growth achieved in recent decades. During the period between 1980 and 1990, the average human population increase in the bioregion was 110 percent, with some cities achieving 200 to 600 percent (Cathedral City, Lancaster, Palmdale, and Hesperia). The average growth rate dropped to 42 percent between 1990 and 2000, but some cities sustained twice that level (for example, Imperial City). In general, human population growth in the deserts has been two to three times greater than in Southern California as a whole during the last two decades. By the year 2020 the total number of people in the bioregion will exceed 3.1 million.

Growth along the edges of the bioregion is also rampant, and expected to accelerate. Of the nation's 20 fastest-growing counties, Maricopa, San Bernardino, San Diego, and Riverside are numbers 4, 8, 9, and 13, respectively. By 2025, another 1,161 square miles of open space will be developed in these four Arizona and California counties alone. Clark County (Nevada) and Los Angeles County will consume another 294 square miles, effectively bracketing the Mojave Desert on its eastern and western borders. By 2030 the total number of people in Southern California as a whole will exceed 26 million, a 34 percent increase compared to 2005.

There are many other human uses for the desert besides habitation, each having unique impacts on the land and its biota. Vehicle tracks and staging areas made by General Patton's forces during World War II are still visible because of soil erosion, surface scarring, and vegetation removal. Even after 40 years, the single passage of a medium-weight M3 tank was enough to increase soil compaction by 50 percent compared to untracked soil. This effect could be measured more than two feet away from and one foot below the track, significantly reducing water penetration and increasing runoff and erosion. Nine major military installations now cover 2.5 million acres of the Mojave Desert and 660 thousand acres of the Sonoran Desert in California. Modern exercises dwarf those of Patton's in scope and duration, involving thousands of soldiers, fleets of armored vehicles, coordinated air strikes,

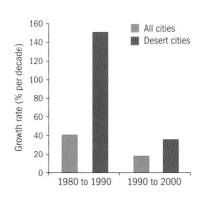

Growth rate of desert cities (red bars) compared to nondesert cities in Southern California. (Data from South California Association of Governments 2005)

and tons of explosives to simulate combat conditions in the world's deserts. It's no surprise, therefore, that training areas at Fort Irwin (580,000 acres in the central Mojave) have fewer Desert Tortoises (*Gopherus agassizii*) than adjacent nontraining areas, with death rates between 1.9 and five percent per year. The base supports the largest known population (87 plants) of Lane Mountain milkvetch (*Astragalus jaegerianus*), which prefers to grow on the tops of rolling hills that make excellent vantage points for maneuvering tanks. Although environmental concerns on bases have been secondary, Army Regulation AR 200-2 requires that long-term impacts of military training on natural resources be reduced or avoided. Recent efforts have attempted to better plan, manage, and recover the unique resources of these vast, de facto reserves.

Sherman tanks delivered to Camp Coxcomb, near Freda (Rice Valley), to prepare for General Patton's invasion of North Africa. These maneuvers involved over a million soldiers between 1942 and 1944 on over 18,000 square miles of desert in California, Nevada, and Arizona. (Unknown photographer, U.S. National Archives)

Agriculture has been a major use of California desert land since ranches were established in the Owens Valley during the 1860s, orchards in the Antelope Valley during the 1890s, and farms in the Imperial Valley during the 1900s. Operations were initially confined to naturally watered meadows and floodplains, but the invention of gasoline engines and well-pumping technologies opened hundreds of thousands of acres to development. Currently, 65,000 acres are under irrigation in the Great Basin and Mojave deserts, which will probably decrease to 45,000 acres by 2020 with urbanization (around Palmdale-Lancaster, Victorville, and Apple Valley). About 75 percent of these lands supply alfalfa and pasture, while another 12 percent grow carrots and onions. Farther south, about 750,000 acres are now under irrigation in the Imperial, Palo Verde, and Coachella valleys, an area that will probably not change much in the near future. Plentiful water from the Colorado River allows C_3 vegetable and melon crops to flourish during the winter and spring. The value of all agricultural commodities in this area exceeds $1.5 billion per year, including citrus, dates, table grapes, Sudan grass, cotton, and cattle. This remarkable productivity supports the expansion of virtually all cities in the American West and is made possible by a transportation system for rapid export. That system has had its own impacts on the bioregion by fragmenting the landscape and promoting the importation of outside agents of detrimental change.

Fragmentation: New Corridors and New Barriers

The wholeness of a pristine landscape is soon lost as roads and highways replace trails. The trail followed by Garcés was more than 200 miles long but less than a foot wide. It could be crossed by any organism regardless of size or stride and was not, therefore, a barrier to dispersal or a death zone to be avoided. Seeds could tumble, beetles amble, lizards

New agricultural fields along the Coachella Canal. (Cherie Northon)

scuttle, and bighorn sheep step across the path on route to nearby patches or distant mountains. In this sense, all places and all resources were virtually connected, and movement of the biota was unobstructed over seasons, years, and millennia. But the trail had become a road by the time Frémont passed, churned and widened by caravans of horses, mules, and wagons. Tollhouses and river crossings were established along the route between Cajon Pass and Barstow by 1863, providing money for additional construction and maintenance. Settlers could then move rapidly along the developing thoroughfare, which simultaneously brought an entourage of nonnative organisms into the bioregion. The road also brought people and desert animals into frequent, often lethal contact. Pronghorn *(Antilocapra americana)* were eventually hunted out, and Desert Bighorn *(Ovis canadensis nelsoni)* cautiously receded into the most isolated ranges. Nevertheless, disruption of the desert was localized, and the old Mojave Road functioned as a corridor for invasion rather than a barrier to mobility.

When such primitive roads were transformed into stagelines, highways, and interstates, the related impacts became much more complex and pervasive. Gradually widening from eight feet to 24 feet to over 100 feet, the ground disturbance required per mile of right-of-way increases from one to three to 12 acres, respectively. This enlarging imprint eventually included multiple lanes, shoulders, median strips, and drainage ditches running to the horizon. And the desert's roads lengthened as they modernized, coalescing into an extensive network that now bisects every valley and mountain range. A conservative inventory found more than 15,000 miles of paved and maintained roads, 21,000 miles of dirt roads, and 7,000 miles of vehicle-accessible washes traversing a desert that is at most 230 miles wide and 430 miles long. Approximately 95 percent of the bioregion is within three miles of a road, so that wilderness areas have become small and insular. Add more than 500 miles of gas pipelines, 1,200 miles of rail, and 3,500 miles of power transmission lines to complete the fragmentation of a once vast, whole, and remote land. The responses of the desert biota to fragmentation are peculiar to each species. Fragmentation creates a corridor for the spread of nonnatives as ancient soil surfaces are scraped, broken, and compacted during construction. The corridor ends isolation between the desert and the outside world as exotic plants and animals arrive and thrive in the new, disturbed habitats (see below). At the same time, fragmentation creates barriers for natives that once moved across an uninterrupted landscape. The seeds of native plants must now move up and over elevated roadbeds to disperse, often becoming trapped on rutted shoulders or steep berms. Small mammals have a particularly strong aversion to crossing paved surfaces. Of eight species studied in the central Mojave Desert, only one male Antelope Ground Squirrel *(Ammospermophilus leucurus)* expanded its home range to the other side of a four-lane highway. Isolation within the desert is also promoted at larger scales as dispersal between adjacent valleys and mountain ranges is reduced. The movement of Desert Bighorn in the western Mojave, for example, was abruptly impeded by construction of the Los Angeles Aqueduct and Highway 395. The steep-sided, water-filled channel has been described as a death trap for wild sheep, while the fenced right-of-way greatly complicated an already uncertain crossing of the lowlands. Reservoirs along the Colorado River have the same effects, splitting large herds into smaller, less stable subpopulations. Wide and busy roads pose greater challenges to small, shy, or slow-moving reptiles that linger on the body-warming pavement. In the western Mojave, the average roadkill rate for Desert Tortoise is one adult or subadult for every two miles of highway each year. The cumulative impact of roadkill on all species must be staggering, although data for highways throughout the California deserts are not uniformly kept. We do know, however, that during each year in Arizona's Saguaro National Park 26,000 reptiles and 17,000 amphibians are killed by automobiles, in addition to 6,500 mammals and 1,400 birds. Could California highways be any less lethal?

But motor vehicles and their impacts are not necessarily limited to highways, or roads or trails for that matter. Touring remote, inaccessible areas began on horseback during the late 1880s but had become motorized by the 1920s. Jeeps that endeared themselves to GIs during World War II were acquired and modified for recreation during the 1950s. Lightweight but powerful "dirt bikes" became commercially available in the 1960s, followed by dune buggies, ATVs, and many kinds of four-wheel-drive trucks and SUVs. By 2004, California had more than 800,000 off-highway motorcycles and ATVs and at least

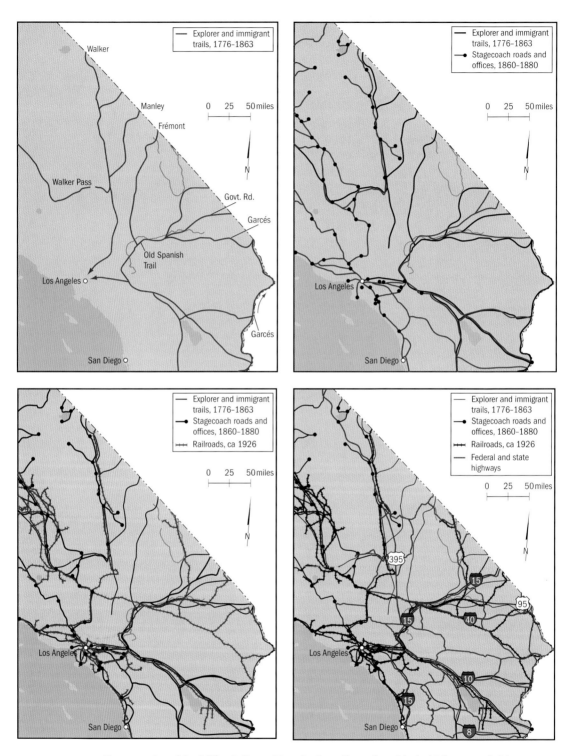

Fragmentation of the California Desert bioregion by trails, roads, rail beds, highways, and cities.
(Based on Beck and Haase 1974)

three million four-wheel-drive vehicles (330 and 1,500 per-cent increases since the 1980s, respectively) In the six ma-jor urbanized counties of Southern California, 519,000 reg-istered off-highway vehicles (OHVs) are within a few hours' drive of almost any desert destination.

Prior to 1980, virtually all of the 12.1 million acres of Cal-ifornia desert land administered by the federal Bureau of Land Management were open to OHVs. Although most enthusiasts preferred roads and trails, the sweep of unbounded arid lands was too much for some to resist. Taking off across untracked bajada, hillside, dune, or playa, a single passage destroys an-cient pavements, wind-packed sands, and cryptogamic crusts, churning more than three quarters to 50 tons of soil per mile, depending on vehicle type and surface hardness. This soil dis-placement amounts to one solid acre of impact after six miles

Soil erosion due to motor-cycles at Dove Springs. (Robert H. Webb)

of travel in a single four-wheel drive vehicle or 20 miles on a single motorcycle. Com-pounding the problem was the precedent set by this single vehicle: subsequent riders would interpret a new, highly visible, and persistent track as a legitimate route across once pris-tine terrain. Multiple passages soon destroy the annual plants and seed banks between the dominant shrubs (usually avoided due to pungent branches and spines). Intensive use near a roadhead, camping area, or challenging slope eventually eliminates the shrubs as well, especially after soil erosion begins to form ruts, gullies, and slumping piles of debris. Hill-sides in the Mojave shed 10 to 20 times more sediment after being subjected to OHV use. This kind of physical disturbance, combined with plant and animal stowaways, has cre-ated the greatest single threat to California deserts: the invasion and spread of nonnative species into once isolated, indigenous natural communities.

Nonnative Species: Agents from Elsewhere

John Frémont was the first trained botanist to enter the bioregion, following portions of the Garcés route during the spring of 1844. His memoirs recorded the occurrence of many plants, some new to science. He had a keen eye for detail and diversity and col-lected about 1,400 specimens. Yet, he makes no mention in his journal of weeds or other familiar, nondesert species along the way. We know that European filaree *(Erodium ci-cutarium)* had already spread north from Mexico because packrat middens in Green-water Valley (near Death Valley) record its first appearance around 1735. Portions of the Frémont trail were already well traveled by horses and cattle, so it is likely that a few other nonnative plants (especially grasses) had become established along the banks of the Mojave River and over Cajon Pass. But across great expanses of arid California, non-native plants and animals had not yet arrived and had not yet begun to alter the com-position and processes of natural communities.

Traveling much of the same route as Frémont, the Death Valley Expedition of 1891

A desert playa appears devoid of life. The halophytic saltbush community abruptly ends at the shoreline, and the cracked, rock-hard sediments do not resemble a fragile, structured soil. Consequently, many playas are designated as "open" to OHVs because impacts to biological resources are not apparent. (Vehicles have been allowed on some sand dunes for the same reason.) But the barren expanses of salt-saturated clay often harbor the dormant eggs of fairy shrimp *(Branchinecta)* and tadpole shrimp *(Triops)*, which turn out to be sensitive indicators of vehicle impact.

This was demonstrated by experimental studies conducted on Bicycle Dry Lake near Fort Irwin, one of the few playas that had not received heavy vehicle use at that time. A relatively lightweight sedan was driven across a section of the playa 20 times, leaving behind a typical, compressed track. The tracks were cored to a depth of an inch, as were untracked sections of playa about six feet away. Since most Alkali Fairy Shrimp eggs reside in the upper layers of sediment, the cores contained a total of 400 to 500 eggs from three species of shrimp.

Careful examination revealed that broken eggs were almost twice as frequent in compressed soils of the track than in uncompressed soils nearby (17.7 percent compared to 10.1 percent, all species included). The eggs of one species, Alkali Fairy Shrimp *(B. mackini)* were more sensitive and likely to break than those of other species. In tracked playa, 25.9 percent of Alkali Fairy Shrimp eggs were broken, compared to 14.7 percent in untracked, control areas. Given that heavily tracked playas may be subjected to hundreds of vehicle passes in a single year, the reduction in egg viability and changes in species composition of the playa community would be significant.

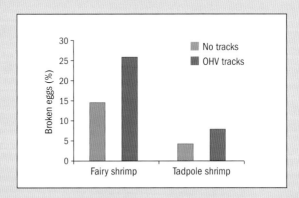

Alkali Fairy Shrimp eggs are almost twice as likely to be broken when the playa surface is compressed by an OHV. The effects on other species are measurable but less pronounced in this experiment. (Based on data from Ericksen et al. 1986)

Left Scraping roadsides to remove vegetation promotes the spread of tumbleweed, the bright green canopies seen here in Deep Springs Valley. (Author)

Right Tumbleweed, or Russian thistle, is a C_4 summer annual that spreads its seeds by tumbling across disturbed soil. (Steve Matson)

catalogued 18 species of weeds. At least six were known from Furnace Creek, which had alfalfa fields by 1875 and irrigated agriculture by 1883. Even in the remote canyons of the Panamint Mountains, white amaranth *(Amaranthus albus)*, goosefoot *(Chenopodium murale)*, and beard grass *(Polypogon monspeliensis)* were abundant, invariably associated with the trails, camping spots, and springs frequented by nineteenth-century travelers. Carried in sacks of grain, lodged in hoofs, and discharged from rumen, nonnative seeds found patches of plowed or otherwise broken soil that allowed establishment. Some were capable of dispersing on their own, such as tumbleweed *(Salsola tragus)*, whose seed-laden adults tumbled into every corner of the region with such speed that they became mistaken icons of the "Old West." Another *entrada* was quietly underway that would ultimately transform and threaten the fragmenting bioregion.

Perhaps no single weed has spread as rapidly or with greater consequence than cheatgrass *(Bromus tectorum)* in the Great Basin. Arriving as a contaminant of wheat, the earliest record for this species was for interior British Columbia in 1889. Within 10 years it was known from northeastern Oregon and southern Idaho, becoming especially abundant along railroad right-of-ways. The foxtail-like seeds also adhered to fur and were carried far into the sagebrush wilderness. By 1930 this annual grass attained its modern dis-

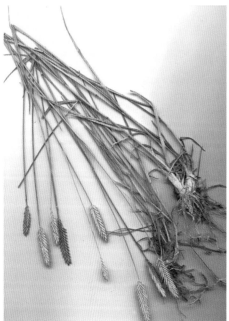

Upper Cheatgrass spreads rapidly after overgrazing or fire. (James M. Andre)

Lower Desert crested wheatgrass *(Agropyron desertorum)* is a native perennial that can be outcompeted by cheatgrass. (Steve Matson)

tribution throughout the semiarid West, becoming a dominant component of many communities (for example, pinyon-juniper woodland, big sagebrush scrub) during the 1950s. Dominance by cheatgrass was achieved by fall germination and winter growth of roots that depleted soil water ahead of the native perennial grasses. Its flowers pollinate themselves by never bothering to open, finally setting seed and dying by July. The standing, dead plants load the community with highly flammable fuel, increasing the frequency and intensity of wildfires. Native shrubs of the Great Basin are destroyed by fire, and the soils become devoid of nutrients and subject to erosion. Cheatgrass changes the successional sequences within these degrading communities, leading to reduced natural diversity and productivity for human and nonhuman uses.

With the advent of roads, train tracks, and highways and soil disturbance on a massive scale throughout the deserts, it should come as no surprise that the number of weed species has increased at a staggering, modern rate. The 2002 *Jepson Desert Manual* lists 214 species from southeastern California, with at least 27 considered noxious by the state of California (that is, to be eradicated on sight). The grass family is the biggest contributor (71 species), followed by the sunflower (25) and mustard (24) families. The majority are prolific annuals that lie dormant in the seed bank during unfavorable hot and dry periods, but some (for example, white amaranth, tumbleweed, and hedgehog grass [*Echinochloa crus-galli*]) are drought-tolerant, summer-active C_4 species that evolved in other arid regions of the globe.

Low, unpredictable rainfall is a major constraint on all species, and weeds can be confined if the soil's armor has not been broken or removed. Intact pavement, varnish, and caliche resist weeds by shedding water and inhibiting penetration by seeds and roots. Open, sparsely vegetated desert habitats for native species are maintained, therefore, by protecting the soil surface from physical disturbance by humans or livestock. An important exception is found in desert riparian communities. Natural disturbance by churning runoff waters allows salt cedar (*Tamarix ramosissima*, also called tamarisk) to invade arroyos and streambeds and

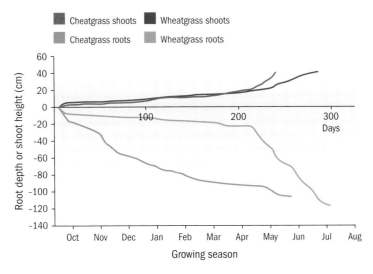

Legend:
- Cheatgrass shoots
- Wheatgrass shoots
- Cheatgrass roots
- Wheatgrass roots

Root depth or shoot height (cm) — vertical axis: 60, 40, 20, 0, -20, -40, -60, -80, -100, -120, -140

Horizontal axis (days): 100, 200, 300 Days

Growing season — Oct, Nov, Dec, Jan, Feb, Mar, Apr, May, Jun, Jul, Aug

Nonnative cheatgrass competes with the native desert wheatgrass by rapid, deep root growth that depletes the available soil water for seedling establishment. Shoots grow at the same rate, so aboveground competition is minor. (Redrawn from Harris 1977)

compete with woody natives by profligate consumption. A pound of salt cedar foliage transpires 60 pounds of water each day, with a single, whole tree dissipating 200 gallons of groundwater from dawn to dusk. Along the upper Mojave River between Forks Reservoir and Afton Canyon, almost a third of the water used by riparian vegetation (an estimated 17,000 acre-feet per year) is transpired by salt cedar alone (rather than Fremont cottonwood [Populus fremontii] or black willow [Salix gooddingii]). In drier stretches near Barstow the native mesquite has been completely displaced. Tolerant of salt, drought, fire, and even toxic boron, very few things inhibit salt cedar growth or reproduction. The seeds are ignored by granivores and produced in such abundance (up to 500,000 per shrub every year) that seedlings form solid green carpets on exposed sandbars. The canopies of arroyo woodlands invaded by salt cedar become dense and continuous, avoided by nesting Black-tailed Gnatcatchers (Polioptila melanura), which favor pure, open stands of blue palo verde (Cercidium floridum) and smoke tree (Psorothamnus spinosus). Along the Colorado River the impenetrable thicket can be hundreds of yards wide, effectively excluding thirsty Desert Bighorn and almost all other natives. Insect biomass, rodent density, and bird species richness are all significantly reduced in a salt cedar thicket compared to native vegetation. The result is a single, monotonous, species-poor riparian community that squanders the desert's most precious resource.

Salt cedar's ability to degrade entire communities is matched by at least a dozen other plants of lesser stature but greater abundance. These are rapidly growing, profusely reproductive spring annuals from arid Eurasia and North Africa, brought here accidentally or intentionally for cattle forage or stabilizing disturbed soils. Many of these species thrive

Upper left Salt cedar is a profligate water user and a prolific seed producer. (Joseph M. Di Tomaso)

Upper right Red brome was introduced from Eurasia. (Author)

Lower The rust-colored skirt around every shrub is red brome. Here it has invaded a carbonate scrub community on the Darwin Plateau, Inyo Mountains. (Author)

where the ground surface has been churned by OHVs, agriculture, or construction. Perhaps evolution in ancient deserts (with long histories of human and megafaunal disturbance) led to the development of aggressive life history traits that put our more recent, delicate herbs at a disadvantage. Grasses, such as cheatgrass in the Great Basin and red brome *(Bromus madritensis* subsp. *rubens)* in the Mojave, have flowers armed with bristles ("awns") or barbs that pierce the skin, cheek pouches, and guts of native herbivores. Tolerance of drought and low soil nitrogen allow Mediterranean grass *(Schismus arabicus*

Sahara mustard is a prolific weed from the Mediterranean region. (Chris Wagner)

An entire creosote bush bajada along Interstate 10 near the Providence Mountains is now dominated by Sahara mustard. (Author)

and *S. barbatus*) to form a wide skirt around almost every creosote bush *(Larrea tridentata)* south of Death Valley. Some forbs have a combination of traits that allows persistence during drought and proliferation during rare, wet years. Sahara mustard *(Brassica tournefortii)* has gel-coated seeds that absorb and sense the available soil moisture before committing to germinate. When a hydration threshold is reached, dormancy breaks, and the rapidly developing seedling allocates resources to building a leafy, productive canopy. Every branch flowers profusely and every flower makes a seed-filled fruit. After death, the stem breaks in a strong wind, allowing the plant to tumble along and sow its crop across the landscape. So many seeds accumulate in the soil that when the next rainy year arrives, the spaces between creosote bushes become lush. Instead of scattered native herbs, each square inch now contains 25 to 56 Sahara mustard *(Brassica tournefortii)* seedlings (175 million to 322 million per acre). The number "billion trillion" and the word "tsunami" have been used to describe this one, newly arrived species in the bioregion.

A flood of weeds is now flowing north from the fields of the Coachella Valley and west from overgrazed grasslands of Arizona, with serious ecological consequences. Once abundant and widespread native plants are becoming uncommon across the fragmented desert.

Although excessive livestock grazing may have contributed, six-weeks fescue *(Vulpia octoflora)* is being rapidly replaced by European grasses (such as species of *Schismus*) that have similar growth forms and physiology. In some areas of the western Mojave, weeds now comprise 50 to 97 percent of the herbaceous plant material produced each spring. Showy wildflowers between Joshua trees have been swamped by a monotonous green sea of red brome and Sahara mustard that contributes little or nothing to the food web. The tough, protein-deficient foliage is eaten by Desert Tortoise only as a last resort, while the seeds are of little value to granivorous ants and rodents. Without animal consumption, the weedy material dies, dries, and accumulates to form a continuous, flammable canopy over thousands of acres (especially along highways). Fires that were once infrequent and burned only patches of desert for lack of fuel are now frequent and catastrophic. Instead of occurring every 30 to 100 years in a particular area, desert wildfires are now recorded about every five years. Between 1980 and 1990 an average of 38 square miles was burned every year in the Mojave Desert. Fires sweep across scrub and woodland communities, incinerating species with little or no tolerance for this new form of disturbance. Unlike their chaparral counterparts, creosote bush does not stump sprout very well, and native desert annuals do not flourish after fire. High temperatures sterilize the soil, killing mycorrhizal fungi necessary for reestablishing many native plants. Desert Tortoises also die in the inferno or die for lack of native, herbaceous foods or shady shrub canopies that shelter 70 percent of all burrows. High mortality of burned Joshua trees reduces the available habitat for night lizards, orioles, and woodrats. Thus a relative few invasive, productive, and unchecked plant species from other arid regions can create a torrent of habitat degradation.

There are fewer nonnative animals than plants in the desert, but the number is not precisely known. No tally exists for invertebrates, but even vertebrates are a little hard to count. This is because fish comprise the largest single category (about 50 nonnative species from southeast Oregon to Baja California), and their desert distributions are difficult to delineate. Most were intentionally introduced as food or bait between 1920 and 1970, although carp *(Cyprinus carpio)* in the Sonoran Desert were established by 1885. Bullfrogs *(Rana catesbeiana)* arrived at Furnace Creek in 1920, one of only two exotic amphibians to invade desert waters. A flock of English House Sparrows *(Passer domesticus)* was released in New York City in 1850, and descendents arrived in California by 1870. Along with European Starlings *(Sturnus vulgaris,* also released in New York), English House Sparrows are probably the most commonly observed birds in desert towns and cities. At least five nonnative mammals are known, including the House Mouse *(Mus musculus),* Burro *(Equus asinus),* and ironically, horse *(E. caballus).*

Only a handful of stout invaders is required to degrade the native species and communities of the desert. One large Bullfrog removed from a spring at Ash Meadows had eight Amargosa Pupfish *(Cyprinodon nevadensis)* in its stomach, representing countless such meals in the past. It takes only a few Burros, say a male and two or three females, to form a viable breeding group capable of producing one or two offspring per year. Ge-

This nonnative Bullfrog, introduced to Amargosa Canyon, has eight Amargosa Pupfish in its gut. (D. W. Sada)

Feral horses left hoofprints along the edge of a spring that trapped and killed these pupfishes. (Jim D. Yoakum)

netic problems from matings between parents and progeny do not appreciably slow the growth of the herd. Without predators or disease, exponential increases in such mobile, generalist herbivores are almost assured. A handful of Burros released by miners in Death Valley during the 1880s became 1,500 strong by 1973. In the Mojave as a whole, the rate of increase ranged between 10 and 20 percent per year, with 12,000 estimated in 1980. Although critical water and forage resources become locally depleted, the landscape is virtually limitless if breeding groups can disperse into new, unoccupied regions. A few Burros colonized Sheep Spring in the Providence Mountains sometime after 1953, supporting more than 20 robust animals by 1981. Given the wide variety of available food plants in such tall mountains, this population became a firmly established member of the "modern megafauna," poised for another round of explosive growth.

Nonnatives invariably begin to degrade the natural communities they invade. Species rich gives way to species poor, as limited resources are consumed by burgeoning, resilient, and unconstrained species. In the case of Burros, the vegetation and water so critical to Desert Bighorn can be virtually destroyed within a few decades. Biologist Fred Jones, working in the Panamint Mountains, wrote in his field notes of July 1955:

Burros have taken all of this over and are ruining the range. The use of *Larrea* [creosote bush] at the lower elevations and the naturally poor quality of feed below 6,500 feet means there is a naturally poor range that has been severely overbrowsed. The end result being practically hopeless for range recovery even under complete protection. . . . *Ambrosia* [burrobush] is nearly a remnant plant—being eaten out. . . . At the higher elevations burros have nearly killed out grasses and such forbs as *Phlox* (which exists only in centers of large shrubs) and are using bush lupine

Feral Burros in Death Valley National Park, 2003. (Joseph Dougherty)

heavily—uprooting much of it. The vegetation is being changed to practically pure sagebrush and *Happlopappus* with some gray horsebush and bush lupine. (Jones 1980)

Around the springs and seeps of desert mountains, certain plants, especially grasses, are completely eliminated or seriously reduced within a radius of one to five miles. This vegetation is thought to provide an "emergency food supply" that the sheep rely upon during their journeys between reliable water sources. Denuded, trampled, and fouled with feces, the springs are subjugated by Burros and usually abandoned by Desert Bighorn. Interactions between the two species are complex, so sweeping statements about competition are difficult to substantiate; however, the strong consensus is that Burros drink more water, eat more forage, congregate about and dominate springs, and often outnumber the native Desert Bighorns, with detrimental consequences. Burros have been implicated in the steady decline of the Cottonwood Mountains population (105 sheep) and the extirpation of the Deep Springs–Eureka Valley population in 1986. Bighorn expert Charles Hansen summarized:

Growth of a feral Burro population at China Lake Naval Weapons Center became exponential after passage of the Wild Horse and Burro Act in 1971. Such explosive growth and the damage it causes are typical of plant and animal "weeds." (Redrawn from McGill 1986)

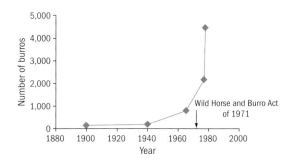

In Death Valley National Monument in 1973 there are only 450 bighorn but about 1,500 burros. Over a 10-year period burros and bighorn have not coexisted; bighorn are on the way out and burros in.

(Jones 1980)

The incessant demands of nonnative animals and plants will force us to choose between Burros and Bighorn, mustards and Tortoise, and Bullfrogs and pupfishes. Along with human incursion and fragmentation, the future of the desert bioregion will be determined by how we decide to manage these aggressive agents of change. Desert waters are now being usurped and squandered. Once common native species are made rare and put at risk of extinction. Natural communities are transformed and impoverished. Without isolation from the larger world, the essential and definitive resources of the desert are readily and ominously depleted.

DEPLETION OF DESERT RESOURCES

Water

The burgeoning population of humans in the bioregion will intensify demand for water. Some desert cities will sustain the 20 to 70 percent growth rates achieved during the 1990s, and their populace will triple compared to 1995. Such growth will require new water sources, reallocation from agriculture, and reclamation to provide the necessary supply.

Currently, humans in the Great Basin and Mojave deserts draw their water equally from surface flows (lakes, rivers, and imports from the State Water Project) and groundwater (aquifers), with less than five percent coming from reclamation (recycling and desalinization). Roughly 50 percent is allocated for agriculture (mostly irrigated pasture or alfalfa), and 16 percent is kept in water bodies to provide habitat, dust control, and recreation (environmental uses). The remaining 34 percent is for domestic and industrial consumption (urban uses). Droughts tend to reduce environmental uses and increase the annual water shortage from 89,000 to 92,000 acre-feet. In contrast, humans of California's Sonoran Desert obtain 90 percent of their water from the Colorado River, seven percent from groundwater, and .3 percent from reclamation. Agriculture accounts for 90 percent of the water use, and less than one percent goes for environmental purposes (essentially all associated with maintaining the Salton Sea). Drought reduces deliveries from the river, increasing the annual shortage from 69,000 to 95,000 acre-feet.

By 2020 urban water use will nearly double in the Colorado and triple in the Great Basin and Mojave deserts, producing annual shortages ranging between 147,000 and 308,000 acre-feet. Water planners for the state predict that some additional water will come from increased use of surface flows (mostly in the north) and reallocation from agriculture. They are trying to hold the line on groundwater extraction and environmental uses and do not assume there will be any gains from reclamation. Nevertheless, drought years could require eight percent more groundwater pumping in the Great Basin and Mo-

This gray band, almost a foot wide, comprises billions of adult alkali flies. It encircles Mono Lake and is an essential part of the food web. (Author)

jave deserts, with the Mojave River likely to be most affected. Groundwater overdrafts lowered the river's watertable by more than five feet during the 1980s, causing 60 to 95 percent mortality of Fremont cottonwood and willows in the riparian woodland. When lowered 10 feet along other stretches, there was 70 percent mortality of mesquite, rapidly shifting the woodland toward dominance by the drought-tolerant, nonnative salt cedar. Without planning and decisive actions to prevent groundwater overdraft, the shady and productive forests of the Mojave River could succumb to increasing human demand.

Human demand has also affected desert lakes and springs. Beginning in 1940, surface water from east-flowing Sierran rivers was diverted from Mono Lake into the Los Angeles Aqueduct. The system could eventually deliver 550,000 acre-feet each year into eight reservoirs and through 12 power plants, providing huge benefits to the rapidly growing metropolis. But ancient Mono Lake, the remnant of Pleistocene Lake Russell, began to shrink toward Holocene oblivion. By 1982 its level dropped 46 vertical feet and its area contracted by 18,000 acres, a loss of 2.2 million acre-feet of water. Negit Island became connected to the desert shore, and once-submerged towers of precipitated carbonate (tufa) were left high and dry for many years. Ground-nesting California Gulls *(Larus californicus)* were no longer safe from Coyotes *(Canis latrans)* and other predators. Even more ominous were the effects on the lake's unique ecosystem. The total salt content of the waters more than doubled (becoming 10 percent, compared to 3.5 percent in seawater), contributing to the near collapse of the endemic Mono Brine Shrimp *(Artemia monica)* population that had usually fed 60,000 breeding gulls, 30,000 migrating Red-necked and Wilson's phalaropes *(Phalaropus lobatus* and *P. tricolor)*, and 750,000 migrating Eared Grebes *(Podiceps nigricollis)*. Overwintering shrimp cysts failed to hatch during the spring of 1981, and without trillions of herbivorous adults, the lake turned green and turbid with algae. Mono Lake Alkali Flies *(Ephydra hians)* and cicadas (Cicadidae) provided alternative food sources, but nevertheless, thousands of fledgling California Gulls died by summer. Whether starvation or unusually high air temperatures were to blame has never been resolved, but the sad condition of Mono Lake in the early 1980s galvanized scientists, activists, and sympathetic legislators and led to restoration of tributary waters by the 1990s.

Other water bodies had also been depleted by development east of the Sierra. Below

Upper   Tens of thousands of California Gulls are at the top of the Mono Lake food web. (William C. Flaxington)

Lower   The Mono Lake food web depends on maintaining freshwater runoff from the Sierra, an ancient connection that sustains the diversity and abundance of desert life. The runoff prevents the concentration of salt and other dissolved minerals from inhibiting the photosynthesis of algae, the consumption of algae by brine shrimp and Mono Lake Alkali Flies, and the consumption of shrimp and flies by gulls, phalaropes, and grebes. Nitrogen is returned to the algae by decomposition of detritus and excrement. (From Hart 1996, used with permission)

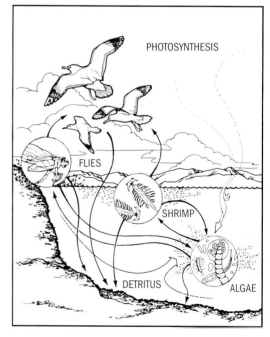

Mono Lake, the Owens River no longer flooded the lush alkali meadows and marshes south of Bishop because it too had been channelized or diverted into the Los Angeles Aqueduct. This drastically reduced habitat for the Owens Pupfish (*Cyprinodon radiosus*) and Owens Chub (*Siphateles bicolor synderi*), as well as a host of unique meadow plants (Owens Valley checkerbloom *[Sidalcea covillei]*, Inyo County star tulip *[Calochortus excavatus]*). The pupfish, which numbered in the millions before 1916, was thought to be extinct by the time it was scientifically described in 1948.

Upper   The Owens River is having its
flows restored after decades of diversion and groundwater pumping into
the Los Angeles Aquaduct. (D. W. Sada)

Lower   The Owens Pupfish was
rediscovered in Fish Slough, north of
Bishop. (D. W. Sada)

Rediscovered among the wet marshes of Fish Slough (north of Bishop) in 1956, 200 were
finally rescued from final desiccation in 1969 by hand-carrying them to a nearby spring.
But Owens Lake, once the terminus of the great river, became a dry, dusty playa by the
1920s. Its food chain of algae, brine shrimp, alkali flies, and countless waterfowl came
to a sudden end after tens of thousands of years of unimaginable productivity. Springflows
around the Owens Valley also began to decline, especially after more than 100 groundwater pumping stations were built between Bishop and Lone Pine. The loss of springs,
no matter how small, will be inevitably joined by corresponding losses of drought-susceptible biodiversity, such as aquatic bivalves (for example, California Floater *[Anodonta
californiensis]*), springsnails *(Pyrgulopsis* and *Tryonia)*, and salamanders *(Batrachoseps)*. And
the scenario may be tragically repeated at Ash Meadows, as unbridled Las Vegas and
Pahrump demand more and more water from the Death Valley aquifer. If the level in
Devils Hole drops more than a foot and a half, the feeding shelf that has for eons sus-

WATER DEVELOPMENT AT DESERT SPRINGS

Past development of desert springs was straightforward; remove the vegetation, install a pump, and take what you need. Such was the case at Jackrabbit Spring in Ash Meadows, when nearby fields of alfalfa required irrigation during the 1940s and 1950s. Subsequent proposals for a massive housing development would have caused even more diversion. Fortunately, protection by the Nature Conservancy and the U.S. Fish and Wildlife Service have allowed natural healing and hands-on restoration to effect recovery. Even the Ash Meadows Pupfish *(Cyprinodon nevadensis mionectes)* returned from exile in an adjacent ditch and became reestablished over the last three decades.

Other springs and their biota will never have the chance to recover. Soda Spring along the Garcés route was apparently destroyed when the Zzyzx resort was built in the 1920s. Lined with cement or piped into tanks, the resource was co-opted exclusively for human use. Overt destruction of wetlands and surface waters is now prevented by federal and state law. But meeting the needs of desert cities will keep demand for water high. Overdrafting the underground supply will lower water levels in many desert springs that share the same aquifer, leading to covert destruction of these precious communities and their species.

Upper   Irrigation pump and drainage ditch installed at Jackrabbit Spring to support Ash Meadows agriculture, 1969. (Jim D. Yoakum)

Center   The pump was turned on and the endemic plants, pupfishes, and ecosystem of Jackrabbit Spring were destroyed. (Jim D. Yoakum)

Lower   Jackrabbit Spring, 1983, after Ash Meadows was acquired by the U.S. Fish and Wildlife Service and restoration had begun. (Author)

tained the endemic Devils Hole Pupfish *(Cyprinodon diabolis)* will be desiccated. The species may persist in concrete refugia or aquaria (as does the Mojave Chub *[Siphateles bicolor mojavensis]*), but its unique and beautiful ecosystem, its evolutionary context, will be destroyed. Continued groundwater decline could reduce flow from as many as 15 springs in the greater Ash Meadows area, affecting another 23 species of endemic animals and plants (one of the highest concentrations anywhere in North America).

But aquatic communities are not the only ones affected by water diversions. Small-scale alterations of runoff down a stony bajada can affect the structure and function of a terrestrial community, even if dominated by drought-tolerant species. This was elegantly demonstrated by studies along the Colorado River Aqueduct at the foot of the Coxcomb Mountains. Completed in 1937, the concrete channel contours across a gravelly bajada that is underlain by a caliche hardpan four feet below the surface. Consequently, storm runoff from the steep escarpment would normally flow over the desert pavement on its way to Chuckwalla Valley. Large amounts of water had to be diverted from the upslope side of the aqueduct to prevent structural damage, but the necessary ditches cut off large areas of desert vegetation from this runoff. After 50 years, creosote bush and burrobush *(Ambrosia dumosa)* in these areas had 30 percent lower density and 20 to 50 percent lower biomass than in adjacent control plots (those with runoff). In addition, the ability of creosote bush to produce clones (the secret to its longevity) was reduced by half. Big galleta grass *(Pleuraphis rigida)*, the shallowly rooted C_4 grass, increased in abundance, but three cacti and four other shrubs tended to decrease. The ripple effects of this reduced plant productivity were not measured, but they are probably significant given the large number of native animals associated with the food web of creosote bush scrub. It is also reasonable to extrapolate beyond this one construction project; every road, canal, and track that diverts water from a downslope arid landscape has probably had similar impacts on ecosystem processes and resident biota.

Air

Traversing the Sonoran Desert from Arizona into California, John Van Dyke wandered over the stark land and beneath an ethereal sky. He enthused (1902):

I ride away through the thin mesquite and the little abode ranch house is soon lost to view. The morning is still and perfectly clear. The stars have gone out, the moon is looking pale, the deep blue is warming, the sky is lightening with the coming day. How cool and crystalline the air! In just a few hours the great plain will be almost like a fiery furnace under the rays of the summer sun, but now it is chilly. And in a few hours there will be rings and bands and scarves of heat set wavering across the waste upon the opalescent wings of the mirage; but now the air is so clear that one can see the breaks in the rocky face of the mountain range, though it is fully twenty miles away. It may be further. Who of the desert has not spent his day riding at a mountain and never reaching its base? This is a land of illusions and thin air. . . .

Desert smog (right) spreads north from the Los Angeles Basin into the Antelope Valley (left). (NASA)

The Barstow to Las Vegas Motorcycle Race attracted hundreds of participants and produced tons of particulate pollutants until it was finally halted in 1990. (Howard Wilshire)

It is the high point to catch the first shaft of the sun. Quickly the light spreads downward until the whole ridge is tinged by it, and the abrupt sides of porphyry begin to glow under it. . . .

That beam of light! Was there every anything so beautiful! How it flashes its color through shadow, how it gilds the tops of the mountains and gleams white on the dunes of the desert. . . . The beast and the bird are not too fond of its heat and as soon as the sun is high in the heavens they seek cover in the canyons; but for all that the chief glory of the desert is its broad blaze of omnipresent light.

The keen eye and philosophical mind of this art professor provided a baseline description of desert air, long before the rise of cities, the proliferation of automobiles, and the diversion of waters into aqueducts. Waste gases and dust are by-products of human population growth, expelled to the atmosphere and exported by the prevailing winds. Export provides relief for those along the smog-choked coast, but these materials don't disappear—they simply migrate from the San Joaquin and San Fernando valleys to China Lake and Palmdale, from Riverside and San Diego to Kelso and Anza-Borrego. A blanket of pollutants, diluted only by a half or a third, builds over the course of a modern desert day. Those with known effects on the biota include alkali dust, ozone, sulfur dioxide, and the various oxides of nitrogen (NO, NO_2). Mountains become obscured, the sky is yellowed, and the omnipresent light is scattered and subdued by a scented, white haze.

Dust, or particulate matter, is lofted by from sources within the desert. On a local scale, thermals create dust devils that move materials over small distances and contribute to the soil-building process. On a bioregional scale, the strong winds generated by weather systems can move mountains, sometimes building dunes and soil pavements, and sometimes creating dust storms that threaten human health. Desiccation of Owens Lake by water diversion now produces up to 10 major loftings of powdery alkali each year, the largest single source of dust in North America. The playa surface, more than 70,000 acres, releases so many tons of fine particulate matter that air quality standards are exceeded more than 50 miles away. The dust itself can affect the respiratory heath of 50,000 people, as can the spores of Coccidiomycosis, a soil fungus associated with creosote bush scrub. Once inhaled the spores produce a potentially lethal lung disease known as valley fever. Similar problems are developing in the Coachella Valley, as water transfers to population centers threaten to expose the bed of the Salton Sea. Childhood asthma and deaths from respiratory disease in this region are already twice the statewide rates. Off-highway vehicle activity can also release large amounts of dust from broken soil surfaces. The 1974 Barstow to Las Vegas motorcycle race produced more than 660 tons of airborne particulates.

Of the 25 most ozone polluted counties in the United States (2004), 13 are in California, and four (San Bernardino, Kern, Riverside, and Los Angeles) are in or adjacent to the desert bioregion. Ozone levels in the central Mojave commonly exceed 100 parts per billion (ppb) when offshore winds blow east from the Los Angeles Basin, compared to 20 to 40 ppb in more remote areas. But even Death Valley is not remote enough, as summertime concentrations have reached 160 ppb (twice the national pollution standard). The American Lung Association has established that lung function of humans (and probably other lunged creatures) is impaired by a one-hour exposure to levels between 90 and 120 ppb. Studies of desert holly *(Atriplex hymenelytra)* demonstrated reduced rates of photosynthesis and water use efficiency when leaves were exposed to these levels under laboratory conditions. Reduced ability to gain carbon with limited water was suggested as the reason whole shrubs were dying at unusually high rates in the valley. Conifers are especially sensitive to ozone pollution, losing chlorophyll, dropping needles, and becoming susceptible to drought and insect attack. Extensive damage to pine forests along the western edge of the desert has been well documented in the San Bernardino and San Gabriel mountains.

Sulfur dioxide is generated largely by power plants that burn coal to generate electricity. One of the largest plants in the southwest is the Mohave Generating Station located in Laughlin, Nevada. It has provided up to three percent of Southern California's electricity while emitting 40,000 tons of sulfur dioxide each year. Although the facility has been scheduled for closure, its effects have been the subject of inquiry and litigation. Respiratory irritation and shortness of breath can occur with exposure to concentrations in the range of 30 to 200 ppb, which can be accentuated by asthma and vigorous physical activity. Large numbers of desert plants, including big sagebrush *(Artemisia tridentata)*, creosote bush, Indian ricegrass *(Achnatherum hymenoides),* and brown-eyed primrose *(Camissonia claviformis)* are very sensitive, suffering leaf injury and reduced growth when exposed to low concentrations. These are among the most productive and characteristic species of the arid West, so the impacts are likely to be transmitted through the food web. Others, such as four-wing saltbush *(Atriplex canescens)* and burrobush are more resistant, so another impact could be a shift in vegetation composition as such species assume dominance in polluted areas.

Contrary to the effects of ozone and sulfur dioxide, the oxides of nitrogen from automobile exhaust actually stimulate plant growth by acting as a fertilizer to the soil. Falling to earth as dry, particulate matter (a principle component of haze), the nitrogen is converted into useful forms by bacteria and made available to insatiable roots. The irony is that nonnative plants seem to benefit more than natives; perhaps they are simply more abundant, better able to hoard the nitrogen, or more efficient in their use of this once-limiting nutrient. As much as 4.5

Although the coal-fired Mohave Generating Station closed in 2005, others are planned for construction throughout the west. (Rick Moore)

grams per square yard of nitrogen can fall per year from the skies around Los Angeles, while only 3 grams is enough to produce increases in the density and biomass of weeds, such as red brome and filaree *(Erodium cicutarium)*. In turn, the fortified weeds are even better able to displace natives, build large fuel loads, increase the intensity and frequency of wildfire, and change the structure and quality of vegetation to the disadvantage of wildlife. This atmospheric fertilization of desert soils is sinister because it is cryptic, incessant, and tied to our love of gasoline combustion.

The carbon dioxide from gasoline combustion will add another, large-scale complication to the future of the bioregion. Atmospheric concentrations of carbon dioxide have already increased by 37 percent over the last 200 years (from 270 ppm to 370 ppm) and are predicted to double (to 540 ppm) by the middle of this century. Global climate change, usually envisioned as an overall warming of the atmosphere, will be accentuated as carbon dioxide and other "greenhouse gases" accumulate and absorb heat energy that would otherwise be radiated into space. Exactly how climate change will manifest itself in California's deserts is not now clear. Strictly speaking, increased mean and extreme temperature could increase the extent of desert, shifting the boundaries of Great Basin, Mojave, and Sonoran communities northward and upslope. These would potentially benefit low-elevation, generalist species while compromising the future of high-elevation and specialist species that may have nowhere else to go. Most accepted climate models predict an average decrease of 1.4 inches of annual rainfall across the southwest by the year 2050, which would have a significant impact on the biota. Greater water stress is likely to reduce stomatal opening and transpiration, thereby limiting photosynthetic productivity. With less moisture moving from plants into the atmosphere, droughted conditions would

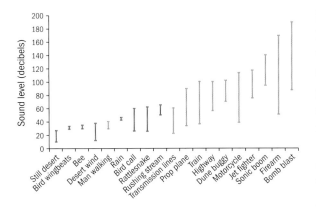

Sound level (decibels) — Y-axis: 0, 20, 40, 60, 80, 100, 120, 140, 160, 180, 200

X-axis labels: Still desert, Bird wingbeats, Bee, Desert wind, Man walking, Rain, Bird call, Rattlesnake, Rushing stream, Transmission lines, Prop plane, Train, Highway, Dune buggy, Motorcycle, Jet fighter, Sonic boom, Firearm, Bomb blast

Comparison of natural sounds and human-made noises in the California deserts. (Redrawn from Brattstrom and Bondello 1995)

be accentuated and possibly made worse. However, there are so many related effects of warming on rainfall, runoff, evapotranspiration, fire frequency, and pollution that simple predictions are virtually meaningless. The response of the bioregion to global warming will unfold before us.

Quiet

The still air of the desert is absolutely quiet. Ancient, pervasive quiet is a resource in short supply across the modern world, a world in need of introspection and spiritual renewal. A quiet *entrada* invites connection to the mysteries of stark creation. John Van Dyke wrote:

What is it that draws us to the boundless and the fathomless? Why should the lovely things of earth—the grasses, the trees, the lakes, the little hills—appear trivial and insignificant when we come face to face with the sea or the desert or the vastness of the midnight sky? . . . They are the great elements. We do not see, we hardly know if their boundaries are limited; we only feel their immensity, their mystery, and their beauty.

And quiet as impressive as the mysteries are the silences. Was there ever such a stillness as that which rests upon the desert at night! Was there ever such a hush as that which steals from star to star across the firmament! You think to break the spell by raising your voice in a cry; but you will not do so again. The sound goes but a little way and then seems to come back to your ear with a suggestion of insanity about it. . . .

Century after century that cry has gone up, mobbing high heaven; and always insanity in the cry, insanity in the crier. What folly to protest where none shall hear! There is no appeal from the law of nature. It was made for beast and bird and creeping thing. Will the human near learn that in the eye of the law he is not different from the things that creep?

The things that creep seldom generate rattles, buzzings, or calls that exceed 40 decibels (dB) of sound pressure (still air in the desert is between 10 and 30 dB). Rainstorms and rushing waters generate some of the loudest natural sounds, between 40 and 60 dB. As humans storm the desert they bring the alien noise of machinery. Propeller aircraft, highways, and motorcycles produce 90 to 110 dB, while jets, sonic booms, and firearms can exceed 120 dB to 140 dB. If exposed to eight minutes of 95 dB of OHV noise (equivalent to being 165 feet from the source), desert vertebrates lose much of their hearing for up to four weeks. Desert Kangaroo Rats *(Dipodomys deserti)* normally hear the approach of a crawling rattlesnake when it is three feet away, but after noise exposure, this distance was lethally reduced to three inches. Couch's Spadefoot Toads *(Scaphiophus couchi)* mistook the same vehicle noise for thunder and emerged from their subterranean burrows in expectation of rain. Prolonged exposure would cause even greater damage to a multitude of hearing-sensitive animals, especially as the vehicles themselves penetrate the most remote fragments of the once quiet desert.

Forage

Although livestock grazing in California began with Spanish missions and land grants, commercial operations did not begin in the deserts until after the Gold Rush. The mining districts of Aurora, Bodie, and Panamint created boomtowns with high demand for fresh meat. Cattle were driven across Tehachapi and Walker passes from the Central Valley in early spring, taking advantage of the western Mojave's productive but ephemeral herbs as forage. Cowboys and steers entered the Owens Valley for the first time in 1859, establishing ranches by 1861 in meadows that had long been irrigated and harvested by the Paiute. Sheep came a little later, brought down from the Sierran high country after overgrazing and other abuses had led to the development of parks and forest reserves in the 1890s. Open range with large numbers of animals in the desert became the practice, and by 1910 there were more than 43,000 sheep, 20,000 cattle, and 5,000 horses in the Owens Valley alone. At about the same time 60,000 sheep and 67,000 cattle were grazing Imperial County. And in between, across the most remote landscapes of the eastern Mojave and Colorado River, the industry was aided by development of railroads and water resources. Virtually every peak, bajada, and major spring was eventually utilized. Production peaked during World War II and then rapidly declined as feedlot operations in other parts of the state became common practice. By 1968 public lands in the entire California desert supported only 138,000 sheep and 25,000 cattle. Stronger federal regulation reduced the extent of grazing to about 4.5 million acres in 1980 and continued the trend toward fewer animals by allowing 60,000 sheep and 10,000 cattle to utilize the forage on public lands.

Attempting to scientifically measure the pervasive effects of livestock on the desert is now a great challenge. After more than a century of widespread impacts, it is difficult to find ungrazed examples of natural communities for comparative purposes. What does an ungrazed Joshua Tree woodland look like? What would its species composition and structure be? We're not entirely sure, except that it would be a lot less weedy. The extreme climate, so inherently variable, makes long-term studies difficult to design, much less execute. Prior to contact with domestic sheep, did Desert Bighorn populations fluctuate in size as much as they do now? Is competition for forage or water most relevant? It's hard to know with any degree of certainty, given the complicating effects of periodic drought. Consequently, we have only begun to discover how and how much livestock have depleted desert resources and when or if recovery will occur. But there is no uncertainly about the obvious impacts of historic overgrazing in the California desert bioregion. Even as early as 1898, H. L. Bentley of the U.S. Department of Agriculture reported, "The ranges [of the southwest] have been almost ruined, and if not renewed will soon be past all hope of permanent improvement." (Bentley 1898) Overgrazing has left a clear legacy of reduced primary productivity, widespread weed invasion, and altered successional responses of entire natural communities.

Reductions in primary productivity from overgrazing have significantly impacted the wildlife resources of the desert and will be very slow to heal. Natural fluctuations in the production of succulent, energy-rich plant tissues already set strict limits on the abundance and activity of desert herbivores (for example, Chuckwalla *[Sauromalus obesus]*, Desert Tortoise, and ground squirrel *[Spermophilus]*). Successive drought years add even greater restrictions, often canceling growth and reproduction entirely and making bare-bones persistence the only attainable goal. Adding large numbers of voracious, nonnative herbivores to the food web makes persistence, growth, and reproduction of native herbivores exceedingly difficult. The single passage of a typical flock of sheep has been shown to reduce annual plant productivity in the Mojave by as much as 60 percent. Such plants and the energy they contain are thus diverted from indigenous mouths into the domesticated protein that supplies distant human populations. The problem is compounded as unpalatable weeds rapidly replace the native plants, further diminishing energy flow through the web. The pavementlike soil is churned by hooves and uprooting, creating a rough, uneven surface that is readily penetrated by germinating weeds. Those weeds often arrive after transport and expulsion from the bowels of the same, roaming animals. It is no coincidence that forage in the western Mojave, which first hosted cattle in 1859, is now 40 to 70 percent nonnative and unable to sustain viable populations of Desert Tortoise.

A recent study has confirmed that cattle can compete directly with Desert Tortoises for forage, even when livestock densities are modest. Comparisons of tortoise and cattle feeding and foraging behavior were made using fenced (without livestock) and unfenced plots in the Mojave. During early spring there was a 38 percent overlap in the diets of these two animals, meaning that the plant species they selected and the proportion of each species eaten were pretty similar. Obviously, the larger, more mobile cattle could consume much more forage than the typical Desert Tortoise, effectively reducing the total forage supply in the habitat. Succulent annuals were preferred, especially the native California dandelion *(Malacothrix californica)*, which was relatively abundant during the first year of the study. But as the soil dried later in the season, tortoises shifted to cacti and other hydrated perennials. This reduced diet overlap to 22 percent because cattle continued to eat the dry "hay" of dead forbs and grasses and avoided the cacti. Drought in the following year, however, produced so few native annuals that tortoises in the unfenced plot had to shift to eating the sparse but green Mediterranean grass that would normally be avoided. They also had to spend more time (and, therefore, energy) trying to find suitable forage than tortoises protected from moderate levels of cattle grazing.

We also know that over time, intensive grazing has altered the process of succession and limited the ability of desert vegetation to recover from disturbance. This has been clearly demonstrated by studies of big sagebrush *(Artemisia tridentata)* communities in the Great Basin. Prior to livestock and weeds, the diverse shrub canopy was interrupted by tall perennial grasses, such as wild rye *(Leymus cinereus)* and needlethread *(Hesperostipa comata)*. Periodic fires, set by lightning or native people, tended to inhibit the shrubs and favor native grasses that resprouted from buds at or below the soil surface. Recovery produced patches of grass-dominated steppe vegetation supporting roving herds of Mule Deer *(Odocoileus hemionus)* and Desert Bighorn. The native grasses, with leaves rich in nitrogen (mostly photosynthetic enzymes) and devoid of herbivore defenses, provided reliable, high-quality forage. With the arrival of intense livestock grazing (for example, many cattle over many years, and less herd movement) these forage species were the first to go. The "protein grasses," even their stems and buds, were so palatable relative to big sagebrush (nauseating oils) and cheatgrass (irritating barbs) that Great Basin steppes had been degraded by the end of the nineteenth century. Sagebrush and rabbitbrush *(Chrysothamnus)* expanded and weeds invaded, but even these would be consumed if overstocking or drought persisted. Soil erosion accelerated where grazing eliminated plant and litter cover or where trampling destroyed the protective cryptogamic crust. The response of degraded sagebrush steppe to fire produces even more degradation, as regrowth is mostly from the weed-dominated seed bank. Succession after heavy livestock grazing in the Great Basin now perpetuates the weeds and woody shrubs that reduce the economic, as well as ecological, benefits of the land.

Other impacts of overgrazing, or of grazing in general, are inconsistent or difficult to quantify. For example, where livestock trample the cryptogamic crust or churn a cemented pavement, the potential for soil erosion is decidedly increased (particularly on slopes). This is of special concern in the desert, where soil nutrients essential for sustaining plant growth are usually concentrated in the upper four inches. The loss of an inch or two of this ancient, enriched soil can further reduce primary productivity for decades, if not centuries. However, it has also been shown that other areas with different soil surface characteristics may not be damaged. Where sheep graze or bed down for the night, the soil is often compacted, with greater surface strength and erosion resistance. This same ambiguity exists with respect to direct impacts of livestock on certain species of wildlife. For example, sheep damaged 10 percent and destroyed four percent of 164 Desert Tortoise burrows found in a one square mile study plot in the Mojave Desert. The remaining, unaffected burrows were located under the protective branches of shrubs where hooves could not trample. And because tortoises often dig new burrows in late spring even if old ones are available, the scientists concluded that the direct effect of the sheep on the burrows was insignificant. Nevertheless, the indirect impacts through reduced productivity, lowered vegetation quality (weeds), and impaired successional responses are significant enough to warrant strict regulation of grazing in the desert.

The first attempt to regulate grazing on nonforested public lands came in 1934 with congressional passage of the Taylor Grazing Act. The act eventually led to establishment

Overgrazing and concentrated use (especially around water sources and corrals) damage soils and vegetation. (Jeff Lovich)

of the federal Bureau of Land Management, which came to administer more than 12.1 million acres of desert land in California (about half the bioregion). Borrowing approaches developed by the U.S. Forest Service, the agency implemented programs for managing and conserving public rangelands on 174 million acres across the American West. This included a system for leasing public lands to private operators, guidelines for evaluating range condition, and regulations for setting site-specific grazing limits. The "animal unit month" (AUM) became the relevant measure of forage economics: the amount of dry plant material required to sustain one cow (and its calf) or five sheep for one month. It amounts to 990 pounds per month, or about six tons for 12 months, which in the Mojave would be every bit of foliage and fruit produced on roughly 22 acres during an average rainfall year. Obviously, only a fraction of this green matter could be consumed as forage without obliterating all traces of the vegetation. Allowances must be made for wildlife use, feral grazers (for example, wild horses and burros), and maintenance of some plant cover. So, in general, it takes about 300 acres of desert to support a cow and calf during an average year, and up to 3,000 acres in a dry year or in areas of minimal forage production. This contrasts with the three to 10 acres required to support the same cow and calf on annual grasslands in the San Joaquin Valley.

By 1980 the BLM had divided its desert lands into 54 grazing allotments, totaling about 4.5 million acres. The allotments had been leased by 63 operators, some of who could trace their heritage to the first generation of desert cowboys. Some were descendents of homesteaders who had established ranches, developed water sources, and took pride in a tradition of stewardship. But for many years that stewardship was based on experiences gained in more productive, less-arid bioregions. Corrals and fences concentrated the impacts of grazing to such a degree that in some areas succession could never overcome the effects of abundant weeds and heavily eroded soils. Thriving populations of nonnative deer, chukar *(Alectoris chukar)*, horses, and Burros were seen by ranchers as evidence of the benefits provided by the plumbing of new wells and concrete-lined springs. Grazing used the abundant protein grass that would otherwise go to waste and deterred the wildfires spread by the profusion of weedy biomass. These arguments assumed the desert would be resilient, readily conforming to practices developed for prairies and woodlands in other parts of the American West.

Even BLM wasn't sure how to regulate grazing on arid lands. Until 1968 the agency based its allocation of AUMs on the assumption that desert forage was produced by the perennial, rather than annual, plants. This constantly overestimated the available feed, permitting too many livestock to be released, year after year, into unreplenished, often droughted lands. (Perennials sacrifice growth for stress tolerance, except in the rare year of abundant rain. It's the annual grasses and forbs that have high rates of photosynthesis and biomass production). Compounding the problem was a lack of enough people to monitor the effects of livestock, with little or no effectual evaluation of how grazing was affecting the vegetation, much less the native wildlife. In 1989 the BLM averaged only one permanent range conservationist per 872,000 acres of leased desert land, with some individuals responsible for as much as 2.5 million acres. The agency has come a long way to rectify these problems, basing most of their permits on "a reasonable potential for growth of annual plants." They no longer assume a minimal standard amount of forage or time for grazing. Instead, they first assess the weather, plant, and soil conditions of an allotment during the winter and then make estimates of AUMs and the length of the coming season. But still, the residual effects of historic overgrazing on native species and natural communities of the bioregion will never be completely erased.

Native Species and Natural Communities

A bioregion is perpetuated by its native species, each a collection of populations that reproduce, migrate, and evolve over time. Characteristic species occur in large, widely distributed populations that thrive under current conditions and determine much about how the bioregion operates. In the California deserts, pinyon pine, creosote bush, Desert Kangaroo Rats, and harvester ants produce the foods, disperse the seeds, channel the water, and distribute the nutrients that affect many other species and their ecosystem context. Such species are relatively common, stress tolerant, and resilient in the face of disturbance, whether human or natural, and will likely persist in desert landscapes of the distant future. They will continue to shift distribution in response to climate change, collect and lose novel genes, and be subjected to the incisive power of natural selection. Characteristic species have evolutionary potential and are unlikely to be irreparably degraded by human activity.

But many species exist in small populations over a sliver of the landscape and do not

Desert species protected by federal and state endangered species laws (clockwise from upper left): Amargosa Vole *(Microtus californicus scirpensis)* (Jennifer L. Neuwald), Inyo California Towhee *(Pipilo crissalis)* (Bob Steele), Coachella Valley Fringe-toed Lizard *(Uma inornata)* (William C. Flaxington), and Cushenberry milkvetch *(Astragalus albens)* (Steve Matson).

make a disproportionate or widespread contribution to the bioregion. They are, however, part of the richness and distinctiveness of the California deserts and may be of local ecological significance. Some are ancient relicts with one or a few, scattered populations that cling to limited patches of suitable habitat. Eureka dunegrass *(Swallenia alexandrae)*, elephant tree *(Bursera microphylla)*, Amargosa Springsnail *(Pyrgulopsis amargosae)*, Devils Hole Pupfish, Panamint Alligator Lizard *(Gerrhonotus panamintensis)*, and Pale Kangaroo Mouse *(Microdipodops pallidus)* are examples of paleoendemics—old, unique species (even genera) persisting within the bioregion. Other species with limited population size and distribution are probably of more recent origin, perhaps the evolutionary products of the Pleistocene-Holocene transition. Borrego milkvetch *(Astragalus lentiginosus* var. *borreganus),* Providence Swallowtail Butterfly *(Papilio indra martini),* and the Palm Springs Pocket Mouse *(Perognathus longimembris bangsi)* are considered neoendemics — new, unique species (often varieties or subspecies rather than fully distinct species) recently evolved within the bioregion. Given their narrow distributions, limited abundance, and special habitat requirements, both paleo- and neoendemics have uncertain futures. They are susceptible to rapid change and can be readily degraded by careless human activities that increase the risk of extinction. These are species of conservation concern, whose evolutionary potential depends on whether the effects of incursion, fragmentation, and nonnatives can be minimized or reversed.

Currently 480 species of vascular plants and vertebrate animals are of conservation concern in the California deserts, or about 19 percent of the total known species (compare tables 3 and 5). If arthropods (insects, spiders, and scorpions), mollusks (snails), and crustaceans (brine shrimp) are added, the number rises to 532 species. Taking into account multiple subspecies and varieties of a species that are also of concern brings the total to 562 as of 2007. This tally is rich in plants (especially *Astragalus,* with 28 species), beetles (12 species, such as *Anomala hardyorum*), springsnails (seven species of *Pyrgulopsis* and *Tyronia),* pupfishes (four species of *Cyprinodon*), riparian birds (21 species, especially flycatchers, gnatcatchers, thrashers), and bats (11 species). In the case of plants, the sheer size of the desert flora and its high degree of endemism are likely to put many species or subspecies at risk. There is practically no limestone outcrop, alkali meadow, mountaintop, or dune in the California deserts without its own expressions of evolutionary diversification. Insects are also diverse but very poorly known. The beetles of concern tend to be found on large, old sand dune systems that have been subjected to intense OHV activity. Springsnails and pupfishes are put at risk, as their aquatic habitats are often modified by nonnative species or water diversion. Riparian birds depend on a healthy, well-watered overstory of native trees for nesting and foraging. The bats are very sensitive to direct disturbance of their roosts by people, often abandoning caves or mines after a single incursion by explorers. Thus, diversity and the pervasive activities of humans put large numbers of unique desert species at risk of extinction.

The problem for conservation biologists is to set priorities when deciding which species to attend to first. Time, money, expertise, and political will are limited, so naturally, rare species farthest from civilization are the lowest priority. For example, the desert ranges of Inyo County (for example, the Panamint, Nelson, Argus, and Inyo mountains) are rich in very rare species that currently have no special legal protection or management. These include the Inyo Slender Salamander *(Batrachoseps campi),* Panamint Alligator Lizard, Argus Kangaroo Rat *(Dipodomys panamintinus argusensis),* a host of endemic butterflies (for example, DeDecker's Blue Butterfly *[Icaricia acmon dedeckera]*), and a multitude of unique plants (for example, limestone monkeyflower *[Mimulus rupicola]* and Gilman's cymopterus *[Cymopterus gilmanii]*). Such obscure species are somewhat protected because their remote habitats receive only a few, intrepid visitors each year. On the other hand,

TABLE 5 Species and Taxa of Conservation Concern in the Great Basin, Mojave, and Sonoran Deserts of California, 2007 (Data from RareFind, CDFG 2007)

	Vascular Plants	Noninsect Invertebrates	Insects	Fish	Amphibians	Reptiles	Birds	Mammals	Sums
Species									
Total	1,836	?	?	43	16	56	425	97	2,473
Conservation concern	363	20	32	12	10	16	47	32	532
Listed	23	0	1	8	3	3	13	5	56
Taxa									
Conservation concern	380	21	32	18	10	16	49	36	562
Listed	25	0	1	10	3	3	15	5	62

valued species that humans know and exploit (for example, Desert Bighorn and saguaro [*Carnegiea gigantea*]) or specialist species that occupy coveted places (for example, springs, riparian floodplains, and mineralized outcrops) need strong legal protection and beneficial management. Otherwise, populations of such species rapidly dwindle as they are hunted, collected, fragmented, or obliterated by habitat destruction. The victims of modern, rapid change, such species warrant the highest priority for legal protection and may require special efforts by scientists, government agencies, and landowners to prevent extinction. But at present only 25 plants and 37 animals in the California deserts are listed under federal or state endangered species laws, even though hundreds are eligible.

Preventing extinction of rare desert plants is difficult at best. Drought-avoiding species fluctuate wildly in abundance, hiding in the seed bank for years and making trends hard to document. Peirson's milkvetch (*Astragalus magdalenae* var. *peirsonii*), known only from Algodones Dunes, is a perennial herb that just about disappears after two or three drought years in a row. Its hard-coated seeds, however, germinate en masse in response to intense fall storms that may occur once a decade. Such an event, 1.5 inches of rain falling in two days, occurred during October 2000. An extensive survey counted only five old plants but 71,900 new plants in the spring of 2001, almost half of which had flowered and produced seeds. By spring of 2003 only 200 of these were still alive, but they left behind a seed bank of two to six million. Many of those seeds responded to the plentiful winter rains of 2005 by producing an estimated 1.83 million plants across the dunes. Yet with the passage of another dry year, these were reduced to 83,000. Such large fluctuations in aboveground population size are buffered only by belowground seeds, which do succumb to granivores, fungi, poor habitat, and old age. So the critical question for conserving this rare plant is how many seeds are required to ensure persistence? We don't know, in part because natural mortality is hidden from view and in part because human-caused mortality adds another level of complexity. More than three million OHV enthusiasts visit the dune habitat of Peirson's milkvetch each year, sometimes exceeding 150,000 riders on a holiday weekend. Heavily used areas are devoid of plants, but vehicles tend to avoid milkvetch populations in steep depressions between dunes. It is also difficult to determine the impact of so many spinning wheels on the seed bank and the tender, cryptic seedlings that emerge during winter months. Such uncertainties have led to great conflict between government agencies, OHV groups, and conservationists.

Perhaps the plight of endangered animals in the bioregion is best illustrated by the Desert Tortoise, which is listed as threatened under both federal and state law. The reasons for its precarious state are complex and multifaceted. Since 1920 the range of this once widespread and common reptile has contracted 50 to 60 percent. Population densities in the western Mojave declined by 90 to 93 percent between 1979 and 1997. The rapid proliferation of roads and vehicles was probably most responsible, in large part because humans could easily and thoroughly permeate the deserts. Roadkill and collection for pets became predictably frequent, but so did senseless vandalism. Between 15 and 29 percent of all carcasses from the western Mojave had obvious gunshot damage. During the same period, less than three percent of carcasses from the less-visited eastern Mojave had been shot. The roads also fragmented and altered the natural communities on which the tortoise depended. Between 40 and 70 percent of the annual production of native annuals (for example, California dandelion), so important in the tortoise diet, has been replaced by less nutritious, less palatable weeds (for example, Mediterranean grass). The weeds also increase the frequency and intensity of devastating wildfires that were virtually unknown to the species and to the bioregion. Tortoise populations in these weed-infested communities are declining at a rate that is substantially greater than populations in less-infested communities. Malnourished animals grow slowly and reproduce less and are likely to have reduced immunity to disease. A respiratory infection, caused by the bacterium *Mycoplasma agassazii,* has been blamed for thousands of Desert Tortoise deaths in the Mojave since the 1990s. Pet tortoises contract the disease while in captivity, spreading it rapidly once illegally released back to the wild by well-intentioned owners. It has been estimated that tens of thousands of Desert Tortoises are kept as pets in Southern California, many collected from the wild and every one an epidemic in the making. Yet another source of mortality selectively targets small, juvenile tortoises, whose empty shells end up strewn across the bajada by the predatory Common Raven *(Corvus corax).* Between 1968 and 1988 the number of desert Common Ravens increased 1,500 percent, fueled by the growth of open garbage dumps and sewage ponds that service the burgeoning cities of Lancaster and Palmdale.

But species are not the only form of biological diversity at risk in the California deserts. Entire communities, rich assemblages of species, can be rare over the landscape and, therefore, susceptible to anthropogenic depletion. Of the 378 recognized types of natural desert communities in the state, 155 (41 percent) are considered by the California Department of Fish and Game as rare and of conservation concern. Examples include sand dune scrub, freshwater marsh, fan palm woodland, and bristlecone pine forest. Each of these depends on small-scale geological features, such as dunes, springs, or high-elevation mountaintops, that create essential conditions to sustain the biota (especially the presence or constancy of moisture). Groundwater pumping and competitive, nonnative species readily alter the essential conditions, leading to progressive and often irreversible changes in community structure and composition. Unfortunately, no law protects rare communities, so their persistence and quality will depend entirely on the actions of land managers and owners.

ECOLOGICAL REMEDIES

When did the tables turn? When did humans pose more of a threat to the desert than the desert posed to humans? Although many events could be considered pivotal (for example, the Garcés *entrada,* publication of Frémont's second expedition report, arrival of agriculture, or railroad construction), it may have been the cultural severance of Indian people from their desert knowledge that shifted all peril. Each family group, each tribe was a repository of place-specific knowledge and values, of resources and a lifeway woven into a coherent whole. Once the people were separated from their place, the lifeway became irrelevant, resources were left defenseless, and the place became vulnerable to deleterious changes originating from outside of the bioregion. Without guardians of indigenous knowledge, there would be no consideration of lost values, allowing degradation of the California deserts to begin.

Serious degradation came as the first nonnative species were established during the latter half of the nineteenth century, as westward expansion and technology promoted human incursion and fragmentation of habitat. But a threshold was crossed in the mid-twentieth century, perhaps with post–World War II migrations to Southern California or the invention of the OHV. That threshold was a marked coalescence of localized, small-scale impacts (damaged soil, deleted vegetation, weed infestations, endangered wildlife) into regionalized transformations of entire landscapes. The scale of this modern disturbance became so great so rapidly that natural healing processes (soil formation, succession, recolonization) would no longer suffice. Healing, if it could happen at all, would now require human assistance. It would require new desert knowledge and new commitment to diminish or reverse threats to the bioregion. How do we develop the ecological remedies that would heal the desert? Through resource-centered management, restoration science, and improved understanding that allows our modern society to value the coherent whole.

The Bureau of Land Management and the California Desert Plan

When the Bureau of Land Management (BLM) was created in 1946, it essentially inherited half the California desert bioregion. These had been federal lands held open for settlement and extensively used for grazing, mining, and military training. Regulatory oversight developed slowly, in part because the agency did not use much science to inform its management (for example, the lack of grazing exclosures) and in part because these remote, "barren" lands did not seem to require much planning, enforcement, and public outreach. This would change by the 1960s as BLM itself became aware that a threshold had been crossed. Obvious degradation and increasing user conflict necessitated congressional action. The BLM lobbied for active management that included scientific inventory of its desert resources, a large-scale planning process, and improved enforcement capabilities. The Federal Lands Policy and Management Act (FLPMA, or "flip-ma"), passed in 1976, transformed the BLM and led to development of the California Desert Plan.

The FLPMA established the 25 million acre California Desert Conservation Area (CDCA), which included federal, state, and private lands. The BLM was charged with preparing and implementing a comprehensive, long-term plan for the management, use, development, and protection of its 12.1 million acres, based upon the principles of multiple use, sustained yield, and the maintenance of environmental quality. This required the largest effort of its kind at the time, establishing a team of more than 130 scientists and resource managers as the newly formed Desert Plan Staff in Riverside. Never before had so many expert botanists, zoologists, wildlife biologists, soil scientists, geologists, archeologists, range conservationists, recreation specialists, and planners been assembled to perform a BLM task. Over a two-year period an advisory committee conducted 15 meetings and seminars across the state to inform the public and gather input. There was no shortage of controversy, from the local citizenry to Congress. More than 40,000 comments were submitted to the Desert Plan Staff for tabulation and analysis.

The massive California Desert Plan (and its seven volumes of appendices) took four years and six million dollars to develop. It included the first comprehensive inventory of soils, plants, animals, natural communities, and archeological sites of the California deserts, a major contribution in and of itself. Desertwide proposals for managing vegetation and wildlife could then be made, with emphasis on endangered species and special habitats (especially those associated with water). Land use controls were developed, from designations of vehicle access routes to wilderness areas and "areas of critical environmental concern" (ACECs). The ACECs protected historical and archeological sites (for example, Yuha rock drawings), unusual vegetation (the Afton Canyon riparian community along the Mojave River), wildlife habitat (Big Morongo Canyon), and endangered species (the Deep Springs Black Toad *[Bufo exsul]* population). Grazing, mining, energy development, recreation, and wild horses and Burros were also addressed to insure the "balance" required by its principal goal:

To provide for the use of the public lands and resources of the California Desert Conservation Area, including economic, educational, scientific, and recreational uses, in a manner which enhances wherever possible—and does not diminish, on balance—the environmental, cultural, and aesthetic values of the Desert and its future productivity.

The plan uses, as its basis for meeting the needs of the country . . . , the best available information about resources of the Desert, in particular its soil, vegetation, water, air, and minerals—the basic and finite things upon which all life depends. Maintenance of the productive potential of these resources on a global scale will determine the future of mankind, thus this must be the heart and foundation of any land-use plan.　　　　　　　　(BLM 1980a)

President Carter signed the plan into law during the final days of his administration. Overall, it was viewed as a success, given the size and complexity of the task, and the nation's first authentic ecosystem management plan. And during the process, the BLM in California had been transformed into a science-based resource agency that responded to a broad spectrum of the public, not just the user groups it regulated. But the political winds had shifted in 1980, and President-elect Reagan was likely to bring more change to the BLM and the plan it was about to implement.

California Desert Protection Act

Built into the Desert Plan was an amendment process that BLM began to use almost immediately after publication. Ideally, amendments would reflect improvements in the information upon which management decisions are based. This is the concept of adaptive management, which provides a formal, decision-making framework that obtains new data from scientifically designed monitoring programs. The plan states:

Since it is plainly impractical to try to learn all there is to know about such a vast and diverse area before completing a plan, or to try to stop and make the world wait until we do know, the Plan carries a major commitment to monitor the effects of decision[s] and to guide future adjustments to those decisions in concert with an ever-increasing body of knowledge.　　　(BLM 1980a)

But the immediacy of the amendments, the lack of an operating adaptive management framework, and a perceived trend toward decreased resource protection began to erode support for the plan. For example, the plan found that 5.7 million acres of BLM land met all the criteria for wilderness protection, yet a 1989 report by the Government Accounting Office (GAO) found that the agency had recommended only 2.3 million acres for designation. About one third of the required wildlife and habitat management plans for the CDCA had been completed (not implemented), in part because the BLM's planning budget had been cut 50 percent between 1981 and 1988. Despite important changes brought to the agency by the California Desert Plan, both in GAO's view and the views of other agencies, BLM has frequently allowed the needs of competing interests, such as recreation and commercial use, to take precedence over wildlife interests when conflicts have arisen.   (Wheat 1999)

It appeared to some that BLM's commitment to science-based resource management had ebbed.

A series of legislative proposals, congressional hearings, and political agreements began in 1986 that would designate wilderness areas and transfer desert lands from the BLM to the National Park Service (NPS). Supporters argued that the BLM's multiple-use mandate and long history of serving the livestock and mining industries would always bias its decision-making process. In contrast, the NPS had a clear protection mandate that would better serve the delicate and degraded resources of the CDCA. Opponents portrayed the legislation as a "lock-up" of public land and a hasty rejection of the Desert Plan. The sheer magnitude and boldness of the proposal generated great political rancor, becoming the largest parks and wilderness campaign to ever affect the lower 48 states. The California Desert Protection Act (CDPA) was finally signed in 1994 by President Clinton, affecting resource management on nearly nine million acres of the CDCA.

The CDPA established 7.7 million acres of wilderness, approximately 3.6 million on BLM lands and 4.0 million on NPS lands. Some of these acres were additions to Death Valley and Joshua Tree national monuments, which were both elevated to national park status. The additions to Death Valley National Park (1.3 million acres) included portions of Eureka, Saline, Panamint, and Greenwater valleys and many intervening ranges, making it the largest federal park (3.4 million acres) outside of Alaska. Joshua Tree gained 245,000 acres of the Little San Bernardino, Cottonwood, Coxcomb, and Eagle mountains that are now fully embraced by the park's boundary (795,000 acres). But the centerpiece of the act was creation of the 1.6 million acre Mojave National Preserve. Extending from Soda Lake to Piute Valley, the preserve encompassed enough climatic, geologic, and topographic diversity that species and communities from all three California deserts, Great Basin, Mojave, and Sonoran, are included. The total number of protected archeological sites has yet to be determined, and about 70 miles of the Garcés footpath can be traced across the preserve.

Changes in land use and agency responsibility go a long way toward reducing threats to the bioregion. Some forms of human incursion are greatly reduced (commercial development, road building, motorized vehicle recreation) or more strictly regulated (hunting, livestock grazing, mining). Others, such as air pollution, go unabated (Joshua Tree was recently designated by the U.S. Environmental Protection Agency as one of eight national parks with excessively high levels of ozone). But parks and wilderness areas draw large numbers of visitors to once remote and isolated areas of the desert (2.8 million in 2003). People arrive in cars, recreational vehicles, socks, and shoes that carry seeds from elsewhere. They desire and deserve contact with desert organisms and long for the solitude of the vast, arid interior. Thus, the challenge of balancing use and protection remains for the NPS, BLM, and all desert landowners. Even the most gentle forms of use will require proactive management: an intervention informed by science, enforced by regulation, and powered by hard work on behalf of sensitive or degraded biological resources.

Proactive Resource Management

The inventory of resources conducted by the BLM for the Desert Plan was the first phase of a science-based conservation process. Knowing species, communities, and environmentally sensitive places is essential—inventory tells the agency what needs to be managed and where it is located. The second phase is a field survey to update the status of those resources, determining which are common or rare, and immediate threats to persistence. The third phase is proactive management, which goes beyond planning to benefit a resource within its natural context. Fencing, vehicle controls, designated campgrounds, and educational signage can be installed where sensitive resources are stationary and localized. But additional measures, more difficult to execute, are needed to reverse historic degradation and to prevent future catastrophe. Among the most important of these measures is removal of nonnative species on a landscape scale.

The need to remove Burros from the desert was long recognized but seldom acted upon. The well-documented threat to Desert Bighorn and other wildlife species was ironically ignored in favor of animals that were perceived by the public as charming or imbued with the mythology of the "Old West." Even the title of the Wild Free-Roaming Horse and Burro Act of 1971 implied a special American status. The act required the BLM (but not the NPS) to "achieve and maintain population levels that insure healthy herds" on its lands while avoiding impacts to wildlife. With a population doubling time of only four years in the CDCA, the Desert Plan successfully argued that removal of 10,000 wild equines would "provide stable, manageable, and healthy herd levels". Roundups on foot, on horse, and by helicopter ensued, with captives funneled to a public adoption program. During the first decade 20,000 Burros were removed, indicating that despite a gross underestimate of population size, the program could be effective on a large scale. As of 2007 there were about 500 Burros total in the CDCA. The BLM has established a goal of 337 in five herd management areas as an appropriate level, with none left in national parks or on most military lands. The potential for explosive growth remains, however, and ongoing removal will be required to counteract this prolific beast and provide a sustained benefit to native species.

The same can be said for nonnative plants, especially salt cedar, which is even more abundant and prolific than the Burros. Attempts to control this highly invasive weed date back to the 1950s and were aimed at increasing water availability for human consumption. The current focus is to enhance habitat for native wildlife and begin the process of ecosystem restoration. A great variety of arduous methods has been developed, from hand-pulling seedlings to bulldozing, burning, cutting, and herbicide application. Lab and field tests of the Salt Cedar Leaf Beetle *(Diorhabda elongata)* have shown promise because this Asian species is a specialist herbivore that will starve to death if offered only native forage. Regardless of control method, resprouting from the root crown is common, and fol-

Colorado River and the "Needles," showing dense riparian vegetation of salt cedar and willow, 2003. (Joseph Dougherty)

low-up treatments are necessary. These labor- and cost-intensive methods have been successfully applied to infestations less than 50 acres in extent. Considering that the problem along the Colorado River alone exceeds 400,000 acres, elimination of salt cedar from the bioregion is unlikely. Nevertheless, enthusiasm and persistence have made a big, local difference, and all desert agencies have embraced "tamarisk bashing." The BLM has had success along the Mojave River in Afton Canyon and in the Coachella Valley at the Dos Palmas Preserve. It has cleared canyons in the Santa Rosa Mountains to make water available for Desert Bighorns. The NPS has virtually eliminated salt cedar from wild portions of Death Valley National Park, just as California State Parks have controlled infestations within Anza-Borrego. Although some have argued that such small-scale weeding efforts are of limited value, they are the first remedy against the plague caused by invading nonnatives. In addition, improvements in habitat quality due to weed removal can be vitally important to small, tenuous populations of rare species.

Some rare species, however, now require extremely high levels of proactive management. Recovery of the Desert Tortoise, required by its 1990 listing as threatened under the Endangered Species Act, affects public and private lands across the entire 25 million acre CDCA. The BLM began to amend its 1980 California Desert Plan, coordinating with the NPS's update of its General Management Plans for Death Valley and the Eastern Mojave

Colorado River near Fort Mojave, showing open floodplain without much riparian vegetation, 1863. (Rudolph D'Heureuse)

Preserve. Both agencies, working with the public and private sectors, will place emphasis on returning viability to Tortoise populations over the next 25 years using some of the same planning and proactive tools that have so far proven effective. A larger palette of "flagship" species, including Mojave Ground Squirrel *(Spermophilus mohavensis)*, Desert Bighorn, California Leaf-nosed Bat *(Macrotus californicus),* sand food *(Pholisma sonorae),* and the Mecca aster *(Xylorhiza cognata)* are also targeted for special action. Degraded natural communities, including arroyo woodland, sand dune scrub, and riparian forest will be managed to favor natives and deter nonnatives. But healing damaged species and degraded communities will require forms of restoration that science has yet to devise.

RESTORATION SCIENCE

Lessons from Natural Healing

If not overwhelmed by the scale, intensity, and frequency of human impacts, the desert can heal itself. Studies of disturbance, population dynamics, and succession tell us that species have an intrinsic ability to recover and communities to recuperate. Processes of dispersal, colonization, soil formation, and vegetation development impart resilience to biological systems that allows persistence. These natural healing processes can be harnessed or emulated if they can be understood by restoration science.

For Desert Bighorn, recovery will require more herds to reclaim mountainous territory relinquished to Burros or depopulated by hunting and disease. More herds over more of the original range will reduce the chance of extinction. But the natural processes of dispersal and colonization of unoccupied habitats have been interrupted by roads and land development, resulting in the isolation of populations that would otherwise spread and establish new herds. Herds isolated by highways for only 40 years have also lost as much as 15 percent of their genetic variation for lack of replenishment by migration. Studies of interacting populations (a metapopulation) have revealed the dynamic linkages that allowed Desert Bighorn to overcome the effects of degradation and demise in the days before fragmentation. Restoration now emulates dispersal and colonization by creating new herds with transplantation and captive breeding programs. Each sheep represents a potential founder of a new population, whose survival and growth can be monitored using radio collars. More than 100 animals have been successfully released into portions of the Santa Rosa and San Jacinto mountains, effectively bypassing lethal, human-made obstacles. Many other species, both plant and animal, depend on metapopulation dynamics for persistence. Each will require its own restoration solutions for mitigating the loss of dispersal and colonization processes in a fragmented desert landscape.

Natural soil formation in deserts requires many organisms acting on parent materials over long periods of time. Microbes and cryptogamic crusts enhance nutrient levels, facilitate root growth, and promote survival of plants colonizing new surfaces. Stems intercept precipitation and roots facilitate its infiltration, as do the burrowing animals that follow. Organic matter accumulates from all of these sources, binding and retaining water and nutrients while supplying the underground food web. When a desert soil is subsequently eroded or compacted, centuries of accumulated biological richness must be restored. As a first step, soil-building microbes and crusts should be protected from further damage. Exclusion of trampling livestock from sagebrush-grass steppe allows remaining "islands" of crust to increase in cover by four to 15 percent in 18 years. In drier areas of the Mojave subjected to heavy vehicle damage, it takes more than 60 years of protection to begin, and one or two centuries to complete, this healing process. Heavy damage may require inoculation with spores of mycorrhizal fungi to rebuild the soil microbial community and promote establishment of colonizing plants. Spreading chunks of bark and wood over the surface provides a slowly decomposing source of food for soil microbes that anchor the food web. Further studies of soil formation will yield other restoration techniques for overcoming a significant constraint on sites that have been severely disturbed.

The development of desert vegetation during succession provides insights for restoration science. Short-lived species that rapidly colonize, grow, and reproduce are pioneers on new or denuded soils. Nitrogen-fixing annuals, such as lupines *(Lupinus)* and milkvetches give an early boost to the soil forming or healing process. These are followed by small but fast-growing shrubs that reproduce just a few years after establishment. Burrobush, cheesebush *(Hymenoclea salsola)*, and rabbitbrush *(Chrysothamnus)* have easily met germination requirements and establish well even after heavy disturbance. The long-lived, stress-tolerant species appear last mostly because they are slow growing. Creosote bush, blackbush *(Coleogyne ramosissima)*, and greenfire *(Menodora spinescens)* may not contribute any cover to the shrub canopy for 100 years, but they will last for centuries once established. This natural pattern forms a generic template for revegetation efforts. Early efforts in the 1970s and 1980s to heal damage caused by construction of highways, powerlines, and aqueducts confirmed that seeds and transplants of short-lived species had the greatest chance of success. But the vagaries of drought, herbivory (especially by jackrabbits *[Lepus]*), and competition with weeds greatly influence the outcomes of revegetation efforts in deserts, as they do during natural succession.

Developing New Approaches and Technologies
In modern Southern California, the self-healing desert is often overwhelmed. The required decades and centuries are simply not available where millions of visitors and residents bring rapid and irreversible change. The desert has become a tortoise in a jackrabbit world.

Under these conditions, restoration science will have to develop new approaches and technologies for healing the damage we cannot prevent.

One such approach comes from the recognition that populations of just about any widespread species are genetically different from one another. Each has been subjected to a unique and quite localized regime of climate, soil, predators, food availability, and other environmental conditions that affect the composition of the gene pool. This evolutionary phenomenon produces adaptive diversity, a kind of fine-tuning that matches organisms to environments on both large and small spatial scales. On a large scale, the south to north progression of chromosome races in creosote bush populations is correlated with success in colonizing very different arid environments, from central Mexico to eastern California. On a smaller scale, populations of Desert Bighorn from near the Owens Valley and the Mojave Desert differ with respect to development of their characteristic horns. Horns begin growing when the Mojave sheep weigh only 12 pounds, whereas the onset in the Owens Valley sheep is at 26 pounds. Restorationists assume that such complex variation is genetically controlled and important to persistence in a given environment. It means that transplanted animals for founding or restoring populations should, indeed must, come from native sources close to the project site. Local populations have been shown to perform better than distant populations of the same species and, therefore, have a greater chance of successful establishment. They also will not introduce poorly adapted forms of genes into a remnant, local population (genetic pollution). Using local genetic sources for all founders has become a creed among restorationists.

Techniques for improving the survival and growth of founding populations are also under development. Irrigation of seeds and container-grown plants is of obvious benefit but difficult to execute in remote, droughted locations. An elaborate, subsurface drip system was installed to help establish a desert saltgrass (*Distichlis spicata* var. *stricta*) meadow across the dusty, barren playa of Owens Lake. Tubing and emitters were sunk into a carefully tilled playa surface and topped with plugs of locally collected saltgrass. Machines designed for agricultural purposes precisely placed these elements of the system together and tamped the clayey surface down to promote rise of water into the root zone. Combined with an equally clever drainage system, irrigation also leached and carried away excessive salts. Although temperatures were high and the soil remained quite salty, this stress-tolerant C_4 species was able to establish a remarkably luxuriant canopy. After just two years saltgrass developed at least 50 percent cover over most of the project's 2,100 acres (which also proved effective in reducing dust emissions). Irrigation is now being reduced, as roots find their way to the shallow groundwater beneath the playa surface.

Adapting other agricultural techniques to desert restoration has been particularly important for healing soil damage. "Ripping" with a tractor-pulled disk harrow can be effectively used to alleviate severe compaction in the upper two feet of a soil. This greatly improves the infiltration of precipitation and penetration by roots. Soil amendments to improve fertility can be helpful, but they can also promote the growth of weeds and inhibit natural recovery of the microbial community. Restorationists prefer inoculation of

A closed road in the Nopah Range before restoration of the vegetation. (Unknown photographer, U.S. Bureau of Land Management)

The same road after restoration with fast-growing, early successional plant species. (Unknown photographer, U.S. Bureau of Land Management)

founding seeds and plants with mycorrhizal fungi. Local sources of native mycorrhizae may still reside within a damaged soil but could require extraction with an auger drill to obtain an inoculum from 10 to 20 feet deep. Surface soils with remnant cryptogamic crusts can be used to inoculate a hydromulch for spraying across a finished revegetation project. Such inoculations reduce the time required for soil restoration and improve the performance of founding populations of native plants.

The importance of controlling nonnative species, both plant and animal, has already been discussed. Techniques for controlling woody weeds, such as salt cedar, are brutal but effective. Bulldozers can clear 100 acres of impenetrable thickets along the Colorado River during a single winter. Hand-cutting along with stump-applied herbicide is needed in more sensitive areas. Herbaceous and grass weeds are more difficult to control because they are so abundant, widespread, and prolific. Hand-weeding red brome can increase the density and biomass of native annuals, but only in small plots where labor-intensive efforts can be used to preserve diverse assemblages of wildflowers. Where such assemblages have been destroyed by construction, it may be better to "fight fire with fire." Research has shown that some native herbs, such as desert marigold *(Baileya multiradiata)*, Palmer's beardtongue *(Penstemon palmeri)*, and desert aster *(Xylorhiza tortifolia)* are able to outcompete, and even exclude, red brome from ripped and seeded sections of an old road. Using native species for weed control can also alter the course of succession, so they, like any other technology, must be thoroughly researched and carefully applied.

Propagation techniques for native desert plants are constantly being improved to increase establishment success and decrease project cost. Experience has shown that seeding many perennial species into a restoration site often fails for lack of rainfall or because rodents and ants quickly gather all the seeds. Transplanting container-grown seedlings of the same species can improve establishment tenfold. One project along a powerline corridor found that only .3 percent of all shrub seeds became established, compared to 26 percent of transplanted seedlings, regardless of irrigation treatment. Even creosote bush can be successfully transplanted, especially if pruned to increase the root-to-shoot ratio. Special growth containers, called plant bands, allow development of a robust root system in founders, a key factor in transplantation success. These open-ended boxes (like long milk cartons) are placed in planting holes and pulled out so that roots are not disturbed. Long-term survival is increased by protecting founders from jackrabbit herbivory or providing a tree shelter (nurse plant surrogate) to shield the plant from wind and sun. Such techniques also help lower the cost of a desert restoration project from $10,000 per acre to a low range of $4,800 to $6,000 per acre. If the biological, educational, aesthetic, or real estate values of the land do not

RESTORATION ON THE 'AHAKHAV TRIBAL PRESERVE

The Mojave and Chemehuevi people still live along the lower Colorado River. Over many decades they saw the waters diverted, floods diminished, forests cleared, and banks choked with salt cedar. Traditional agriculture and fisheries were displaced, along with mesquite woodlands, cottonwood riparian, and the backwater wetlands that supported a rich assemblage of cultures and creatures. The people were relocated to higher ground, but they remained connected to their long history of river dwelling.

That connection was renewed in 1994 by Dennis Patch, a Mojave Indian who grew up on the Colorado River Indian Reservation. Inspired by childhood memories and the stories told by elders, Patch

Replacing salt cedar with native cottonwood and willow on the 'Ahakhav Tribal Preserve. (Fred Philips)

had a vision: to establish a preserve that restored people to the river and recovered lost biological resources. The vision was bold, a conviction that saw potential in a degraded landscape others had long abandoned. Instead of sweltering weed thickets, stagnant meanders, and channelized watercourses, Patch dreamt of a nature park where tribal members would gather to relax, fish, and picnic in the shade of *gugvap* (cottonwood) and *vimaka* (mesquite). And with his master's degree in education, he was well aware that this nature park could inspire generations yet to come.

warrant this kind of expenditure, a minimum treatment to facilitate natural healing may be the best approach. This could include soil ripping or roughening, weed-free composting, and planting "islands" of a few irrigated founders at a cost of $500 to $2,000 per acre.

Overcoming the effects of incursion and fragmentation on the desert biota will be an ongoing challenge. Barrier fences and underpasses have demonstrated effectiveness in reducing roadkill mortality in Desert Tortoise, sometimes by as much as 75 percent along critical sections of highway. But it is unknown if such devices alone can ameliorate all effects of fragmentation. Connecting preserves and parks with intervening corridors of high-quality or restored habitat may reestablish the metapopulation dynamics of long-isolated herds of Desert Bighorn. Maybe even Pronghorn could spread south from the Owens

Egrets use the newly restored wetland and riparian vegetation of the 'Ahakhav Tribal Preserve. People have also returned. (Fred Philips)

But realizing the vision required a diverse coalition of talents with relentless determination. Skeptics on and off the reservation had to be persuaded. Permits, environmental impact statements, grants, and technical plans had to be written and approved. Consultations with the tribal council, elders, and reservation residents ensured that restoration designs would reflect the broadest possible consensus and build a strong foundation of support. Fred Phillips, then a landscape architect student at Purdue University, led an army of students on a two-year effort that brought a bulldozer, native plant nursery, sediment dredge, and local workforce to the banks of the river in 1996.

Working in phases, the first clearing and replanting of riparian habitat was done on 124 acres. Salt cedar and other nonnatives were selectively removed by a bulldozer that could plow through the dense thickets. More than 228,000 cubic yards of sediments and stagnant muck were dredged from adjacent backwater wetlands and spread across the riparian clearing. The sediments provided a rich, organic supplement that would prepare the soil for replanting. Cuttings of native species from local populations had been inoculated with mycorrhizal fungi from local soils and allowed to establish themselves in one-gallon pots. Tens of thousands of these founders of the new riparian vegetation were planted in specific spots that soil

➤

Valley if contiguous habitat could be managed for this purpose. Obviously, large-scale planning efforts that attempt to unite habitat islands into ecosystem archipelagos can benefit many species at one time.

The research needed to develop these approaches and techniques began in the 1970s, two centuries after Garcés witnessed the last zenith of biological diversity and ecological integrity in the bioregion. It flourishes in academia, government agencies, and consulting firms, attempting to maintain, if not restore, that diversity and integrity. If sustained and expanded, restoration science will continue learning from the desert and innovating ecological remedies. Of equal importance will be the training of skilled practitioners and zealous guardians of a new, indigenous knowledge.

testing indicated would be optimal for growth and survival. A drip irrigation system and tree shelters allowed roots to reach the water table and shoots to endure herbivores and the intense summer sun. The hard work, often on days that exceeded 120°F, was accomplished by Mojave, Chemehuevi, Hopi, and Navaho people from the reservation, along with students from Purdue.

The restoration brought transformation. Cottonwoods and mesquite grew almost an inch per day, establishing a new canopy that was surprisingly tall (15 to 36 feet) and shady (100 percent cover) after only three or four years. Survival of founding trees exceeded 80 percent overall. The number of bird species observed within the restoration area has doubled, and even deer have returned. And people returned as well, taking advantage of the preserve's recreation and education programs. A trained staff now hosts more than 1,000 youths and adults each year, leading canoe trips, interpretive hikes, tree planting, and other outdoor activities that build community support and ownership of the 1,042 acre preserve. An abandoned, depauperate landscape has become a cultural classroom, and the values of the native river are taught once again. The project is also serving as a model for the Lower Colorado River Multispecies Conservation Plan, as well as for Indian tribes throughout the country that perform ecological restoration.

Reversing the damage of the past, damage to ecosystems and damage to people, is a great challenge. Interpersonal and institutional conflict took their toll, and Phillips left the preserve in 1999. Reflecting on the project's tangible benefits, he wrote:

> The other night I walked through the 'Ahakhav. The smell had changed; it's
> cooler than it used to be here. Our two-year-old cottonwoods towered 35 feet
> above me. It is amazing what can be done when a community comes
> together and takes action as a whole. Let the historic cultural visions con-
> tinue to guide us.

Discovery and rediscovery go on. We have already discovered that California deserts can be understood by science and explored for new species, natural communities, and ecological processes. We have already rediscovered that California deserts can be cherished for their life-giving utility and conquered only when their limits are known and respected. In 230 years we have made a good start. New national parks and preserves will bring desert knowledge to more and more people who will come and make their own observations and have their own revelations beneath the "broad blaze of omnipresent light." Many will be informed, some will be inspired, and a few will care enough to become guardians. The tamarisk-bashing ecologist John Rodman, who has led work parties into the desert for decades, has described this personal, as well as ecological, transformation:

The moment of truth arrives when people out for a Sunday walk come down the trail in the nature preserve, stop, stare, and ask who we are and why we are cutting down the nice flowering shrubs [salt cedar]. Who are we, indeed? No longer mere esthetes entranced by pretty pink flowers, no longer mere birdwatchers or backpackers who pass like angelic, incorporeal tourists leaving no trace upon the land—though we hope to see more birds when the tamarisk has been replaced by riparian natives. But do we grit our teeth and commit violence now in the hope of harmony after the revolution? The truth is that we enjoy what we are doing. We all have our private motives, but we have also tasted what it feels like to participate once again as actors in a natural system, and neither the place nor we will be the same again. Not even George, a sober senior citizen who has extended his range through successive tamarisk bashes until he has now driven all the way to Amargosa Canyon to work two days in order to take home one trailer load of what he admits is terrible firewood. Tamarisk bashing has crept into his blood. . . .

If, at the end of the day, there is no more tamarisk standing between the trail and the arroweed, or perhaps no tamarisk left standing at all in a small palm oasis, then the volunteers can contemplate with satisfaction the remarkable (sometimes unexpected) transformation.

Basketwoman of Olancha, 1931. (C. Hart Merriam)

Discovery and rediscovery are being woven into a new basket. The basket has a weft of values that recognize the irreplaceable benefits of diverse and self-sustaining deserts. Such a basket takes a long time for our society to weave, but once formed, its strength and integrity will be hard to deny. It will hold water and the seeds of subsistence and even endure the careless lapses of a learning species. More importantly, the knowledge and values woven into the basket will favor a sovereign future for this arid bioregion, governed by evolutionary and ecological processes.

REFERENCES

PREFACE

Baldwin, B. G., S. Boyd, B. J. Ertter, R. W. Patterson, T. J. Rosatti, and D. H. Wilken. 2002. *The Jepson Desert Manual: Vascular Plants of Southeastern California.* University of California Press, Berkeley.

Jaeger, E. C. 1938. *The California Deserts.* Stanford University Press, Stanford, CA.

MacMahon, J. 1985. *Deserts.* Audubon Society Nature Guides. A. Knopf, New York.

Miller, A. H., and R. C. Stebbins. 1973. *The Lives of Desert Animals in Joshua Tree National Monument.* University of California Press, Berkeley.

Morhardt, S., and E. Morhardt. 2004. *California Desert Flowers: An Introduction to Families, Genera, and Species.* University of California Press, Berkeley.

Phillips, S. J., and P. W. Comus. 2000. *A Natural History of the Sonoran Desert.* Arizona-Sonora Desert Museum Press, Tucson, and University of California Press, Berkeley.

INTRODUCTION: THE LOST BASKET

Anderson, M. K. 2005. *Tending the Wild: Native American Knowledge and the Management of California's Natural Resources.* University of California Press, Berkeley.

Bettinger, R. L. 1991. Native land use: Archeology and anthropology. In C. A. Hall Jr. (ed.), *Natural History of the White-Inyo Range, Eastern California,* pp. 463–486. University of California Press, Berkeley.

Fowler, D. D. 1986. History of research. In W. L. D'Azevedo (ed.), *Great Basin.* Vol. 11, *Handbook of North American Indians,* pp. 15–30. Smithsonian Institution, Washington, DC.

Liljeblad, S., and C. S. Fowler. 1986. Owens Valley Paiute. In W. L. D'Azevedo (ed.), *Great Basin*. Vol. 11, *Handbook of North American Indians*, pp. 412–434. Smithsonian Institution, Washington, DC.

Thomas, D. H., L. S. A. Pendleton, and S. C. Cappannari. 1986. Western Shoshone. In W. L. D'Azevedo (ed.), *Great Basin*. Vol. 11, *Handbook of North American Indians*, pp. 262–283. Smithsonian Institution, Washington, DC.

Wilke, P. J., M. DeDecker, and L. E. Dawson. 1979. *Dicoria canescens* T. & G., an aboriginal food plant in the arid west. *Journal of California and Great Basin Anthropology* 1: 188–192.

EYE OF THE BEHOLDER

Tuohy, D. R. 1986. Portable art objects. In W. L. D'Azevedo (ed.), *Great Basin*. Vol. 11, *Handbook of North American Indians*, pp. 227–237. Smithsonian Institution, Washington, DC.

Wallace, W. J. 1957. A clay figurine from Death Valley National Monument, California. *The Masterkey* 31: 131–134.

REDISCOVERY

Austin, M. 1903. *The Land of Little Rain*. Houghton Mifflin, Boston.

Beck, W. A., and Y. D. Haase. 1974. *Historical Atlas of California*. University of Oklahoma Press, Norman.

Beidleman, R. G. 2006. *California's Frontier Naturalists*. University of California Press, Berkeley.

Blake, W. P. 1858. *Report of a Geological Reconnaissance in California, Made in Connection with the Expedition to Survey Routes in California to Connect with the Surveys of Routes for a Railroad from the Mississippi Top. Engineer's, in 1853*. H. Bailliere, New York.

Bolton, H. E. 1930. *Anza's California Expeditions*. Vol. 2, *Opening a Land Route to California*. University of California Press, Berkeley. Pp. 323–360.

Brewer, W. H. 1974. *Up and Down California*. Third edition. University of California Press, Berkeley.

Brooks, G. R. 1977. *The Southwest Expedition of Jedediah S. Smith: His Personal Account of the Journey to California, 1826–1827*. Arthur Clark, Glendale, CA. Pp. 75–93.

Campbell, E. W. C., and W. H. Campbell. 1937. The archeology of Pleistocene Lake Mojave. The Lake Mojave site. *Southwest Museum Papers* 11: 9–44.

Chalfant, W. A. 1930. *Death Valley: The Facts*. Stanford University Press, Stanford, CA.

Cline, G. G. 1963. *Exploring the Great Basin*. Reprinted 1988. University of Oklahoma Press, Norman.

Cous, E. (trans. and ed.). 1900. *On the Trail of a Spanish Pioneer, the Diary and Itinerary of Francisco Garcés (Missionary Priest) in His Travels through Sonora, Arizona, and California, 1775–1776*. F. P. Harper, New York.

Coville, F. V. 1893. *Botany of the Death Valley Expedition*. Contributions to the U.S. National Herbarium 4. U.S. Government Printing Office, Washington, DC.

D'Azevedo, W. L. (ed.). 1986. *Great Basin*. Vol. 11, *Handbook of North American Indians*. Smithsonian Institution, Washington, DC.

Ebeling, W. 1986. *Handbook of Indian Foods and Fibers in Arid America*. University of California Press, Berkeley.

Farquhar, F. P. (ed.). 1966. *Up and Down California in 1860–1864. The Journal of William H. Brewer*. University of California Press, Berkeley. Pp. 387–396.

Fisher, A. K. 1893. Report on the ornithology of the Death Valley Expedition of 1891, comprising notes on the birds observed in Southern California, southern Nevada, and parts of Arizona and Utah. *North American Fauna* 7: 7–158.

Fitch, C. H. 1892. General route of the expedition. In C. H. Merriam (ed.) *The Death Valley Expedition. A Biological Survey of Parts of California, Nevada, Arizona and Utah. North American Fauna 7 (1893)*: Map 1.

Frémont, J. C. 1845. *Report of the Exploring Expedition to the Rocky Mountains and to Oregon and California*. Blair and Rives, Washington, DC.

Heap, G. H. 1854. *Central Route to the Pacific; from the Valley of the Mississippi to California: Journal of the Expedition of E. F. Beale, Superintendent of Indian Affairs in California, and Gwinn Harris Heap, from Missouri to California, in 1853*. Lippincott, Grambo, and Co., Philadelphia.

Heizer, R. F. 1978. *California*. Vol. 8, *Handbook of North American Indians*. Smithsonian Institution, Washington, DC.

Houghton, S. G. 1976. *A Trace of Desert Waters: The Great Basin Story*. A. H. Clark, Glendale, CA.

Jackson, D. 1975. *Sagebrush Country*. Time-Life Books, New York.

Jackson, D., and M. L. Spence. 1970. *The Expeditions of John Charles Frémont*. Vol. 1, *Travels from 1838 to 1844*. University of Illinois Press, Urbana. Pp. 672–776.

Jaeger, E. C. 1940. *Desert Wild Flowers*. Stanford University Press, Palo Alto, CA.

Jaeger, E. C. 1961. *Desert Wildlife*. Stanford University Press, Palo Alto, CA.

James, G. W. 1914. *California, Romantic and Beautiful*. The Page Co., Boston.

Kroeber, A. L. 1925. *Handbook of the Indians of California*. California Book Co., Berkeley, CA.

Kurzius, M. A. 1981. *Vegetation and Flora of the Grapevine Mountains, Death Valley National Monument, California-Nevada*. Contribution CPSU/UNLV 017/06. U.S. National Park Service, Washington, DC, and University of Nevada, Las Vegas.

Latta, F. 1979. *Death Valley '49ers*. Bear State Books, Exeter, CA.

Lindsay, D. 1973. History in the California Desert: The creation of the Anza Borrego Desert State Park—largest in the United States. *Journal of San Diego History* 19: 14–26 .

Lingenfelter, R. E. 1986. *Death Valley and the Amargosa: A Land of Illusion*. University of California Press, Berkeley.

Lummis, C. F. 1892. *A Tramp across the Continent*. Schribner's, New York.

Lummis, C. F. 1925. *Mesa, Canon, and Pueblo. Our Wonderland of the Southwest*. Century, New York.

Manley, W. L. 1894. *Death Valley in '49*. Reprinted 1929. Wallace Hebberd, New York.

McGrath, R. D. 1988. No goodee cow man. In Friends of the Eastern California Museum (compilers), *Mountains to Desert: Selected Inyo Readings*, pp. 17–73. Eastern California Museum, Independence, CA.

Merriam, C. H. 1893. Notes on the distribution of trees and shrubs in the deserts and desert ranges of southern California, southern Nevada, northwestern Arizona, and southwestern Utah. *North American Fauna* 7: 285–359.

Olmsted, Jr., F. L. 1929. *Report of State Park Survey of California*. California Printing Office, Sacramento, CA, pp. 51–52.

Palmer, T. S. 1893. List of localities visited by the Death Valley Expedition. *North American Fauna* 7: 361–384.

Perkins, E. B. 1922. *The White Heart of Mojave: An Adventure with the Outdoors of the Desert*. Boni and Liveright, New York. Pp. 93–95.

Riley, C. V. 1893. Report on a small collection of insects made during the Death Valley Expedition. *North American Fauna* 7: 235–268.

Russell, I. C. 1889. The Quaternary history of Mono Valley, California. In *Eighth Annual Report of the U.S. Geological Survey*, pp. 267–400. U.S. Geological Survey, Washington, DC.

Shelton, R. 1982. *Selected Poems 1969–1981*. University of Pittsburg Press, Pittsburgh, PA.

Smith, L. M. 1978. Edmund C. Jaeger, dean of the American desert. *Fremontia* 6: 21–24.

Stearns, R. E. C. 1893. Report on the land and fresh-water shells collected in California and Nevada by the Death Valley Expedition, including a few additional species obtained by Dr. C. Hart Merriam and assistants in parts of the southwestern United States. *North American Fauna* 7: 269–283.

Steinbeck, J. 1962. *Travels with Charley, in Search of America*. Viking Press, New York. Pp. 187–193.

Stejneger, L. 1893. Annotated list of the reptiles and batrachians collected by the Death Valley Expedition in 1891, with descriptions of new species. *North American Fauna* 7: 159–228.

Thompson, D. G. 1929. The Mohave Desert region, California. A geographic, geologic, and hydrologic reconnaissance. *U.S. Geological Survey Water Supply Paper* 578.

Van Dyke, D. 1927. A modern interpretation of the Garcés route. *Historical Society of Southern California* 13: 353–359.

Van Dyke, J. C. 1902. *The Desert. Further Studies in Natural Appearances*. Schribner's, New York.

Wild, P. (ed.). 2004. *True Tales of the Mojave Desert: From Talking Rocks to Yucca Man*. Center for American Places, Santa Fe, NM.

ALONG THE MOJAVE RIVER IN 1863

Casebier, D. G. 1999. *Mojave Road Guide, An Adventure through Time*. Tales of the Mojave Road Publishing Company, Essex, CA.

Duffield-Stoll, A. Q. 1994. *Zzyzx: History of an Oasis*. California Desert Studies Consortium, California State University, Fullerton.

Heap, G. H. 1854. *Central Route to the Pacific; From the Valley of the Mississippi to California: Journal of the Expedition of E. F. Beale, Superintendent of Indian Affairs in California, and Gwinn Harris Heap, from Missouri to California, in 1853*. Lippincott, Grambo, and Co., Philadelphia.

Lines, G. C. 1999. Health of native riparian vegetation and its relation to hydrologic conditions along the Mojave River, southern California. *U.S. Geological Survey Water Resources Investigations Report* 99-4112.

REDISCOVERY: DESERT FISHES

Brown, T. W. 1978, *Fishes, Amphibians, and Reptiles of the Lower Mojave River System*. Bureau of Land Management Desert Plan Staff, Riverside, CA.

Howard, H. 1955. Fossil birds from Lake Manix, Californa. *U.S. Geological Survey Professional Paper* 264-J.

Lovich, J. 1998. *Mojave Tui Chub*. Prepared for West Mojave Plan: A Habitat Conservation Plan and California Desert Conservation Area Plan Amendment. U.S. Bureau of Land Management, Moreno Valley, CA. www.blm.gov/ca/pdfs/cdd_pdfs/tuichub1.PDF

McGinnis, S. M. 2006. *Freshwater Fishes of California*. University of California Press, Berkeley.

Snyder, J. O. 1918. The fishes of Mohave River, California. *Proceedings of the U.S. National History Museum* 54: 297–299.

Waucoba4. 2006. Field trip to Pleistocene Lake, Manix, California. http://members.aol .com/Waucoba5/manix/manixlake.html.

WITHIN THE MAGIC CIRCLE

Jaeger, E. C. 1961. *Desert Wildlife*. Stanford University Press, Palo Alto, CA

A CONSPIRACY OF EXTREMES

Bainbridge, D. A., and R. A. Virginia. 1995. Desert soils and soil biota. In J. Latting and P. G. Rowlands (eds.), *The California Desert: An Introduction to Natural Resources and Man's Impact*, pp. 59–67. June Latting Books, Riverside, CA.

Bender, G. L. 1982. Introduction. In G. L. Bender (ed.), *Reference Handbook on the Deserts of North America*, pp. 1–6. Greenwood Press, Westport, CT.

California Geological Survey. 2006. Simplified Geologic Map of California, Map Sheet 57. California Department of Conservation.

Crosswhite, F. S., and C. D. Crosswhite. 1982. The Sonoran Desert. In G. L. Bender (ed.), *Reference Handbook on the Deserts of North America*, pp. 163–295. Greenwood Press, Westport, CT.

Dimmitt, M. A. 2000. Biomes and communities of the Sonoran Desert region. In S. J. Philips and P. W. Comus (eds.), *A Natural History of the Sonoran Desert*, pp. 3–18. Arizona-Sonora Desert Museum Press, Tucson, AZ.

Fiero, B. 1986. *Geology of the Great Basin*. University of Nevada Press, Reno.

Fowler, D., and D. Koch. 1982. The Great Basin. In G. L. Bender (ed.), *Reference Handbook on the Deserts of North America*, pp. 7–63. Greenwood Press, Westport, CT.

Hart, J. 1996. *Storm over Mono: The Mono Lake Battle and the California Water Future*. University of California Press, Berkeley.

Harvey, A. M., P. E. Wigand, and S. G. Wells. 1999. Response of alluvial fan systems to the late Pleistocene to Holocene climatic transition: Contrasts between the margins of pluvial lakes Lahontan and Mojave, Nevada and California, USA. *Catena* 36: 255–281.

Hill, M. 2006. *Geology of the Sierra Nevada*. University of California Press, Berkeley.

Howald, A. 2000. Plant communities. In G. Smith (ed.), *Sierra East: Edge of the Great Basin*, pp. 94–207. University of California Press, Berkeley.

Hunt, C. B. 1976. *Death Valley: Geology, Ecology, Archaeology*. University of California Press, Berkeley.

Jaeger, E. C. 1938. *The California Deserts*. Stanford University Press, Stanford, CA.

Jennings, C. W. 1977. *Geological Map of California: Geological Data Map 2*. California Division of Mines and Geology, Sacramento.

Kroeber, A. L. 1925. *Handbook of the Indians of California*. California Book Co., Berkeley.

Kuchler, A. W. 1976. Natural vegetation of California. In M. G. Barbour and J. Major (eds.), *Terrestrial Vegetation of California*. John Wiley and Sons, New York.

MacMahon, J. A. 1988. Warm deserts. In M. G. Barbour and W. D. Billings (eds.), *North American Terrestrial Vegetation*, pp. 231–264. Cambridge University Press, Cambridge, UK.

McAuliffe, J. R. 2000. Desert soils. In S. J. Philips and P. W. Comus (eds.), *A Natural History of the Sonoran Desert*, pp. 87–104. Arizona-Sonora Desert Museum Press, Tucson, AZ.

Miller, M. B., and L. A. Wright. 2004. *Geology of Death Valley: Landforms, Crustal Extension, Geologic History, Road Guides*. Kendall/Hunt Publishing, Dubuque, IA.

Nelson, C. A. 1971. *Waucoba Spring Geological Quadrangle*. U.S. Geological Survey, Washington, DC.

NOAA (National Oceanic and Atmospheric Administration). 1971–2000. *Climatography of the U.S., No. 81: California*. National Climatic Data Center, U.S. Department of Commerce, Washington, DC. http://cdo.ncdc.noaa.gov/cgi-bin/climatenormals/climatenormals.pl.

Norris, R. M., and R. W. Webb. 1976. *Geology of California*. John Wiley and Sons, New York.

NREL (National Renewable Energy Laboratory). 2003. Dynamic maps, GIS data, and analysis tools. U.S. Department of Energy, Washington, DC. www.nrel.gov/gis/solar.html.

Rowlands, P. G. 1995. Regional bioclimatology of the California Desert. In J. Latting and P. G. Rowlands (eds.), *The California Desert: An Introduction to Natural Resources and Man's Impact*, pp. 95–136. June Latting Books, Riverside, CA.

Rowlands, P. G., H. Johnson, E. Ritter, and A. Endo. 1982. The Mojave Desert. In G. L. Bender (ed.), *Reference Handbook on the Deserts of North America*, pp. 103–145. Greenwood Press, Westport, CT.

Scarborough, R. 2000. The geologic origin of the Sonoran Desert. In S. J. Philips and P. W. Comus (eds.), *A Natural History of the Sonoran Desert*, pp. 71–86. Arizona-Sonora Desert Museum Press, Tucson, AZ.

Sharp, R. P., and A. F. Glazner. 1997. *Geology Underfoot in Death Valley and Owens Valley*. Mountain Press, Missoula, MT.

Smith, S. D., R. K. Monson, and J. E. Anderson. 1997. *Physiological Ecology of North American Desert Plants*. Springer-Verlag, Berlin.

Soltz, D. L., and R. J. Naiman. 1978. *The Natural History of Native Fishes in the Death Valley System*. Natural History Museum of Los Angeles County, Los Angeles.

West, N. E. 1988. Intermountain deserts, shrub steppes, and woodlands. In M. G. Barbour and W. D. Billings (eds.), *North American Terrestrial Vegetation*, pp. 209–230. Cambridge University Press, Cambridge, UK.

Whitford, W. G. 2002. *Ecology of Desert Systems*. Academic Press, San Diego.

MUD VOLCANOES OF THE SALTON TROUGH

Blake, W. P. 1858. *Report of a Geological Reconnaissance in California: made in connection with the expedition to survey routes in California to connect with the surveys of routes for railroad from the Mississippi Top. Eng'rs, in 1853*. H. Bailliere, New York.

James, G. W. 1918. *The Wonders of the Colorado Desert*. Little, Brown, and Co., Boston.

Norris, R. M., and R. W. Webb. 1976. *Geology of California*. John Wiley and Sons, New York.

Thompson, D. G. 1929. The Mohave Desert region, California. A geographic, geologic, and hydrologic reconnaissance. *U.S. Geological Survey Water Supply Paper* 578.

RAIN SHADOW AND WIND MACHINE

Blake, W. P. 1858. *Report of a Geological Reconnaissance in California: Made in Connection with the Expedition to Survey Routes in California to Connect with the Surveys of Routes for Railroad from the Mississippi Top. Eng'rs, in 1853.* H. Bailliere, New York. Pg 91.

Center for Land Use Interpretation. 2006. San Gorgonio Pass wind array. http://ludb.clui.org/ex/i/CA4930/.

Manley, W. L. 1894. *Death Valley in '49.* Reprinted 1929. Wallace Hebberd, New York.

OPERATIONS AND ORIGINS

Axelrod, D. I. 1979. *Age and Origin of Sonoran Desert Vegetation.* Occasional Papers of the California Academy of Sciences 132. California Academy of Science, San Francisco.

Axelrod, D. I. 1983. Paleobotanical history of the western deserts. In S. G. Wells and D. R. Haragan (eds.), *Origin and Evolution of Deserts,* pp. 113–130. University of New Mexico Press, Albuquerque.

Bailowitz, R. A., and M. P. Sitter. 2000. Butterflies. In S. J. Philips and P. W. Comus (eds.), *A Natural History of the Sonoran Desert,* pp. 328–332. Arizona-Sonora Desert Museum Press, Tucson, AZ.

Beck, C., and G. T. Jones. 1997. The terminal Pleistocene/Early Holocene archaeology of the Great Basin. *Journal of World Prehistory* 11: 161–236.

Buchmann, S. L. 2000. Bees. In S. J. Philips and P. W. Comus (eds.), *A Natural History of the Sonoran Desert,* pp. 341–344. Arizona-Sonora Desert Museum Press, Tucson, AZ.

Cline, G. G. 1963. *Exploring the Great Basin.* Reprinted 1988. University of Nevada Press, Reno.

Davidowitz, G. 2000. Grasshoppers. In S. J. Philips and P. W. Comus (eds.), *A Natural History of the Sonoran Desert,* pp. 309–312. Arizona-Sonora Desert Museum Press, Tucson, AZ.

Davidson, D. W., M. Bowker, D. George, S. L. Phillips, and J. Belnap. 2000. Treatment effects on performance of N-fixing lichens in disturbed soil crusts of the Colorado Plateau. *Ecological Applications* 12: 1391–1405.

Davis, E. L. 1970. Archaeology of the north basin of Panamint Valley, Inyo County, CA. *Nevada State Museum Anthropological Papers* 15: 85–141.

Ebeling, W. 1986. *Handbook of Indian Foods and Fibers of Arid America.* University of California Press, Berkeley.

Ebert, T. A., and P. H. Zedler. 1984. Decomposition of ocotillo *(Fouquieria splendens)* wood in the Colorado Desert of California. *American Midland Naturalist* 111: 143–147.

Fonteyn, P. J., and B. E. Mahall. 1978. Competition among desert perennials. *Nature* 275: 544–545.

Fowler, D., and D. Koch. 1982. The Great Basin. In G. L. Bender (ed.), *Reference Handbook on the Deserts of North America,* pp. 7–63. Greenwood Press, Westport, CT.

Frank, C. L. 1988. The influence of moisture content on seed selection by kangaroo rats. *Journal of Mammology* 69: 353–357.

Grant, C. 1980. The desert bighorn and aboriginal man. In G. Monson and L. Sumner (eds.), *The Desert Bighorn, Its Life History, Ecology, and Management,* pp. 7–39. University of Arizona Press, Tucson.

Grayson, D. K. 1993. *The Desert's Past. A Natural Prehistory of the Great Basin.* Smithsonian Institution Press, Washington, DC.

Grayson, D. K. 2007. Deciphering North American Pleistocene extinctions. *Journal of Anthropological Research* 63: 185–213.

Harvey, A. M., P. E. Wigand, and S. G. Wells. 1999. Response of alluvial fan systems to the late Pleistocene to Holocene climatic transition: Contrasts between the margins of pluvial lakes Lahontan and Mojave, Nevada and California, USA. *Catena* 36: 255–281.

Hibbard, C. W., D. E. Ray, D. E. Savage, D. W. Taylor, and J. E. Guilday. 1965. Quaternary mammals of North America. In H. E. Wright Jr. and D. G. Frey (eds.), *The Quaternary of the United States,* pp. 509–525. Princeton University Press, Princeton, NJ.

Hill, M. 2006. *Geology of the Sierra Nevada.* University of California Press, Berkeley.

Ivanyi, C., J. Perry, T. R. Van Devender, and H. Lawler. 2000. Reptile and amphibian accounts. In S. J. Philips and P. W. Comus (eds.), *A Natural History of the Sonoran Desert,* pp. 533–585. Arizona-Sonora Desert Museum Press, Tucson, AZ.

Jaeger, E. C. 1961. *Desert Wildlife.* Stanford University Press, Stanford, CA.

Jameson Jr., E. W., and H. J. Peeters. 2004. *Mammals of California.* University of California Press, Berkeley.

Jennings, J. D. 1986. Prehistory: Introduction. In W. L. D'Azevedo (ed.), *Great Basin.* Vol. 11, *Handbook of North American Indians,* pp. 15–30. Smithsonian Institution, Washington, DC.

Kirkland Jr., G. L. 1999. Bailey's pocket mouse *(Chaetodipus baileyi).* In D. E. Wilson and S. Ruff (eds.), *The Smithsonian Book of North American Mammals,* pp. 507–508. Smithsonian Institution, Washington, DC.

Lines, G. C. 1999. Health of native riparian vegetation and its relation to hydrologic conditions along the Mojave River, southern California. *U.S. Geological Survey Water Resources Investigations Report* 99-4112.

Lines, G. C., and T. W. Bilhorn. 1996. Riparian vegetation and its water use during 1995 along the Mojave River, southern California. *U.S. Geological Survey Water Resources Investigations Report* 96-4241.

MacMahon, J. A. 1988. Warm deserts. In M. G. Barbour and W. D. Billings (eds.), *North American Terrestrial Vegetation,* pp. 231–264. Cambridge University Press, Cambridge, UK.

MacMillen, R. E. 1999. Desert woodrat *(Neotoma lepida).* In D. E. Wilson and S. Ruff (eds.), *The Smithsonian Book of North American Mammals,* pp. 604–606. Smithsonian Institution, Washington, DC.

Madsen, D. B. 2002. Great Basin peoples and Late Quaternary aquatic history. *Smithsonian Contributions to the Earth Sciences* 33: 387–405.

Margulis, L., D. Chase, and W. L. Nutting. 1980. The symbiotic microbial community of the Sonoran Desert termite *Pterotermes occidentalis. Biosystems* 13: 109–137.

Martin, P. S., and R. G. Klein. 1984. *Quaternary Extinctions: A Prehistoric Revolution.* University of Arizona Press, Tucson.

McAuliffe, J. R. 1988. Markovian dynamics of simple and complex desert plant communities. *American Naturalist* 131: 459–490.

McCarten, N., and T. R. Van Devender. 1988. Late Wisconsin vegetation of Robber's Roost in the western Mojave Desert. *Madrono* 35: 226–237.

Mehringer Jr., P. J. 1967. Pollen analysis of the Tule Springs area, Nevada. *Nevada State Museum Anthropological Papers* 13: 132–200.

Merlin, P., and P. Siminski. 2000. Mammals. In S. J. Philips and P. W. Comus (eds.), *A Natural History of the Sonoran Desert*, pp. 473–507. Arizona-Sonora Desert Museum Press, Tucson, AZ.

Norris, R. M., and R. W. Webb. 1976. *Geology of California*. John Wiley and Sons, New York.

Noy Meir, I. 1973. Desert ecosystems: Environment and producers. *Annual Review of Ecology and Systematics* 4: 25–41.

Polis, G. A. 1991. Food webs in desert communities: Complexity via diversity and omnivory. In G. A. Polis (ed.), *The Ecology of Desert Communities*, pp. 383–438. University of Arizona Press, Tucson.

Pough, F. H., C. M. Janis, and J. B. Heiser. 2004. *Vertebrate Life*. Prentice Hall, New York.

Rowlands, P. G. 1995. Vegetation dynamics of the California Desert Conservation Area. In J. Latting and P. G. Rowlands (eds.), *The California Desert: An Introduction to Natural Resources and Man's Impact*, pp. 185–212. June Latting Books, Riverside, CA.

Rowlands, P. G., H. Johnson, E. Ritter, and A. Endo. 1982. The Mojave Desert. In G. L. Bender (ed.), *Reference Handbook on the Deserts of North America*, pp. 103–145. Greenwood Press, Westport, CT.

Rundel, P. W., and A. C. Gibson. 1996. *Ecological Communities and Processes in a Mojave Desert Ecosystem*. Cambridge University Press, Cambridge, UK.

Sharp, R. P., and A. F. Glazner. 1997. *Geology Underfoot in Death Valley and Owens Valley*. Mountain Press, Missoula, MT.

Sherbrooke, W. C. 2003. *Introduction to Horned Lizards of North America*. University of California Press, Berkeley.

Smith, R. L. 2000. Termites. In S. J. Philips and P. W. Comus (eds.), *A Natural History of the Sonoran Desert*, pp. 316–319. Arizona-Sonora Desert Museum Press, Tucson, AZ.

Smith, S. D., R. K. Monson, and J. E. Anderson. 1997. *Physiological Ecology of North American Desert Plants*. Springer-Verlag, Berlin.

Spaulding, G. 1985. Vegetation and climate of the last 45,000 years in the vicinity of the Nevada Test Site, south-central Nevada. *U.S. Geological Survey Professional Paper* 1329.

Van Devender, T. R. 2000. The deep history of the Sonoran Desert. In S. J. Philips and P. W. Comus (eds.), *A Natural History of the Sonoran Desert*, pp. 61–69. Arizona-Sonora Desert Museum Press, Tucson, AZ.

Webb, R. H., J. W. Steiger, and E. B. Newman. 2001. The response of vegetation to disturbance in Death Valley National Monument, California. *U.S. Geological Survey Bulletin* 1793.

West, N. E. 1988. Intermountain deserts, shrub steppes, and woodlands. In M. G. Barbour and W. D. Billings (eds.), *North American Terrestrial Vegetation*, pp. 209–230. Cambridge University Press, Cambridge, UK.

Wheeler, D. E., and S. W. Rissing. 2000. Ants. In S. J. Philips and P. W. Comus (eds.), *A Natural History of the Sonoran Desert*, pp. 349–351. Arizona-Sonora Desert Museum Press, Tucson, AZ.

Whitford, W. G. 2002. *Ecology of Desert Systems*. Academic Press, San Diego.

Wigand, P. E., and D. Rhode. 2002. Great Basin vegetation history and aquatic systems: The last 150,000 years. *Smithsonian Contributions to the Earth Sciences* 33: 309–367.

DESERT FOSSILS

Howard, H. 1955. Fossil birds from Manix Lake California. *U.S. Geological Survey Paper* 264-J.

Jefferson, G. T., and L. Lindsay (eds.). 2006. *Fossil Treasures of the Anza Borrego Desert.* Sunbelt Publications, El Cajon, CA.

Marenco, P. J., F. A. Corsetti, D. J. Bottjer, and A. J. Kaufman. 2002. Chemostratigraphy of the Union Wash Formation: Implications for the early Triassic recovery from the Perimian Triassic mass extinction. Geological Society of American Annual Meeting, Denver, CO. Paper 222–12, http://gsa.confex.com/gsa/2002AM/finalprogram.

Stone, P., C. H. Stevens, and M. J. Orchard. 1991. Stratigraphy of the Lower and Middle (?) Triassic Union Wash Formation, East-Central California. *U.S. Geological Survey Bulletin* 1928.

Waucoba4. A visit to the Waucoba Spring geologic section. http://members.aol.com/Waucoba5/dv/wsgeology.htm.

Winters, H. H. 1954. The Pleistocene fauna of the Manix beds in the Mojave Desert, California. M.S. thesis, California Institute of Technology, Pasadena.

MEASURING PHOTOSYNTHESIS IN DEATH VALLEY

Ebeling, W. 1986. *Handbook of Indian Foods and Fibers of Arid America.* University of California Press, Berkeley. Pp. 151–154, 439–451, selection on page 449, para 2.

Ehleringer, J. 1985. Annuals and perennials of warm deserts. In B. F. Chabot and H. A. Mooney (eds.), *Physiological Ecology of North American Plant Communities,* pp. 162–180. Chapman and Hall, New York.

Went, F. 1968. The mobile laboratories of the Desert Research Institute. *Bioscience* 18: 293–297.

REMARKABLE BIOTA

Al-kahtani, M. A., C. Zuleta, E. Caviedes-Vidal, and T. Garland, Jr. 2004. Kidney mass and relative medullary thickness of rodents in relation to habitat, body size, and phylogeny. *Physiological and Biochemical Zoology* 77: 346–365.

Baldwin, B. G., and R. L. Moe. 2002. Floristic diversity in the California Deserts. In B. G. Baldwin, S. Boyd, B. J. Ertter, R. W. Patterson, T. J. Rosatti, and D. H. Wilken. *The Jepson Desert Manual: Vascular Plants of Southeastern California,* pp. 40–46. University of California Press, Berkeley.

Barker, D. H., L. R. Stark, J. F. Zimpfer, N. D. Mcletchie, and S. D. Smith. 2005. Evidence of drought-induced stress on biotic crust moss in the Mojave Desert. *Plant, Cell, and Environment* 28: 939–947.

Bartholomew, G. A., and J. W. Hudson. 1961. Desert ground squirrels. *Scientific American* 205: 107–116.

Brown, L. R., and L. H. Carpelan. 1971. Egg hatching and life history of a fairy shrimp *Branchinecta mackini* Dexter (Crustacea: Anostraca) in a Mohave Desert Playa (Rabbit Dry Lake). *Ecology* 52: 41–54.

Best, T. E. 1999. Desert kangaroo rat *(Dipodomys deserti)*. In D. E. Wilson and S. Ruff (eds.), *The Smithsonian Book of North American Mammals,* pp. 525–527. Smithsonian Institution, Washington, DC.

BLM (Bureau of Land Management). 1980. *California Desert Plan. Final Environmental Impact Statement and Proposed Plan.* Appendix Vol. E, *Wildlife and Vegetation.* BLM Desert Plant Staff, Riverside, CA.

Bowers, J. E. 1994. Natural conditions for seedling emergence of three woody species in the northern Sonoran Desert. *Madrono* 41: 73–84.

Bowers, J. E. 1996. Environmental determinants of flowering date in the columnar cactus *Carnegia gigantea* in the northern Sonoran Desert. *Madrono* 43: 69–84.

Carpelan, L. H. 1995. Invertebrates of the California desert. In J. Latting and P. G. Rowlands (eds.), *The California Desert: An Introduction to Natural Resources and Man's Impact,* pp. 275–282. June Latting Books, Riverside, CA.

Crosswhite, F. S., and C. D. Crosswhite. 1982. The Sonoran Desert. In G. L. Bender (ed.), *Reference Handbook on the Deserts of North America,* pp. 163–295. Greenwood Press, Westport, CT.

Dimmitt, M. A. 2000. Araceae (Palmae) (palm family). In S. J. Philips and P. W. Comus (eds.), *A Natural History of the Sonoran Desert,* pp. 165–167. Arizona-Sonora Desert Museum Press, Tucson, AZ.

Dimmitt, M. A. 2000. Fouquieriaceae (ocotillo family). In S. J. Philips and P. W. Comus (eds.), *A Natural History of the Sonoran Desert,* pp. 240–243. Arizona-Sonora Desert Museum Press, Tucson, AZ.

Dimmitt, M. A. 2000. Plant ecology of the Sonoran Desert Region. In S. J. Philips and P. W. Comus (eds.), *A Natural History of the Sonoran Desert,* pp. 129–151. Arizona-Sonora Desert Museum Press, Tucson, AZ.

Dimmitt, M. A. 2000. Zygophyllaceae (caltrop family). In S. J. Philips and P. W. Comus (eds.), *A Natural History of the Sonoran Desert,* pp. 261–264. Arizona-Sonora Desert Museum Press, Tucson, AZ.

Dudley, T. 2000. Aquatic insects of the Sonoran Desert. In S. J. Philips and P. W. Comus (eds.), *A Natural History of the Sonoran Desert,* pp. 357–363. Arizona-Sonora Desert Museum Press, Tucson, AZ.

Ehleringer, J. 1985. Annuals and perennials of warm deserts. In B. F. Chabot and H. A. Mooney (eds.), *Physiological Ecology of North American Plant Communities,* pp. 162–180. Chapman and Hall, New York.

England, A. S., and W. F Laudenslayer Jr. 1995. Birds of the California desert. In J. Latting and P. G. Rowlands (eds.), *The California Desert: An Introduction to Natural Resources and Man's Impact,* pp. 337–372. June Latting Books, Riverside, CA.

Evens, J., and I. Tait. 2005. *Introduction to California Bird Life.* University of California Press, Berkeley.

Frommer, S. 1976. Arthropods. In I. P. Ting and B. Jennings (eds.), *Deep Canyon, a Desert Wilderness for Science,* pp. 131–137. Philip L. Boyd Deep Canyon Research Center, Palm Desert, CA.

Hafner, D. J. 1992. Speciation and persistence of a contact zone in Mojave Desert Ground Squirrels, subgenus *Xerospermophilus. Journal of Mammology* 73: 770–778.

Harris, J. H., and P. Leitner. 2004. Home-range size and use of space by adult Mojave Ground Squirrels, *Spermophilus mohavensis. Journal of Mammology* 85: 517–523.

Hill, R. W., G. A. Wyse, and M. Anderson. 2004. *Animal Physiology*. Sinauer Associates, Sunderland, MA.

Huang, Y., R. Tracy, G. E. Walsberg, A. Makkinje, P. Fang, D. Brown, and A. N. Van Hoek. 2001. Absence of aquaporin-4 water channels from kidneys of the desert rodent *Dipodomys merriami merriami*. *American Journal of Physiology* 280: F794–F802.

Inouye, R. S. 1991. Population biology of desert annual plants. In G. A. Polis (ed.), *The Ecology of Desert Communities*, pp. 27–54. University of Arizona Press, Tucson.

Jaeger, E. C. 1938. *The California Deserts*. Stanford University Press, Stanford, CA.

Jaeger, E. C. 1961. *Desert Wildlife*. Stanford University Press, Stanford, CA.

Jameson Jr., E. W., and H. J. Peeters. 2004. *Mammals of California*. University of California Press, Berkeley.

Krausman, P. R., and R. T. Bowyer. 2003. Mountain sheep. In G. A. Feldhamer, B. C. Thompson, and J. A. Chapman (eds.), *Wild Mammals of North America: Biology, Management, and Conservation*, pp. 1095–1115. Second edition. John Hopkins University Press, Baltimore.

Latting, J., and P. G. Rowlands (eds.). 1995. *The California Desert: An Introduction to Natural Resources and Man's Impact*. June Latting Books, Riverside, CA.

Laudenslayer Jr., W. F. 1995. Mammals of the California desert. In J. Latting and P. G. Rowlands (eds.), *The California Desert: An Introduction to Natural Resources and Man's Impact*, pp. 373–402. June Latting Books, Riverside, CA.

Lovich, J. E., P. Medica, H. Avery, K. Meyer, G. Bowser, and A. Brown. 1999. Studies of reproductive output of the Desert Tortoise at Joshua Tree National Park, the Mojave National Preserve, and comparative sites. *Park Science* 19: 22–24.

Lummis, C. F. 1925. *Mesa, Canon, and Pueblo. Our Wonderland of the Southwest*. Century, New York.

MacMahon, J. C. 1985. Annuals and perennials of warm deserts. In B. F. Chabot and H. A. Mooney (eds.), *Physiological Ecology of North American Plant Communities*, pp. 162–180. Chapman and Hall, New York.

Madson, D. B. 2002. Great Basin peoples and late Quaternary aquatic history. *Smithsonian Contributions to the Earth Sciences* 33: 387–405.

Manolis, T. 2003. *Dragonflies and Damselflies of California*. University of California Press, Berkeley.

Mayhew, W. W. 1995. Amphibians of the California desert. In J. Latting and P. G. Rowlands (eds.), *The California Desert: An Introduction to Natural Resources and Man's Impact*, pp. 305–316. June Latting Books, Riverside, CA.

Miller, A. H., and R. C. Stebbins. 1973. *The Lives of Desert Animals in Joshua Tree National Monument*. University of California Press, Berkeley.

Nobel, P. S. 1985. Desert succulents. In B. F. Chabot and H. A. Mooney (eds.), *Physiological Ecology of North American Plant Communities*, pp. 181–197. Chapman and Hall, New York.

Ohmart, R. D., and B. W. Anderson. 1982. North American desert riparian ecosystems. In G. L. Bender (ed.), *Reference Handbook on the Deserts of North America*, pp. 433–466. Greenwood Press, Westport, CT.

Pough, F. H., C. M. Janis, and J. B. Heiser. 2004. *Vertebrate Life*. Seventh edition. Prentice Hall, New York.

Raven, P. H., and D. I. Axelrod. 1978. *Origin and Relationships of the California Flora.* University of California Publications in Botany 72. University of California Press, Berkeley.

Rowlands, P. G. 1995. Floristics of the California Desert Conservation Area. In J. Latting and P. G. Rowlands (eds.), *The California Desert: An Introduction to Natural Resources and Man's Impact,* pp. 213–274. June Latting Books, Riverside, CA.

Sada, D. W., and J. E. Deacon. 1994. *Spatial and Temporal Variability of Pupfish* (Cyprinodon): *Habitat, Populations, and Microhabitat Use at Salt Creek and Cottonball Marsh, Death Valley National Monument, CA.* Report to U.S. National Park Service, DVNM, Coop. Agreement No. 8000-2-9003. U.S. National Park Service, Death Valley National Monument, CA and NV.

Sharifi, M. R., E. T. Nilsen, and P. W. Rundel. 1982. Biomass and net primary production of *Prosopis glandulosa* (Fabaceae) in the Sonoran Desert of California. *American Journal of Botany* 69: 760–767.

Siminski, P. 2000. The desert adaptations of birds and mammals. In S. J. Philips and P. W. Comus (eds.), *A Natural History of the Sonoran Desert,* pp. 367–372. Arizona-Sonora Desert Museum Press, Tucson, AZ.

Smith, G. R., T. E. Dowling, K. W. Gobalet, T. Lugaski, D. K. Shiozawa, and R. P. Evans. 2002. Biogeography and timing of evolutionary events among Great Basin fishes. *Smithsonian Contributions to the Earth Sciences* 33: 175–234.

Smith, S. D., T. L. Harsock, and P. S. Nobel. 1983. Ecophysiology of *Yucca brevifolia,* an arborescent monocot of the Mojave Desert. *Oecologia* 60: 10–17.

Smith, S. D., R. K. Monson, and J. E. Anderson. 1997. *Physiological Ecology of North American Desert Plants.* Springer-Verlag, Berlin.

Solbrig, O. 1982. Plant adaptations. In G. L. Bender (ed.), *Reference Handbook on the Deserts of North America,* pp. 419–432. Greenwood Press, Westport, CT

Soltz, D. L., and R. J. Naiman. 1978. *The Natural History of Native Fishes in the Death Valley System.* Natural History Museum of Los Angeles County, Los Angeles.

Spira, T. P. 1987. Alpine annual plant species in the White Mountains of Eastern California. *Madroño* 34: 315–323.

Stark, L. R. 2003. Mosses in the desert? *Fremontia* 31: 26–33.

Stebbins, R. H. 1995. Desert reptiles. In J. Latting and P. G. Rowlands (eds.), *The California Desert: An Introduction to Natural Resources and Man's Impact,* pp. 317–336. June Latting Books, Riverside, CA.

Turner, J. C., and R. A. Weaver. 1980. Water. In G. Monson and L. Sumner (eds.), *The Desert Bighorn, Its Life History, Ecology, and Management,* pp. 100–112. University of Arizona Press, Tucson.

Van Devender, T. R., and H. Lawler. 2000. Desert Tortoise. In S. J. Philips and P. W. Comus (eds.), *A Natural History of the Sonoran Desert,* pp. 545–547. Arizona-Sonora Desert Museum Press, Tucson, AZ.

Wehausen, J. D., and R. R. Ramey II. 1993. A morphometric reevaluation of the Peninsular bighorn subspecies. *Transactions of the Desert Bighorn Council* 37: 1–10.

Wehausen, J. D., and R. R. Ramey II. 2000. Cranial morphology and evolutionary relationships in the northern range of *Ovis canadensis. Journal of Mammology* 81: 145–161.

West, N. E. 1988. Intermountain deserts, shrub steppes, and woodlands. In M. G. Barbour and W. D. Billings (eds.), *North American Terrestrial Vegetation*, pp. 209–230. Cambridge University Press, Cambridge, UK.

Whitford, W. G. 2002. *Ecology of Desert Systems*. Academic Press, San Diego.

Wilson, D. E., and S. Ruff (eds.). 1999. *The Smithsonian Book of North American Mammals.* Smithsonian Institution, Washington, DC.

Wullschleger, J., and W. Van Liew. 2006. Devils Hole revisited: Why are pupfish numbers and water level dropping again? *ParkScience* 24(2). www2.nature.nps.gov/parkscience/index .cfm?ArticleID=51.

Yensen, E., and P. W. Sherman. 2003. Ground squirrels. In G. A. Feldhamer, B. C. Thompson, and J. A. Chapman (eds.), *Wild Mammals of North America: Biology, Management, and Conservation*, pp. 211–231. Second edition. Johns Hopkins University Press, Baltimore.

Zak, J. C., and D. W. Freckman. 1991. Soil communities in deserts: Microarthropods and nematodes. In G. A. Polis (ed.), *The Ecology of Desert Communities*, pp. 55–88. University of Arizona Press, Tucson.

DEALING WITH HEAT

Bartholomew, G. A., and J. W. Hudson. 1961. Desert ground squirrels. *Scientific American* 205: 107–116.

Mooney, H. A., J. Ehlringer, and O. Bjorkman. 1977. The energy balance of leaves of the evergreen desert shrub *Atriplex hymenelytra*. *Oecologia* 29: 301–310.

Secor, S. M., and K. A. Nagy. 1994. Bioenergetic correlates of foraging mode for the snakes *Crotalus cerastes* and *Masticophis flagellum*. *Ecology* 75: 1600–1614.

Sherbrooke, W. C. 2003. *Introduction to Horned Lizards of North America*. University of California Press, Berkeley. P. 88, panting.

Siminski, P. 2000. The desert adaptations of birds and mammals. In S. J. Philips and P. W. Comus (eds.), *A Natural History of the Sonoran Desert*, pp. 367–372. Arizona-Sonora Desert Museum Press, Tucson, AZ. P. 369, jackrabbit ears.

Whitford, P. G. 2002. *Ecology of Desert Systems*. Academic Press, San Diego. P. 143, tenebrionids.

GREATER THAN THE SUM OF THE PARTS

Armstrong, W. P. 1980. Sand food: A strange plant of the Algodones Dunes. *Fremontia* 7: 3–9.

Barbour, M. G., B. M. Pavlik, F. Drysdale, and S. Lindstrom. 1994. *California's Changing Landscapes: Diversity and Conservation of California Vegetation*. California Native Plant Society, Sacramento.

Bean, L. J., and K. S. Saubel. 1972. *Temalpakh: Cahuilla Indian Knowledge and Usage of Plants*. Malki Museum, Banning, CA.

Best, T. E. 1999. Panamint kangaroo rat *(Dipodomys panamintensis)*. In D. E. Wilson and S. Ruff (eds.), *The Smithsonian Book of North American Mammals*, pp. 539–540. Smithsonian Institution, Washington, DC.

Blake, B. H. 1999. Panamint chipmunk *(Tamias panamintinus)*. In D. E. Wilson and S. Ruff (eds.), *The Smithsonian Book of North American Mammals*, pp. 373–375. Smithsonian Institution, Washington, DC.

Blake, W. P. 1858. *Report of a Geological Reconnaissance in California: Made in Connection with* the *Expedition to Survey Routes in California to Connect with the Surveys of Routes for a Railroad from the Mississippi Top. Engineer's, in 1853*. H. Bailliere, New York.

Bowers, J. E. 1981. Catastrophic freezes in the Sonoran Desert. *Desert Plants* 2: 232–236.

Bowers, J. E. 1994. Natural conditions for seedling emergence of three woody species in the northern Sonoran Desert. *Madrono* 41: 73–84.

Bradley, W. G., and J. E. Deacon. 1967. The biotic communities of southern Nevada. *Nevada State Museum Anthropology Paper 13*, Part 4: 202–295.

Burk, J. H. 1988. Sonoran Desert. In M. G. Barbour and J. Major (eds.), *Terrestrial Vegetation of California*, pp. 869–889. California Native Plant Society, Sacramento.

Cornett, J. W. 1984. *The Desert Palm Oasis*. Educational Bulletin 84-1. Desert Protective Council Publications, Spring Valley, CA.

Cornett, J. W. 1986. Spineless petioles in *Washingtonia filifera* (Arecaceae). *Madrono* 33: 76–78.

Cornett, J. W. 1988. Naturalized populations of the desert fan palm, *Washingtonia filifera*, in Death Valley National Monument. In C. A. Hall Jr. and V. Doyle-Jones (eds.), *Plant Biology of Eastern California*, pp. 167–174. University of California Press, Los Angeles.

Crosswhite, F. S., and C. D. Crosswhite. 1982. The Sonoran Desert. In G. L. Bender (ed.), *Reference Handbook on the Deserts of North America*, pp. 163–295. Greenwood Press, Westport, CT.

des Lauriers, J., and M. Ikeda. 1986. An apparent case of introgression between pinyon pines of the New York Mountains, eastern Mojave Desert. *Madrono* 33: 55–62.

Dimmett, M. A. 2000. Agavaceae (agave family), Nolinaceae (nolina family). In S. J. Philips and P. W. Comus (eds.), *A Natural History of the Sonoran Desert*, pp. 155–164. Arizona-Sonora Desert Museum Press, Tucson, AZ.

Dimmitt, M. A. 2000. Cactaceae (cactus family). In S. J. Philips and P. W. Comus (eds.), *A Natural History of the Sonoran Desert*, pp. 183–218. Arizona-Sonora Desert Museum Press, Tucson, AZ.

Dimmett, M. A. 2000. Fabaceae (legume family). In S. J. Philips and P. W. Comus (eds.), *A Natural History of the Sonoran Desert*, pp. 227–239. Arizona-Sonora Desert Museum Press, Tucson, AZ.

Dimmett, M. A. 2000. Fouquieriaceae (ocotillo family). In S. J. Philips and P. W. Comus (eds.), *A Natural History of the Sonoran Desert*, pp. 240–243. Arizona-Sonora Desert Museum Press, Tucson, AZ.

Elliott-Fisk, D. L., and A. M. Peterson. 1991. Trees. C. A. Hall Jr., *Natural History of the White-Inyo Range, Eastern California*, pp. 87–107. University of California Press, Berkeley.

Evens, J., and I. Tait. 2005. *Introduction to California Bird Life*. University of California Press, Berkeley.

Forbes, H. C., W. R. Ferren Jr., and J. R. Haller. 1988. The vegetation and flora of Fish Slough and vicinity, Inyo County, California. In C. A. Hall Jr. and V. Doyle-Jones (eds.), *Plant Biology of Eastern California*, pp. 99–138. White Mountain Research Station, University of California, Los Angeles.

Fowler, C. S. 2000. "We live by them": Native knowledge of biodiversity in the Great Basin of Western North America. In P. E. Minnis and W. J. Elisens (eds.), *Biodiversity and Native America*, pp. 99–132. University of Oklahoma Press, Norman.

Franzreb, K. E. 1978. Breeding bird densities, species composition, and bird species diversity of the Algodones Dunes. *Western Birds* 9: 9–20.

Fraser, J., and C. Martinez. 2002. Restoring a desert oasis. *Endangered Species Bulletin* 27(2): 18–19.

Gordon, S. A. 1980. Analysis of twelve Sonoran Desert seed species preferred by the desert harvester ant. *Madroño* 27: 68–78.

Hanson, R. B. 2000. Nature watching in the Sonoran Desert Region. In S. J. Philips and P. W. Comus (eds.), *A Natural History of the Sonoran Desert*, pp. 29–50. Arizona-Sonora Desert Museum Press, Tucson, AZ.

Henrickson, J., and B. Prigge. White fir in the mountains of eastern Mojave Desert of California. *Madrono* 23: 164–168.

Howald, A. 2000. Plant communities. In G. Smith (ed.), *Sierra East: Edge of the Great Basin*, pp. 94–207. University of California Press, Berkeley.

Hunt, C. B. 1966. Plant ecology of Death Valley, California, with a section on distribution of fungi and algae by C. B. Hunt and L. W. Durrell. *U.S. Geological Survey Professional Paper* 509.

Ivanyi, C., J. Perry, T. R. Van Devender, and H. Lawler. 2000. Reptile and amphibian accounts. In S. J. Philips and P. W. Comus (eds.), *A Natural History of the Sonoran Desert*, pp. 533–585. Arizona-Sonora Desert Museum Press, Tucson, AZ.

Jameson Jr., E. W., and H. J. Peeters. 2004. *Mammals of California*. University of California Press, Berkeley.

Johnson, D. H. 1943. Systematic review of the chipmunks (genus *Eutamias*) of California. *University of California Publications in Zoology* 48: 63–148.

Johnson, N. K., and C. Cicero. 1986. Richness and distribution of montane avifaunas in the White-Inyo Region, California. In C. A. Hall Jr. and V. Doyle-Jones (eds.), *Plant Biology of Eastern California*, pp. 137–159. White Mountain Research Station, University of California, Los Angeles.

Jones, W. 1979. The severe freeze of 1978–79 in the southwestern United States. *Desert Plants* 1: 37–39.

Karban, R., M. Huntzinger, and A. C. McCall. 2004. The specificity of eavesdropping on sagebrush by other plants. *Ecology* 85: 1846–1852.

Madsen, D. B. 2002. Great Basin peoples and late Quaternary aquatic history. *Smithsonian Contributions to the Earth Sciences* 33: 387–405.

Nabhan, G. P., and J. L. Carr (eds.). 1994. *Ironwood: An ecological and cultural keystone of the Sonoran Desert*. Conservation International Occasional Paper 1. Conservation International, Washington, DC.

Ohmart, R. D., and B. W. Anderson. 1982. North American desert riparian ecosystems. In G. L. Bender (ed.), *Reference Handbook on the Deserts of North America*, pp. 433–466. Greenwood Press, Westport, CT.

Patencio, F. 1943. *Stories and Legends of the Palm Springs Indians*. Times-Mirror Press, Los Angeles.

Pavlik, B. M. 1985. Sand dune flora of the Great Basin and Mojave deserts, California. *Madrono* 32: 197–213.

Phillips, E. A., K. K. Page, and S. D. Knapp. 1980. Vegetational characteristics of two stands of Joshua tree woodland. *Madroño* 27: 43–46.

Raguso, R. A., and M. A. Willis. 2000. Moths. In S. J. Philips and P. W. Comus (eds.), *A Natural History of the Sonoran Desert*, pp. 333–340. Arizona-Sonora Desert Museum Press, Tucson, AZ.

Raven, P. H., and D. I. Axelrod. 1995. *Origins and Relationship of the California Flora*. California Native Plant Society Press, Sacramento.

Rhode, D. 2002. *Native Plants of Southern Nevada: An Ethnobotany*. University of Utah, Salt Lake City.

Sada, D. W. 2000. Native Fishes. In G. Smith (ed.), *Sierra East: Edge of the Great Basin*, pp. 246–264. University of California Press, Berkeley.

Sawyer, J. O., and T. Keeler-Wolf. 1995. *A Manual of California Vegetation*. California Native Plant Society, Sacramento.

Smith, R. S. U. 1982. Sand dunes in the North American deserts. In G. L. Bender (ed.), *Reference Handbook on the Deserts of North America*, pp. 481–524. Greenwood Press, Westport, CT.

Spaulding, G. 1985. Vegetation and climate of the last 45,000 years in the vicinity of the Nevada Test Site, south-central Nevada. *U.S. Geological Survey Professional Paper* 1329.

Sugden, E. 2000. Arthropods. In G. Smith (ed.), *Sierra East: Edge of the Great Basin*, pp. 208–245. University of California Press, Berkeley.

Titus, J. H., L. B. Aniskoff, J. Griffith, L. Garrett, and B. Glatt. 2003. Depth distribution of arbuscular mycorrhizae associated with mesquite. *Madrono* 50: 28–33.

Tomback, D. F. 2000. Birds. In G. Smith (ed.), *Sierra East: Edge of the Great Basin*, pp. 290–389. University of California Press, Berkeley.

Trombulak, S. C., and M. L. Cody. 1980. Elevational distributions of *Pinus edulis* and *P. monophylla* (Pinaceae) in the New York Mountains, eastern Mojave Desert. *Madrono* 27: 61–67.

Udvardy, M. K. 1977. *The Audubon Society Field Guild to North American Birds*. Alfred Knopf, New York.

Vasek, F. C. 1995. Ancient creosote rings and yucca rings. In J. Latting and P. G. Rowlands (eds.), *The California Desert: An Introduction to Natural Resources and Man's Impact*, pp. 83–86. June Latting Books, Riverside, CA.

Vasek, F. C., and M. G. Barbour. 1988. Mojave desert scrub vegetation. In M. G. Barbour and J. Major (eds.), *Terrestrial Vegetation of California*, pp. 835–867. California Native Plant Society, Sacramento.

Vasek, F. C., and R. F. Thorne. 1988. Transmontane coniferous vegetation. In M. G. Barbour and J. Major (eds.), *Terrestrial Vegetation of California*, pp. 797–832. California Native Plant Society, Sacramento.

Wallace, A., and E. M. Romney. 1972. *Radioecology and Ecophysiology of Desert Plants at the Nevada Test Site*. National Technical Information Service, U.S. Department of Commerce, Springfield, VA.

West, N. E. 1988. Intermountain deserts, shrub steppes, and woodlands. In M. G. Barbour and W. D. Billings (eds.), *North American Terrestrial Vegetation*, pp. 209–230. Cambridge University Press, Cambridge, UK.

Whitford, W. G. 2002. *Ecology of Desert Systems*. Academic Press, San Diego.

Wigand, P. E., and D. Rhode. 2002. Great Basin vegetation history and aquatic systems: The last 150,000 years. *Smithsonian Contributions to the Earth Sciences* 33: 309–367.

Young, J. A., R. A. Evans, and J. Major. 1988. Sagebrush Steppe. In M. G. Barbour and J. Major (eds.), *Terrestrial Vegetation of California*, pp. 763–796. California Native Plant Society, Sacramento.

ASSEMBLING RODENT COMMUNITIES

Reichman, O. J. 1991. Desert mammal communities. In G. A. Polis (ed.), *The Ecology of Desert Communities*, pp. 311–347. University of Arizona Press, Tucson.

Whitford, W. G. 2000. *Ecology of Desert Systems*. Academic Press, San Diego.

BUTTERFLY ENDEMISM

Emmel, J. F., and T. C. Emmel. 1998. A new subspecies of *Papilio indra* (Lepidoptera: Papilionidae) from northwestern California. In T. C. Emmel (ed.), *Systematics of Western North American Butterflies*, pp. 701–706. Mariposa Press, Gainesville, FL.

Emmel, J. F., and B. M. Griffin. 1998. A new subspecies of *Papilio indra* (Lepidoptera: Papilionidae) from the Muddy Mountains of southern Nevada. In T. C. Emmel (ed.), *Systematics of Western North American Butterflies*, pp. 707–710. Mariposa Press, Gainesville, FL.

Emmel, J. F., T. C. Emmel, and B. M. Griffin. 1998. A new subspecies of *Papilio indra* (Lepidoptera: Papilionidae) from the Dead Mountains of southeastern California. In T. C. Emmel (ed.), *Systematics of Western North American Butterflies*, pp. 711–716. Mariposa Press, Gainesville, FL.

Emmel, J. F., T. C. Emmel, and S. O. Mattoon. 1998. New Polyommatinae subspecies of Lycaenidae (Lepidoptera) from California. In T. C. Emmel (ed.), *Systematics of Western North American Butterflies*, pp. 171–200. Mariposa Press, Gainesville, FL.

Emmel, J. F., T. C. Emmel, and S. O. Mattoon. 1998. New subspecies of Pieridae (Lepidoptera) from California, Nevada, and Baja California. In T. C. Emmel (ed.), *Systematics of Western North American Butterflies*, pp. 127–138. Mariposa Press, Gainesville, FL.

THE SAND FOOD COMMUNITY

Armstrong, W. P. 1980. Sand food: A strange plant of the Algodones Dunes. *Fremontia* 7: 3–9.

Ebeling, W. 1986. *Handbook of Indian Foods and Fibers of Arid America*. University of California Press, Berkeley.

Jaeger, E. C. 1941. *Desert Wild Flowers*. Stanford University Press, Stanford, CA.

Nabhan, G. P. 1980. *Ammobroma sonorae*, an endangered parasitic plant in extremely arid North America. *Desert Plants* 2: 188–196.

Wiesenborn, W. D. 2003. Insects on *Pholisma sonorae* (Lennoaceae) flowers and their conspecific pollen loads. *Madrono* 50: 110–114.

VARIATIONS IN RIPARIAN COMMUNITIES

Evens, J. 2001. Vegetation in watercourses of the eastern Mojave Desert. *Fremontia* 29(2): 26–35.

Lines, G. C., and T. W. Bilhorn. 1996. Riparian vegetation and its water use during 1995 along the Mojave River, southern California. *U.S. Geological Survey Water Resources Investigations Report* 96-4241.

Anderson, B. 1998. The case for salt cedar. *Restoration and Management Notes* 16: 130–134.

Avery, H. W. 1999. Livestock grazing in the Mojave Desert in relation to the Desert Tortoise. In *U.S. Geological Survey Mojave Desert Science Symposium Proceedings*. University of Nevada, Las Vegas. www.werc.usgs.gov/mojave-symposium/abstracts.html.

Bainbridge, D. A., and R. A. Virginia. 1995. Desert soils and soil biota. In J. Latting and P. G. Rowlands (eds.), *The California Desert: An Introduction to Natural Resources and Man's Impact*, pp. 59–67. June Latting Books, Riverside, CA.

Bainbridge, D. A., M. Fidelibus, and R. MacAller. 1995. Techniques for plant establishment in arid ecosystems. *Restoration and Management Notes* 13: 190–197.

Baldwin, B. G., S. Boyd, B. J. Ertter, R. W. Patterson, T. J. Rosatti, and D. H. Wilken (eds.). 2002. *The Jepson Desert Manual: Vascular Plants of Southeastern California*. University of California Press, Berkeley.

Barrows, C. 1994. Tamarisk control: A success story. *Fremontia* 22(3): 20–22.

Barrows, C. 1998. The case for wholesale removal [of salt cedar]. *Restoration and Management Notes* 16: 135–138.

Beck, W. A., and Y. D. Haase. 1974. *Historical Atlas of California*. University of Oklahoma Press, Norman.

Bentley, H. L. 1898. Cattle ranges of the Southwest: A history of the exhaustion of the pasturage and suggestions for its restoration. U.S. Department of Agriculture, *Farmer's Bulletin* No. 72.

Berry, K. H. 1997. The desert tortoise recovery plan: An ambitious effort to conserve biodiversity in the Mojave and Colorado deserts of the United States. *Conservation, Restoration, and Management of Tortoises and Turtles: An International Conference*, pp. 430–440. New York Turtle and Tortoise Society, Orange, NJ.

Berry, K. H. 1999. Desert Tortoise research projects in the Mojave and Colorado deserts of California: Status, trends, demography, and habitats. Presented at the Center for Conservation Biology, University of California, Riverside, Mojave Desert Science Symposium, February 1999.

Berry, K. H., J. Mack, R.W. Murphy and W. Quillman. 2006. Introduction to the special issue on the changing Mojave Desert. *Journal of Arid Environments* 67, 5–10.

BLM (Bureau of Land Management). 1980a. *The California Desert Conservation Area: Final Environmental Impact Statement and Proposed Plan*. Desert Planning Staff, Riverside, CA.

BLM. 1980b. *The California Desert Conservation Area: Plan Alternatives and Environmental Impact Statement*. Draft. Desert Planning Staff, Riverside, CA.

BLM. 2000. *Desert Conservation: A Management Showcase*. BLM-CA-GI-91-003-2000. Bureau of Land Management, Riverside, CA.

BLM. 2002. *Proposed Northern and Eastern Colorado Desert Coordinated Management Plan and Final Environmental Impact Statement*. BLM-CA-ES-2002/004+1790+1600. Bureau of Land Management, Riverside, CA.

Boarman, W. I. 1999. Subsidized predators in the Mojave Desert. Presented at the Center for Conservation Biology, University of California, Riverside, Mojave Desert Science Symposium, February 1999.

Boarman, W. I. 2002. *Threats to Desert Tortoise populations: A critical review of the literature.* U.S. Geological Survey, Western Ecological Research Center, Sacramento, CA.

Brattstrom, B. H., and M. C. Bondello. 1995. Natural sounds and man-made noise in the desert. In J. Latting and P. G. Rowlands (eds.), *The California Desert: An Introduction to Natural Resources and Man's Impact,* pp. 437–461. June Latting Books, Riverside, CA.

Brooks, M., and K. Berry. 1999. Ecology and management of alien annual plants in the California desert. *CalEPPC News* 7(1): 4–6.

Brooks, M. L. 2000. Competition between alien annual grasses and native annual plants in the Mojave Desert. *American Midland Naturalist* 144: 92–108.

Brooks, M. L. 2004. Fifteen years of research on disturbance effects in Desert Tortoise habitat. Presented at the U.S. Geological Survey, Western Ecological Research Center, Desert Tortoise Council Symposium, February 2004.

Brooks, M. L., and B. Lair. 2005. *Ecological effects of vehicular routes in a desert ecosystem.* U.S. Geological Survey, Western Ecological Research Center, Henderson, NV.

California Department of Fish and Game. 2003. *List of Terrestrial Natural Communities Recognized by the California Natural Diversity Database.* Wildlife and Habitat Branch, Vegetation Classification and Mapping Program, Sacramento, CA.

California Department of Fish and Game. 2007. RareFind 3.1 (October 2007). California Natural Diversity Database, Biogeographic Data Branch, Sacramento. www.dfg.ca.gov/bdb/.

California Department of Water Resources. 1999. *California Water Plan Update. Eastern Sierra and Colorado River Regions.* Bulletin 160–98. California Department of Water Resources, Sacramento.

California Department of Water Resources. 2005. *California Water Plan Update.* Vol. 3, *Regional Reports.* California Department of Water Resources, Sacramento.

Carle, D. 2004. *Introduction to Water in California.* University of California Press, Berkeley.

Carle, D. 2006. *Introduction to Air in California.* University of California Press, Berkeley.

Cole, K. L., and R. H. Webb. 1985. Late Holocene vegetation changes in Greenwater Valley, Mojave Desert, California. *Quaternary Research* 23: 227–235.

Cooper, D. S., and D. L. Perlman. 1997. Habitat conservation on military installations. *Fremontia* 25: 3–8.

Cragen, D., and G. Schumacher. 1969. *Deepest Valley: Guide to Owens Valley and Its Mountain Lakes, Roadsides, and Trails,* pp. 167–200. Wilderness Press, Berkeley, CA.

DeFalco, L. A., and M. L. Brooks. 1999. Ecology and management of exotic annual plant species. Presented at the Center for Conservation Biology, University of California, Riverside, Mojave Desert Science Symposium, February 1999.

Dickey, J., M. Hall, M. Madison, J. Smesrud, M. Griswold, Q. Cotton, M. Heilmann, G. Roland, J. Jordahl, R. Harasick, W. Bamossy, R. Coles, L. Wheeler, P. Brown, K. Burton, R. Fornelli, I. Anderson, M. Riedel-Lehrke, R. Tiller, and J. Richards. 2005. Stabilizing Owens Dry Lake surface with irrigated saltgrass. Parts 1 and 2. *Ecesis* 1(2): 1, 6–7, 9 and 1(2): 1, 5–7, 9.

Epps, C. W. 2005. Highways block gene flow and cause a rapid decline in genetic diversity of desert bighorn sheep. *Ecology Letters* 8: 1029–1038.

Eriksen, C. H., G. E. Prettyman, and J. E. Moeur. 1986. The effects of soil disturbance by off-road vehicles on the eggs and habitat of playa lake crustaceans. In R. G. Zahary (ed.), *Desert*

Ecology 1986: A Research Symposium. Southern California Academy of Sciences and the California Desert Studies Consortium, Fullerton.

Ewing, R., J. Kostyack, D. Chen, B. Stein, and M. Ernst. 2005. *Endangered by Sprawl: How Runaway Development Threatens America's Wildlife.* National Wildlife Federation, Smart Growth America, and NatureServe, Washington, DC.

Feinstein, D. 2004. Celebrating the desert. Celebrating the tenth anniversary of the California Desert Protection Act. *National Parks* 78: 38–40.

Fisher, D. 1990. Statement for the High Desert Cattlemen's Association. In *Hearing before the Subcommittee on Public Lands, National Parks, and Forests of the Committee on Energy and Natural Resources, United States Senate, on S.11 to Provide for the Protection of Public Lands in the California Desert,* pp. 434–439. U.S. Government Printing Office, Washington, DC.

Haley, J., and D. Bainbridge. 1999. Desert restoration: Do something or wait a thousand years. Presented at the Center for Conservation Biology, University of California, Riverside, Mojave Desert Science Symposium, February 1999.

Hamin, E. M. 2003. *Mojave Lands. Interpretive Planning and the National Reserve.* Johns Hopkins University Press, Baltimore.

Harris, G. A. 1977. Root phenology as a factor of competition among grass seedlings. *Journal of Range Management* 30: 172–176.

Hart, J. 1996. *Storm over Mono. The Mono Lake Battle and the California Water Future.* University of California Press, Berkeley.

Hartman, S., and I. Anderson. 1999. California deserts in transition: Ecosystem planning. *Fremontia* 27: 13–17.

Jones, F. L. 1980. Competition. In G. Monson and L. Sumner (eds.), *The Desert Bighorn, Its Life History, Ecology, and Management,* pp. 197–216. University of Arizona Press, Tucson.

Kroeber, A. L. 1925. *Handbook of the Indians of California.* California Book Co., Berkeley, CA.

Lee, M. 2005. Lines drawn in the desert. Borrego plan rekindles familiar land-use debate. *San Diego Union-Tribune,* February 11, 2005.

Legge, A. H., H.,-J. Jager, and S. V. Krupa. 1998. Sulfur dioxide. In R. B. Flagler (ed.), *Recognition of Air Pollution Injury to Vegetation: A Pictorial Atlas,* Chapter 3. Second edition. Air and Waste Management Association, Pittsburgh.

Leland, J. 1986. Population. In W. L. D'Azevedo (ed.), *Great Basin.* Vol. 11, *Handbook of North American Indians,* pp. 608–619. Smithsonian Institution, Washington, DC.

Leonard, B. 2004. Desert destinations. *National Parks* 78: 42–46.

Lines, G. C. 1999. Riparian vegetation along the Mojave River. Presented at the Center for Conservation Biology, University of California, Riverside, Mojave Desert Science Symposium, February 1999.

Lovich, J. E., and D. Bainbridge. 1999. Anthropogenic degradation of the southern California desert ecosystem and prospects for natural recovery and restoration. *Environmental Management* 24: 309–326.

Mack, R. N. Alien plant invasion into the intermountain West: A case history. In Mooney, H. A. and J. A. Drake (eds.), *Ecology of Biological Invasions of North America and Hawaii,* pp. 191–213. Springer-Verlag, New York.

Madsen, D. B. 2002. Great basin peoples and Late Quaternary aquatic history. In R. Hershler,

D. B. Madsen, and D. R. Currey (eds.), *Great Basin Aquatic Systems History,* pp. 387–405. Smithsonian Contributions to the Earth Sciences 33. Smithsonian Institution, Washington, DC.

McGill, T. J. 1986. Federal equine management on federal lands. In R. G. Zahary (ed.), *Desert Ecology 1986: A Research Symposium,* pp. 169–174. Southern California Academy of Sciences and the Southern California Desert Studies Consortium, Fullerton.

McGrath, R. D. 1988. No goodee cow man. In Friends of the Eastern California Museum (compilers), *Mountains to Desert: Selected Inyo Readings,* pp. 17–73. Eastern California Museum, Independence, CA.

National Park Service. 2005. Land protection plan for Death Valley National Park. Appendix B. www.nps.gov/moja/devaplan/devaappb.html.

Philips III, A. M., and D. J. Kennedy. 2003. The ecology of *Astragalus magdalenae* var. *peirsonii:* Distribution, reproduction, and seed bank. Report to the American Sand Association, LaVerne, CA.

Philips III, A. M., and D. J. Kennedy. 2003. The ecology of *Astragalus magdalenae* var. *peirsonii:* Germination and survival. Report to the American Sand Association, LaVerne, CA.

Prose, D. V. 1985. Persisting effects of armored military maneuvers on some soils of the Mojave Desert. *Environmental Geology and Water Science* 7: 163–170.

Rae, C. 1992. *East Mojave Desert: A Visitor's Guide.* Olympus Press, Santa Barbara, CA.

Reilly, M. 2007. Dry future ahead for the US Southwest. *NewScientist* 194: 15.

Rodman, J. 1980. Reflections on tamarisk bashing. In Hughes, H. G. and T. M. Bonnicksen (eds.), *Restoration '89: The New Management Challenge,* pp. 59–69. Society for Ecological Restoration, Madison, WI.

Sada, D. W. 1984. *Land Protection Plan: Proposed Acquisition to Establish Ash Meadows National Wildlife Refuge, Nye County, Nevada.* United States Fish and Wildlife Service, Portland, OR.

Sanders, A., and R. Minnich. 2000. *Brassica tournefortii.* In C. C. Bossard, J. M. Randall, and M. M. Hochovsky, *Invasive Plants of California's Wildlands.* University of California Press, Berkeley.

Schlesinger, W. H., and C. S. Jones. 1984. The comparative importance of overland runoff and mean annual rainfall to shrub communities of the Mojave Desert. *Botanical Gazette* 145: 116–124.

Schlesinger, W. H., P. J. Fonteyn, and W. A. Reiners. 1989. Effects of overland flow on plant water relations, erosion, and soil water percolation on a Mojave Desert landscape. *Soil Science Society of America Journal* 53: 1567–1572.

Soltz, D. L., and R. J. Naiman. 1978. *The Natural History of Native Fishes in the Death Valley System.* Natural History Museum of Los Angeles County, Los Angeles.

Southern California Association of Governments. 2005. Population growth by city for SCAG region, 1980–1990, 1990–2000. www.scag.ca.gov.

Thompson, C. R. 1995. Air pollution effects on desert plants. In J. Latting and P. G. Rowlands (eds.), *The California Desert: An Introduction to Natural Resources and Man's Impact,* pp. 481–488. June Latting Books, Riverside, CA.

U.S. Fish and Wildlife Service. 2005. Threats to desert tortoises. www.fws.gov/nevada/desert_tortoise/dt_threats.html.

Van Dyke, J. C. 1902. *The Desert: Further Studies in Natural Appearances.* Charles Scribner's Sons, New York.

Walker, L. R., and E. A. Powell. 1999. Effects of seeding on road revegetation in the Mojave Desert, southern Nevada. *Ecological Restoration* 17: 150–155.

Webb, R. H., and S. S. Stielstra. 1979. Sheep grazing effects on Mojave Desert vegetation and soils. *Environmental Management* 3: 517–529.

Webb, R. H., K. H. Berry, and D. E. Boyer. 2001. Changes in riparian vegetation in the southwestern United States: Historical changes along the Mojave River, California. *U.S. Geological Survey Open-File Report* 01-245.

Wehausen, J. D. 1988. The historical distribution of mountain sheep in the Owens Valley Region. In Friends of the Eastern California Museum (compilers), *Mountains to Desert: Selected Inyo Readings,* pp. 97–115. Eastern California Museum, Independence, CA.

Wehausen, J. D. 1991. Some potentially adaptive characters of mountain sheep populations in the Owens Valley region. In C. A. Hall, V. Doyle-Jones, and B. Widawski (eds.), *Natural History of Eastern California and High-Altitude Research,* pp. 256–267. Symposium 3. White Mountain Research Station, Los Angeles.

West, N. E. 1988. Intermountain deserts, shrub steppes, and woodlands. In M. G. Barbour and W. D. Billings (eds.), *North American Terrestrial Vegetation,* pp. 209–230. Cambridge University Press, Cambridge, UK.

Wheat, F. 1999. *California Desert Miracle: The Fight for Desert Parks and Wilderness.* Sunbelt Publications, San Diego.

Wilshire, H. G. 1980. Study results of 9 sites used by off-road vehicles that illustrate land modifications. *U.S. Geological Survey Open-File Report* 77-601.

Wilshire, H. G., K. A. Howard, C. M. Wentworth, and H. Gibbons. 1996. Geologic processes at the land surface. *U.S. Geological Survey Bulletin* 2149.

HIDDEN EFFECTS OF OHVS ON A "LIFELESS" PLAYA

Eriksen, C. H., G. W. Prettyman, and J. E. Moeur. 1986. The effects of soil disturbance by off-road vehicles on the eggs and habitat of playa lake crustaceans. In R.G. Zahary (ed.), *Desert Ecology 1986: A Research Symposium.* Southern California Academy of Sciences and the California Desert Studies Consortium, Fullerton.

RESTORATION ON THE 'AHAKHAV TRIBAL PRESERVE

Kroeber, A. L. 1925. *Handbook of the Indians of California.* California Book Co., Berkeley. Pp. 742–743.

Phillips, Fred. 1998. The 'Ahakhav Tribal Preserve. Colorado River Indian tribes initiate a major riparian restoration program. *Restoration and Management Notes* 16: 140–148.

Thompson, J. W. 2000. Desert passage. Wanted: One student for grueling project with uncertain outcome, no funding in hand, on Indian reservation. *Landscape Architect* 3: 56–65.

ART CREDITS

JOSEPH DOUGHERTY 80, 270, 295

STEPHEN DOWLAN, (c) 2006 173, 234

ARTHUR V. EVANS AND JAMES N. HOGUE 150, 184, 218, 234

WILLIAM C. FLAXINGTON 117, 118, 124, 183, 231, 248, 273, 286

DR. DANIEL L. GEIGER, (c) 2004 117

SHAWN GOODCHILD, courtesy of the US Fish and Wildlife Service 228

GEORGE HAWXHURST, courtesy of the California Academy of Sciences 43

RUDOLPH D'HEUREUSE, courtesy of the Bancroft Library, University of California 33, 34, 35, 296

RICHARD HIETT 35

MARC C. HOSHOVSKY 227

ANGELA HYDER, (c) 2006 49, 61

DR. LLOYD GLENN INGLES, courtesy of the California Academy of Sciences 115, 119, 135, 150, 176, 189, 216

G. W. JAMES, courtesy of the Autry National Center, Southwest Museum, Los Angeles 38

GARY JENSEN 90

CHARLES E. JONES, (c) 2004 110

C. KOPPEL, courtesy of the Bancroft Library, University of California 142

ALFRED KROEBER, courtesy of the Phoebe Apperson Hearst Museum of Anthropology and the Regents of the University of California 236

JEFF LEMM 219, 221

JEFF LOVICH 284

QT LUONG/TERRAGALLERIA.COM, Terra Galleria 25

DAVID L. MAGNEY 227

STEVE MATSON, (c) 2005 5, 10, 74, 263, 264, 286

SAM MCGINNIS 50

C. HART MERRIAM, courtesy of the Bancroft Library, University of California 303

MARLI BRYANT MILLER 67, 77, 79, 85, 94

H. B. MOLHAUSEN, courtesy of the Bancroft Library, University of California 17

GARY A. MONROE, (c) 1992, 2000 27

HAROLD MOONEY 107

RICK MOORE 279

TOM G. MURRAY, courtesy of the Riverside Metropolitan Museum 59

JENNIFER NEUWALD 286

RON NIEBRUGGE/WILDNATUREIMAGES.COM, (c) 113, 219, 241

CHERIE NORTHON, PH.D 253, 258

DOMINIC OLDERSHAW, courtesy of the Desert Repeat Photography Collection, US Geological Survey 123

unknown, courtesy of the US Geological Service 84, 94

unknown, courtesy of the US National Archives 257

unknown, courtesy of USC Special Collections Library 19

T. R. VAN DEVENDER 135

GLENN AND MARTHA VARGAS, courtesy of the California Academy of Sciences 169, 190, 195

W. A. A. VEATCH courtesy of the Bancroft Library, University of California 86

CHRIS WAGNER, SBNF 267

JOHN WALTER AND NANCY PETERSON WALTER 206

DEE E. WARENYCIA, (c) 2005, 2006 116, 154

WAUCOBA4@AOL.COM 131, 132

ROBERT H. WEBB, courtesy of the US Geological Survey 261

CHARLES WEBBER, courtesy of the California Academy of Sciences 30, 80, 115, 179, 201, 232, 238, 240

MATT WEISER, (c) 220

STEPHEN H. WILLARD, courtesy of (c) Palm Springs Art Museum 62, 72, 81, 235

H. G. WILSHIRE, courtesy of the US Geological Survey 277

YEAGER AND WOODWARD, courtesy of the US National Park Service 123

JIM D. YOAKUM 269, 275

RICHARD ZMASEK, (c) 2005 128, 129

TIM ZUROWSKI, enature.com 202, 205

INDEX

Abies
   concolor, 136, 213
   concolor var. *concolor,* 213
   concolor var. *lowiana,* 213
Abronia villosa, 110 (plate), 168, 249
acacia, 130
Acacia, 130
   greggii, 227
Acari, 119, 122
ACECs (Areas of Critical Environmental
   Concern), 291
Achnatherum
   hymenoides, 14, 114, 222, 278
   speciosum, 217
acorns, 21, 22, 146, 236
adaptive diversity, 298
adaptive management, 292
Aeronautes saxatalis, 174
Aesculus, 133
Afton Canyon, 21, 21 (plate), 32, 137, 265, 291,
   295
agave, 146, 187 (plate), 244
Agave deserti, 146, 187 (plate), 244
Agile Kangaroo Rat, 205

agriculture, 38–39, 54, 56, 87, 106, 146, 247,
   257, 258 (plate), 263
  Indian, 146, 166, 255
  water use, 38, 39, 159 (plate), 257, 271, 275
Agropyron desertorum, 264 (plate), 265 (fig.)
'Ahakhav Tribal Preserve restoration project,
   300–302
air pressure, 75 (map), 78
air quality, 109, 276–279, 293
aiwa. See Indian ricegrass
Alamo River, 87
albedo, 183–184, 187 (plate), 207
Alectoris chukar, 285
algae, 91, 156, 226, 228, 230, 272, 274
  blue-green algae, 131, 171, 226
  fossil algae, 131
  green algae, 171, 226
  See also cryptogamic crusts
Algodones Dune sunflower, 248 (plate), 249
Algodones Dunes, 20, 245, 245 (plate), 248,
   249, 288–289
  sand food community, 246–247, 246 (plate)
alkali, alkali dust, 85, 277–278
Alkali Bee, 225

Alkali Fairy Shrimp, 171, 171 (plate), 262

alkali flies, 272, 272 (plate), 273 (fig.), 274

alkali meadow, 225, 226, 226 (plate), 237

alkali pink, 225

alkali sacaton, 224–225, 226 (plate), 237

alkalinity, 90, 91

Allenrolfea occidentalis, 141, 224

allscale, 224

alluvial soils, 89, 90, 92, 227, 233

    See also bajadas

Alnus incana tenuifolia, 200

alpine ecosystems, 127

Altithermal, 141–145, 205, 216, 220 (fig.)

amaranths, 102

    Torrey's amaranth, 104 (plate), 106 (fig.)

    white amaranth, 263, 264

Amaranthus, 102

    albus, 263

Amargosa Pupfish, 158, 268, 269 (plate)

Amargosa River, 27, 28, 68, 93, 93 (plate), 94, 137, 158

Amargosa River Pupfish, 158, 159–160

Amargosa spiny caper, 27–28

Amargosa Springsnail, 286

Amargosa Vole, 286 (plate)

Amboy Crater, 81

Ambrosia dumosa, 108, 108 (fig.), 175, 220–221, 221 (plate), 269, 276

Ambrysus

    amargosus, 228 (plate)

    mormon, 229

amino acids, 121–122

ammonium, 120

ammonoids, 131–132, 131 (plate)

Ammoperoix heyi, 190

Ammospermophilus leucurus, 184, 259

Amnicola, 41

amoebae, 119

amphibians, 46–47, 49, 152 (table), 230, 231 (plates)

    nonnative species, 268

    See also individual genera and species

amphipods, 229

Ancient Bison, 140

Andreas Canyon, 238

Anemopsis californica, 21 (plate)

animal consumption (carnivory), 111, 115–119

    See also Indian diets; predators

animal interactions. *See* animal consumption; competition; predators

animal unit month (AUM), 284, 285

animal-plant interactions. *See* plant consumption; plant-animal interactions; *specific plants, animals, and community types*

Anna's Hummingbird, 241 (plate)

annuals, 109, 121, 166–169, 166 (fig.), 297

    as animal food source, 111, 171–172, 175, 282, 284, 289

    Mojave Desert, 27, 212, 221, 222–223, 222 (plates), 224, 268

    nonnative species, 265–267

    restoration techniques, 299

    sand dune annuals, 248

    in succession process, 123, 125, 297

    See also forbs; herbs; *specific plants*

Anodonta, 41

    californiensis, 274

Anomala hardyorum, 287

Antelope, 22, 24, 25, 33, 38. *See also* Pronghorn

antelope bitterbrush, 202, 207, 207 (plate), 208

Antelope Ground Squirrel, 184, 259

Antelope Valley, 22, 23, 25 (plate), 38–39, 70, 84 (plate), 239, 256, 257

    Frémont expedition in, 24–25

Antelope Valley California Poppy State Reserve, 25

Anthocharis cethura, 214

Antilocapra americana, 141, 151, 208, 258

ants, 218, 222

    See also harvester ants

Anza, Juan Bautista, 20

Anza-Borrego Desert, 133, 169, 233, 237

Anza-Borrego Desert State Park, 59, 84 (plate), 140 (plate), 233 (plate), 295

aphids, 111

Apodemia, 113

Apple Valley, 70

aquatic habitats, 94–95, 125, 156–158, 171, 202, 229

aquifers. *See* Death Valley Aquifer; groundwater

Arcan, Abigail, 31

archaeology, 45

Archeocyathids, 131

Archillete, 28

arctic ecosystems, 127

Arctomecon merriamii, 184 (plate)

Areas of Critical Environmental Concern
    (ACECs), 291

arenas, 88

Argia moesta, 156–157, 156 (plate)

Argus Kangaroo Rat, 287

Arid Land Termite, 116 (plate)

aridisols, 89

arrow weed, 79 (plate), 229, 233, 237

Arroyo Chub, 52

arroyo willow, 201, 237

arroyo woodland, 233–237, 233 (plates), 265, 296
    riparian, 227

arroyos, 85, 89, 90, 197

Artemia monica, 272

Artemisia, 22, 102, 237
    nova, 207
    tridentata, 70, 105, 202, 278, 282

arthropods, 122, 189, 287

Asbolus verrucosus, 184 (plate)

Ash Meadows, 29, 31, 50, 50–54, 96, 114 (plate),
    157
    springs and water depletion, 229 (plate),
        274–276, 275 (plates)

Ash Meadows Naucorid, 228 (plate)

Ash Meadows Pupfish, 50–51, 51 (plate),
    158–159, 275

ashes, 137
    desert ash, 213
    velvet ash, 237

aspen, quaking, 200, 201 (plate), 202 (plate)

Asteraceae, 207

asters
    desert aster, 299
    limestone aster, 199
    Mecca aster, 296

asthma, 278

Astragalus, 52, 120, 287
    albens, 286 (plate)
    jaegerianus, 257
    kentrophyta, 199
    lentiginosus var. *borreganus*, 286–287
    lentiginosus var. *fremontii*, 167
    magdalenae var. *peirsonii*, 249, 288–289

atmospheric fertilization, 279

Atriplex, 52, 102, 175, 224
    canescens, 224, 278
    confertifolia, 113, 217
    hymenelytra, 183, 184 (plate), 185 (fig.), 224,
        224 (plate), 278
    polycarpa, 224

AUM (animal unit month), 284, 285

Auriparus flaviceps, 162, 190, 234

Austin, Mary, 56 (plate), 57–58

Australian Dotterel, 190

avocado, 133

Axelrod, Daniel, 209–210

Azotobacter, 120

Baccharis sergiloides, 227, 229

bacteria, 101, 229, 297
    cyanobacteria, 91, 120, 158
    decomposing, 89, 112 (fig.)
    nitrogen-fixing, 109, 114, 120, 124
    salt-tolerant, 226, 226
    soil, 88, 91, 114, 151, 171, 189, 226
    varnishes, 91, 92

Badwater, 91 (plate)

Bailey, Vernon, 47 (plate), 52

Baileya, 172
    multiradiata, 299

Bailey's Pocket Mouse, 113, 115 (plate)

Baja peninsula, 132

bajadas, 85, 85 (plate), 88 (plate), 94, 123,
    221 (plate)
    soils, 89, 90, 91, 120, 223

Bald Eagle, 51

Baltic rush, 226 (plate)

barrel cactus, 125, 186, 187 (plate), 195 (plate),
    241
    in Mojave communities, 221, 244
    See also bisnada; California barrel cactus

Barstow, 22, 27, 39, 52, 259

Barstow to Las Vegas motorcycle race,
    277 (plate), 278

basalt, 79, 81, 84 (plate), 212

basketry, 141, 146
    granaries, 236 (plate), 237

Batrachoseps, 272
    campi, 287

bats, 287
    California Leaf-nosed Bat, 296

Beale, Edward F., 33, 51
Bear Flag Rebellion, 27–28
beard grass, 263
beardtongues, 173
    Palmer's beardtongue, 299
    See also penstemons
bears, 133
Beatty, 57
Beauveria densa, 228
beavers, 23, 232
beavertail cactus, 34, 34 (plate), 105 (plate), 221,
    244
bedrocks, 79–80, 82 (map), 83 (map), 120
    See also specific types
bedstraws, 141
    Parish's bedstraw, 213
bees, 47, 179, 200, 234, 240
    Alkali Bee, 225
beetles, 208, 287
    Desert Ironclad Beetle, 184 (plate)
    Giant Palm Borer, 150 (plate), 239, 239 (plate)
    Mesquite Beetle, 234–235
    Moapa Riffle Beetle, 229
    naucorid beetles, 228 (plate), 229
    Salt Cedar Leaf Beetle, 294
bellyplants, 27, 28, 222 (plates)
Bembix rugosa, 246–247, 247 (plate)
Bembix Wasp, 246–247, 247 (plate)
Bennett, Sarah, 31
Bentley, H. L., 281–282
Betula, 137
    occidentalis, 200
biatatk, 247
    See also sand food
Bicycle Dry Lake, 262
big galleta grass, 217, 222, 240, 276
Big Morongo Canyon, 291
big sagebrush, 108, 112, 202, 204, 278
    chemical defenses, 208–209, 209 (fig.), 283
    migrations, 136, 142, 205
    photos, 70 (plate), 208 (plate)
    See also big sagebrush scrub
big sagebrush scrub, 105, 201, 201 (plate),
    206–209, 207 (plate)
    nonnative species in, 263–264, 283
bighorn sheep, 22, 70, 133, 163
    Indian hunting, 3, 7, 141, 145
    See also Desert Bighorn

biological communities. *See* communities;
    specific types
biological diversity, 59–60, 111, 149, 151–152,
    152 (table), 298
    See also plant diversity; species richness
birches, 137
    water birch, 200
birds, 30, 118, 162, 184, 190
    Death Valley Expedition observations, 49, 52
    diversity, 152 (table), 197 (fig.), 223
    forest and woodland communities, 200, 205,
        218
    fossil species, 132, 133
    in Indian diets, 231
    mesquite associates, 234
    nonnative species, 268
    riparian communities, 201–202, 265, 287,
        302
    torpor in, 173–174
    wetlands, 230, 272, 274
    See also individual species
Bishop, 76
bisnada, 28
Bison, Ancient, 140
Bison bison antiquus, 140
bitter springs, 96
black cottonwood, 200, 201
black sagebrush, 207
Black Toad, 230, 231 (plate), 291
black willow, 237, 265
blackbirds, 46
blackbush, 124–125, 124 (plates), 217, 223, 297
blackbush scrub, 125
black-stemmed rabbitbrush, 227, 227 (plate)
Black-tailed Gnatcatcher, 190, 234, 265
Black-tailed Jackrabbit, 111–112, 113 (plate), 145
bladderpod, 240
Blake, William P., 40–42, 77–78, 86–87,
    235–236
blister beetles, 208
BLM. *See* Bureau of Land Management
blue palo verde, 115, 233, 233 (plate), 265
blue-green algae, 131, 171, 226
boa constrictors, 118, 130, 232
body size, 191–192, 210–211
Bodie, 76, 281
Bombus, 240
Bonanza King Dolomite, 5, 8, 10, 210

Bonytail, 50

Bootettix argentatus, 113, 113 (plate), 195

borates, 85, 120

borers

    Giant Palm Borer, 150 (plate), 239, 239 (plate)

    Mesquite Borer, 234, 234 (plate)

Borrego milkvetch, 286–287

bostrychid beetles, 239

Botrytis carnea, 226

boxthorn, 173

brachiopods, 131

Branchinecta, 262

    gigas, 171

    mackini, 171, 171 (plate), 262

Brassica tournefortii, 267, 267 (plates)

Brewer, William, 45

Brier, Juliette, 30–31

brine shrimp, 274, 287

    Mono Brine Shrimp, 272, 273 (fig.)

bristlecone pine, 136, 142, 198–199, 199 (plate), 212

bristlecone pine forest and woodland, 166 (fig.), 198–200, 199 (plates), 290

brittlebush, 221, 240

    virgin brittlebush, 227

brome grasses, 124

    red brome, 266, 266 (plates), 268, 279, 299

Bromus, 124

    madritensis subsp. *rubens*, 266, 266 (plates)

    tectorum, 263–264, 264 (plate)

brown-eyed primrose, 104 (plate), 106 (fig.), 168, 278

browsers, 111

Bruchus desertorum, 234–235

buckeye, 133

buckhorn cholla, 244

buckwheats, 24–25, 52, 113, 141, 171–172

    California buckwheat, 240

    dune buckwheat, 246, 249

    Hermann's buckwheat, 216

    napkinring buckwheat, 211

    sulfur-flowered buckwheat, 203

Buenaventura River, 22, 23

Bufo

    exsul, 230, 291

    punctatus, 230

bugseed, 5, 10, 11, 14, 249

    Clark's bugseed, 11 (plate), 13, 169

Bull Salmon, 50, 50 (plate)

Bullfrog, 268

bulrushes, 137

bumblebees, 240

bunchgrasses, 42, 196–197, 202–203, 222

Bureau of Land Management (BLM), 261, 291, 294

    California Desert Plan, 151, 291–293, 294, 295

    Desert Tortoise recovery efforts, 295–296

    grazing regulation, 283–285

Burro, 191, 192, 270 (plate), 284, 285, 291

    population growth and impacts, 268–271, 270 (fig.)

    removal of, 294

burrobush, 142, 175, 221 (plates), 269, 276, 278–279

    as creosote bush associate, 220–221, 221 (plate), 240, 242–243

    water use, 108, 108 (fig.)

burrowing animals, 90, 91, 128, 174, 192, 297

    See also specific animals

Bursera microphylla, 233, 286

Butler Peak, 32

butterflies, 113, 214–215, 246, 287

    DeDecker's Blue Butterfly, 9 (plate), 214–215, 287

    Desert Orangetip, 214

    Desert Swallowtail Butterfly, 214–215 (plates), 215, 215 (map)

    host plants, 214–215

    Monarch, 214

    Navaho Giant Yucca Skipper, 217–218, 219 (plate)

    Providence Swallowtail Butterfly, 287

C_3 photosynthesis, 100 (fig.), 101–102, 103 (table), 105

    influences on, 106 (fig.), 107 (fig.)

    plants using, 102, 169

C_4 photosynthesis, 101 (fig.), 102, 103 (table), 105

    influences on, 106 (fig.), 107 (fig.)

    plants using, 102, 169, 183

cacti, 72 (plate), 130, 140, 153, 181, 185–188, 249

    beavertail cactus, 34, 34 (plate), 105 (plate), 221

    as food source, 112, 141, 172, 282

    hedgehog cactus, 217, 244

cacti (cont.)
    old man cactus, 202
    pencil cactus, 244
    pincushion cactus, 244
    scrub communities, 221, 240, 244
    water depletion impacts, 276
    water uptake by, 185–186, 186 (fig.)
    woodland communities, 203, 217, 223
    See also barrel cactus; cactus scrub; chollas
Cactus Mouse, 191, 192
cactus scrub, 243–244, 244 (plate)
Cahuilla people, 38 (plate), 41–42, 146, 165–166,
    235–237, 235 (plate), 247, 255
Cajon Pass, 23, 25, 46, 259, 261
Cajon Pass Tollhouse, 33 (plate)
calcium, 90, 120, 121
calcium carbonate, 89, 91, 92
calderas, 81
caliche, 89, 128, 264
California barrel cactus, 34, 34 (plate), 125,
    186 (fig.), 188, 244
California buckwheat, 240
California croton, 240
California dandelion, 282, 289
California Desert Conservation Area (CDCA),
    291
California Desert Plan, 291–293, 294, 295
California Desert Protection Act, 292–294
California fan palm, 154–155, 154 (plate),
    237–239
    See also fan palm woodland; fan palms
California Floater, 274
California Gull, 272, 273 (plate)
California juniper, 204
California Leaf-nosed Bat, 296
California poppy, 24, 25, 25 (plate)
California sycamore, 237
California Towhee, Inyo, 286 (plate)
California Treefrog, 230
Calliope Hummingbird, 202
Callisaurus draconoides, 116–117, 117 (plate)
Calochortus excavatus, 273
Calypte
    anna, 241 (plate)
    costae, 49, 49 (plate), 52, 173–174, 173 (plate)
CAM photosynthesis, 102 (fig.), 103 (table), 104,
    105, 244
    plants using, 153, 181, 185–188

camels, 80, 133, 134, 134 (fig.), 140, 190, 233, 237
Camelus dromedarius, 80, 190
Camissonia claviformis, 104 (plate), 168, 278
Camp Cady, 33, 34 (plate)
Camp Coxcomb, 257 (plate)
Camp Independence, 45
Campbell, Elizabeth, 45
Campbell, William, 45
Canis
    latrans, 111, 118, 119 (plate), 164, 230–231, 272
    latrans mearnsi, 118
canyon oak, 213, 216, 227
canyons, 83, 85
carbon dioxide, 279–280
carbon fixation, 101, 102, 108
    See also photosynthesis
carbon gain. *See* primary productivity; water use
    efficiency
carbonate scrub, 209–212, 209 (plate)
carbonates, 79, 80, 90, 215, 223, 224
    See also dolomites; limestones
Carnegiea gigantea, 188, 233, 287–288
carnivory. *See* animal consumption
Carp, 268
carpenter bees, 240
Carr, Milton, 33–34
carrizo, 22
Carson, Kit, 23
Carson River, 137
Carter, Jimmy, 292
Casa del Desierto, 39
Castilleja applegatei subsp. *martinii,* 200
catclaw, 227, 240
Catostomus, 157, 228
cattails, 137, 138, 197, 229, 230 (plate)
    as food source, 141, 230, 231
cattle, 281, 282
Caulanthus, 214
CDCA (California Desert Conservation Area),
    291
Cedar Spring, 21
Cenozoic Era, 129
    fossil fauna, 132–133
centipedes, 117, 119, 121 (plate)
Centrocercus urophasianus, 208, 208 (plate)
Cerambycidae, 208
Cercidium
    floridum, 115, 233, 265

floridum subsp. *floridum*, 71
   microphyllum, 244
Cercocarpus intricatus, 199
Chaetodipus
   baileyi, 113
   penicillatus, 235
chaparral shrubs, 204
Charleston Peak, 40, 53 (fig.)
Chautauquan magazine, 46
cheatgrass, 263–264, 264 (plate), 265 (fig.), 266, 283
checkerbloom, Owens Valley, 226 (plates), 273
cheesebush, 125, 175, 221, 227, 297
cheetah, 133
Chemehuevi people, 33, 40, 50, 300, 302
chemical defenses of plants, 208–209, 209 (fig.)
Chenopodiaceae, 207, 224
Chenopodium murale, 263
Chihuahuan Desert, 220
Chilopsis linearis, 227
China Lake Naval Weapons Center, 270 (fig.)
Chionactis occipitalis, 117–118, 118 (plate), 249
Chipmunk, Panamint, 216, 216 (plate)
Chisel-tooth Kangaroo Rat, 113, 191 (fig.)
Chlorella vulgaris, 226
chloride, 90, 120
Chocolate Mountains, 71
chollas
   buckhorn cholla, 244
   teddy-bear cholla, 221, 244, 244 (plate)
   See also silver cholla
Chrysothamnus, 112, 283, 297
   nauseosus, 125, 202
   paniculatus, 227, 227 (plate)
   viscidiflorus, 199
chubs, 157, 228
   Arroyo Chub, 52
   Mojave Chub, 276
   Mojave Tui Chub, 51–52, 52 (plate), 133
   Owens Chub, 273
Chuckwalla, 172, 221, 221 (plate)
Chuckwalla Mountains, 71, 276
Chukar, 285
chuparosa, 173, 233, 233 (plate)
cicadas (Cicadidae), 272
cinchweed, 168 (plates), 169
cinder cones, 81

Cirsium mohavense, 225
Clark Mountain, 213
Clark's bugseed, 11 (plate), 13, 169
Clark's Nutcracker, 205, 205 (plate)
climate, 45, 67, 69 (table), 71–79, 75 (maps), 100
   current/future climate change, 279–280
   effects on sensitive species, 240–241
   ET/P ratios, 69 (table), 72–73
   factors influencing, 73–77, 75 (maps)
   Holocene oscillations and Altithermal, 129, 139, 141–145, 205, 213, 216, 220 (fig.)
   Pleistocene, 129, 132–133, 134, 136–137
   Tertiary, 130, 131
   wind, 76–78, 79 (plate)
climate adaptations, 207
   heat coping mechanisms, 182–185, 241
Clinton, Bill, 293
Clokey paintbrush, 200
clones, 200, 220 (plate), 244 (plate)
Clovis culture, 139, 144 (plate)
Coachella Valley, 36, 39, 86, 111, 278
   agriculture and urbanization, 39, 256 (plate), 257, 258 (plate)
Coachella Valley Fringe-toed Lizard, 286 (plate)
Coachwhip, 182–183, 183 (plate)
Coccidiomycosis, 278
Cocopa people, 247
cold air drainage, 76–77, 223, 240
cold desert phlox, 203
coldenia, 249
Coleogyne ramosissima, 124–125, 297
Collembola, 122
Colorado Desert, 71
   See also Sonoran Desert
Colorado Fringe-toed Lizard, 248 (plate), 249
Colorado Pikeminnow, 50, 50 (plate)
Colorado River, 35, 50 (plate), 70, 71, 86, 133, 232
   'Ahakhav Tribal Preserve restoration project, 300–302
   fish species, 50, 50 (plate)
   Garcés exploration, 19–20
   riparian communities, 265, 295, 295 (plate), 296 (plate)
   as sand source, 245, 248
   water use/diversions, 87, 257, 271
Colorado River Aqueduct, 276
Common Raven, 289
common reed, 229

communities, 195–249, 285
    analysis and classification methods, 210, 227
    fragmentation, 259, 260 (maps), 261,
        301–302
    Merriam's life zones, 53 (fig.), 53 (plate), 54
    nonnative species impacts, 263–264, 265,
        267–271, 281–284, 289, 290
    nurse plants, 242–243
    overview, 195–198, 196 (table)
    See also Great Basin communities; Mojave
        communities; Sonoran communities;
        threatened communities; *specific types*
competition, 100, 105, 108, 108 (fig.), 121, 122,
    128, 155, 188, 210–211, 239, 243
    from nonnative species, 263–265, 265 (fig.),
        269–271, 279, 281–282, 297
conifer forest, 70
    migrations, 136, 137 (fig.), 139, 139 (fig.), 142,
        212–213
conifers
    ozone sensitivity, 278
    See also conifer forest; *individual genera and*
        species
conservation
    California Desert Plan, 291–293, 294, 295
    California Desert Protection Act, 292–294
    challenges, 288–289, 293–294
    development of conservation ethic, 59–60
    restoration approaches, 296–302
    setting priorities, 287–289
    threatened species, 287–289, 288 (table),
        295–296
Contopus sordidulus, 201–202
convergence, 207
cores. *See* pollen analysis
cormorants, 51
corn, 22, 35, 102
Corvus corax, 289
Coso, 49–52
Costa's Hummingbird, 49, 49 (plate), 52,
    173–174, 173 (plate)
Cotonopus cooperi, 200
Cottonball Marsh, 160 (plate)
Cottonball Marsh Pupfish, 159, 160 (plate)
Cottonwood Mountains Desert Bighorn, 270
cottonwoods, 22, 133, 137, 237, 302
    black cottonwood, 200, 201
    See also Frémont cottonwood

Couch's Spadefoot Toad, 280–281
Coville, Frederick V., 47, 52–53
Coxcomis Mountains, 204, 276
Coyote, 27, 118, 119 (plate), 235, 237
    Desert Coyote, 118
    as predator, 111, 164, 230–231, 272
crassulacean acid metabolism. *See* CAM
    photosynthesis
creosote bush, 34, 109, 125, 178–181, 221, 297
    air pollution impacts, 278
    as animal food source, 112
    associated plants, 221, 242–243, 267
    King Clone, 220 (plate), 221
    migrations, 142, 151, 219–220, 220 (fig.)
    nonnative species impacts, 268, 269
    photos, 34 (plate), 71 (plate), 88 (plate),
        92 (plate), 179 (plates), 195 (plate)
    photosynthesis, 102, 106 (fig.), 180
    in pinyon-juniper woodland, 204
    in the Sonoran Desert, 240, 243
    transplantation, 300
    as water competitor, 108
    water depletion impacts, 276
    See also creosote bush scrub
Creosote Bush Grasshopper, 113, 113 (plate), 195
creosote bush scrub, 219–223, 221 (plate), 232,
    243–244, 254
    arborescent, 239–243, 240 (plate), 244
    Coccidiomycosis, 278
    nonnative species in, 266–267
    water depletion impacts, 276
Crossidium, 177–178, 178 (plates)
Crotalus cerastes, 182
croton
    California croton, 240
    Wiggin's croton, 249
Croton
    californicus, 240
    wigginsii, 249
crows, 46
crustaceans, 229, 287
cryptantha, 213 (plate)
Cryptantha tumulosa, 213 (plate)
cryptogamic crusts, 91, 92 (plate), 120, 203, 283,
    297, 299
Cushenberry milkvetch, 286 (plate)
Cutthroat Trout, Lahontan, 202, 202 (plate)
cyanobacteria, 91, 120, 158

cymopterus, 215
Cymopterus, 215
Cymopterus gilmanii, 287
Cyperaceae, 141
Cyperus esculentus, 146
Cyprinodon, 13, 13 (plate), 137, 153, 157–162, 228,
    287
    diabolis, 157–158, 157 (plate), 229, 274, 276
    nevadensis, 158, 268, 269 (plate)
    nevadensis amargosae, 158, 159–160
    nevadensis calidae, 158
    nevadensis mionectes, 50–51, 51 (plate),
        158–159, 275
    nevadensis nevadensis, 158
    nevadensis pectoralis, 158
    nevadensis shoshone, 158
    radiosus, 95 (plate), 273–274, 274 (plate)
    salinus milleri, 159, 160 (plate)
    salinus salinus, 160, 161 (plate), 162 (fig.)
Cyprinus carpio, 268

dace, 157, 228
Daggett, 33, 40, 46
daisy, naked-stemmed, 210
Danaus plexippus, 214
dandelion, 71 (plate), 282, 289
Daylight Pass, 57 (plate), 58
Dead Mountains, 215, 227 (plate)
Death Valley, 57 (plate), 68, 79 (plate)
    air quality, 278
    archaeological finds, 12–13
    burros in, 269–270, 270 (plate), 271
    climate, 73, 75
    early crossings, 30–31, 31 (plate), 35–36
    fan palm groves, 237
    fossil fauna, 132–133
    lakebed polygons, 91 (plate)
    petroglyphs, 145, 145 (plate)
    saltbush scrub, 224 (plate)
    wetlands communities, 229–231
    See also specific locations and features
Death Valley Aquifer, 96, 158, 161–162, 274
Death Valley Expedition, 13, 46–49, 47 (plate),
    48 (map), 52–54, 216, 236
Death Valley Fault, 94
Death Valley National Monument, 59, 271, 293
Death Valley National Park, 230, 293, 295
decomposition, 88–89, 120 (plate), 122, 226

DeDecker, Mary, 7–11, 7 (plate)
DeDecker, Paul, 7–10, 7 (plate)
DeDeckera Canyon, 3, 10
Dedeckera eurekensis, 7–9, 9 (plate), 10–11, 210,
    214–215
DeDecker's Blue Butterfly, 9 (plate), 214–215,
    287
Deep Canyon, 151
Deep Springs, 291
Deep Springs Black Toad, 230, 231 (plate), 291
Deep Springs Valley, 231 (plate), 263 (plate)
Deep Springs–Eureka Valley Desert Bighorn,
    270
deer, 141, 195, 285, 302
    Mule Deer, 143, 205, 208, 283
deer mice, 141
dehydration, 165. *See* desiccation; drought;
    water stress
Descurainia, 214
desert agave, 146, 187, 187 (plate), 244
desert almond, 227
desert ash, 213
desert aster, 299
desert baccharis, 227, 229, 233
Desert Bighorn, 163–165, 191, 192, 265
    feeding and watering habits, 111, 163–164,
        205, 208, 230, 235
    habitat fragmentation, 258, 296, 301–302
    nonnative fauna and, 269–271, 281, 283, 294
    petroglyphs, 145, 145 (plate)
    photos, 149 (plate), 164 (plate)
    population variation, 164–165, 298
    predators and hunting, 164, 230–231, 258
    recovery efforts, 296
    threatened status, 287, 296
Desert Coyote, 118
desert crested wheatgrass, 264 (plate),
    265 (fig.)
desert dandelion, 71 (plate)
Desert Drywood Termite, 115
Desert Harvester Ant, 114 (plate), 222
desert holly, 183, 184 (plate), 185 (fig.), 224,
    224 (plate), 278
Desert Horned Lizard, 116, 116 (plate), 182,
    182 (plate)
Desert Iguana, 150 (plate)
Desert Ironclad Beetle, 184 (plate)
desert ironwood, 132, 233, 240 (plate), 240, 243

Desert Kangaroo Rat, 113, 190–192, 191 (fig.), 210, 280
  photos, 115 (plate), 190 (plate)
Desert Kit Fox, 119, 119 (plate), 182
desert marigold, 299
desert mistletoe, 114 (plate), 234, 234 (plate)
desert mosses, 177–178
desert needlegrass, 217
Desert Night Lizard, 218, 219 (plate)
Desert Orangetip, 214
desert origins, 99, 129–146
  Holocene ecosystems, 19, 130 (fig.), 133–134, 139–146
  Pleistocene ecosystems, 130 (fig.), 133–139
  Tertiary ecosystems, 129, 130–132
desert pavement, 91, 92, 92 (plate), 264, 283
desert peach, 124
desert pepper weed, 114 (plate)
Desert Pocket Mouse, 191 (fig.), 235
desert riparian forest, 201–202
  See also riparian communities
desert sage, 227
desert saltgrass, 224, 229, 298
desert shadscale, 113, 217, 223, 224, 225 (plate)
desert shrews, 119
desert snails, 153
Desert Studies Center, 52
desert sunflower, 167 (plates), 168
Desert Swallowtail Butterfly, 214–215 (plates), 215, 215 (map)
Desert Tortoise, 90, 171–173, 174, 257, 268
  feeding habits, 111, 171–172, 222, 268, 282, 289
  livestock competition, 282, 283
  photos, 99 (plate), 171 (plate)
  recovery efforts, 295–296, 301
  roadkill rates, 259, 289, 301
  threatened status, 289
desert trumpet, 29
desert varnish. See varnished soils
desert willow, 227, 233
Desert Woodrat (Packrat), 14, 135–136, 135 (plates)
desert-lavender, 240, 244
desiccation tolerance, 177, 188
Devil's Cornfield, 79 (plate)
Devil's Garden, 62 (plates)
Devils Hole, 157–158, 158 (plates), 159 (figs.), 274

Devils Hole Pupfish, 157–158, 157 (plate), 229, 274, 276
Devils Playground, 70
D'Heureuse, Rudolph, 34
Dichelostemma capitatum, 146
Dicoria, 10
  canescens, 249
  canescens subsp. clarkiae, 5, 13, 169
Dinapate wrighti, 150 (plate), 239, 239 (plate)
dinosaurs, 132
Diorhabda elongata, 294
Dipodomys, 111, 112–113, 190–191
  agilis, 205
  deserti, 113, 190–192, 190 (plate), 191 (fig.), 210, 280
  ingens, 192
  merriami, 210
  microps, 113
  panamintinus, 216, 216 (plate)
  panamintinus argusensis, 287
Dipsosaurus dorsalis, 150 (plate)
dire wolves, 133
discharge playas, 96
Distichlis, 137
  spicata var. stricta, 224, 298
disturbance, 92, 122, 125, 158, 159 (fig.), 178, 248, 254, 264–266, 276, 287, 290, 296
Dodecatheon pulchellum, 225
dolomites, 79, 120, 209
  See also Bonanza King Dolomite
dormancy
  nematodes, 188
  seed dormancy, 167–168, 169
  torpor in animals, 173–174, 176
Dos Palmas Preserve, 295
Dove Springs, 261
dragonflies, 156–157
  Mexican Amberwing, 156 (plate), 157
  Powdered Dancer, 156–157, 156 (plate)
drought, 88, 152–153, 271–272
  Altithermal, 141–145, 205, 216, 220 (fig.)
  current/future climate change and, 279–280
  tolerance and adaptations, 153–154, 166–168
drought-avoiding species, 153, 166–176
  Alkali Fairy Shrimp, 171, 171 (plate), 262
  annual herbs, 166–169
  Costa's Hummingbird, 49, 49 (plate), 52, 173–174, 173 (plate)

drought-deciduous shrubs, 169–171, 223
   See also Desert Tortoise; Mojave Ground
      Squirrel
drought-susceptible species, 153, 154–166
   birds, 162–163
   desert pupfishes, 157–162
   dragonflies, 156–157
   humans, 165–166
   trees, 154–156
   See also Desert Bighorn
drought-tolerant species, 153, 177–192
   cacti, 181, 185–188
   desert mosses, 177–178
   evergreen shrubs, 178–181
   Greater Roadrunner, 162, 189–190,
      189 (plate)
   nematodes, 188–189
   See also Desert Kangaroo Rat
dugongs, 133
dune buckwheat, 246, 249
dune weevils, 249
dunes. *See* sand dunes
dust, dust storms, 277–278
dust devils, 78, 79 (plate), 277
Dutton, Charles, 68

eagles, 51
Eared Grebe, 272
"eavesdropping" plants, 209, 209 (fig.)
Ebbets Pass, 23
Echinocactus polycephalus, 186, 186 (fig.),
   187 (plate), 188, 221, 244
Echinocereus engelmannii, 217
Echinochloa crus-galli, 264
ecosystem operations, 99–100
   models of, 125–128
   See also energy flow; nutrient cycling; primary
      productivity; succession
ecotones, 71 (plate)
   fan palm woodland transitions, 237
   Great Basin–Mojave, 68–69, 216–217
   Mojave Desert as, 212
   Mojave-Sonoran, 70–71, 239
   sagebrush scrub, 206
   woodland-scrub, 204–205, 223
effigies, 12–13
egrets, 301 (plate)
El Garcés Hotel, 39, 39 (plate)

Eleocharis rostellata, 225
elephant tree, 232 (plates), 233, 241, 286
elevation
   Merriam's life zones, 53 (fig.), 53 (plate), 54
   species richness and, 197 (fig.)
Elymus elymoides, 199
Empetrichythys, 157, 228
Encelia
   farinosa, 221
   virgenensis, 227
Enceliopsis
   nudicaulis, 210
endangered species. *See* threatened and
   endangered species
endemism, endemic species, 151–152, 166,
   286–287
   amphibians, 231 (plates)
   butterflies, 214–215, 287
   carbonate scrub plants, 209–212
   Mojave species, 212, 214–215, 216
   sand dune communities, 246–247, 249
energy flow, 110–119
   food webs, 110–111, 112 (fig.), 115–116
   inefficiencies in, 115
   reserve concept, 126–127
   See also animal consumption; plant
     consumption
English House Sparrow, 268
entrada, 20, 22, 254, 280, 290
ephedra
   Mormon tea, 112
   Nevada ephedra, 124, 207, 208, 217
Ephedra, 112
   nevadensis, 124, 207
Ephedraceae, 207
Ephydra hians, 272, 272 (plate)
Equus
   asinus, 191, 192, 268
   caballus, 268
   occidentalis, 140
Erigeron uncialis, 199
Eriogonum, 52, 113, 171–172
   deserticola, 249
   fasciculatum, 240
   heermannii var. *floccosum,* 216
   inflatum, 29
   intrafractum, 211
   ovalifolium, 203

Eriophyllum wallacei, 222 (plate)

Erodium cicutarium, 124, 261, 279

erosion, 82–85, 257, 261, 283

    wave erosion, 94, 94 (plate)

    wind erosion, 77–78, 79 (plate), 123, 125

    See also soils

ET/P, 69 (table), 72–73

Eureka dunegrass (old man grass), 5, 11 (plate),

    14, 150 (plate), 286

Eureka Dunes, 3–7, 14

Eureka Valley, 220 (fig.)

European exploration

    Garcés expedition, 19–22, 146, 231, 254, 293

    See also explorations; human impacts; human

        presence

European Starling, 268

Evans, George, 36–37

evaporation, 85, 88, 182

    See also transpiration

evaporative cooling, 155, 162, 183–184, 191–192

evapotranspiration-to-precipitation ratio. *See*

    ET/P

evergreen shrubs, 178–181

evolution of desert biota, 129

    fossil biota, 80, 131–133, 154–155

    Tertiary species, 130, 131–132

    See also desert origins; genetic divergence;

        plant migrations; speciation

exotic species. *See* nonnative species

explorations, 19–29

    archaeological study, 45

    Death Valley Expedition, 13, 46–49,

        47 (plate), 48 (map), 52–54, 216

    Frémont expedition, 23–29, 28 (map), 60,

        68, 70, 261

    Garcés expedition, 19–22, 146, 231, 254, 293

    Mono Lake, 42–45

    railroad surveys, 38, 40–42, 51–52, 235–236

    Smith and Ogden, 22–23

extinctions, 151

    Indian tribes, 255

    Permian-Triassic, 131–132

    Pleistocene, 139 (fig.), 140, 254, 255

    rate of change and, 254

    See also threatened and endangered species

extreme deserts, 72, 73

facilitation, 242–243

Fairbanks Springs, 50

fairy shrimp, 171, 171 (plate), 262, 262 (fig.)

Falco mexicanus, 182

Falcon, Prairie, 182

fan palm woodland, 237–239, 238 (plate), 290

fan palms, 132, 153

    California fan palm, 154–155, 154 (plate),

        237–239

faults, faulting, vi (map), 80, 84 (plate),

    85 (plate), 94

    Salton Trough mud volcanoes, 86–87

Federal Lands Policy and Management Act

    (FLPMA), 291

feeding relationships. *See* animal consumption;

    food webs; plant consumption

Ferocactus cylindraceus, 28, 34, 34 (plate), 125,

    244

filaree, 124, 261, 279

fire, 265, 285

    fire frequency, 144, 268, 289

    impacts on native plants, 237, 239, 264, 268,

        283

    Indian use of, 239, 283

firs, 137, 139

    See also white fir

Fish Slough, 95 (plate), 274

fish traps, 42

Fisher, Albert K., 47 (plate), 49, 52

fishes, 49, 50–52, 228–229

    diversity, 152, 152 (table), 157

    fossil species, 132, 133

    nonnative species, 268

    See also individual genera and species

flamingos, 51, 133

Flat-tailed Horned Lizard, 248 (plate)

flies, 47, 246, 247

    alkali flies, 272, 272 (plate), 273 (fig.), 274

    sand flies, 246, 247 (plate)

floods, flooding, 83, 87, 89, 91, 225

FLPMA (Federal Lands Policy and Management

    Act), 291

fluxes (nutrient transfer processes), 119

flycatchers, 230, 287

    Olive-sided Flycatcher, 200

Font, Pedro, 19–20

food webs, 99 (plate), 110–111, 112 (fig.), 115–116,

    118, 135, 229, 246–247

    aquatic, 158, 158 (plate), 171, 202, 229–230

belowground, 114–115, 119, 122, 189, 207
    Mono Lake, 272, 273 (fig.)
    sand dune communities, 249
    See also energy flow
foothill palo verde, 244
forbs, 164, 175, 269–270, 285
    nonnative, 267, 269
forests and woodlands, 196 (table)
    forest/woodland distinction, 197–198
    Great Basin, 198–206
    migrations, 136, 137 (fig.), 139, 139 (fig.), 142,
        144–145, 204–205, 212–213
    Mojave, 212–214, 216–219, 227
    Sonoran, 233–239
    See also specific types
Fort Irwin, 141, 257, 262
Fort Mojave, 22
Fort Yuma earthquake, 86
fossil biota, 51, 80, 131–133, 134–135, 154–155, 198
Fouquieria, 127 (fig.), 130
    splendens, 71, 115, 170, 233
Fouquieriaceae, 170
four-wing saltbush, 224, 278
foxes
    Desert Kit Fox, 119, 119 (plate), 182
    Gray Fox, 118
fragmentation, 152, 257–259, 260 (maps), 261,
        297, 301–302
Fraxinus, 137
    anomala, 213
    velutina, 237
freezing sensitivity, 71, 75, 170, 188, 239, 242
Frémont, John C., 23, 24 (plate), 27–28
    1844 California expedition, 23–29, 28 (map),
        60, 68, 70, 261
Frémont cottonwood, 26, 201, 227, 232, 265
    photos, 26 (plate), 238 (plate)
Frémont's indigobush, 27, 27 (plates)
Frémont's milkvetch, 167
Freund, Leslie, 11
fringe-toed lizards
    Coachella Valley Fringe-toed Lizard,
        286 (plate)
    Colorado Fringe-toed Lizard, 248 (plate), 249
frogs, 46–47
    Bullfrog, 268
    California Treefrog, 230
frosts, 74, 75, 239, 240–241

Funeral Mountains, 30
fungi, 91, 114, 119, 122, 234
    aquatic, 229
    cryptogamic crusts, 91, 92 (plate), 120, 203,
        283, 297, 299
    salt-tolerant, 226
    soil fungi, 88, 114, 119, 151, 226, 268, 278,
        297, 299–300
Funston, Frederick, 47, 52–53
Furnace Creek, 52, 54, 263, 268

Galium, 141
    parishii, 213
Gambelia, 151
Garcés, Francisco, 19–22, 19 (plate), 146, 231,
        302
    1776 desert crossing, 20–22, 146, 254, 293
Garlock Fault, vi (map), 80, 84 (plate)
generalist herbivores, 111–112
genetic divergence, 149–150, 155 (fig.), 172–173,
        176, 181, 214–215, 298
genetic pollution, 298
Geococcyx californianus, 162, 189–190, 189
        (plate)
geography, vi (map), 67, 68–71, 69 (table)
    climate and, 73–76
geology, 67, 69 (table), 79–88
    bedrocks, 79–80, 82 (map), 83 (map), 120
    canyons and bajadas, 83, 85, 88
    Salton Trough mud volcanoes, 86–87
    topographic processes, 80–81, 83, 85, 130–131
    ventifacts, 77 (plate), 78
    See also specific landform types
geothermal springs and geysers, 96
Geraea canescens, 167 (plate), 168
Gerrhonotus panamintensis, 286
Giant Ground Sloth, 134 (fig.), 140, 218
Giant Kangaroo Rat, 192
Giant Palm Borer, 150 (plate), 239, 239 (plate)
Gila elegans, 50
Gilia, 172
gilias, 172
Gilman's cymopterus, 287
Girvanella, 131
glacial activity, 133, 134, 136, 137, 138, 145
    Mono Lake and, 42–43, 43 (plate)
global warming, 279–280
glycophytes, 90

gnatcatchers, 287
  Black-tailed Gnatcatcher, 190, 234, 265
gold discovery, gold seekers, 29, 30, 281
Golden Eagle, 51
Golden-crowned Kinglet, 200
goosefoot, 263
goosefoot family, 207
Gopherus agassizii, 90, 111, 171, 257
Gorman Hills, 25
Government Road, 33–34, 33 (plate)
Government Springs, 33
granitic rocks, 24–25, 79, 80, 81 (plate), 83, 120,
  130, 215
granivory, 111, 112–113, 222
  nonnative plant species, 265, 268
  rodent communities, 210–211
  seeds in Indian diets, 5, 21, 37, 141, 144, 146,
    236–237, 238–239
  See also pinyon nuts; *specific animals*
grape soda lupine, 124
Grapevine Mountains, 33, 85 (plate)
grasses, 120, 130, 263, 264, 269–270
  as food source, 111, 112, 114, 134 (fig.), 141
  in Joshua tree woodland, 217, 223
  migrations, 142, 144
  native, grazing and, 283, 285
  nonnative species, 261, 263, 264, 264 (plates),
    266–267, 266 (plates), 268
  Pleistocene, 137, 140
  in riparian communities, 201
  in scrub communities, 224–225, 240
  wetlands grasses, 197
  See also grazing; *individual genera and species*
grasshoppers, 47, 118
  Creosote Bush Grasshopper, 113, 113 (plate),
    195
grassland communities, 196–197, 196 (table),
  232
  alkali meadow, 225, 226, 226 (plate), 237
  steppes, 197, 198, 206, 283
Gray, Andrew, 247
Gray Fox, 118
Grayia spinosa, 124, 175, 207
grazers, 111–112
grazing, 268, 281–285, 284 (plate)
greasewood, 224, 225 (plate)
Great American Desert, 29, 39
Great Basin communities, 70 (plate), 198–212

bristlecone pine forest, 198–200
  grasslands, 197, 198, 283
  leaf area index, 105
  pinyon-juniper woodland, 202–206, 243
  riparian forest, 198, 200–202
  scrub communities, 206–212, 264, 283
Great Basin Desert, 67–68, 68 (map)
  ancient flora and fauna, 136, 142, 143
  climate, 73 (fig.), 74, 75 (maps), 76
  nonnative species in, 263–264
  physical environment, 68, 69 (table),
    70 (plate)
  productivity, 109, 109 (fig.)
  water use/depletion, 271–272
  See also Great Basin communities
Greater Roadrunner, 162, 189–190, 189 (plate)
Greater Sage-Grouse, 208, 208 (plate)
Grebe, Eared, 272
green algae, 171, 226
greenfire, 297
Greenwater Valley, 261
ground sloths, 133, 134, 140
  Giant Ground Sloth, 134 (fig.), 140, 218
ground squirrels
  Antelope Ground Squirrel, 184, 259
  Round-tailed Ground Squirrel, 176, 176 (map),
    176 (plate), 205
  See also Mojave Ground Squirrel
groundwater, 92, 93, 96, 159, 224
  agricultural irrigation, 38, 39, 257, 271, 275
  Death Valley Aquifer, 96, 158, 161–162
  human demand and depletion, 271–272,
    274–276, 290
  See also water uptake/transport
guard cell. *See* stomata
Gutierrezia sarothrae, 112
Gymnorhinus cyanocephalus, 162–163, 205,
  205 (plate)
gypsum, 85
Gypsum Cave, 134

habitat corridors, 301–302
habitat degradation
  fragmentation, 258–259, 260 (maps), 261,
    301–302
  nonnative species impacts, 264, 265, 267–271
  See also human impacts
Halictidae, 240

Halimolobos diffusa var. *jaegeri*, 213

halophytes, 90
> *See also* salt-tolerant biota

halophytic saltbush scrub, 224–225, 225 (plate), 262

Hancock's Redoubt, 33–34

Hannahs, Charlotte, 58

Hansen, Charles, 270–271

Happlopappus, 270

hares, 21, 23, 25
> *See also* jackrabbits

harvester ants, 113, 114 (plate), 116, 117, 128
> Desert Harvester Ant, 222

Heap, Gwynne, 32–33, 51

heat coping mechanisms, 157, 159–160, 162 (fig.), 163, 172, 174 (fig.), 179–180, 182–185, 207, 241

Hecastocleis shockleyi, 210–211

hedgehog cactus, 217, 244

hedgehog grass, 264

Heintzelman, Maj., 86–87

Helianthus niveus subsp. *tephrodes*, 249

Hemileuca
> *hera*, 208, 208 (plate)
> *nuttalli*, 208

Hera Moth, 208, 208 (plate)

herbivory. *See* plant consumption

herbs, 166–169, 198, 201, 225
> *See also* annuals; forbs

Hermann's buckwheat, 216

herons, 230

Hesperostipa comata, 283

Heteromyidae, 210
> *See also individual genera and species*

Heuchera rubescens var. *pachypoda*, 213

hibernation, 176

Holocene climate, 129, 139, 141–145, 205, 213, 216, 219–220, 220 (fig.)

Holocene ecosystems, 19, 130 (fig.), 133–134, 139–146

Homo sapiens. *See* explorations; human impacts; human presence; Indians

Homoptera, 111

honey mesquite, 22, 109, 155–156, 155 (fig.), 229, 233–237, 235 (plate)

Hoover Dam, 71

Hopi people, 302

hop-sage, spiny, 124, 175, 207

Horn, Dr., 45

horned lizards
> Desert Horned Lizard, 116, 116 (plate), 182, 182 (plate)
> Flat-tailed Horned Lizard, 248 (plate)

horses, 80, 133, 134, 140, 151, 233
> nonnative feral horses, 268, 269 (plate), 281, 284, 285, 291

House Mouse, 268

House Sparrow, English, 268

human impacts, 63, 253–290
> agricultural/industrial development, 38–39, 54, 247, 257, 258 (plate), 261, 263, 275
> air pollution, 109, 276–279, 293
> climate change, 279–280
> grazing, 268, 281–285
> military installations, 256–257, 257 (plate)
> noise, 280–281
> overviews, 253–254, 290
> roads, 33–34, 36, 257–263, 260 (maps), 276, 289, 296
> threatened species and conservation priorities, 285–290
> vehicle use, 247, 256, 259, 261, 262, 277, 278, 279, 280–281, 289
> water use and depletion, 271–276, 281
> *See also* human presence; Indians; land management; nonnative species

human presence, 19–63, 146, 196
> arrival of humans in North America, 134, 138–139
> desert appreciation and conservation ethics, 55–63, 276–277, 280
> early American travelers and settlers, 22–23, 29–31, 35–39, 50–51, 261, 263
> popular accounts of desert travels, 45–46, 54–55
> tourism, 39, 58–59
> urbanization and population growth, 254–256, 256 (fig.), 274, 275, 278
> *See also* explorations; human impacts; Indians

Humboldt River, 137

humidity, 72

hummingbirds, 200, 240
> Anna's Hummingbird, 241 (plate)
> Calliope Hummingbird, 202
> Costa's Hummingbird, 49, 49 (plate), 52, 173–174, 173 (plate)

Hunt, Charles, 226
Hunt, Jefferson, 29
hunting, 258
    See also Indian diets
hybridization, 144 (fig.), 176, 176 (fig.), 202 (fig.)
Hyla cadaverina, 230
Hymenoclea salsola, 125, 175, 227, 297
Hyptis emoryi, 240

Ibex Hills, 28
Icaricia
    acmon dedeckera, 9 (plate), 214–215, 287
ice ages, 133
    Little Ice Age, 145, 146
iceplants, 104
Icterus parisorum, 218
Iguana, 132
iguanas, 132
    Desert Iguana, 150 (plate)
ily, 237
    See also honey mesquite; mesquite
Imperial Valley, 38 (plate), 39, 86, 87, 248, 257
Independence, 37, 45
Indian diets, 19–20, 21, 139
    acorns, 21, 22, 146, 236
    agriculture, 146, 255
    animals and fish, 3, 7, 21, 23, 50, 139,
        140–141, 145, 231
    bugseed, 5
    fan palm seeds, 237, 238–239
    Indian ricegrass, 3–6, 4 (plate), 6 (plate), 146
    mesquite, 235–237
    mobility and foraging, 19, 144, 145–146,
        165–166, 231
    pinyon nuts, 37, 146, 205–206, 206 (plates)
    plants and seeds in, 37, 141, 144, 145–146,
        196, 231
    sand food, 247
    seed grinding technologies, 140 (plate), 144,
        206
    shifts in, 140–141, 143–144, 196, 255
    tending plants, 3
    wetlands habitats, 146, 231
    worms, 37
Indian ricegrass *(aiwa),* 3, 5 (plate), 10 (plate),
        14, 114, 222
    air pollution impacts, 278

as Indian food source, 3–6, 4 (plate),
        6 (plate), 146
Indian Wells, Valley, 36
Indians, 303 (plate)
    American contacts with, 22, 23, 29, 33–36, 35
        (plate), 36–39
    archaeological study of, 45
    arrival in North America, 134, 138
    basket found in DeDeckera Canyon, 9–10,
        11–14, 11 (plate)
    Bighorn petroglyphs, 145, 145 (plate)
    clay effigy finds, 12–13
    desert in myth and song, 40, 42, 43
    desert knowledge, 14, 17, 290
    European contact impacts, 255
    European contacts with, 19–22, 231
    migration. *See* mobility
    population estimates, 254–255, 254 (fig.)
    projectile points, 139, 144, 144 (fig.), 145
    rabbit hunt, 22
    trade networks, 20, 21, 146
    tribal and linguistic territories, 18 (map)
    use of fire, 239
    water needs/availability, 165–166, 231
    See also Indian diets
indigobush, Frémont's, 27, 27 (plates)
Indio, 76, 84 (plate), 239
Indio hills, 80
infrared gas analysis, 106–107
insects, 47, 151, 287
    creosote bush associates, 179
    fan palm pests, 239
    insect herbivory, 111, 113
    as prey, 116, 117, 118
    sand food pollinators, 246–247
    See also specific communities and insects
Inyo California Towhee, 286 (plate)
Inyo County geology, 83 (map)
Inyo County star tulip, 273
Inyo Mountains, 80 (plate), 131, 200
Inyo Slender Salamander, 231 (plate), 287
iodine bush, 141, 224, 229
iris, wild, 225
Iris missouriensis, 225
iron, 120
irrigation
    revegetation projects, 298, 300

See also agriculture

isolation, 151–152, 214, 247, 259, 271

Isomeris arborea, 240

Jackrabbit Spring, 275, 275 (plates)

jackrabbits, 133, 141, 184, 195 (plate)
    Black-tailed Jackrabbit, 111–112, 113 (plate),
        145
    herbivory, 170, 195, 208, 247, 297, 300

Jaeger, Edmund, ix, 59–61, 59 (plate)

Jaeger's mustard, 213

jaguars, 133

James, George Wharton, 38–39

Jayhawkers, 30

Jefferson's Mammoth, 140

Jeffrey pine, 136, 200, 201 (plate)

jewelflower, 214

Joaquin Jim, 37

Joe Walker Trail, 36

jojoba, 113, 115 (plate), 240

Jones, Fred, 269–270

Joshua tree, 68, 102, 204
    animal interactions, 134 (fig.), 217–219,
        218 (plate)
    Jaeger's Magic Circle, 59, 60–61
    migrations, 140, 142
    photos, 61 (plate), 71 (plate), 142 (plate),
        143 (plate), 218 (plate)
    See also Joshua tree woodland

Joshua Tree National Park, 81 (plate), 293

Joshua tree woodland, 68, 70, 206–207, 216–219,
       217 (plate), 218 (plate), 223, 243–244
    fire impacts, 268

Juglans pseudomorpha, 133

July gold, 5, 7–9, 9 (plate), 10–11, 187, 210,
    214–215

jumping cholla. *See* teddy-bear cholla

Juncus, 201
    balticus, 225

juniper berries, 204 (plate), 205

juniper woodland, 139–140, 144
    See also pinyon-juniper woodland

junipers, 137, 145, 220 (fig.)
    California juniper, 204
    in sagebrush ecotones, 206
    seed cones, 204 (plate), 205, 216 (plate)
    western juniper, 203–204

See also Utah juniper

Juniperus
    californica, 204
    occidentalis, 203–204
    osteosperma, 136, 202

Justicia, 173
    californica, 233

kangaroo mice, 210
    Pale Kangaroo Mouse, 113, 150 (plate),
       191 (fig.), 286

kangaroo rats, 111, 112–113, 126, 133, 190–191,
      211
    Agile Kangaroo Rat, 205
    Argus Kangaroo Rat, 287
    Chisel-tooth Kangaroo Rat, 113, 191 (fig.)
    Giant Kangaroo Rat, 192
    in human diet, 141
    landscape influence, 127, 128
    Merriam Kangaroo Rat, 210
    Panamint Kangaroo Rat, 216, 216 (plate)
    See also Desert Kangaroo Rat

Kelso Depot, 39

Kelso Wash, 22

kidney function, 160–161, 191 (fig.)

King Clone, 220–221, 220 (plate)

Kinglet, Golden-crowned, 200

Kingston Mountains, 212–213, 216

Kitanemuk people, 255

Kochia californica, 224

Krascheninnikovia lanata, 208

Kroeber, Alfred, 40

La Brea Tar Pits, 133, 134

Lahontan Cutthroat Trout, 202, 202 (plate)

Lake Cahuilla, 41–42, 41 (plates), 42 (plate),
    86–87, 235–236, 248, 254

Lake Cronise, 137

Lake Hill, 139

Lake Lahontan, 137

Lake Manix, 51, 133, 134, 137

Lake Manley, 94, 95, 137, 160

Lake Mojave, 45, 137

Lake Mojave culture, 139

Lake Owens, 137

Lake Panamint, 137, 139

Lake Rogers, 133 (plate)

Lake Russell, 42, 44 (map), 93, 95, 137, 272
Lake Silver, 137
Lake Soda, 137
Lake Tahoe, 202
Lake Tecopa, 28
lakes, 40–45, 93–95, 137–138, 138 (map)
    See also Pleistocene lakes; *specific lakes*
land management
    grazing regulation, 283–285
    OHV access, 261, 262
    resource-centered management, 291–296
    restoration approaches, 296–302
Lane Mountain milkvetch, 257
Lanfair Valley, 22
Larrea, 34, 34 (plate), 71 (plate), 151, 269
    divaricata, 181
    tridentata, 102, 178–181, 179 (plate), 204, 267
Larus californicus, 272
Last Chance Mountains, 209 (plate)
Las Vegas, 23, 29, 134, 137, 274, 277 (plate),
    278
Latta, Frank, 31, 35–36
laurel, 133
leaf area index, 104–105
leaf-cutter bees, 240
leaves
    creosote bush, 179–180
    desert holly, 183, 184 (plate), 185 (fig.)
    heat coping mechanisms, 183–184, 185
    leaf area index, 104–105
    ocotillo, 170
    palms, 154
    turgor, 180–181
Lee Vining Canyon, 201 (plate)
leopard lizards, 151
Leptoconops, 246, 247 (plate)
Leptodactylon pungens, 199
Leptotyphlops humilis, 117, 117 (plate)
Lepus, 170, 195, 208, 297
    californicus, 111–112, 113 (plate)
Leymus cenereus, 283
life zone classification system, 53 (fig.), 53 (plate),
    54
Liliaceae, 216
lily family, 216
limber pine, 136, 139, 198
limestone aster, 199
limestone monkeyflower, 7, 8 (plate), 211, 287

limestone penstemon, 211
limestones, 79, 80, 80 (plate), 120, 209, 227
    fossil biota, 131–132, 131 (plate)
Linanthus parryi, 222 (plate)
Little Ice Age, 145, 146
Little Lake, 81, 217
little-leaf mahogany, 199
livestock grazing, 268, 281–285, 284 (plate)
lizards, 46, 116, 150, 246
    Panamint Alligator Lizard, 286, 287
    Side-blotched Lizard, 116
    Zebra-tailed Lizard, 116–117, 117 (plate)
    See also fringe-toed lizards; horned lizards;
        iguanas; night lizards
llamas, 134, 233
lodgepole pine, 200
lomatium, 215
Lomatium, 215
longevity, 179, 199, 221, 240, 242
longhorn beetles, 208
Los Angeles Aqueduct, 259, 272, 273
Lower Colorado River Multispecies Conservation
    Plan, 302
Lucerne Valley, 70, 221
Lucy's Warbler, 190
Lummis, Charles, 54–55, 55 (plate), 165
lupines, 112, 120, 172, 269–270, 297
    grape soda lupine, 124
    patch-mosaic example, 127–128, 128 (plates),
        129 (plate)
    silver lupine, 199–200
Lupinus, 112, 172, 297
    argenteus var. *tenellus,* 199–200
    excubitus, 124
Lycium, 173, 223
    andersonii, 124

Macedonia Canyon, 20 (plate), 21
MacGillivray's Warbler, 202
Macrotus californicus, 296
Magic Circle census, 59, 60–61
magnesium, 120, 121
maize, 146
Malacothrix californica, 282
mammals
    Death Valley Expedition collections, 49, 216
    diversity, 152 (table), 197 (fig.)
    fossils, 132–133

habitat fragmentation, 258–259
in Mojave transition zones, 223
nonnative species, 268
Pleistocene fauna, 134–135, 134 (fig.), 136, 139 (fig.), 140, 254
See also individual genera and species
Mammillaria, 244
mammoths, 133, 237
Jefferson's Mammoth, 140
Mammut americanum, 140
Mammuthus jeffersoni, 140
manganese, 120
Manley, William, 29–30, 30 (plate), 36, 50–51, 76
maps
air pressure and precipitation patterns, 75
California deserts, vi, 68
Death Valley Expedition route, 48
fragmentation, 260
geology, 82, 83
ground squirrel species distribution, 176
Indian territories, 18
Lake Russell (Mono Lake) and Sierra glaciers, 44
map used by Frémont expedition, 28
Mojave River system, 32
Pleistocene lakes and rivers, 138
solar radiation, 75
swallowtail butterfly subspecies, 215
trail and road development, 260
Marble Mountains, 233 (plate)
marigolds, 172
desert marigold, 299
marine fossils, 131, 133
Marl Springs, 33
marshes, 197, 233, 290
See also wetlands
Masticophis flagellum, 182–183, 183 (plate)
Mastodon, 80, 140, 151
Mecca aster, 296
Mecca Hills, 80, 85 (plate)
Mediterranean grass, 266–267, 282, 289
Megachilidae, 240
Megacyliene antennata, 234, 234 (plate)
Megathymus yuccae navajo, 217–218
Meloidae, 208
melons, 146
Menodora spinescens, 297

Merriam, C. Hart, 47 (plate), 216
life zone classification system, 53 (fig.), 53 (plate), 54
Merriam Kangaroo Rat, 210
Mesozoic Era, 129, 130 (fig.)
dinosaurs, 132
mesquite, 28, 33, 57, 58, 120, 146, 237, 302
animal associates, 112, 113, 140, 233–235
honey mesquite, 109, 155–156, 155 (fig.), 229, 233–237, 235 (plate)
Indian use of, 146, 235–237
screw bean mesquite, 229
threats to, 265, 272
Mesquite Beetle, 234–235
Mesquite Borer, 234, 234 (plate)
Messor, 113
metabolic water, 190–191
metalmark butterflies, 113
metamorphic rocks, 79
metapopulations, 296–297
methyl-jasmonate, 209
Mexican Amberwing, 5, 156 (plate), 157
mice, 141, 210, 211
Cactus Mouse, 191, 192
House Mouse, 268
Pinyon Mouse, 174
See also kangaroo mice; pocket mice
Micrarionta, 153
Microdipodops, 210
pallidus, 113, 150 (plate), 286
Microtus californicus scirpensis, 286 (plate)
midden analysis (woodrats), 135–136, 142, 143, 144, 202, 220 (fig.)
military installations, 256–257, 257 (plate)
milkvetches, 52, 120, 297
Borrego milkvetch, 286–287
Cushenberry milkvetch, 286 (plate)
Frémont's milkvetch, 167
Lane Mountain milkvetch, 257
mountain milkvetch, 199
Peirson's milkvetch, 249, 288–289
millipedes, 117
Miloderes, 249
Mimulus rupicola, 7, 211, 287
minerals, 120, 128
buildup in animals, 172, 190
See also nutrient cycling; *specific minerals*
Mirabilis bigelovii, 113 (plate)

mirages, 78

Moapa Riffle Beetle, 229

mobility
    endemism and, 214
    Indian mobility and foraging, 19, 144,
        145–146, 165–166, 231

moha, 70
    See also Desert Bighorn

Mohave Generating Station, 278, 279 (plate)

Mojave Chub, 276

Mojave communities, 71 (plate), 179, 212–231
    annuals in, 212, 221, 222–223, 222 (plates),
        224, 268
    creosote bush scrub, 219–223, 221 (plate),
        243–244
    endemism in, 212, 214–215, 216
    Joshua tree woodland, 216–219, 223,
        243–244
    leaf area index, 105
    riparian communities, 26–27, 26 (plate),
        228, 265, 272
    saltbush scrub and alkali meadow, 223–226,
        228
    wetlands, 228–231
    white fir forest, 212–214, 216

Mojave Desert, 67–68, 68 (map), 70–71, 165
    air quality, 278
    ancient flora and fauna, 136, 137 (fig.), 142,
        143
    climate, 73 (fig.), 74, 75 (maps)
    Garcés expedition, 19–22, 146, 231, 254, 294
    military installations, 256, 257
    nonnative species in, 268, 269, 282, 283,
        289
    physical environment, 68–69, 69 (table)
    productivity, 109, 109 (fig.)
    water use/depletion, 271–272
    See also Mojave communities

Mojave Ground Squirrel, 174–176, 174 (fig.), 175
    (plate), 176 (map), 184, 221, 296

Mojave National Preserve, 293

Mojave Patchnose Snake, 118

Mojave people, 17 (plate), 22, 35 (plate), 40, 50, 146
    'Ahakhav Tribal Preserve restoration project,
        300–302
    early European and American contacts,
        20–21, 34–35
    impacts of contact, 39, 255

Mojave River, 26 (plates), 32, 32 (map), 34 (plate),
        93, 137, 146, 165, 176, 216
    agriculture along, 38
    alternate names, 21, 22, 32, 146
    early expeditions along, 21–23, 24, 26–27,
        31–35, 51–52, 261
    fish species, 51–52, 52 (plate)
    groundwater overdraft impacts, 272
    narrows, 25, 26 (plate), 34, 51
    riparian communities, 265, 272
    salt cedar removal, 295

Mojave Road, 258
    See also Old Spanish Trail

Mojave thistle, 225

Mojave Tui Chub, 51–52, 52 (plate), 133

Mojave yucca, 34, 34 (plate), 222

mollusks, 47, 49, 198, 287
    Lake Cahuilla, 41, 41 (plate)

Monarch, 214

monkeyflower, limestone, 7, 8 (plate), 211

Mono Brine Shrimp, 272, 273 (fig.)

Mono Lake, 42–45, 43 (plate), 93, 137,
        203 (plate), 207 (plate)
    food web, 272, 272 (plate), 273 (fig.),
        273 (plate)
    water diversion impacts, 272

Mono Lake Alkali Fly, 272, 272 (plate), 273 (fig.)

Monoptilon belliforme, 222 (plate)

montane riparian forest, 200–201
    See also riparian communities

Mormon tea, 112, 140

mosses, 177–178

moths, 214
    Hera Moth, 208, 208 (plate)
    Nuttall's Sheep Moth, 208
    Yucca Moth, 218–219

Mount San Jacinto, 62 (plates)

mountain alder, 200

mountain building, 79, 80, 129, 130–131

mountain leapfrogging, 200, 213, 216

Mountain Lion, 118–119, 163, 164, 231

mountain milkvetch, 199

mud volcanoes, 86–87

Muddy Mountains swallowtails, 215

Muhlenbergia richardsonis, 199

Mule Deer, 143, 205, 208, 235, 283

Mule Springs limestone, 131

Mus musculus, 268

mustard family, 264
mustards, 214
    Jaeger's mustard, 213
    Sahara mustard, 267, 267 (plates), 268
    tansy mustard, 214
Mycoplasma agassazii, 289
mycorrhizae, 114, 226, 234, 268, 297
    inoculation with, 298–299
Mylodon, 140

naked-stemmed daisy, 210
Nama demissum, 222 (plate)
napkinring buckwheat, 211
nasal salt glands, 172, 190
National Park Service (NPS), 293, 294, 295
    Desert Tortoise recovery efforts, 295–296
Native Americans. *See* Indians
Nature Conservancy, 275
naucorid beetles, 229
    Ash Meadows Naucorid, 228 (plate)
Navaho Giant Yucca Skipper, 217–218,
        219 (plate)
Navaho people, 302
Needles, 20, 39, 60, 70, 295 (plate)
needlethread, 283
nematodes, 114, 119, 188–189, 208
neoendemics, 286–287
    See also endemism
Neotoma, 218
    lepida, 14, 135–136, 135 (plates)
Nevada ephedra, 124, 207, 208, 217
Nevadan Hills, 130
New River, 87
New York Mountains, 70, 136, 212–213,
        213 (plate), 216, 227 (plate)
night lizards, 268
    Desert Night Lizard, 218, 219 (plate)
nightshade, 24
nitrates, 120, 121
nitrifying bacteria, 121
nitrogen, 108–109, 279, 283
nitrogen fixation, nitrogen-fixing bacteria, 109,
        114, 120, 124, 226, 236, 297
nitrogen oxides, 277, 279
Nitrophila occidentalis, 225
nocturnal animals, 191–192
noise, 280–281, 280 (fig.)
Nomia melanderi, 225

nonnative species, 34, 172, 254, 261, 263–271,
        290
    annuals, 265–267
    community impacts, 263–264, 265, 267–271,
            281–284, 289, 290
    early arrivals, 52, 54, 261, 263
    factors facilitating spread of, 258, 261, 263,
            264, 264–266, 279
    grasses, 261, 263, 264, 264 (plates),
            266–267, 266 (plates), 268
    introduced livestock, 281–285
    removal/control of, 294–295, 299, 303
    See also Burro; salt cedar; *other genera and
        species*
Nopah Range, 299 (plates)
Nothrotheriops, 140
    shastensis, 134 (fig.), 218
NPS. *See* National Park Service
Nucifraga columbiana, 205, 205 (plate)
nurse plants, 242–243, 242 (plate)
nuthatches
    Pygmy Nuthatch, 200, 200 (plate)
    Red-breasted Nuthatch, 200
nutrient cycling, 119–122
    patch-mosaic model and, 128
    pulse-reserve model, 126–127, 126 (fig.), 127
nutrient levels/availability, 90, 91, 120–121, 128
    species richness and, 212
nutrient uptake, 119–122
Nuttall's Sheep Moth, 208

oak woodland, 139–140
oaks, 204
    canyon oak, 213, 216, 227
    Sonoran scrub oak, 213, 227 (plate)
ocotillo, 71, 130, 169–171, 173
    as food source, 115, 241 (plate)
    photos, 50 (plate), 169 (plate), 170 (plate)
    in Sonoran Desert, 233, 240, 243, 244
Odocoileus, 141
    hemionus, 143, 205, 283
off-road vehicle use. *See* OHVs
Ogden, Peter Skein, 23
OHVs, 247, 259, 261, 261 (plate), 262,
        277 (plate), 278, 280, 289
Olancha, 68
old man cactus, 202
old man grass, 5, 14

Old Spanish Trail, 22, 29, 146, 258, 260 (maps)
early immigrant parties, 29–31, 35–36
Old Woman Mountains swallowtails, 215
Olive-sided Flycatcher, 200
Olmsted, Frederick Law, 59
Olneya tesota, 132, 233
Oncorhynchus
clarki henshawi, 202, 202 (plate)
mykiss, 161
Oporornis tolmiei, 202
Opuntia, 112
acanthocarpa, 244
basilaris, 34, 34 (plate), 105 (plate), 221
bigelovii, 221
echinocarpa, 34, 34 (plate), 185–186,
187 (plate), 217
erinacea, 202
ramosissima, 244
orioles, 268
Scott's Oriole, 218, 219 (plate)
orogeny. *See* mountain building
ostracods, 229
Ostrich, 190
Ovis canadensis nelsoni, 111, 163, 205, 258
Owens Chub, 273
Owens Lake, 37, 274, 277–278, 298
Owens Pupfish, 95 (plate), 273–274, 274 (plate)
Owens River, 21, 93, 273, 274 (plate)
Owens Valley, 23, 45
agriculture and grazing, 36, 166, 257, 281
alkali meadow, 225, 226 (plate)
Great Basin–Mojave transition, 68, 70
riparian woodland, 201
settlement and conflict in, 36–37
Owens Valley checkerbloom, 226 (plates), 273
Owens Valley Paiute, 36–37, 146, 205–206
Oxystylis, 27–28
ozone, 277, 278, 293

Packrat (Desert Woodrat), 14, 135–136, 135 (plates),
202
paintbrush, Clokey, 200
Paiute people, 14
See also Owens Valley Paiute; Southern
Paiute
Palafoxia arida subsp. *gigantea*, 249
Pale Kangaroo Mouse, 113, 150 (plate), 191 (fig.),
286

paleoendemics, 150 (plate), 286
See also endemism; relict species
Palm Borer, Giant, 150 (plate), 239, 239 (plate)
Palm Desert, 253 (plate)
Palm Springs, 96
Palm Springs Pocket Mouse, 287
Palmdale, 36, 38, 217, 289
Palmer, T. S., 13, 47 (plate)
Palmer's beardtongue, 299
Palmoxylodon mohavensis, 132
palms. *See* fan palm woodland; fan palms
palo verde, 71, 130, 233, 243
blue palo verde, 115, 233, 233 (plate), 265
foothill palo verde, 244
in Sonoran creosote bush scrub, 240, 241
Palo Verde Valley, 257
Panamint Alligator Lizard, 286, 287
Panamint Chipmunk, 216, 216 (plate)
Panamint Kangaroo Rat, 216, 216 (plate)
Panamint Mountains, 75–76, 124, 200, 215, 216
nonnative species in, 263, 269
Panamint Valley, 36, 53 (plate), 138, 139
panic grass, 249
Panicum urvilleanum, 249
Papilio
indra, 214–215 (plates), 215, 215 (map)
indra martini, 287
parasitic plants
desert mistletoe, 114 (plate), 234, 234 (plate)
sand food, 246–247, 246 (plate)
Parish's bedstraw, 213
Parker, 40
Parry, C. C., 236
Passer domesticus, 268
Patch, Dennis, 300
patch-mosaic ecosystem model, 127–128, 127
(fig.), 128 (plates), 129 (plate), 243
Patencio, Francisco, 237–238
Patton, George S., 256
pavement, 91, 92, 92 (plate), 264, 283
Pa-vi-o-osi people, 43
pea family, 27, 120
Pectis papposa, 168 (plate), 169
Peewee. *See* Western Wood-Peewee
Peirson's milkvetch, 249, 288–289
Pelocoris biimpressus, 229
Peltohyas australis, 190
pencil cactus, 244

Peninsular Ranges, 136
Penstemon, 173
   calcareus, 211
   palmeri, 299
penstemons
   limestone penstemon, 211
   Palmer's beardtongue, 299
PEP carboxylase, 102, 104
Pepsis, 126, 234
perennials, 225, 285
   in succession process, 123, 125, 127–128,
      127 (fig.)
   See also phreatophytes; shrubs; *individual*
      genera and species
Perithemis intensa, 156 (plate), 157
Perkins, Edna Brush, 57 (plate), 58
Permian-Triassic extinction, 131–132
Perognathus, 210
   longimembris bangsi, 287
Peromyscus, 141
   eremicus, 191, 192
   truei, 174
Persea coalingensis, 133
Petrophyton caespitosum, 213
pets, tortoises as, 289
Phainopepla, 234, 234 (plate)
Phainopepla nitens, 234, 234 (plate)
phalaropes, 272
   Red-necked Phalarope, 272
   Wilson's Phalarope, 272
Phalaropus
   lobatus, 272
   tricolor, 272
Philadelphia Company, 34–35, 34 (plates),
   35 (plates)
Phillips, Fred, 301–302
phlox, 141
   cold desert phlox, 203
   spiny phlox, 199
Phlox, 141, 269
   stansburyi, 203
Pholisma sonorae, 246–247, 246 (plate), 296
Phoradendron californicum, 114 (plate), 234,
   234 (plate)
Phormidium tenue, 226
phosphorus, 212
photorespiration, 101–102, 104
photosynthesis, 100–109

annuals, 166, 168
cacti, 153, 181, 185–188
measuring, 104, 106–107
nitrogen availability and, 108–109
ocotillo, 170
ozone pollution and, 278
phreatophytic trees, 154, 155, 233
types, 101–104, 103 (table)
water availability and, 105, 108
Phragmites, 137
   australis, 229
   communis, 22
phreatophytes, 154–156, 155 (fig.), 229, 233
   See also individual genera and species
Phrynosoma
   mcallii, 248 (plate)
   platyrhinos, 116, 116 (plate), 182, 182 (plate)
Physa, 41
Pikeminnow, Colorado, 50, 50 (plate)
pincushion cactus, 244
pine nuts, 22, 37, 141, 146, 162–163, 205–206
pines, 137, 139, 142, 201, 278
   bristlecone pine, 136, 142, 198–199, 199
      (plate)
   Jeffrey pine, 136, 200, 201 (plate)
   limber pine, 136, 139, 198
   lodgepole pine, 200
   ponderosa pine, 200
   See also pinyon nuts; pinyon pines
pink currant, 201
Pintwater Cave, 134
Pinus
   contorta subsp. *murrayana,* 200
   edulis, 213
   flexilis, 136, 198
   jeffreyi, 136, 200
   longaeva, 136, 198–199, 199 (plate)
   monophylla, 25, 102, 151, 202
   ponderosa, 200
Pinyon Jay, 162–163, 205, 205 (plate)
Pinyon Mouse, 174
pinyon nuts, 22, 141, 162–163, 205
   Indian use of, 37, 146, 205–206, 206 (plates)
pinyon pines, 25, 70 (plate), 76, 102, 130, 151,
   202, 203 (plate), 227
   migrations, 145, 205
   in sagebrush ecotones, 206
   two-leaf pinyon, 213

pinyon pines (cont.)
  in woodrat middens, 136
  See also pinyon nuts; pinyon-juniper
      woodland
pinyon-juniper woodland, 166 (fig.)
  geographic variations, 203–205
  Great Basin, 202–206, 203 (plate), 243
  migrations, 136, 142, 145, 204–205, 219, 232,
      254
  Mojave, 212
  Mojave transition zones, 223
  nonnative species in, 264
Pipilo crissalis, 286 (plate)
plankton, 133
Planorbis, 41
plant communities. *See* communities; Great
      Basin communities; Mojave communities;
      Sonoran communities; threatened
      communities
plant consumption (herbivory), 110–115, 297
  butterfly larval food plants, 214–215
  livestock grazing, 268, 281–285
  of nonnative species, 172, 265, 268
  plants' chemical defenses, 208–209,
      209 (fig.)
  shrub responses to, 208–209
  See also granivory; Indian diets
plant distribution. *See* vegetation patterns
plant diversity, 52, 152 (table)
  See also species richness
plant interactions
  facilitation, 242–243
  See also competition; succession
plant migrations
  Altithermal climate change and, 141 145, 151,
      216, 219–220, 220 (fig.)
  conifer forest, 136, 137 (fig.), 139, 139 (fig.),
      142, 212–213
  pinyon-juniper woodland, 136, 142, 145,
      204–205, 219, 232
  Sonoran species, 232–233
  spread of creosote bush scrub, 219–221
Plantago insularis var. *fastigiata*, 222
plantains, 222
plant-animal interactions, 128, 195–196, 198
  See also plant consumption; *specific plants,
      animals, and community types*
Platanus racemosa, 237

playas, 85, 85 (plate), 88, 89, 90 (plate), 120,
      142, 149
  Alkali Fairy Shrimp, 171, 171 (plate), 262
  as lake remnants, 95–96
  OHV impacts, 262
  plant communities, 224–225, 262
  soils, 89, 223, 224, 262
Pleistocene ecosystems, 130 (fig.), 133–139
  climate, 134, 136–137
  fauna, 133, 134–135, 134 (fig.), 136, 139 (fig.),
      140
  human arrival, 134, 138–139
  plants, 134, 135–136, 137–138
Pleistocene extinctions, 139 (fig.), 140, 254
Pleistocene lakes, 42–43, 45, 93–95, 133,
      137–138, 138 (map)
  Holocene climate change and, 142–143, 144
  See also specific lakes
Pleuraphis rigida, 217, 276
Pluchea sericea, 79 (plate), 229
pocket mice, 210
  Bailey's Pocket Mouse, 113, 115 (plate)
  Desert Pocket Mouse, 191 (fig.), 235
  Palm Springs Pocket Mouse, 287
Podiceps nigricollis, 272
Pogonomyrmex. See harvester ants
Point of Rocks Spring, 229 (plate)
Poleta Formation, 131
Polioptila melanura, 190, 234, 265
pollen, 113, 195, 198, 200, 208, 225, 234, 242
pollen analysis, 134, 137, 139 (fig.), 142, 144
pollination, 200, 218–219, 225, 234, 241 (plate),
      242, 246–247
polygons, 88, 91 (plate), 142
Polypogon monspeliensis, 263
ponderosa pine, 200
poolfishes, 157, 228
population figures
  current population and growth, 255–257,
      256 (fig.)
  Indian populations, 254–255, 254 (fig.),
      255 (fig.)
Populus, 133
  balsamifera subsp. *trichocarpa*, 200
  fremontii, 26, 26 (plate), 265
  tremuloides, 200
potash, 85
potassium, 120, 121, 172, 190

potentilla, 216

Potentilla patellifera, 216

pottery, 146

Powdered Dancer, 156–157, 156 (plate)

power plants, 278, 279 (plate)

Prairie Falcon, 182

precipitation. *See* rainfall; snow

predators, 111, 115–119, 163–164

    humans as, 140–141

    See also specific animals

prickle-leaf, 210–211

primary productivity, 100–110, 226, 268

    climate change and, 279–280

    grazing and, 282, 283, 289

    measurements of, 104–105, 109–110,
        109 (fig.)

    water and nutrient limitations, 105, 108–109

    See also photosynthesis

primary succession, 122–125

proactive resource management, 293–296

productivity. *See* energy flow; primary
    productivity

Pronghorn, 141, 143, 151, 208, 258, 301–302

Prosopis

    glandulosa var. *torreyana*, 109, 155–156,
        155 (fig.), 229

    pubescens, 229

protected species, 286 (plates), 288, 289,
    295–296

    See also threatened and endangered species

proteins, 121–122

    in mesquite beans, 236

Providence Mountains, 21, 22, 40, 70, 136,
    212–213, 215, 269

Providence Spring, 36

Providence Swallowtail Butterfly, 287

Prunus fasciculata, 227

psammophytes, 248–249

Psorothamnus

    fremontii, 27, 27 (plates)

    spinosus, 120, 227, 265

Pterotermes occidentalis, 115

Ptychocheilus lucius, 50, 50 (plate)

puddle mirages, 78

pulse-reserve ecosystem model, 126–127,
    126 (fig.)

Puma concolor, 118–119, 163, 164, 231

Pumilia, 132

pupfishes, 13, 13 (plate), 137, 153, 157–162, 228,
    229, 287

    Amargosa Pupfish, 158, 268, 269 (plate)

    Amargosa River Pupfish, 158

    Ash Meadows Pupfish, 50–51, 51 (plate),
        158–159, 275

    Cottonball Marsh Pupfish, 159

    Devils Hole Pupfish, 157–158, 157 (plate),
        229, 274, 276

    Owens Pupfish, 95 (plate), 273–274,
        274 (plate)

    Salt Creek Pupfish, 160, 161 (plate), 162 (fig.)

    Saratoga Springs Pupfish, 158

    Shoshone Pupfish, 158

    Tecopa Pupfish, 158

    Warm Springs Pupfish, 158

Purshia tridentata, 202

Pygmy Nuthatch, 200, 200 (plate)

Pyramid Lake, 202

Pyrgulopsis, 274, 287

    amargosae, 286

    carinifera, 229

quaking aspen, 200, 201 (plate), 202 (plate)

Quaternary, 42–43, 129, 133

    See also Holocene *entries*; Pleistocene *entries*

Quercus, 204

    chrysolepis, 213, 216

    turbinella, 213

quiet, 280–281

rabbitbrushes, 112, 283, 297

    black-stemmed rabbitbrush, 227, 227 (plate)

    rubber rabbitbrush, 125, 202, 207, 208

    yellow rabbitbrush, 199, 208

rabbits, 21, 22, 23, 30, 118, 141

Racetrack, 90 (plate)

railroad surveys, 38, 40–42, 51–52, 235–236

railroads, 38, 281

rain roots, 186 (fig.)

rainfall, 45, 69 (table), 71–75, 73 (fig.), 75 (maps)

    future climate change and, 279

    landforms and, 81, 83–85

    Pleistocene, 134

    productivity and, 109 (fig.)

    rain shadow, 73–74, 76–77

    thunderstorms, 75, 78–79

rain shadow, 73–74, 76–77

Rana catesbeiana, 268

Rancho La Brea fauna, 133, 134–135

Rancho Santa Ana Botanical Garden, 10

rare and threatened species. *See* threatened and
    endangered species

rats. *See* kangaroo rats; woodrats

rattlesnakes, 46, 118, 280
    Sidewinder, 182, 183 (plate)

Raven, Common, 289

Raven, Peter, 209–210

Razorback Sucker, 50

Reagan, Ronald, 292

recharge playas, 96

red brome, 266, 266 (plates), 268, 279, 299

red heuchera, 213

red mites, 120 (plate)

Red-breasted Nuthatch, 200

rediscovery, 3, 12, 14, 17–19, 40–42, 50–54, 59,
    63, 125, 146, 151, 239, 274, 303–304

Red-naped Sapsucker, 201, 202 (plate)

Red-necked Phalarope, 272

redoubts, 33–34, 34 (plate)

Red-spotted Toad, 230, 231 (plate)

reed, common, 229

Reed Formation, 198, 199 (plate)

Regulus satrapa, 200

relict species, 8–11, 150 (plate), 151, 286
    Algodones Dunes, 249
    California fan palm, 154–155, 154 (plate)
    Mojave Tui Chub, 51–52, 52 (plate), 133
    ocotillo, 71, 169–171, 169 (plate), 170 (plate)
    See also endemism

reptiles, 46–47, 49, 223
    diversity, 152 (table), 197 (fig.)
    See also individual genera and species

"Requiem for Sonora" (Shelton), 64

reserves, 126–127, 126 (fig.)

reservoirs (of nutrients), 119

resource depletion, 254, 271–290
    water, 271–276

resource-centered management, 291–296

respiratory disease, 278

Resting Springs, 29

restoration, 299 (plates)
    'Ahakhav Tribal Preserve project, 300–302
    Jackrabbit Spring, 275, 275 (plates)
    natural healing processes, 290, 296–297, 301
    new approaches, 297–302

nonnative species removal, 294–295
    population dynamics and, 296–297, 298
    soil restoration, 297
    succession patterns and, 297

reverse osmosis, 160

Rhinichthys, 157, 228

Rhizobium, 120

rhizosheaths, 114, 120

rhyolite, 80

Ribes nevadense, 201

Richardson's mulygrass, 199

riparian communities, 93 (plate), 196 (table),
    197, 227 (plates), 232, 295 (plate)
    'Ahakhav Tribal Preserve restoration project,
        300–302
    Great Basin, 198, 200–202
    Mojave, 26–27, 26 (plate), 227, 264–265, 272
    nonnative species in, 264–265, 272, 294–295
    Sonoran, 237, 265
    threatened status, 287, 296

rivers and streams, 68, 92, 95, 96, 146
    Holocene climate change and, 142–143
    See also riparian communities; *specific rivers
        and streams*

rixford rockwort, 210

roadkill, 259, 301

roadrunners, 172
    Greater Roadrunner, 162, 189–190,
        189 (plate)

roads, 33–34, 36, 257–260, 260 (maps), 276,
    289, 296
    restoration of, 299 (plates)
    See also Old Spanish Trail; vehicle impacts

rock spiraea, 213

Rock Springs, 34, 35 (plates)

Rocky Mountain white fir, 213

rodents, 210–211, 216, 222, 223
    See also individual genera and species

Rodman, John, 303

Rogers, John, 36

root systems, 114, 155 (fig.), 155–156, 169, 180,
    185–186, 186 (fig.), 234, 243, 265 (fig.)
    competition for soil moisture, 105, 108,
        108 (fig.), 265 (fig.), 264, 265
    nutrient uptake, 121–122
    See also water uptake/transport

Rosa woodsii var. *ultramontana,* 201

Rosaceae, 207

rose, wild, 201

rose family, 207

Round-tailed Ground Squirrel, 176, 176 (map), 176 (plate), 205

rubber rabbitbrush, 125, 202, 207, 208

RUBP carboxylase, 101, 104, 108

runoff, 71, 88, 120, 137, 257, 276

rushes, 201, 225, 237
    Baltic rush, 225, 226 (plate)

Russell, Israel, 42–45

Russian thistle. *See* tumbleweed

rusty molly, 224

saber-tooth cats, 133, 134

Saccharum, 102

sage, desert, 227

sagebrush woodland, 139

sagebrushes, 22, 42, 102, 137, 270, 283
    black sagebrush, 207
    See also big sagebrush; big sagebrush scrub

Sage-Grouse, Greater, 208, 208 (plate)

saguaro, 132, 241, 242 (plate), 287–288
    associated plants, 127 (fig.), 243, 244
    frost sensitivity, 188, 241
    range and migrations, 188, 233

Sahara mustard, 267, 267 (plates), 268

salamanders, 274
    Inyo Slender Salamander, 231 (plate), 287

Saline Valley, 3, 6

salinity, 90

Salix, 93 (plate), 133, 200
    gooddingii, 237, 265
    lasiolepis, 201

Salsola tragus, 263, 263 (plates)

salt(s)
    Indian trade, 146
    in playa soils, 96, 224
    salt ponds and streams, 96, 160
    See also salt-tolerant biota; sodium

salt balance, 160–161, 183, 189–190, 248

salt cedar (tamarisk), 34, 264–265, 266 (plate), 294–295, 295 (plate)
    impacts on native communities, 264–265, 272, 300
    removal efforts, 294–295, 299, 300, 301, 303

Salt Cedar Leaf Beetle, 294

Salt Creek, 160, 161 (plate)

Salt Creek Hills, 27

Salt Creek Pupfish, 160, 161 (plate), 162 (fig.)

salt glands, 172, 190

saltbush scrub, 166 (fig.), 223–225, 226, 228, 262
    photos, 224 (plate), 225 (plate)

saltbushes, 52, 102, 113, 140, 175, 224, 237
    four-wing saltbush, 224, 278
    migration of, 142
    See also desert holly; desert shadscale

saltgrass, 230 (plate)
    desert saltgrass, 224, 229, 298

Salton Basin, 40–42, 80, 86–87, 92 (plate), 151, 166, 237, 247

Salton Sea, 71, 271, 278

Salton Trough, 41 (plates), 86
    mud volcanoes, 86–87

salt-tolerant biota, 90, 224–226, 228, 237, 265
    fishes, 160–161, 228–229

Salvadora hexalepis mohavensis, 118

Salvia dorrii, 227

San Andreas Fault, vi (map), 80, 84 (plate), 86

San Gorgonio Pass, 36, 62 (plate), 77–78

San Xavier del Bac, 20

sand dune scrub, 245, 248–249, 290, 296

sand dunes, 77, 85, 89 (plate), 248, 287
    formation, 123, 142–143, 149, 152, 245

sand flies, 246, 247 (plate)

sand food, 246–247, 246 (plate), 296

sand grass. *See* Indian ricegrass

Sand Partridge, 190

sand sheets, 88

sand verbena, 110 (plate), 168, 249

sandstones, 79, 80, 132

Santa Ana River, 22

Santa Rosa Mountains, 70, 204

Saratoga Springs, 141 (plate), 230, 230 (plate)

Saratoga Springs Pupfish, 158

Sarcobatus vermiculatus, 224

Sauromalus obesus, 221, 221 (plate)

sauropods, 132

savannas, 206

scale insects, 111

Scaphiophus couchi, 280–281

Schismus, 268
    arabicus, 266–267
    barbatus, 266–267

Scientific American, 45–46

scientific expeditions. *See* explorations

Scirpus
    acutus, 197
    acutus subsp. *occidentalis,* 137, 229
    americanus, 137
Scopulophila rixfordii, 210
scorpions, 56
Scott's Oriole, 218, 219 (plate)
screw bean mesquite, 229
scrub communities, 196, 196 (table)
    Great Basin, 206–212
    Mojave, 219–223
    Sonoran, 239–245, 248–249
    See also big sagebrush scrub; creosote bush
        scrub; saltbush scrub
scrub oak, Sonoran, 213, 216, 227 (plate)
Scyphophorus yuccae, 217
sea cows, 133
Sea of Cortez, 80, 86, 232
Searles Valley, 36
sea turtles, 133
secondary succession, 123, 125
sedges, 141, 201, 225
sedimentary rocks, 79, 80 (plate), 85 (plate)
sedum, 213
Sedum niveum, 213
seed bank, 126 (fig.), 126–127, 169, 172, 222,
        283, 288–289
seed consumption. *See* granivory
seed dispersal, 111, 128, 222, 259, 263
    creosote bush, 220–221
    fan palms, 237–238
    Joshua tree, 218, 219
seed germination
    annuals, 127–128, 167–168, 169, 267
    revegetation projects, 299–300
seed grinding technologies, 140 (plate), 144, 206
seed predators. *See* granivory
seedling facilitation, 242–243
seeps, 96
seepweed, 224
semideserts, 72
Serrano people, 22, 255
shadscale, 113, 217, 223, 225 (plate)
sheep, 281, 282, 283
    See also bighorn sheep; Desert Bighorn
Sheep Spring, 269
Shelton, Richard, 64
shooting star, 225

Shoreline Butte, 94, 94 (plate)
Shoshone people, 4 (plate), 14, 46, 57
Shoshone Pupfish, 158
Shreve, Forrest, 122
shrews, 119
shrimp, 133
    See also brine shrimp; fairy shrimp
shrubs, 144, 264
    as animal food source, 111, 172, 175
    in arborescent creosote bush scrub, 240, 242
    climate adaptations, 207
    convergence in, 207
    drought-deciduous, 169–171
    evergreen, 178–181
    fire impacts, 268
    in forest communities, 198
    in Joshua tree woodland, 217, 223
    nutrient storage, 121–122
    productivity, 109–110
    restoration techniques, 299–301
    sand dunes, 249
    in succession process, 125, 297
    water depletion impacts, 276
    See also scrub communities; *individual genera
        and species*
Sidalcea covillei, 226 (plates), 273
Side-blotched Lizard, 116
Sidewinder, 182, 183 (plate)
Sierra Nevada, 79, 130–131, 137
    glacial activity and Mono Lake, 42–43,
        44 (map)
    Smith crossing, 23
Sierran white fir, 213
silver cholla, 34, 185–186, 217, 221
    photos, 34 (plate), 49 (plate), 187 (plate)
silver lupine, 199–200
Simmondsia chinensis, 113, 115 (plate), 240
single-leaf pinyon. *See* pinyon pines
Siphateles, 157, 228
    bicolor mohavensis, 276
    bicolor synderi, 273
    mojavensis, 51–52, 52 (plate), 133
    orcutti, 52
Sitta
    canadensis, 200
    pygmaea, 200, 200 (plate)
six-weeks fescue, 268
Skidoo, 123 (plates)

skinks, 130

sloths, 237

   See also ground sloths

Smith, Jedediah, 22–23

smog, 277, 277 (plate). *See* air quality

smoke tree, 120, 227, 233, 233 (plate), 265

snails, 153

   See also springsnails

snakes, 47, 117, 118, 223

   boa constrictors, 118, 130, 232

   Coachwhip, 182–183, 183 (plate)

   Mojave Patchnose Snake, 118

   Sidewinder, 182, 183 (plate)

   Western Blind Snake, 117, 117 (plate)

   Western Shovelnose Snake, 117–118,
      118 (plate), 249

snakeweed, 112

snow, 74, 75–76, 163, 198, 206, 207, 216, 223,
   239

Soda Lake, 21, 21 (plate), 23, 32

Soda Spring, 275

Soda Springs, 52

sodium, 90, 120, 121

   See also salt(s)

sodium carbonate, 91

soil microorganisms, 114, 119, 122, 189

   bacteria, 91, 92, 121, 122

   fungi, 114, 119, 226, 268, 278, 297, 299–300

   mites, 119, 120 (plate), 122

   nematodes, 114, 119, 188–189, 208

   salt-tolerant, 226

soil roundworms. *See* nematodes

soils, 67, 88–92, 90 (plate), 91 (plate), 92 (plate)

   chemistry, 85, 88, 90, 92, 120–121

   compaction, 125, 256

   disturbance and nonnative plant species, 259,
      261, 263, 264, 264–266

   fire impacts, 268

   formation, 88–89, 91–92, 123–124, 297

   grazing impacts, 283, 284 (plate)

   moisture in, 89–90, 91, 152

   nitrogen in, 108–109, 114

   nutrient levels/availability, 90, 120, 121, 128

   patch-mosaic model, 127–128

   pH, 90, 91

   restoration techniques, 297, 298–299

   road and vehicle impacts, 256, 259, 261–263,
      264

surface features, 88, 90–92, 283

texture, 89–90, 121

   See also erosion; nitrogen fixation; soil
      microorganisms; water
      uptake/transport

solar energy/radiation, 75 (map), 76–77, 91, 100

Soledad Canyon, 36

Sonoran communities, 72 (plate), 179, 232–249

   arborescent creosote bush scrub, 239–243,
      240 (plate), 244

   arroyo woodland, 233–237

   cactus scrub, 243–244

   fan palm woodland, 237–239, 290

   leaf area index, 105

   sand dune scrub, 245, 248–249, 290

Sonoran Desert, 67–68, 68 (map)

   ancient flora and fauna, 136, 143

   climate, 73 (fig.), 74–75, 76

   evolution of, 131–132, 142

   military installations, 256

   nonnative species in, 265, 268

   physical environment, 69 (table), 71

   productivity, 109, 109 (fig.)

   water use, 271

   See also Sonoran communities

Sonoran scrub oak, 213, 216, 227 (plate)

sounds, 280–281, 280 (fig.)

Southern Paiute, 33

Spanish bayonet, 222

Spanish needle, 249

sparrows

   English House Sparrow, 268

specialist carnivores, 115

specialist herbivores, 113–114

speciation, 129, 151, 155, 157, 172–173, 176, 181,
   214–215

species richness, 151–152, 152 (table)

   annuals, 166 (fig.)

   birds, 230

   carbonate scrub communities, 211–212

   Death Valley soils, 226, 228

   elevation and, 197 (fig.)

   Mojave communities, 223

   Sonoran communities, 233

Spermophilus

   mohavensis, 174, 221

   tereticaudus, 176, 176 (map), 177 (plate), 205

Sphyrapicus nuchalis, 201

spikerushes, 225

spiny hop-sage, 124, 175, 207

spiny phlox, 199

Sporobolus airoides, 224–225

springs, 96, 125, 159

    as animal water sources, 163–164, 230–231

    development/depletion of, 236, 274, 275

    nonnative species impacts, 268, 270

    See also groundwater; wetlands; *specific springs*

springsnails, 228 (plate), 229, 274, 287

    Amargosa Springsnail, 286

springtails, 120 (plate), 122

squash, 146

squirreltail grass, 199

star tulip, Inyo County, 273

Stark, Dr., 34–35, 34 (plate), 35 (plate)

Starling, European, 268

Steelhead, 161

Steinbeck, John, 60–63

Stejneger, Leonhard, 46–47

Stellula calliope, 202

Stenelmis moapa, 229

steppes, 197, 198, 206, 283

stomata, 154 (plate), 156, 166, 170, 177, 180–181, 186

stonecrops, 104

storks, 51, 133

Streptanthus, 214

Struthio camelus, 190

Sturnus vulgaris, 268

Suaeda moquinii, 224

succession, 122–125

    facilitation, 242–243

    overgrazing and, 282–283, 285

    patch-mosaic model, 127–128, 127 (fig.), 243

    pulse model and, 127

    restoration models, 297, 299

succulents, 104

    See also cacti; CAM photosynthesis

suckers, 157, 228

    Razorback Sucker, 50

sugarcane, 22, 23, 102

sulfur, 120

sulfur dioxide, 277, 278–279

sulfur-flowered buckwheat, 203

sun spiders, 119

sunflower family, 207, 264

sunflowers, 130

    Algodones Dune sunflower, 248 (plate), 249

    desert sunflower, 167 (plates), 168

Susan River, 137

Swallenia alexandrae, 14, 150, 286

sweat bees, 240

Swift, White-throated, 174

sycamore, California, 237

Sylvilagus, 141

tamarisk. *See* salt cedar

Tamarix ramosissima, 264–265

Tamias panamintensis, 216, 216 (plate)

tansy mustard, 214

tarantula hawks, 126, 234

tarantulas, 46, 119

Taylor Grazing Act, 283

Tecopa, 23, 28

Tecopa Pupfish, 158

Tecopa Springs, 29

tectonic processes, 80, 86–87

    See also faults; mountain building; *specific faults*

teddy-bear cholla, 221, 244, 244 (plate)

Tegeticula paradoxa, 218–219

Tejon Canyon, 23

Tejon Canyon pass, 25 (plate), 48 (map)

Tejon Pass, 22, 142 (plate), 143 (plate)

Tejon Ranch, 25

Telescope Peak, 29, 30 (plate), 53 (plate), 212

temperatures, 69 (table), 72, 73 (fig.), 74–75, 76–77

    heat coping mechanisms, 182–185, 207, 241

    potential climate change, 279

    soil temperatures and reradiation, 78

tenebrionid beetles, 184

termites, 114–115, 116, 117, 122, 128, 218

    Arid Land Termite, 116 (plate)

    Desert Drywood Termite, 115

Tertiary, 129, 130–132, 130 (fig.)

thelypodium, 214

Thelypodium, 214

thermal springs, 159

thermals, 78, 277

theropods, 132

Thousand Palms, 238

thrashers, 287

threatened and endangered species, 285–290, 288 (table), 296

carbonate scrub species, 209–211
    legally protected species, 286 (plates), 288,
        289, 295–296
threatened communities, 290, 296
    natural healing processes, 290, 296–297,
        301
thunderstorms, 75, 78–79, 83, 177, 239
Timbishu Shoshone, 46
Tin Mountain, 204 (plate)
tinajas, 163
Tiquilia plicata, 249
Titanothere, 132–133, 132 (plate)
Titanothere Canyon, 132
toads, 46–47
    Black Toad, 230, 231 (plate), 291
    Couch's Spadefoot Toad, 280–281
    Red-spotted Toad, 230, 231 (plate)
toiwaitu, 165
Tonopah and Tidewater Railroad, 93 (plate)
topographic processes, 80–85
    See also faults; geography; volcanic activity
torpor, 173–174, 176
Torrey, John, 29
Torrey's amaranth, 104 (plate), 106 (fig.)
tortoises, 130
    See also Desert Tortoise
tourism, 39, 58–59
Towne Pass, 30
transition zones. *See* ecotones
transpiration
    cacti, 181, 183–184, 185, 186–187
    creosote bush, 179–180
    desert holly, 183, 185 (fig.)
    ocotillo, 170–171
    phreatophytic trees, 154, 155
Transverse Ranges, 136, 142
Travels with Charley (Steinbeck), 60–63
trees. *See* forests and woodlands; phreatophytes;
    individual genera and species
trilobites, 131
trout
    Lahontan Cutthroat Trout, 202, 202 (plate)
    See also Steelhead
Truckee River, 137, 202
true deserts, 71, 72, 73
Tryonia, 228 (plate), 272
    clathrata, 229
Tulare Lake, 22, 142

Tule Springs, 36
tules, 137, 138, 141, 197, 229, 230, 230 (plate)
tumbleweed, 263, 263 (plates), 264
turgor, leaves, 180–181
Twentynine Palms, 75
two-leaf pinyon, 213
Typha, 197
    angustifolia, 137
    latifolia, 137

Uma
    inornata, 286 (plate)
    notata, 249
Umbellularia salicifolia, 133
Union Wash Formation, 131, 132
Upper Narrows of the Mojave River, 25, 26
    (plate), 51
urban water use and demand, 271–272, 274, 275
urbanization, 255–257, 274, 275, 278
urchins, 133
Urocyon
    cinereoargenteus, 118
    cinereoargenteus scottii, 118
U.S. Army
    Government Road project, 33–34
    Owens Valley conflict, 36–37
U.S. Fish and Wildlife Service, 275
Uta stansburiana, 116
Utah juniper, 202, 203 (plate), 204 (plates), 213,
    216 (plate)
    migrations, 136, 142, 205, 220 (fig.)
    See also pinyon-juniper woodland

Vallecitos Mountains, 70
Valley Fever, 278
Van Dyke, John, 55–57, 56 (plate), 61, 276–277,
    280
Vanyume people, 21–23, 37–38, 255
varnished soils, 91, 92, 120, 264
vegetation patterns
    evolution of, 129
    facilitation/competition and, 243
    Holocene, 139–140, 142, 144–145
    leapfrogging, 213, 216
    Mojave riparian communities, 227
    patch-mosaic model, 127–128, 127 (fig.), 128
        (plates), 129 (plate), 243
    Pleistocene, 134, 135–136, 137–138

vegetation patterns (cont.)
  Pliocene, 133
  Tertiary, 130, 131–132
  See also communities; plant migrations;
    specific community types
vehicle impacts, 256, 279, 280–281
  OHVs, 247, 259, 261, 261 (plate), 262,
    277 (plate), 278, 280–281, 289
  See also roads
velvet ash, 237
ventifacts, 77 (plate), 78
Verdin, 162, 190, 234
Vermivora luciae, 190
Veromessor, 113
  pergandei, 222
Victorville, 165
virgin brittlebush, 227
volcanic activity, 79–80, 81
  Death Valley, 94
  Salton Trough mud volcanoes, 86–87
  springs and geysers, 96
Vontrigger Spring, 22
Vulpes macrotis, 119, 119 (plate), 182
Vulpia octoflora, 268

Walcott, Charles Doolittle, 131
Walker Lake, 23, 202
Walker River, 137
Walker Trail, 36
Wallace, William, 12–13
walnut, 133
walruses, 133
warblers
  Lucy's Warbler, 190
  MacGillivray's Warbler, 202
Warm Springs Pupfish, 158
wash riparian communities, 227
Washingtonia, 153
  filifera, 154–155, 154 (plate), 237–239
wasps, 246
  Bembix Wasp, 246–247, 247 (plate)
  tarantula hawks, 126, 234
water(s), 69 (table), 92–96, 149
  diversions and depletion, 271–276, 281, 290
  Holocene climate change and, 142–143
  human use statistics, 271
  human water needs, 165–166
  landforms and, 81–83

metabolic water, 190–191
sand food as source of, 247
soil infiltration, 89–90, 91
water availability, 90, 109–110, 126–127,
  143–145
water conservation adaptations, 173–174, 178,
  180–181, 190–192
water stress, 105–108, 166, 180–184, 187–188
  See also groundwater; lakes; rivers and
    streams; springs; water
    uptake/transport; wetlands
water birch, 200
water temperatures, 159–160, 162 (fig.)
water uptake/transport
  annuals, 166
  cacti, 185–186, 186 (fig.)
  competition for soil moisture, 105, 108,
    108 (fig.), 154, 243, 264–265, 265 (fig.)
  creosote bush, 181
  drought-deciduous shrubs, 169, 170–171
  phreatophytic trees, 155–156, 233, 237
  salt cedar, 264–265
water use efficiency, 105, 107
  ozone pollution and, 278
watering holes, 163–164, 230–231
weathering, 120, 121
weeds. *See* nonnative species
weevils
  dune weevils, 249
  Yucca Weevil, 217, 218 (plate)
Weins, Del, 10–11
welded tuff, 80
Western Blind Snake, 117, 117 (plate)
western juniper, 203–204
Western Shoshone people, 4 (plate)
Western Shovelnose Snake, 117–118, 118 (plate),
  249
Western Wood-Peewee, 201–202
wetlands, 95 (plate), 165, 196 (table), 197, 233,
  290
  Great Basin, 198
  Holocene climate oscillations and, 143, 144,
    145, 165
  Mojave communities, 228–231
  Pleistocene, 137–138
  water depletion impacts, 273
  See also riparian communities; springs
Whipple Mountains, 233, 243, 244

white amaranth, 263, 264
white bear poppy, 184 (plate)
white fir, 136, 137 (fig.), 139, 213
    Rocky Mountain white fir, 213
    Sierran white fir, 213
white fir forest, 212–214, 216
White Mountains, 68, 142
    bird species, 200, 201
    bristlecone pine forest, 199, 199 (plate)
White-Inyo Range, 23
White-throated Swift, 174
Wiggin's croton, 249
Wild Free-Roaming Horse and Burro Act,
        270 (fig.), 294
wild hyacinth, 146
wild iris, 225
wild rose, 201
wild rye, 283
wilderness designations, 293
wildfires. *See* fire
Williams, Minnie, 206 (plates)
Williamson, R. S., 40
willows, 93 (plate), 133, 137, 200, 209 (fig.), 295
        (plate)
    arroyo willow, 201, 237
    black willow, 237, 265
    See also desert willow
Wilson's Phalarope, 272
wind, 76–78, 79 (plates), 277
    influence on soils and landforms, 77–78, 79
        (plate), 85, 91, 123, 245
wind power generation, 78
Wingate Pass, 137
winnowing, 6 (plate)
winterfat, 208, 217
wolfberry, 223
woodlands, 197
    forest/woodland distinction, 197–198
    See also forests and woodlands; *specific types*
woodrat middens, 135–136, 142, 143

woodrats, 141, 218, 268
    Desert Woodrat, 14, 135–136, 135 (plates)
worms
    in Indian diet, 37
    See also nematodes
wormwood, 22, 237

Xantusia, 46
    vigilis, 218
xerophytic saltbush scrub, 224, 224 (plate)
Xylocarpa, 240
Xylorhiza
    cognata, 296
    tortifolia, 299
Xyrauchen, 157
    texanus, 50

yellow nut sedge, 146
yellow rabbitbrush, 199, 208
yerba manza, 21 (plate)
yucca, 221–222
    Mojave yucca, 34, 34 (plate), 222
    Spanish bayonet, 222
    See also Joshua tree
Yucca, 221–222
    baccata, 222
    brevifolia, 68, 102, 204
    schidigera, 34, 34 (plate), 222
Yucca Moth, 218–219
Yucca Weevil, 217, 218 (plate)
Yuma, 20, 36, 37–38, 50
Yuma people, 20, 22, 247

Zea mays, 102
zebras, 133
Zebra-tailed Lizard, 3, 116–117, 117 (plate)
zone classification systems
    Merriam's life zones, 53 (fig.), 53 (plate), 54
Zzyzx, 52, 275

ABOUT THE AUTHOR

Bruce Michael Pavlik received his Ph.D in botany from the University of California at Davis, working on the physiological ecology of grasses with Professor Michael Barbour. His research has focused on the ecology and physiology of plants native to western North America, including the conservation of endangered species. Ecological restoration has become central to his research program, and recent projects have emphasized the design and active management of populations and communities using field-based, experimental approaches. Most of his projects have been associated with grasslands and deserts, but unusual ecosystems (dunes, geothermal springs, serpentinite outcrops, vernal pools) have received special attention.

Author (left) and brother Bob, near Victorville, 1968. (LaVerne Pavlik)

The author was called to testify before House and Senate committees of the U.S. Congress during hearings on the California Desert Protection Act. The act increased protections on more than seven million desert acres by creating national parks and wilderness areas.

Mr. Pavlik is currently Professor of Biology at Mills College in Oakland, California, and author or coauthor of more than 50 scientific and popular publications, including *Oaks of California* (1991, Cachuma Press), *California's Changing Landscapes* (1993, California Native Plant Society), and the fifth edition of the *Inventory of Rare and Endangered Vascular Plants of California* (1994, California Native Plant Society). He has recently established a science consulting firm (BMP Ecosciences) specializing in biological resource management.

Text: 9.5/14 Scala
Display: Scala Sans and Bauer Bodoni
Compositor: Jane Rundell
Illustrator: Dartmouth Publishing
Indexer: Thérèse Shere
Printer and binder: Oceanic Graphic Printing, Inc.